Arrogance
on the Battlefield

Arrogance
on the Battlefield
A Primary Cause of Defeat, 1755–1991

J. Lee Ready

ARMS AND
ARMOUR

Arms and Armour Press
An Imprint of the Cassell Group
Wellington House, 125 Strand, London WC2R 0BB

Distributed in the USA by Sterling Publishing Co. Inc.,
387 Park Avenue South, New York, NY 10016-8810.

Distributed in Australia by Capricorn Link (Australia)
Pty. Ltd, 2/13 Carrington Road, Castle Hill, NSW 2154.

British Library Cataloguing-in-Publication Data:
a catalogue record for this book is available from
the British Library

ISBN 1-85409-319-3

Designed and edited by DAG Publications Ltd.
Designed by David Gibbons; layout by Anthony A.
Evans; edited by Philip Jarrett; printed and bound
in Great Britain by Hartnolls Limited, Bodmin, Cornwall

Contents

Acknowledgements

It would be dishonest of me to claim sole praise for this book, though I do claim sole responsibility for all mistakes and opinions. A list of all who have helped me would be a book in itself.

Certain institutions have been exceedingly kind and professional:

In Britain: the Public Record Office; the Imperial War Museum; British Museum; British Library; the London Library; the National Army Museum; University of Lancaster; University of Manchester; University of London; London School of Economics and Political Science; Lancashire Library; Merseyside Library.

In the USA: the Smithsonian Washington DC; Gilcrease Museum Tulsa; Oklahoma University; the Trans-Mississippi Rifles; University of Tulsa; Tulsa Library; and the Crow Nation, who impeccably maintain the Little Big Horn National Park and gave valuable assistance to me despite being in the middle of a 'Cheyenne uprising'.

There are also a few individuals who have made a tremendous impact on this work: my mother Constance T. Horan; father Jack A. Ready, mentor Marvin Lowe, fellow scholar and comrade Jerry Kirk, standard bearer Christopher V. Stafford, my daughter Louise, and above all my patient wife Kay.

J. Lee Ready
Preston, England

PART 1

The veteran of battle has every right to wonder why I am taking up the pen to describe the performance of commanders on battlefields at which I was not present. Am I the ultimate armchair general?

Perhaps so, but as each battle is different, though I shall attempt to show similarities, then surely only by actually becoming Braddock on that fateful day on the Monongahela or becoming Custer on the Little Big Horn could anyone give an accurate description of what they would have done instead.

Therefore, we are left with a dilemma. Should we never criticise anyone, because such body transference is impossible? Every film critic is therefore an armchair director and every sports commentator an armchair player.

It is my contention that anyone who does anything opens himself up to criticism, including myself of course. What we should ask is whether the criticism has merit, seems logical, or opens up new dimensions. If my criticism of these commanders can open up new thought on the matter, can perhaps stir the imagination to want to know more, then I have done my job, regardless of whether or not anyone agrees with my criticisms.

Military commanders bear the greatest burden of all in that their errors may cost many lives, may cost the nation dearly, indeed may destroy the nation. Battlefield pressure is greater than any sports final, college exam or surgical operation.

It would seem logical, therefore, that commanders are better trained to cope with stress and the many variables of the battlefield. Oddly this is not the case, except in rare instances. Indeed on occasion absolute imbeciles have been given armies to play with. The political leaders who gave them the armies bear the greater guilt.

Even great commanders make mistakes: Lee at Gettysburg, Napoleon at Lodi, Grant at Cold Harbor, Tito at Jablanica. Their successes overshadow their errors and they were great enough to learn from them, though not necessarily humble enough to admit them.

Commanders make errors for all sorts of reasons, but try to go into battle with a modicum of a plan. The military rule book has a plan for everything from how to make a bed, fold clothes and cross a street in column to how to fight a battle. A battle plan involves grand strategy (the art of managing a campaign), strategy (the art of getting to the battlefield or luring the enemy to the battlefield) and tactics (the art of fighting the battle), which strategists and tacticians have been writing about regularly in the West since the sixteenth century and in China from two millennia before that. Every good battle plan expects nothing to go according to plan. Emergencies necessitate rule bending, but plans need to be made all the same otherwise chaos reigns.

The common soldier may cuss his sergeants and disrespect his officers, but he almost always expects the man at the top to be above petty squabbles and to react accordingly.

The majority of leaders do the best they can, but errors can be brought about by many causes: impetuosity, pride, timidity, cowardice, inability to delegate, insanity, senility, emotional disturbance, stupidity, anger, superstition, religion, illness, wounds, exhaustion, politics. Unscrupulous leaders may do the wrong thing because of treason, corruption, feuding or jealousy.

This book studies those errors brought about by arrogance. We do this by looking at each battle in a methodical fashion more or less in the same manner, beginning with a background to the conflict, then tackling the war, grand strategy, the commander(s), the battlefield, strategy, the army, causes of arrogance, the approach or countdown, the enemy, the battle, aftermath, appraisal, an alternative strategy, the consequences of the battle and the battle's place in history.

Part One covers those battles fought in what we sophisticated people of the late twentieth century like to call the simpler times, before life and all its expectations became complicated to the point of madness.

1755

The Monongahela

Background: Those native American Indian tribes whose land was invaded by the Spaniards from 1492 onwards were most unfortunate, because almost all the Spaniards saw them merely as potential slaves, whereas those Indians who watched with curiosity as the English, Dutch, Swedes and French began landing on the Atlantic shore of North America from 1607 onwards were fortunate as these white men came to trade and learn. To this day descendants of those early English settlers celebrate the manner in which Indians fed them and cared for them through the first harsh winters in the rite of Thanksgiving.

The English, who unlike the other Europeans came from a land long at peace, used the term 'king' to describe any Indian tribal chief and recognised these tribes as sovereign nations.

For fifteen years there was peace and friendship between the English and the Indians, and also intermarriage for the Englishmen did not bring any of their own womenfolk across the Atlantic until 1620. This is all the more remarkable because the tribes warred with each other and some were positively bloodthirsty.

The honeymoon period ended on 22 March 1622 when the Indians of the Powhattan confederacy attacked the English settlements in Virginia without warning. The peaceful colonists were helpless against this sudden onslaught by their Indian neighbours and within days fully one third of the colony's men, women and children had been massacred. It was the worst atrocity suffered by English townships since the Viking raids six centuries earlier.

Though they initially relied upon armour, swords, pikes and primitive firearms, the Virginia settlers learned to survive by adopting Indian methods of warfare. Most importantly for future generations they began to wage war as brutally as did the Indians, wiping out entire villages and enslaving thousands either for their own plantations or selling them to the Spaniards. The Indian had taught the settlers a new type of war.

The English government in London refused to be dragged into this conflict or any of the Indian wars that followed. The landed gentry in England believed the settlers had probably instigated the troubles anyway and were only getting their just deserts. The settlers, who increasingly referred to themselves as Americans, learned that when it came to self-preservation they were on their own. So in the war against the Pamunkey in Virginia in 1632, the Naragansetts and Pequot in Massachusetts in 1636, the Susquehannock in Virginia in 1641 and the Powhattan again in 1644–46 the settlers waged war without the approval or assistance of the government in London.

Indeed from 1642 to 1651 the London government had its own problems, a series of civil wars. Not only did no English troops come to America to protect the Americans, but some Americans went to England to fight.

Still small in number the Americans had to seek aid from Indian allies, thereby becoming involved in centuries old intertribal feuds.

In 1655 the Dutch turned on the Swedes and conquered their colony and nine years later an English fleet came to America to conquer the Dutch colony. Swedish and Dutch settlers now lived under English rule. The English-speaking Americans were pleased with the trade opportunities this conquest opened up. To Boston and Jamestown they now added the Dutch town of New Amsterdam, renaming it New York.

Settlements continued to expand as their birth rate was high and there was a constant influx of English families seeking a better life than that offered by war-ravaged and nobility-ruled England. This expansion continually moved the frontier (the line where European civilisation ended) ever westwards, so that as early as 1675 when war broke out on the Virginia frontier between new settlers and the Susquehannock and the Delaware-Nanticokes, the sedentary residents of the east coast towns and plantations saw this as none of their concern and refused to aid the frontier settlers. They exhibited the same attitude to the frontier as did the residents of England. When a mob of frontiersmen marched to Jamestown to seek redress they were met by force from the Virginia militia. Jamestown was destroyed in the fight and it took intervention by the Maryland militia before the rebellion was quelled.

Only now did English troops arrive by sea, but they came not to protect the frontier settlers from the Indians, but to hunt down the frontier rebels and hang them!

Yet, just thirteen years later when England went to war against France and Spain, the London government expected the Americans to participate in this war by joining with Indian allies and raiding the French in the north and west (Canada) and the Spaniards in the south (Florida). The Americans soon found they had no choice as they were subjected to raids by the French and Spaniards and their Indian allies.

This War of the League of Augsburg ended in 1697, but five years later was followed by a repeat affair, the War of the Spanish Succession until 1713. War against Spain 1718–20 was followed in 1740 by another major conflict against France and Spain, the War of Jenkins' Ear which in 1744 became the War of the Austrian Succession. All of these wars began and ended in Europe. The Americans showed what they thought of them by the names they gave them, such as King William's War, Queen Anne's War and King George's War.

By 1748, when peace finally came, the Virginia militia had a military pedigree of 126 years, longer in fact than any of the regiments that made up the English Army. By this date all Americans, whether of English, Dutch, Swedish, Scots, Welsh, Irish, German or African ancestry were considered to be British, subjects of the king in London. Not counting Indians, the population of the British colonies in North America exceeded 1,500,000.

Yet the king's Parliament which made the laws and levied the taxes consisted of members who represented constituencies in Ireland, Wales, Scotland and England only, and were dominated by those from England. Increasingly in the taverns and coffee shops of British America the cry was heard 'no taxation without representation' meaning that the Americans felt that if they paid import and export taxes to Parliament, they ought to have representatives there to influence how that money was spent.

The American cities of Boston, Philadelphia, New York and Charleston were as cosmopolitan as most European cities and the lifestyle of their inhabitants was indistinguishable from that of London or Dublin. Life in these cities was far removed from the knife-edge existence of the frontier settlers who were constantly expanding westwards.

The War: Some of this expansion was uncontrolled so that groups of families entered virgin territory and set up townships overnight answering to no law but that which they brought with them, using the Bible as a reference manual.

Other settlements were much more orderly and structured and were set up by private business speculators, who surveyed the land, picked the best locations for townships and farms and often laid roads. This land was then sold to the incoming settlers. Sawmills and community general stores provided another source of revenue for the land speculator.

In 1754 Governor Dinwiddie of Virginia sent a survey team led by 22-year-old George Washington into the land north-west of Virginia across the Ohio River. Dinwiddie had given permission for the Ohio Company, a speculative venture, to organise colonisation into this area once the survey was complete. It was no coincidence that Dinwiddie and Washington were partners in the company.

Washington knew his team would be going into land already claimed by the French and by several Indian tribes, but his main concern was to get there ahead of any survey teams that Pennsylvania might send out.

On 28 May 1754 Washington and 120 of his map-makers and woodsmen ran into a party of Frenchmen and though there was no formal state of hostilities between England and France Washington knew that such niceties did not exist on the frontier. He ordered his men to use their hunting rifles on the Frenchmen: they killed ten and captured 21.

Washington's men built a defensive fort to lay their claim to the region, naming it Fort Necessity, but on 3 July the entire 400-man survey team was attacked by a large body of French and Indians. After suffering thirteen killed and 54 wounded, young Washington swallowed his pride and surrendered on condition that he and his men were allowed to go home to Virginia. The French kept their word.

Grand Strategy: As soon as Dinwiddie learned of the fate of his venture he declared a de facto state of war with the French and mobilised his militia. He also asked London for help and must have been surprised when London notified him he would receive royal troops. This would enable him to make a show of force in order to impress the French so that he could delineate a border favourable to Virginia.

The Commander: To command the two regiments that were to sail to America and to take control of Dinwiddie's militia, the London government chose Major General Edward Braddock.

Born in Scotland in 1695 he had been a mere boy when Scotland formally acknowledged rule by the London parliament and at the ripe old age of fifteen he had joined the British Army, his family buying him a commission, as was the custom at the time. Moreover they placed him in the Coldstream Guards, an élite regiment.

However, his military career was most undistinguished and it was 1746 after 36 years service before he saw action: as a lieutenant-colonel against the French in the Netherlands. His star then swiftly ascended as he became a friend of the Duke of Cumberland, who was not only a general but a son of King George II. This friendship may have come initially from membership of the Freemasons. In the mid-eighteenth century Freemasonry rules were almost as important in some regiments as the king's regulations.

By 1753 Braddock had sold his lieutenant-colonelcy and bought the rank of colonel and in the following year through his connections at the royal court he was given command of the American expedition and was promoted twice to major general.

Thus for only the third time in 148 years of English presence in North America a royal army expedition was being sent into the vastness of that land, and it was placed in the hands of an overweight 60-year-old officer who had never commanded on the battlefield and whose only qualification was his influence at court. This boded ill for the expedition, unless Braddock was the sort of open-minded individual who would listen to advice and if he was accompanied by thinking officers, not yes-men, and if his troops were experienced and well trained.

The Army: When he arrived in Virginia in February 1755 having sailed from England Braddock took stock of his human material. The 44th and 48th Regiments had been raised in England some fourteen years earlier, and while a few of the older men had seen action, most were unblooded. Recently stationed in Ireland the regiments had taken in Protestant Irish recruits to replace the ill and the discharged and just before sailing, in order to make up the numbers, the regiments had asked other units for the loan of men. The result had been an intake of the poorest grade of soldier as the other regiments saw the opportunity to unload their trouble-makers. Upon reaching Virginia the regiments were still not at full strength and they recruited about 300 Americans.

Therefore, though Braddock would have on paper 1,400 regulars, almost half were newcomers to the two regiments and a quarter were fresh recruits. He also had 100 regular artillerymen and 30 sailors to man cannon.

Like Braddock, his senior officers were a product of the purchase system, such men as his aide Captain Orme, the commander of the 44th Colonel Sir Peter Halket, commander of the 48th Colonel Thomas Dunbar, Major Thomas Gage, Colonel Burton, Colonel John St Clair and Lieutenant-Colonel Horatio Gates his senior staff officer. Almost no one in the army was promoted because he was a good officer. Yet, Braddock was not dismayed by these failings, for he did not see them as failings.

He was dismayed by the militia he found in Virginia. When on campaign militia members took the title 'provincials', but not all were veteran militiamen. Too often militiamen liked the respect from society folk that a fancy uniform gained them, and did not mind the weekly or monthly drills, but they hated the idea of going to war. Therefore, many made excuses and allowed new recruits to take their place. Hence the term 'provincial' became a derogatory word in polite society.

Braddock thought the militia officers uncouth and many of them too young, such as Colonel George Washington the militia commander, though even Braddock could hardly have failed to notice that Washington was an intellectual far better educated than himself or any of his regular officers.

The 450 provincials from the militias of Virginia, Maryland and North Carolina may have looked like soldiers in their blue frock coats pinned back at the tail and their buff breeches and vest waistcoats and black tricorn hats, but their manner was boisterous, almost anarchic, compared to the disciplined, quiet bearing of the redcoated white breeched regulars. Braddock described them as 'slothful' and 'languid'. None were frontiersmen. Days before they had been shopkeepers, farm labourers, blacksmiths, sawmillers, foundry workers and recent immigrants. Thus there were Englishmen in militia uniform and Americans in regular uniform.

British regulars were trained to stand on the battlefield in the open, almost shoulder to shoulder, where their bright red coats and white breeches could be seen a mile away. With their clothes tight fitting and their hair powdered white and tied back to the coat they moved stiffly and did not crumple when shot, but sort of toppled over. Each man carried a thirteen-pound muzzle-loading musket with a 46-inch barrel that fired a .69 calibre ball. After closing with the enemy to a range of less than a hundred yards they would line up in two or three ranks, the men in the rear ranks standing just to the left of the man in front and they would point their muskets at the enemy. A sergeant would line up the muskets using a short pike and at their officer's command an entire company would fire at once. This was known as volley fire. Such was the amount of smoke from a volley that it was difficult for a soldier to see if he had hit anything. However, by the time he had reloaded, 20 to 30 seconds, the smoke had cleared. Throughout this time the soldiers were subjected to the enemy's cannon and musket fire.

Only when ordered to charge did they fix bayonets. It was difficult to load a musket with the bayonet already fixed and the added weight made it difficult to hold at firing position until the sergeant was satisfied with the rank's aim.

Braddock did not think to change his men's training for they were going up against Frenchmen and the only Frenchmen he knew fought in the same manner, though they had a tendency to fire by rank not by company. The militia were undergoing training to fight in the same manner.

Washington and others mentioned that many of the Frenchmen were in fact born and bred in America and fought more like Indians, but this did not alter Braddock's attitude.

There was low morale among the regulars. The sudden induction of new men into the 44th and 48th had upset the 'family' life of the regiments, and as expected the troublemakers from the other regiments made trouble. The new recruits were not yet trained when the march began and the veterans were not happy at the prospect of going into action while nursemaiding a quarter of their men. Furthermore they did not like the look of the militia and did not look forward to placing their flanks into the care of these unsoldierly farmhands. Last but not least, as they marched westwards and began to see the immense size of this land they realised that if something went wrong it would be a long walk back to civilisation.

There was low morale among the militia, because when they finally met the famed redcoats they were mightily disappointed. They saw them as mostly inflexible, illiterate machine-like men, who seemingly had no thoughts either way as to what this war was about. Militia officers were known to their men, having earned respect in trade, politics or owning great estates, yet were willing to talk to their men as equals. Whereas the regular officers came across as effete and snobbish.

Braddock thought the 300 civilians who went with them as teamsters (wagon drivers), carpenters, lumberjacks, cooks and construction workers were most important for he was told he would have to clear a path through forests for his wagons and he intended to build forts. A handful of the civilians were Negroes, but none of the soldiers were Negroes.

Braddock did not seem to want to take advantage of his excellent intelligence sources, namely the Indians who knew the area and the enemy; and George Washington, who had first hand knowledge of the region from a military perspective.

Braddock did agree to accept a few Indians as guides, but wanted no tribal 'army' to accompany him. After all, the purpose of the expedition was to show the flag: to make an impression on the French garrison of Fort Duquesne, so that they would negotiate a treaty. With 2,300 men he would outnumber the French at Fort Duquesne by ten to one.

The Approach: On 10 June 1755 the 2,300 strong expedition left the last community on the frontier, Fort Washington (later Cincinnati), and began marching north from the Ohio River through the forest in warm weather. The lumberjacks were only occasionally needed, because the trees were usually sparse enough to allow wagons through. Still, after eight days they had covered just 30 miles.

Braddock now received intelligence that 500 French were on their way towards Fort Duquesne. He decided to act on this news and called a conference of his regular and militia officers. He was not an unintelligent man and he knew his wagons were slowing him down, so he chose to divide his force into two, a heavy (slow) column and a light (fast) column. Colonel Dunbar was given command of the heavy column with the majority of the wagons, most of the civilians and 600 regulars and militia. Braddock would take command of the light column with the remaining soldiers, 30 wagons, some pack horses and ten cannon: all told 86 officers and 1,373 soldiers and civilians.

However, it took until 8 July for Braddock to get within eight miles of Fort Duquesne, so he had not travelled all that much faster than he would have done had he kept his force intact.

Still, it did seem he had caught the French by surprise. On the morning of the 9th as the column crossed the Monongahela River at its confluence with Turtle

Creek near the home of a trader, they could quite clearly hear the French chopping wood.

Causes of Arrogance: Believing he was about to win a victory Braddock suddenly seems to have thrown caution to the wind. He dispersed his force as he approached the fort, surely firm evidence that his arrogance had got the better of him. This arrogance stemmed from several beliefs. For one, he came from a better class than the enemy commander, for he was a British Army officer, a general no less who was welcomed at court and who had been entrusted with an important mission by his king, his parliament and his friend, the king's son. Also he believed his redcoats to be the finest soldiers on the planet, far superior to the French in Europe and certainly superior to the half-savage backwoodsmen French he was now up against. His militia, though poor quality for a European battlefield, were more than adequate for today's affair. After all, they were at least white and not the naked savages whom the French called allies. Last but not least he outnumbered the enemy seven times. He did not count Indians, for they would run when he brought his artillery into play, surely.

The Enemy: The enemy was stronger than Braddock anticipated. Colonel Contrecoeur had 70 French regulars and 140 French militia at the fort, but he and his officers had been trying to convince as many tribes as possible to help them. The French were traders not farmers, they said, and they would not interfere with the Indian way of life, which was generally a true statement. As a result on this day there were no less than 650 warriors at the fort belonging to several of the Delaware tribes plus the Seneca, Ottawa, Eel, Pottawatomie, Piankashaw, Huron, Ojibway, Shawnee and Menominee. Some were noted fighters, like Pontiac of the Ottawa. Some of the Indians wore warpaint, very much a personal thing. One warrior might have a couple of stripes across his face, another might have his entire body painted in garish colours. A few had their heads shaven, except for a long lock, known as a scalp lock, but others wore long hair, braided with leather and beads. Some wore one or two feathers. The Ojibway were noted for their grass and feather hats, looking like someone at a carnival, and they favoured nose rings. These warriors possessed a motley collection of firearms from modern accurate flintlock rifles to muskets, old wheel-locks and even hundred-year-old match-locks. They also had knives and steel hand-axes and traditional weapons of bows, spears, wooden war clubs and stone tomahawks.

The French carried rifles, steel hand-axes and long knives and were trained to fight like Indians. The Indian hid behind a bush or tree and fired, often from a kneeling or prone position, then he moved, for the gunsmoke had given away his position, and hid while he reloaded. He would then reappear in a different spot and fire from there.

Everyone knew of Braddock's approach – his column made as much noise as a circus parade – and the Indians were nervous, such was the reputation of the famed redcoats.

The Battle: Braddock sent Major Gage ahead with a body of mounted militia, followed by some infantry. Several hundred yards behind Gage would come St Clair with the civilians, pack horses and waggons and two light cannon. This placed 350 men in a string about a mile in length. A mile behind them rode Braddock himself accompanied by a body of mounted militia and his mounted staff officers. Following was the main body of the light column: first a squad comprising an officer and twenty infantrymen, the sailors and a heavy cannon, a company of grenadiers (the tallest soldiers of each regiment), then the main body of infantry and militia, followed by the remainder of the artillery, some infantry, a company of grenadiers and some mounted militia to round up stragglers in this 90°F heat.

On either flank of the long column were squads and some half-squads of a sergeant and ten infantrymen, some of them as much as a half mile from the main body. The terrain was sparsely wooded and the soldiers could see each other up to about 400 yards distant.

They marched with the Monongahela on their left and a hill to their right. Braddock made no attempt to place a covering force on the hill, nor did he make any attempt to sneak up on the French. Indeed just in case the enemy was deaf as well as blind Braddock ordered his musicians to play.

Several officers rode up to Braddock to point out that this was no way to attack an enemy and that king's regulations gave specific instructions for moving in wooded terrain in the face of the enemy. He ignored all advice. Having been cautious for a month he now discarded caution at the moment he needed to be most cautious. Furthermore, he gave no orders as to what to do if they met the enemy!

Ahead of Gage there was a stream gully and there the French and Indians lay in wait. Captain Beaujeu and Captain Dumas had harangued the Indians for hours and had temporarily gained their confidence. These officers stripped to the waist and vowed to fight Indian-style, thus flattering the Indians.

Braddock's men on the other hand were stifling in their uniforms in the hot weather. The militia had been allowed to take off their coats, and probably some regulars had done so too. The civilians were in shirt sleeves. Already several soldiers were down with heat exhaustion. They were certainly visible to the French in their colourful garb and British grenadiers wore metal plates on their hats, which reflected sunlight and made an excellent target.

Suddenly Beaujeu gave the order and 860 French and Indians began running towards the front of Gage's force.

The leading mounted militia were the first to see the attackers and they rode back to warn Gage, firing a parting shot as they went. Gage's infantry were startled by the sight of a mass of bare-chested people running towards them. Even to hardened Indian-fighting frontiersmen the sight and sound of a mass of Indians whooping and screaming was unnerving. To Braddock's men it was an absolutely terrifying spectacle.

Most likely the civilians turned and ran at once. They were not cowards, but they had not signed on to fight. One of them, Daniel Boone, was no faint heart, but he was sensible. He ran. They had heard enough stories round the campfire to know that if caught they might be burned at the stake or flayed alive.

Gage ordered his infantry to form double ranks and they did so; then waited for the sergeants to line up their musket barrels. Their first volley may have knocked down one or two of the charging enemy, but then many of the French and some of the Indians stopped and took cover behind foliage to open up a steady fire upon Gage's massed ranks. Soon perhaps a hundred or more were on Gage's flanks firing into the redcoats who were helpless against this onslaught.

Gage also brought his cannon into play and they did some damage. Beaujeu fell early in the fight, his head split apart by a ball. The cannon were primarily useful for the noise they made, reassuring the redcoats and unnerving the Indians.

Still horsed, Gage surveyed all beneath him, while he sent officers to inform Braddock of the attack. His redcoats were falling continually, but they were maintaining their ranks and placing volley after volley into the enemy. Some Frenchmen began to fall back.

A few warriors, usually teenagers eager to earn laurels, waited until the red-coats were reloading and then ran up the ends of the ranks and caved in the head of a redcoat with a war club, and then ran back into the foliage hollering with excitement, to disappear before any soldier could fire back.

Braddock had no need of messengers to tell him of the battle for he could clearly hear the shooting and minutes later he witnessed the panicked flight of the civilians running towards and then past him. Close on the heels of the civil-ians was a mob of Indians, who had run past Gage's men. Some of Braddock's soldiers wondered if Gage's men had not already fallen and these were victori-ous Indians coming to repeat their massacre.

Braddock swiftly ordered Halket to guard the wagons and pack-horses, while he advanced with the remainder of the men to aid Gage. He gave no thought to the hill on his right flank, but was magnetised by the sound of Gage's struggle like a moth to a flame. Forming his redcoat infantry and grenadiers and the mili-tia into columns he then led them on horseback forward at a run, ignoring the withering fire of rifle and musket balls that came their way from the Indians who were by now on all sides.

Gage had in fact ordered a withdrawal, hoping to find Braddock waiting for him in dense ranks shooting massed volleys into charging Indians, but he was amazed suddenly to see Braddock with a few staff officers calmly riding alone towards him and was further amazed to see in the distance Colonel Burton lead-ing the infantry towards him, running stiffly in their restricted clothing in col-umn, having as yet inflicted no damage on the enemy.

Here and there militiamen ceased to run and sweating and puffing in the sti-fling heat they took cover behind a bush and opened fire on the Indians, but their officers screamed at them and beat them with the flat of the swords to chase them back into the column.

Those squads and half squads who had been as much as a half mile from the main column when the shooting began were only now just reaching the battle-field having run through the timber and foliage, but they ran into a solid wall of Indians between them and safety and they died in twos and threes at the hand of war club, tomahawk and arrow. A few may have been struck by musket balls fired by scared militiamen.

An entire militia company swerved to the side and knelt down in ranks to open fire on the enemy on the flank and a minute later a redcoat company fol-

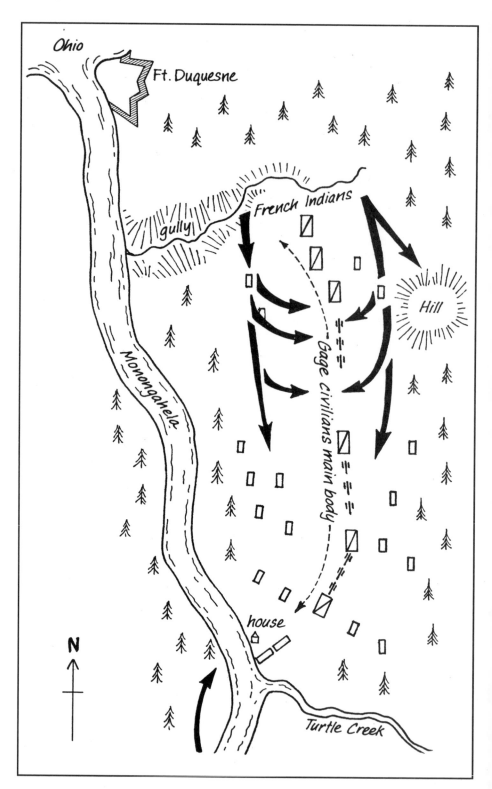

lowed suit right behind them, but their aim was so inaccurate they shot into the backs of the militiamen.

Most of the militiamen now began to take cover and fire singly and in pairs. The regular officers verbally abused any of their men who attempted the same, calling the militiamen cowards, and pushing with their horses they chased the redcoats back into the column, until eventually Gage's and Braddock's regulars were massed together. Now they began to pour volley after volley into the trees and scrub in all directions. The Indians simply lay on the ground until a volley of musket balls winged their way overhead, then calmly knelt and took careful aim to bring down one more redcoat. Then they ran off to reload in safety. Indians were notoriously poor shots for they never had enough practice ammunition, but at ranges of 20 to 30 yards they could not miss.

Braddock rode up and down the line hounding regulars and militiamen back into ranks and waving his sword. Suddenly his horse crumpled beneath him and the fat 60-year-old was thrown sprawling. His aide, Orme, rode up to him. Regaining his wind, and replacing his powdered wig and hat the general borrowed a horse and within a minute was off again hounding some other poor devil. Orme marvelled at the man's courage.

Not having had the benefit of a regular army education some of the Indians decided it would be a good idea to occupy the hill and shoot at the massed ranks below. St Clair noticed this when one of their shots felled him. He sent a messenger to Braddock, who responded by ordering the hill taken. Captain Waggoner charged up the slope with a company of militiamen, but was quickly repulsed, whereupon Colonel Burton grabbed a company of regulars and individual militiamen and led them up the slope. Astride his horse he was too tempting a target to miss and he was knocked off his horse by a ball. His men retreated.

Again a horse under Braddock collapsed in a heap and he was slammed into the hard baked earth. Regaining his wind, he borrowed yet another horse. Seeing the general yelling at someone in the bushes, Washington rode up to him and asked permission to lead his militia as he saw fit, namely to fight 'Indian-style'. Braddock must have thought this colonial a third his age to be impudent in the extreme and he replied that if Washington suggested such a thing again he would run him through with his sword. Disgusted, Washington rode off.

Yet many other British regular officers were thinking along the same lines as Washington as they watched their men fall one by one. Halket rode up to Braddock to suggest similar, but before Braddock could say what he thought of such a request a ball spun Halket off his horse. Halket's son, also an officer, rode up and dismounted to mourn his dying father, but was instantly shot and fell over his father's body.

Braddock was already off charging around, having survived four horses shot from under him by now. The bodies of his men were all around in red coats or coatless and their white shirts covered in blood or in blue coats or civilian work shirts. Already soldiers were rummaging through the knapsacks of the dead searching for powder and ball as they had run out. Bankrupt of ideas Braddock bellowed once again for his men to get back into ranks. Suddenly he was toppled from his horse as a ball passed through his lung.

Orme organised a wagon and the troops heaved the heavy, wounded general into it. Washington, was sought for he was now the first ranking officer. Washington surveyed the scene from his horse. For three hours the army had fought bravely, if not wisely, but three-quarters of the officers were down as were more than half the men. Washington knew he could not order a surrender, for there would be no gentlemen's agreement this time: the Indians' blood was up and they would massacre all prisoners. Seeing some militiamen and regulars fleeing to the rear towards Turtle Creek, the direction which most of the civilians had taken, he realised he had little time left to make a decision. He ordered a retreat.

Dunbar ordered the baggage burned as the men reformed and withdrew in relatively good order. The Indians did not chase after them: indeed they were happy to see them leave; this had been the biggest battle either of these tribes had ever fought! They too were in shock.

Fifteen of the Indians had been killed and several wounded, and eight of the Frenchmen had fallen.

Braddock had put 86 officers and 1,373 others onto the battlefield and of these 23 officers and 459 men survived to retreat, many of whom like Gates were wounded.

Aftermath: Five days later, as the column continued to retreat, Braddock died: almost his last words as he lay cradled by Orme were: 'We shall better know how to deal with them another time.' It is not known if by 'them' he meant the French, the Indians or the militia. Washington ordered him buried and all signs of his grave erased, in case any following Indians found him and dug him up.

Once safely at Fort Washington, Orme wrote to the Duke of Cumberland describing Braddock's conduct as kindly as possible, but he could not hide the fact that Braddock had shown as much incompetence as he had courage.

Appraisal: Braddock was responsible for errors in twelve major categories that can be designated: training, counsel, morale, intelligence, ground, reconnaissance, plan, dispersal, tactics, psyops, sufficiency of manpower and command ability.

He failed to ensure his recruits and militia were adequately trained.

He failed to take counsel to train everyone in the style of fighting that Washington and others suggested.

He did nothing to maintain morale among his regulars and militia.

He refused advice from those with intelligence of the terrain and the enemy.

He ignored the usefulness of the hill and allowed the enemy to possess it.

He sent out no reconnaissance unit which could have surprised the enemy waiting in the gully.

He forgot his own plan of caution once in range of the enemy.

He divided his forces into a light and a slow column, then dispersed the light column into several sections in the vicinity of the enemy.

He placed his civilians between his main body and the enemy, approached as if on parade and gave no contingency orders.

He made no attempt to use psyops (psychological operations) to damage the fragile morale of the various Indian tribes.

He refused to contemplate using Indian allies.

Once under fire he exhibited courage, but also stubbornness, glued to a mode of fighting that was suicidal.

When Benjamin Franklin, a well known American intellectual, heard the news, he said Braddock: 'was I think a brave man and might have made a good figure in some European war, but he had too much self-confidence and had too high an idea of the validity of European troops and too low a one of Americans and Indians.'

Indeed so much of the blame has fallen on Braddock's shoulders that the battle is remembered two centuries later as 'Braddock's Defeat'. No doubt none of the surviving officers was willing to accept blame and the government in London was willing to blame a dead officer, for it saved the embarrassment of a court martial.

An Alternative: It is possible that Braddock might have defeated the enemy, perhaps by keeping his forces together, approaching with good reconnaissance and cautiously beginning a siege of Fort Duquesne even with the French reinforcements inside it; until the Indians got bored and went home, as was their habit in siege warfare. By that time he would still have had three times as many troops as the French and then, if he offered the garrison a parole on the same lines as that offered to Washington the previous year, he might have able to end the whole affair. If so the story of his expedition would probably have been confined to the dusty archives of some government record office and quickly forgotten by the public.

Consequences: Braddock's defeat created a clamour for vengeance, for the London government believed it could not allow the defeat to stand by itself. Thus Washington's War turned into a major Anglo-French War and ended only eight years later after the redcoats had redeemed their honour on many battlefields in Europe and in North America, most notably at the capture of Quebec, with the result that the French Army was expelled from all of North America! The northern French lands known as Canada became British territory and the western French lands known as Louisiana went to Spain.

The Battle's Place in History: The chief result of Braddock's battle was that the reputation of the British regulars, who had been feared for a century, was thoroughly shattered. The realisation that a handful of white men fighting frontier-style together with a few hundred poorly armed Indians could repel an expedition three times their number based upon regulars was a startling discovery. It gave some of the more radical Americans the first glimmer of hope that if their political arguments with parliament resulted in armed rebellion they might just stand a chance in battle against the redcoats.

It was certainly an alarming thought that the battlefield tactics of naked, savage redskins were superior to that of educated Europeans, for this concept challenged the very foundation of white expansion across America, which was based upon the belief that the white man was superior to the red man, which no white-skinned person had hitherto doubted.

1777

Saratoga

Background: Once the French armies, though not their settlers, had been removed from North America, there was really no major European threat to the American colonies. The Indians remained hostile, but only shot at those Americans who encroached upon their land. By 1775 some of the 2,200,000 non-Indians in North America felt secure enough to challenge the London authorities.

The eighteenth century in Western Europe and North America was known as the Enlightenment and the Age of Reason. Great thinkers such as Rousseau, Voltaire, Samuel Johnson and Thomas Jefferson were shaking the foundations of established society. In music Mozart was rebelling against rules that often put a composer in prison if he disobeyed them. Edward Gibbon published (1776) the first volume of his *Decline and Fall of the Roman Empire*, with its obvious comparison to contemporary empires, the first really modern history. Quakers, Moravians and Methodists were challenging conformist Protestantism and Catholicism alike. In art, science and politics rebels were searching for new freedoms. Many of these people were intellectuals of an astoundingly high order, conversing philosophy in classical Greek, and many were members of the Freemasons, a secretive society that had spawned such notables in the seventeenth century as Isaac Newton and Christopher Wren and by 1775 had become so public that leading rebels in America openly used Freemasonry emblems and slogans.

It is true that the American political revolutionaries only demanded freedom for white, property owning, Christian men, leaving non-Christians, Indians, Negroes and women out in the cold, yet among their supporters were women, Negroes, Indians and Jews, who believed that freedom for a few was better than no freedom at all.

This is not to say that Americans openly challenged their king, for that would have been treason, and few Americans gave any thoughts about independence. Indeed they saw their desire for greater freedoms to be a natural direct result of current British political thought and experimentation.

They had their detractors in England to be sure, notably supporters of the Tories, currently in power in Parliament, but they also had English supporters, especially among the Whig party. The new American movement was not a class one, as its supporters came from all classes: landed gentry, merchants, farm hands, textile workers, indentured servants, seamstresses, slaves, shopkeepers; and it was not nationalist, for among its supporters were Americans, Englishmen, and immigrants to America. The most vociferous rabble rouser in America was Thomas Paine, recently come from England. Among others from Britain who keenly supported the cause were Charles Lee, John Paul Jones, James Wilson, Arthur St Clair, Richard Montgomery and Horatio Gates. Montgomery (a Protestant Irishman) had served in the regular army and distinguished himself at Quebec, then married into the Schuylers, a respected family in upper New York descended from Dutch colonists. Gates, having survived his wound received at 'Braddock's Defeat', had retired and bought land near Washington's home in Virginia. A studious man who wore thick spectacles, he enjoyed the life of the Virginia gentry with servants and slaves, for his mother had been a servant girl, a fact which had hindered his attempts to enter English society.

There were also Americans who had chosen the Tory cause such as William Franklin, who had parted company with his father, Benjamin Franklin a keen supporter of the new movement. Washington's best friend was a Tory.

Hostilities were put off as long as possible because everyone knew this would not be a conflict between Briton and American, but a civil war between friends, father versus son, brother versus brother.

The War: On a cool day in April 1775 Major General Thomas Gage, veteran of 'Braddock's Defeat' and now commander of the redcoat garrison in Boston, ordered the seizure of the munitions of a Massachusetts body known as the Minutemen. The Massachusetts Militia could not allow this, for they had defended themselves for over 150 years before the London government ever thought of sending regulars to Boston. To protect these munitions a handful of men gathered in civilian clothing with their hunting pieces at Lexington Common to block the advance of the redcoat column. Someone fired a shot, probably accidentally, and the redcoats panicked and poured a volley into the civilians, felling seventeen of them.

These were truly shots heard round the world. Massachusetts militiamen flocked to the scene and by nightfall had besieged Gage and his regulars in Boston.

Within a month militiamen throughout the colonies, calling themselves 'patriots', declared their support for the Massachusetts 'rebels' and they set up patriot governments, known as congresses, in each colony: New Hampshire (including Vermont), Massachusetts (including Maine), New York, Connecticut, Rhode Island, New Jersey, Pennsylvania, Maryland, Delaware, Virginia, North Carolina, South Carolina and Georgia.

However, there were no open rebellions in the colonies of Newfoundland, Nova Scotia, Canada, North West Territory (Illinois, Indiana, Ohio), West Florida (Mississippi and Alabama) or Florida. Moreover, within the rebellious colonies only about a third of the populace supported the rebellion, a third remained loyal to the crown (known as Tories or loyalists) and another third tried to maintain neutrality, not knowing or caring what the argument was about.

The Patriots also set up an all-continent congress at Philadelphia and they employed George Washington as Commander-in-Chief of the Patriot armies. He accepted his friend and neighbour Horatio Gates as chief of staff. Washington's plan was to borrow existing militia regiments to create a body known as the Continental Army, answerable to the Continental Congress in Philadelphia, rather than to the colonies' congresses. Additionally each colony would retain some militia regiments for its own use.

While Gage was besieged in Boston, Benedict Arnold a Connecticut officer gathered 261 men to capture Fort Ticonderoga and its precious cannon. He did it without serious bloodshed, for the redcoat garrison knew nothing of the rebellion. Then Arnold pleaded for support to invade Canada and raise the flag of rebellion there.

After arguments with superiors, followed by a series of adventures Arnold managed to assemble an army outside the walls of Quebec by November, while Richard Montgomery besieged Montreal.

Following Montgomery's capture of Montreal he joined Arnold and together the two forces attacked Quebec on New Year's Eve. The affair was a fiasco and Montgomery was killed, Arnold wounded and 426 patriots were captured.

However, Major General Sir Guy Carleton, who had fled Montreal for Quebec, remained inside the walls of Quebec and was not succoured until May 1776 when a British fleet arrived with reinforcements.

Having realised they would get nowhere within the British system the Patriot leaders asked Thomas Jefferson to write a Declaration of Independence, which they published on 4 July. The thirteen rebellious colonies were henceforth thirteen sovereign, albeit temporarily united, states.

Crown supporters, British as well as American, were astounded at the impudence of the Patriots and vowed to scour the land seeking out these traitors. Carleton was ordered to invade New York with two columns, one down Lakes Champlain and George and the other from Lake Ontario, using altogether 17,000 regulars, Indians, American loyalists and militia from Canada, Nova Scotia and Newfoundland, while Major General Howe launched an amphibious invasion of New York through Staten Island, Long Island, Manhattan Island and then the Hudson Valley, using 34,000 regulars, American loyalists and Germans. The Germans were either Hanoverians, and therefore as much 'British' as anyone, or soldiers lent to the British by their own rulers. The patriots erroneously called them mercenaries.

By autumn 1776 Major General Philip Schuyler and his field commander Major General Horatio Gates were in command in upper New York facing Carleton. The memory of 'Braddock's Defeat' through a lack of caution was strong in Gates' mind and he was determined to be extremely cautious in this his first combat command.

Carleton was also cautious, indeed much too cautious for his deputy Major General John Burgoyne, who wanted to charge ahead at once. Carleton not only overruled Burgoyne, but left behind fully 4,000 troops to guard Quebec and sailed south initially with only 700 regulars, 200 German artillerymen and 1,000 Indians in 24 ships and 200 canoes.

Faced with Burgoyne's consistent complaints, Carleton left him behind on 9 October. Two days later Carleton's fleet was ambushed by an American fleet on Lake Champlain and though Carleton was victorious he ordered a retreat.

Burgoyne had had enough. He resigned and sailed for England.

The Commander: John Burgoyne was 54 years old. An Englishman of good family he had entered the army in 1740 at the age of eighteen, his family buying him a lieutenancy. Stationed in Preston, England he soon became a favourite at the Mitre Inn, Red Lion and the Bull and Royal and at the gaming tables in the town's coffee houses. A friend from schooldays of the son of the Earl of Derby he visited his friend's home at Knowsley Hall some 30 miles distant for weekends and became enamoured of the Earl's daughter. Lady Charlotte Stanley fell for the handsome lieutenant, who was known as a dandy or macaroni because he dressed outlandishly, for example he wore the requisite powdered wig and was clean shaven, but he allowed his natural hair to dangle in locks at the side and wore side whiskers – considered devilish in polite society.

After Burgoyne had been turned down as a prospective son-in-law by the Earl, he and Lady Charlotte eloped. This caused a scandal for he had 'betrayed' the hospitality of one of his noble superiors. His bride brought enough money with her to buy him a promotion to captain.

Three years later, to escape creditors the gambling macaroni resigned his commission and he and his wife fled to France. The fact that he resigned in the middle of a war and moved to the enemy's country did not go down well among his superior officers.

Following ten years of rich French food, too much wine and the attentions of creditors, and probably irate French fathers of pretty French maids, he returned to England on condition that his father-in-law bought him out of his predicament. He rejoined the army and made a name for himself killing Frenchmen.

By 1762 he had raised himself to Brigadier General and entered politics as a Tory Member of Parliament. He became an oft-sighted figure at the fashionable balls and dinners in London society and was so successful he was soon solvent. In 1766 he paid Sir Joshua Reynolds to paint a flattering portrait of himself. As a macaroni with a scandalous past he was a much sought after guest by bored noble ladies.

His gambling and womanising were public, he had his friend (now the new Earl of Derby) buy him the Member of Parliament's seat for Preston, and he took to writing plays for the theatre (his biggest 'hit' was *The Heiress*). In 1773 he achieved the distinction of being condemned in Parliament for his scandalous lifestyle. In 1775 still a serving officer he was ordered to America, possibly to get him out of London.

Grand Strategy: Now in the winter 1776–77 Burgoyne was suddenly back in London and complaining about Carleton's excessive caution and claiming he could whip the rebels quickly, stating: 'There are no men of military science on the rebel side.' Burgoyne pointed out that Howe had been successful, defeating Washington's Continental Army at Brooklyn Heights and other battles and driving him westwards into Pennsylvania. This excellent campaign was in stark contrast to Carleton's failure.

Burgoyne proposed to invade upper New York along the same routes as Carleton's columns, while Howe advanced up the Hudson Valley to meet him, thus trapping the Patriot forces of Schuyler between them. This would also cut off the New England Patriots from the other rebel colonies.

Because they took him at his word, or possibly just to get rid of him, Parliament gave him field command of Carleton's forces.

The Army: Upon reaching Quebec Burgoyne organised his invasion. His western invasion force was made up of 1,000 New York loyalists, 300 regulars and 500 Indians of the Iroquois confederacy under the command of Colonel Barry St Leger. They were to sail down the St Lawrence River and across Lake Ontario to Fort

Oswego, then make their way eastwards up the Oswego River towards the Hudson Valley.

Burgoyne would command the northern invasion force personally, which consisted of: Brigadier General Phillip's brigade of the 9th, 47th and 53rd Regiments of regulars; Brigadier General Hamilton's brigade of the 20th, 21st and 62nd Regiments of regulars; and Major General Baron Friedrich von Riedesel's brigade of loyalists and Canadians in two regiments (King's Royal Regiment and Butler's Rangers) and two outfits of Germans (Prince Friedrich's Regiment and a provisional battalion of grenadier companies from several Brunswick regiments). Each regiment possessed at least one light infantry company, which was armed not with muzzle-loading muskets, but with the new Ferguson .60 calibre breech-loading rifle. In addition to the brigades Colonel Simon Fraser commanded a grenadier and two light infantry companies from the 24th Regiment. Fraser in fact acted more like a deputy to Burgoyne despite the presence of three generals. Burgoyne also possessed a very large artillery train of 138 cannon, and lastly a force of 650 Indians of the Iroquois and Abenaki confederacies accompanied the force.

The regulars wore red coats with white breeches, the Germans blue coats with yellow facings and white breeches and the loyalists wore green coats with buff or brown breeches. The Indians wore traditional clothing.

In addition to combatants Burgoyne was taking along no less than 2,000 civilian men and women as sailors, teamsters, lumberjacks, construction workers, cooks, hunters, laundresses, carpenters and such.

The soldiers soon learned that Burgoyne did not believe in mistreating his men. In fact he had earned the complimentary soubriquet 'Gentleman Johnny'.

In fine spring weather the troops, Indians and civilians embarked aboard ships, small boats and canoes for the leisurely sail down Lake Champlain, the rivers and Lake George.

On 30 June they reached Fort Ticonderoga.

The Enemy: The Patriots were waiting for them: Arthur St Clair (pronounced sinclair) had placed his 3,000 militia in the fort. St Clair was a Scot, who had come to America in 1757 at the age of 21 in a most unusual manner. He had bought a commission in the Royal American Regiment, a regular army unit recruited solely in America. Following the defeat of the French in 1763 he had married an American and settled in Pennsylvania. In 1775 he chose the Patriot cause and on the basis of his regular army experience achieved an appointment as a major general.

The Patriots wore uniforms when they could get them, but the uniforms varied. Brown coats with red facings were popular, but also dark or light blue coats, light green coats and a variety of breeches. To make this even more confusing musicians traditionally wore opposite colours: for example, if a Crown regular regiment wore red coats with blue facings its musicians wore blue coats with red facings and if a Patriot regiment wore blue coats with red facings its musicians wore red coats with blue facings. Arnold always wore a red coat.

St Clair was most fortunate to have with him a Polish engineer trained by the French Army, Tadeusz Kosciuszko, who pointed out a hilltop overlooking the fort. However, St Clair was an obstinate man who ignored advice and he did not fortify the hilltop.

The Approach: Burgoyne's staff spied the significance of the hill at once and dragged guns up the slope. Before they could open fire, St Clair decided he could not hold the fort now and he ordered a retreat! Burgoyne felt very smug. In weeks without a casualty he had done more than Carleton had done in five months. His men rejoiced by singing Yankee Doodle: 'Yankee Doodle came to town upon his little pony, stuck a feather in his hat and called it macaroni.' This was sung to insult the rebels: it meant Yankee Doodle (American fool) was so stupid he thought all he had to do to become a macaroni (outlandish dresser) was stick a feather in his hat. The song had originally been written to insult Cromwell.

Leaving the 53rd and most of Prince Friedrich's Regiment and some cannon to garrison Fort Ticonderoga and assigning the 47th to guard the vessels on the river, Burgoyne set out overland with separate columns to follow the Patriots who evidently had retreated in several directions.

The forests of this area were almost virgin, lush and green and somewhat claustrophobic as they admitted little sunlight except in glades, but Burgoyne's men had no time to judge the beauty of the scenery, for they were too worried about the possibility of a Patriot sniper awaiting them.

A column of loyalists under Fraser, seconded by Lord Balcarres, cautiously edged eastwards into Vermont and near a tiny settlement called Hubbardton caught up with a rearguard. Fraser's loyalists were fought to a standstill until von Riedesel arrived with 80 grenadiers of Prince Friedrich's Regiment. The tall Germans charged and took up good firing positions. Though trained in European-style open ground fighting, they were also good skirmishers. Within an hour they tipped the scales and defeated the Patriots, though Seth Warner's Vermont boys withdrew in good order.

The Crown forces had killed about 40 Patriots and captured 320, but it cost them 180 killed and wounded. Balcarres was one of the wounded.

Meanwhile St Leger's expedition was besieging 750 New York militia and some continentals inside Fort Stanwyx. Knowing the Patriots would attempt to rescue the fort, St Leger put some loyalists under Sir John Johnson and Indians under their chief Thayendanega (known to the whites as Joseph Brant) in a blocking position on Oriskany Creek. This was a good move for they intercepted and defeated a relief force of 800 Patriots belonging to a New York militia regiment and three continental regiments. The Patriot commander, Brigadier General Nicholas Herkimer, having lost a quarter of his men, and being wounded, ordered a retreat. However, the fort's garrison had sortied and scared the Indians, who fell back to study the situation.

Burgoyne gathered his columns together again and made slow progress on his southward march and often had to await provisions coming along his tenuous supply line. He was also hindered by Patriot snipers and by trees deliberately felled in his path.

In August he risked sending Lieutenant-Colonel Friedrich Baum and 374 Germans, 50 British, 150 Canadians, 100 loyalists and 50 Indians into Vermont to acquire supplies and possibly recruit any loyalists they might find. Winding their way through the sparsely populated Green Mountains the column was ambushed on the 15th near Bennington by New Hampshire and Vermont militia under Colonel John Stark. Baum sent a courier for reinforcements and Burgoyne replied by sending von Breymann and 642 Germans. They arrived late on the 16th to find Baum dead and his force in disarray. Von Breymann ordered a counter-attack, and the slaughter was terrific as the Patriots fought gallantly. When von Breymann was wounded he ordered his men to fall back. The whole affair had cost Burgoyne 207 killed and 700 missing and four guns and four ammunition wagons lost.

The news of this action was morale-shattering for Burgoyne and his men. Obviously the rebels could stand and fight when they wanted to. Already the tedious march, the never ending expanse of forest and the fear of snipers had frayed everyone's nerves. The regular officers were bored and made it obvious they wished to be home in England. This angered the loyalists who were fighting for their homes. Burgoyne seems to have spent much of his time gambling in his tent and dallying with Mrs Rousseau, the wife of one of his officers. There were desertions among the soldiers and civilians.

Burgoyne then learned that St Leger had abandoned his attempt to invade western New York!

In early September most of Burgoyne's Indians deserted. The whole campaign was proving to be a disaster.

Burgoyne held a staff conference. With no western invasion, an eighth of his own men dead, wounded, missing or sick and the rebels obviously full of fight, he could have honourably turned back. He chose to continue.

Causes of Arrogance: Burgoyne's reasons for confidence, if not absolute arrogance, were that he had proved, he believed, at Ticonderoga that he was tactically brilliant compared to the Patriot generals. He had forced the enemy to disperse east and south. He still retained his excellent regulars and Germans, and faced not continentals but untrained and mostly unblooded militia. Furthermore he knew that Howe would now be advancing up the Hudson to meet him as he advanced down it.

Moreover, scouts and spies informed Burgoyne that Schuyler and St Clair had been dismissed and he was now up against Gates and Arnold who had set up a defensive position on Bemis Heights on the Hudson. This was excellent news, for the rebels had placed themselves between Burgoyne and Howe and were thus trapped.

The Battlefield: As Burgoyne's column approached within twelve miles of the heights they were met by some loyal New Yorkers including John Nielsen, who owned Freeman's Farm just two miles north of the rebel position. He gave invaluable assistance about the nature of the ground, though it is probable he misled Burgoyne somewhat so that the battle would not take place on his cultivated land.

Burgoyne had to attack soon. Carleton in Quebec could not or would not send sufficient provisions. Burgoyne had run out of fodder and his horses were dying of malnutrition. With his men manhandling some wagons and guns his column was advancing only one mile per day! In two and a half months his column had covered only a hundred miles.

On 17 September rebel sniping increased dramatically as the column, having dwindled to 6,200 troops and circa 1,800 civilians came within two miles of Freeman's Farm.

The Battle: Next day Burgoyne called a council of war and was in buoyant mood despite his problems: insufficient horses, scarce provisions, his plan gone astray, low morale among the troops, a stretched line of communication to Quebec. Yet he made no serious reconnaissance of the area, relying on Nielsen and other locals. He was confident his regulars could handle the New York militia in front of him.

His plan was to march straight across Freeman's Farm with 3,000 regulars, while Fraser took the loyalists, some regular riflemen, the remaining Indians and a few Germans, for a total of 2,200, off to the right (west) to strike the enemy on their left (west) flank. The camp with its baggage, supplies and civilians would be guarded by 800 Germans.

Marching off on the morning of the 19th the two columns encountered thick fog. Most of the soldiers surely suspected they could be walking into an ambush, but Burgoyne rode past on horseback seemingly without a care.

By 11.00am when the fog lifted Fraser realised he was lost, despite having a road to follow, and he soon came under rifle fire from the south and west. As men stumbled and convulsed when struck by a heavy rifle ball, Fraser ordered a withdrawal. He had in fact been ambushed by Arnold leading a reconnaissance in force of Morgan's Pennsylvania/Virginia Regiment and Dearborn's Regiment, both of them riflemen of the Continental Army.

Minutes later Burgoyne's main force saw Morgan's riflemen charging towards them, clearly visible through the trees as they wore white hunting smocks. Burgoyne placed his men in double ranks and they met the Patriots with volley fire, soon sending them fleeing into the thick woods.

At last the pain and frustration of the march gave way to elation as the redcoats cheered, believing they had routed an untrained militia band. Burgoyne ordered his men to fix bayonets and walk forward across a clearing.

Suddenly redcoats began to drop, felled at 1,000 yards range by rifle balls of .45 to .65 calibre.

After eight minutes of walking they were within 500 yards of the Patriot riflemen, having stepped over the bodies of numerous redcoats, and the fire was more accurate now, so much so that regulars began scattering to the woods on both flanks. The accuracy of Morgan's rifles from the front (south) was joined by the accuracy of Dearborn's rifles from the right (west) and both were quickly joined by the intensity, though not accuracy, of the muskets of Poor's Massachusetts Brigade and half of Larned's New York/New Hampshire Brigade firing from the woods to the left (east). Thus Burgoyne's regulars were being shot down by seven regiments from three directions and had yet to fire back.

As some redcoats moved into the trees for cover this uncovered their artillery which was in rear and a body of patriots wearing several styles and colours of uniforms tried to capture the guns, but were chased off the field by redcoats at bayonet point.

Burgoyne and his officers rode up and down chastising their troops for skulking in the woods and ordered them back into ranks, the foremost of which had come within 150 yards of Morgan's men and were now at last shooting volleys into the woods.

Fraser's men reassembled and rushed to the sound of battle, running into the rear of Scammel's Brigade led in person by Arnold. The Patriots turned and counter-attacked and Fraser's Indians ran, but the Germans and loyalists stood their ground.

After four hours of standing in the clearing, Burgoyne seems to have come to the conclusion it was not a good idea, so, not knowing where Fraser was, he ordered von Riedesel to bring up 500 of his Germans from the camp and attack the enemy right (east) flank.

The baron complied, but his men reached an impassable gully and therefore swerved westwards. They ran straight into the rear of Poor's Brigade.

Arnold had to plead humiliatingly with Gates for permission to counter-attack the Germans with the unused half of Larned's Brigade, but once this had been approved Larned's men became lost and attacked in the west not the east, meeting Fraser's troops. Fraser fell back.

Finally as darkness rapidly fell in this area of tall trees both sides retired from the battlefield.

It was hours before all of Burgoyne's men could find the camp and some wandered around all night. The moans of undiscovered wounded sounded like the wailing of ghosts throughout the night. It was chilling to the bone.

Burgoyne ordered earthworks erected while he held a council of war. Of his 5,700 men engaged 620 had been killed or wounded. His 62nd Regiment had caught the full force of the enemy riflemen and had lost 290 of its 350 men (Patriot losses were about 330.) The atmosphere was somewhat subdued as the regular officers realised they had been outfought. Only now did they fully understand they had not been facing hastily assembled militia, but veteran regiments on loan from Washington's Continental Army.

A few days later Burgoyne learned that his lines of supply had been raided by Patriots and over 200 boats lost. His plan now was to await Howe. The civilians were deserting in droves and in frustration Burgoyne ordered captured deserters to be given a thousand lashes, often a fatal punishment. The men no longer called him 'Gentleman Johnny'.

Unknown to Burgoyne the Patriot 'victory' caused bitter wrangling among them and Gates dismissed Arnold. Every line officer but one demanded his reinstatement, angry that Gates who had done nothing to fight the battle should behave this way towards a gallant and resourceful officer. Gates ignored them. Morale in the Patriot camp improved somewhat when they were reinforced by Lincoln's Division.

It was galling for Burgoyne's men, who were close to starving, to look across Freeman's Farm and see unharvested corn, but to venture forth risked a sniper's rifle ball.

On 4 October Burgoyne held another council of war, in which Rousseau, his commissary, said they had only nine days' food left at half rations. Some officers wanted to bypass the Patriots and attack 22 miles to the south-west to Albany, the capital city of New York, where they would find food aplenty. Fraser and von Riedesel urged immediate retreat. Burgoyne vacillated for two days then agreed to a harvest expedition and stated if Howe did not arrive by the 11th he would surrender.

At 10.00am on the 6th Burgoyne's harvest expedition left the earthworks with 1,500 regulars and 600 loyalists. After advancing 2,000 yards under sniper fire

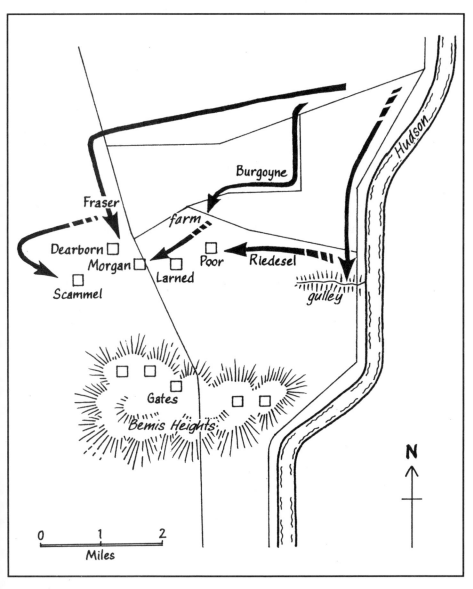

they spread out to give cover to the civilians who now rushed out to harvest the corn.

At noon Burgoyne noticed movement in the woods on his left and right and he ordered his artillery to play hell with the massing Patriots. In the thick woods the cannon balls rebounded to ground and did little damage.

At 2.30pm continentals from Connecticut, New York and New Hampshire marched into full view at the bottom of a slope and Burgoyne ordered his Grenadier Guards to charge them at bayonet point. The grenadiers did so and hollered as they approached the zombie-like Patriots who just stood and watched. Only when the redcoats were 40 yards from the Patriots did the wax dummies spring into life and fire a volley. The musket balls ripped into the grenadiers and the survivors halted in stunned shock, whereupon the Patriots fixed bayonets and charged. Patriot and redcoat stood toe to toe and stabbed each other until the grenadiers eventually broke and ran uphill to the rear.

Now Burgoyne's right (west) came under deadly fire from Morgan's riflemen, who were so far back in the woods they were invisible but for their gunsmoke. Fraser reacted by ordering the green-coated loyalists into the woods to hunt them down, American versus American.

Lord Balcarres rode up and down in front of his troops calming them under Morgan's fire, but then Dearborn's rifles joined in the killing. Balcarres' men stood it for a few minutes, but then withdrew to the north-east against orders.

Burgoyne could easily see this from horseback and despite rifle balls whizzing through his open coat he rode towards the men to stem the rout. Unable to do so, he agreed to a withdrawal.

The civilians fled to the earthworks and the regulars followed, backing up and firing every few minutes. Soon the loyalists extricated themselves from the woods and retreated too.

A party of Germans were stuck out on their own and they were now attacked by Larned's men, who against Gates' wishes were taking orders from Arnold. The Germans repelled one charge, but ran at the second one.

Fraser then set up a rearguard with his loyalists, but was fiercely charged by Arnold leading Poor's, Larned's and Morgan's men. As the two sides battled at 40 yards range a rifle ball in the stomach almost tipped Fraser off his horse. An aide led the dying colonel away.

Falling back under the cover of artillery fire, the loyalists reached the earthworks, but the Patriots charged the nearest corner, a miniature fort held by Colonel von Breymann and 200 of the blue-coated Germans. Breaking into the fort, the Patriots were met by a vicious fire from the Germans on the walls. Arnold was shot down and carried off the field wounded. Von Breymann was killed and only a counter charge by redcoats saved the Germans. The Patriots at last withdrew.

Aftermath: Burgoyne was in a dither again. His day's losses totalled 600 killed and wounded and he had lost ten guns. Snipers were still picking off his sentries and the enemy was too close for him to escape to the other side of the river.

Next day he withdrew the army seven miles north to Saratoga Heights, hoping to cross the river there, but then dithered again for several days, until he learned on the 13th that patriots were on the east bank. He was surrounded.

Sending emissaries to Gates, he asked for terms. They were generous: all his men could go home if they promised not to make war on the Patriots again. Burgoyne agreed and he and his 5,728 armed men, almost 1,000 of them wounded, marched temporarily into captivity.

Appraisal: Burgoyne was badly let down by Howe, who attacked late and was still 120 miles to the south on 13 October. Nonetheless Burgoyne, the first Crown general to surrender to the Patriots, had made errors in seven major categories: intelligence, reconnaissance, equipment, dispersal, pace, tactics, command ability.

He made no attempt to gain trustworthy intelligence about his enemy's strength or quality.

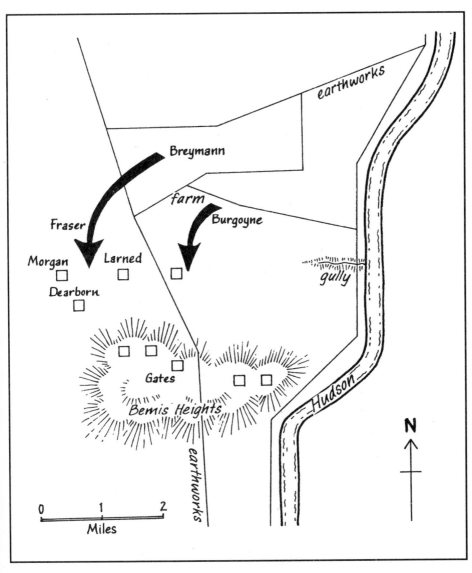

He did not reconnoitre ahead of his advance, nor reconnoitre the prospective battlefield and was therefore unaware of gullies and such or of the enemy's advanced positions.

He had not brought sufficient horses.

He had diverted forces to Vermont on loose intelligence in search of a supply depot and had reinforced this diversion, when he should have kept his eye firmly on his goal, the Hudson Valley. His use of only 2,100 men on 6 October was foolish.

The entire pace of his advance was extremely slow.

His tactics of keeping his troops in the open under fire was fatal.

His command ability was too often indecisive, giving the enemy plenty of time to manoeuvre, resupply and reinforce.

Alternatives: There were several alternatives open to Burgoyne once he had entered New York: to withdraw, to change direction of advance, to stay put.

Withdrawing would have saved his army, but extended the war another year with no significant Crown victory and it may have lost Burgoyne his command, though his capture of Ticonderoga was certainly in his favour. It would certainly have been more acceptable than surrendering, which not only extended the war, but lost an army and gave the Patriots cannon, firearms and munitions and most importantly new heart.

He could have stayed put eating all his horses to await Howe and that would have forced Gates to maintain his army in the field throughout a New York winter. Patriot regiments were notorious for losing men through unauthorised leave in the winter months and Burgoyne's tenacity may have produced fruit in the form of a link up with Howe and a retreat by Gates devoid of much of his manpower. It would certainly have been preferable to the surrender, which released Gates to turn against Howe.

There were four directions in which Burgoyne could have advanced, once the Hudson Valley was denied him by Gates: south-westwards to Albany with its warehouses full of provisions and its government offices; westwards along the Mohawk Valley to ravage the settlements there and possibly link up with St Leger; eastwards over the Green Mountains into Vermont; or south-eastwards across the Taconic Mountains into Massachusetts. Any one of these moves would have caused panic among the Patriots and forced Gates to chase him, leaving Howe free to roam southern New York.

Consequences: Burgoyne went home, but not his men, for the Patriots went back on their word and imprisoned everyone but Burgoyne. Burgoyne was greeted in the streets of London by an irate mob yelling: 'General Swagger' and 'That Martial Macaroni'.

He was stripped of his commission, whereupon he switched his political allegiance to the Whigs. Loyalty was not one of Burgoyne's strongpoints. Now a widower, he set up house with Susan Caulfield, a popular singer, and was soon once again a figure in London society.

The Battle's Place in History: Neither Gates, nor Arnold, nor Burgoyne could have foreseen the importance of Burgoyne's defeat. Benjamin Franklin had been in France drumming up support for the Patriot cause, but the French king was unwilling to ally with rebels who might surrender at any moment. But when the news of the surrender at Saratoga reached France the mood changed and the king soon authorised a new war against the British and an alliance with the Patriots. Saratoga was the turning point of the war.

North West War

Background: In 1783 the London government ended hostilities in America by recognising the independence of the various United States. Additionally Florida went to Spain. However, Canada remained British.

The Canadians who had joined the Patriot cause felt betrayed: so did the American loyalists. They passed each other as they resettled. Benedict Arnold was homeless too, having defected to the loyalist cause, believing his endeavours were not appreciated by the fickle Continental Congress.

Gates had gone on to fight and lose other battles and eventually retired a bitter man. Arthur St Clair, militarily compromised by his abandonment of Fort Ticonderoga, entered politics and became President of the Continental Congress. After the war Washington became President of the Articles of Confederation, not so much ruling the states as regulating them.

The Army: One of Washington's problems was that the Continental Army was disbanded in 1783, leaving him with only words to back up his decrees. The states still retained their militias and saw no need for a joint army. Washington was able to compromise by establishing a regiment of militia volunteers: Pennsylvania offered 260 men, Connecticut 165, New Jersey 110 and New York 165; but few showed up and none from New York.

The leader of the Pennsylvanians, Josiah Harmar, was made colonel. Though educated by Quakers and only 22 when the revolutionary war had begun he had risen to the command of the 2nd Pennsylvania Continentals.

Each of the volunteers, white men only, was issued a handsome blue coat with red facings, but they rarely wore it, being forced to spend their time building forts on the frontier.

As the states had shown no real interest in Washington's 'private army', he asked for volunteers to enlist direct and Congress gave him enough money to raise a few hundred men.

Harmar's patience was sorely tried as he had to fight for every requisition of provisions and supplies. His men were bored, overworked and paid intermittently and the regiment suffered 16% desertions in the first year. Yet, between 1784 and 1790 these 700 men were responsible for the peace of the North West Territory: 248,000 square miles of prairie, forests, rivers and mountains; a region more than twice the size of Britain and Ireland.

By 1787 it was obvious that the Articles of Confederation were not working and politicians from every state decided to create one sovereign nation. Meeting for a month in Philadelphia they created a constitution for the new country and Washington was elected President of the Republic of the United States.

As far as Harmar was concerned this meant an expansion to 1,216 soldiers, but not much of an improvement in supplies or pay. Despite unification the states argued that they could handle any war that might come their way and had no need of Harmar's men.

The War: Yet, as far as the frontier settlers were concerned war had come, brought about by the presence of the British. The American War of Independence had ended in 1783, but the British still garrisoned several forts in flagrant violation of the peace treaty: Pointe au Fer, Oswegatchie, Oswego and Niagara in upper New York and Miami, Detroit and Michilimackinac in Michigan.

Within the political spectrum in England were the Whigs, who were eager to turn the United States into allies, the Tories who begrudgingly dealt with the Americans as equals, and a hardcore faction within the army, supported by displaced loyalists, who believed the new nation would soon fall apart and they could take up where they had left off, hence their refusal to abandon the garrisons in New York, the colony which had provided the highest number of loyalists, and Michigan, from which they could continue to influence the Indians of the North West Territory.

Most Americans really did not care if the garrisons remained: in New York they traded with them; but the few settlers who were trying to make a home in the North West were passionate about the situation, because the Shawnee were raiding the settlers' homes and farms, and the settlers strongly suspected the Shawnee were being supplied by the British with arms and ammunition.

During the revolution the British had encouraged Indians to raid American homesteads and massacre men, women and children, knowing the Indians did not ask if they were loyalists or Patriots. However, the vast majority of Americans refused to believe that now, years after the war, the British were still encouraging such heartless butchery. As a result the settlers' complaints were ignored.

Grand Strategy: Besides politics, Arthur St Clair had gone into business, becoming a director of the new Ohio Company, which like its predecessor of 35 years earlier was trying to colonise the land north of the Ohio River, known as the North West Territory. In 1787 he had talked his Congress into passing the Northwest Ordinance making him that territory's first governor.

However, prospective settlers were scarce owing to the stories of Shawnee massacres. Once in office St Clair was overwhelmed by petitions from his constituency and shaken by their pleas when he rode as far west as the Mississippi River to see them. Between 1784 and 1790 the settlers of the territory suffered 1,500 killed at the hands of the Shawnee, a tremendous amount of suffering for a population (1790) of just 4,280 whites and Negroes, including French families who had remained after 1763.

Angry that a couple of hundred Shawnee warriors were blocking the march of progress, St Clair wrote to George Washington and Thomas Jefferson, demanding Harmar's regiment join with local militia to eradicate the Indian menace once and for all. This was agreed.

In the summer of 1790 Harmar organised a two-pronged offensive: Major J. F. Hamtramck led an expedition from Vincennes, while Harmar gathered 353 of his regulars and 1,133 militia from Kentucky, Virginia and Pennsylvania and assembled them at Fort Washington. He told them that much was riding on this expedition: the future of his 'army' and the future of westward expansion by the American people. In theory the land as far west as the Mississippi River was American soil, but with the Shawnee and other Indians running wild, this land was denied the American people. The fledgling nation could not allow such a situation to continue, thus the United States Army's one and only general (he had been recently promoted) was to lead his country's first military expedition.

The Approach: As expected, provisions were slow in arriving and it was September before Harmar's command could leave the fort. He planned to follow the Maumee and Miami Rivers until he reached the Shawnee villages, which he thought they would defend. His intelligence as to whether or not this would happen, or whether any other tribes would see this as an invasion and oppose him, was non-existent. He was blundering forward, but felt he had little choice, for there was much political pressure on him to seek a victory. As long as he kept his force together the few hundred hostiles could not hurt him.

On 18 October they reached a hastily abandoned village. Excitedly the men destroyed and burned lodges, drying frames, animal skins, fur rugs, canoes, cooking pots and such items the Shawnee would need for winter.

Over the next four days they destroyed four more abandoned villages. It galled them that the Shawnee would not fight and that while they were here some Shawnee war party might be elsewhere massacring helpless settlers. Anxious that the Shawnee would evade him, though he was by now 150 miles inside their land, Harmar chose to divide his forces to search for them, by sending out two detachments of over a hundred men each.

Days later a score of survivors from the two detachments came running into his camp with bloodcurdling stories of harrowing escapes. No less than 75 regulars and 108 militiamen had been killed or captured when the detachments bumped into hostile war parties. Harmar, shaken by this news and knowing winter was fast approaching, ordered a retreat to Fort Washington.

Renewed Grand Strategy: St Clair was livid. The federal government's one and only general had proven to be incompetent and it would be several months before another expedition could be formed. He demanded the federal government do something about this sad state of affairs and suggested that he himself take command next time, failing to mention his own abysmal war record.

Congress was also flabbergasted, though they should not have been and were very much at fault through their penny pinching naivety. The problem was that these congressmen still thought of themselves as Virginians, Georgians, Pennsylvanians and such, not as Americans in the federal sense, and they aimed to please their home state governments as much as possible. They hated to spend money on something that was solely of federal benefit, or of benefit to only one state.

Yet they had to do something and, like many a Congress since, they decided to throw some money at the problem to solve it. They authorised the recruitment of a second regiment of regulars of 912 men on three-year enlistments and the creation of a Corps of Levies of 2,000 men to be enlisted for six months. Furthermore they accepted St Clair's offer of his services.

The Commander: St Clair was eager to get to grips with the enemy, whom he knew were the Shawnee plus perhaps a few other tribes and he too was beginning to suspect British involvement. Most important, though, at the age of 54 he was about to achieve that great military victory that had always eluded him since he had left Scotland 33 years earlier.

At Fort Washington he gathered Harmar's regulars, militiamen and new recruits and attempted to train the well-meaning but awkward soldiers. Fortunately some were veterans of the American War of Independence.

Coming to the conclusion that his army would not be ready for some time, he chose to make a preliminary strike and in June 1791 sent out 750 Kentucky militia to raid the hostiles. They destroyed a Wea village for the loss of just five wounded, but there had never been proof that the Wea were responsible for outrages. He may have simply added to his enemies.

In August he sent 500 militia to repeat the affair and they successfully destroyed a village at a cost of two killed and one wounded.

Causes of Arrogance: St Clair was confident. He had a British Army education and his regulars were as well trained as he could make them. He had shown that troops in large bodies could survive in enemy territory and punish the enemy. His total force of 2,700 men with their .45 calibre rifles and .69 calibre muskets were trained in skirmishing and volley fire and would be more than a match for all the Shawnee and any other tribe that chose to ally with them. None of the tribes in the North West could muster more than a hundred warriors each, the Shawnee being the exception, and in any case on any given day some warriors would be away hunting, trading or on a war party, and some would have to be left behind to defend the women and children, so an entire tribe could really not muster an 'army' of more than 50 or so.

Even after fighting Indians for 169 years the whites still had an innate sense of racial superiority over them which extended to the battlefield. They saw Indians as good scouts, but thought they really could not manage a battle without white leadership.

It does not seem to have occurred to St Clair that the North West tribes might band together under one leader for self-defence, as the Powhattan, Abenaki and Iroquois had done in the previous century. The North West tribes had in fact united once before, in 1763 under a warrior called Pontiac, but because that had been so unusual St Clair believed the Indians, who spent much of their time fighting each other, could never produce another 'Pontiac'.

The Expedition: It was September before St Clair's 718 regulars and 1,574 Corps of Levies were ready, and after leaving 300 to garrison Fort Washington he marched northwards at the head of his army, which included 418 Kentucky and Pennsylvania militia.

A few days inside the territory he stopped to build a fort as he wanted secure lines of communication. Construction took ten days. He was able to leave his sick here, but naturally the fort required a garrison and this came out of his 2,400 man complement, leaving him with less than 2,000 as they marched on.

By late October the weather was turning chilly and rain dispirited the men. They had joined to fight Indians not march and build forts. The knowledge that Indians were watching them at all times made the atmosphere tense and frustrating. Each morning's roll call uncovered the desertion of two or three men.

By the first morning of November St Clair had covered only 100 miles in 48 days, and this morning he learned that 70 militiamen had deserted the night before. Cursing his troops as: 'offscourings, enervated by idleness, debaucheries and every species of vice'; St Clair decided to send a unit to arrest the deserters. Considering his regulars to be the only reliable soldiers he had, he sent 262 of them off after the deserters. This left him with just 1,400 men in camp, of which by his own admission only about 300 or so were reliable.

The Enemy: St Clair was wrong in his judgement of Indian capabilities. Harmar's two detachments had not stumbled into war parties, but had been deliberately attacked in two well planned ambushes, which were themselves part of a larger strategy. This had been coordinated by Little Turtle, a 44-year-old Eel, whose appearance, as he dressed in robes with the front half of his head shaven and his hair long, was that of a philosopher not a warrior. He was the 'new Pontiac' whom St Clair believed did not exist.

Little Turtle knew exactly what he was doing. Daily his scouts reported to him all the activities of St Clair's column. He refused to countenance an attack, and told his warriors to await the right moment.

He had indeed been supplied by the British, who were encouraging raids on American homesteads with such offers as British recognition of an Indian buffer state between the USA and Canada.

His leadership had overawed other chiefs, who for their war against the white invaders agreed to put aside tribal feuds and animosities. Hence Little Turtle's army consisted of the Eel, Shawnee, Wea, Ojibway, Ottawa, Pottawatomie, Huron, Kickapoo, Piankashaw, and the thirteen bands of the Delaware, an assembly of well over 1,000 warriors. Each tribe chose several warriors as sub-commanders for the coming battle: for example, Tecumseh of the Shawnee.

When Little Turtle's scouts reported to him that St Clair had reduced his main force by 262 regulars who had gone after the deserters, he knew this was the moment to strike.

The Battle: In the early morning hours of 4 November the Indian army approached St Clair's camp. They did not whoop and holler or fire their rifles, but obeyed Little Turtle's orders to creep silently and stealthily with a discipline that any élite European regiment would have been proud of. When they were almost upon the sleeping soldiers a white sentry fired a warning shot and now the Indians let out spine-chilling screams and charged the tents and bedrolls and using knives, war clubs, tomahawks and steel axes they stabbed, slashed and cudgelled the dazed soldiers as they emerged from sleep. Many soldiers never escaped their tents.

The soldiers along the perimeter did not stand a chance, but those in the middle rallied around St Clair and half-dressed they lined up in ranks and met the charging Indians with volley fire in the nick of time.

The warriors fell back and hiding behind tents, bushes and trees they began shooting at the massed troops with their rifles and bows. A few solders left the main body and fought individually, but St Clair and his officers managed to keep most of the men together.

Now and then an American panicked and darted into the woods in flight only to be followed by a grinning warrior who planned to hang the man's scalp on his lodge pole that night. Some captured soldiers could be heard screaming in agony as Indians tortured them.

After two hours of slaughter St Clair ordered a bayonet charge with the object of taking the Indians by surprise long enough for his army to escape. The manoeuvre was in fact highly successful, and some may have wondered how the day would have gone if they had done this immediately. Cutting their way through, the troops did not stop for breath until they were clear of the camp. Only a handful of Indians followed them at a distance hoping to take prisoner any soldiers who could not keep up.

Little Turtle's warriors remained in camp looting it and telling each other embellished stories of their heroism in the fight. They were suffering from trauma as this was the biggest battle any of them had ever known, apart from a few old men who had fought Braddock. Their casualties were less than a hundred, but as these Indians lived in villages of less than a hundred men, women and children the number of dead and wounded Indians lying on the field appeared overwhelming.

It was day's end before St Clair could take an account: 657 men were dead or missing and 271 of his remaining 743 were wounded. His expedition of 2,400 men had been reduced to just 472 able-bodied men with no provisions and some not even fully clothed.

Appraisal: Harmar had made errors in four categories: intelligence, psyops, reconnaissance and dispersal.

He made little or no attempt to find out who his enemy was, their strength or location.

He made no attempt to woo any of the chiefs, or to offer a chance for them to distance themselves from the Shawnee depredations.

To be sure he was right to have reconnaissance parties searching for the enemy, but these should have been parties of, say, three men perhaps a mile or so from each other looking in all directions, so if one party found the enemy their struggle might alert the others, and he would risk only a few of his men at a time. Instead he searched in only two directions, in parties so numerous that their stumbling through thickets and woods made too much noise to surprise any Indian, but if attacked were not large enough to survive. Moreover parties this large could be seen leaving his camp. He knew the Shawnee were watching him, or he would not have found their villages abandoned.

This constituted dispersal of his forces in the face of the enemy, leaving both parties and his main column in jeopardy.

St Clair was angered by Harmar's failure, but he himself made errors in seven major categories: intelligence, psyops, counsel, morale, dispersal, reconnaissance and tactics.

He made no attempt to gain serious intelligence about the enemy, totally ignoring the enemy's potential, believing that without white commanders the Indian could not fight a stand up battle or use strategy, despite much evidence to the contrary, and disbelieving the tribes could unite or produce another 'Pontiac'.

He made no attempt to use psyops, which might have damaged the unity of Little Turtle's shaky military alliance. In fact his raid on the Wea might have backfired, sending a message to the peaceful tribes that they too were in danger.

He had access to professional Indian fighters, Indians, frontiersmen and others who knew the enemy's ways, but it is obvious he took little counsel from them.

He knew his army's morale was bad and did nothing to correct it. He despised his men and they knew it.

He dispersed his forces by garrisoning an unnecessary fort and then by sending 262 reliable regulars to hunt 70 unreliable deserters, not only denuding his own army of half its best men, but risking the lives of those regulars.

It is doubtful if any reconnaissance teams could have found the enemy so that he could ambush them, but certainly a spread of reconnaissance teams on the morning of the 4th could have acted as trip-wire units, engaging Little Turtle's army before it could surprise the camp.

He failed to realise that even in camp he was engaged in tactics: he did not have his men sleep in shifts, so that a third were armed and alert at any one moment nor did he place sentries outside his perimeter.

Consequences: St Clair was ridiculed. This was the worst defeat of a white expedition at the hands of an Indian-led army in 184 years. St Clair remained governor, but like Harmar he lost his commission. Harmar became a civil servant. St Clair spent the rest of his life trying to excuse his defeat and died in poverty at the age of 81.

The consequences of St Clair's defeat were twofold. The British Army was encouraged that its policy of making war on the Americans by proxy was working and they not only increased the flow of war material to the tribes, but began sending 'advisers' with them on war parties, thus escalating the proxy war into a real war, which for political reasons both Parliament and Congress refused to admit actually existed.

The second consequence was that Congress agreed to raise another army and to provide a general who had actually won a battle before. They chose Anthony Wayne, whose vigour in the revolutionary war, some said rashness, had gained him the nick-name 'Mad Anthony'.

He recruited 3,578 personnel into his Legion of the United States and he literally whipped them into shape with floggings and executing captured deserters. He did not enter the territory until October 1793 and then only to build Fort Greenville 75 miles north of Fort Washington. In December he reached the St Clair battleground and built Fort Recovery. Fighting skirmishes he never once let his guard down.

Wayne showed that there could be an alternative result when a white army met Little Turtle. On 20 August 1794 with 2,000 legion regulars and 1,500 Kentucky and Virginia militia at the site of a tornado touchdown on the Maumee River known as Fallen Timbers he was attacked by Little Turtle's army and a contingent of a hundred British 'advisers'. Wayne's men held their ground, though suffering 70 casualties, then charged with the bayonet. Killing 40 Indians and wounding scores more they broke the military back of the North West tribes.

The Indians fled to a British fort, but the British commander barred the gates.

Over the next weeks individual chiefs surrendered to Wayne and a year later at Fort Greenville British emissaries agreed to give up the idea of an Indian buffer state and to withdraw their troops from US soil. The Indians were forced to move several hundred miles to the north and west.

The Battle's Place in History: Truthfully the battles fought by Harmar and St Clair in themselves have no place in history, for they have been consigned to that dustbin of failures that every nation keeps hidden. Fallen Timbers is remembered by the Americans, but not the war in which it was fought. The war was an embarrassment both to Britons and Americans and remains so to this day.

The war was well remembered by the North West Indians, but as none of these tribes were literate, their great accomplishments against Harmar and St Clair were sung only as long as the singers remained alive. When old age claimed the last of them this oral history was lost.

1814

New Orleans

Background: The British accepted their defeat at Fallen Timbers gracefully because from 1793 onwards they were involved in a major struggle with France.

French royal support for the American patriots had backfired: the French bourgeoisie perceived the victory of the patriots over a tyrannical king and nobility as a victory for themselves too, and in 1789, just six years after the American victory, they overthrew their king and nobility.

John Locke, a seventeenth century English philosopher, had urged respect for 'life, liberty and property': ('property' meant the results of one's own labour). Jefferson wanted to quote him, but by 1776 'property' had its modern connotation, so he wrote 'life, liberty and the pursuit of happiness', and added that 'all men are created equal'. The French revolutionaries adapted his words as 'fraternity, liberty, equality'.

The British landed gentry did not care who ruled France, but this did seem to be a disturbing trend, first America, now France, and they feared a revolt in Britain. Radical Whigs were already handing out American and French revolutionary literature and with a king currently suffering from 'madness' and unable to help them, the British ruling class appeared weak. Therefore, they made war on France to restore the French king.

The revolutionaries in France got out of hand, being far more radical than their American counterparts. Indeed in 1799 war broke out between France and the United States: a war that was fought only at sea. For two years the Americans and British were in effect allies, though no formal alliance was made.

Ultimately power in France fell into the hands of Napoleon Bonaparte who defeated Austria, his arch enemy on land, then made peace with the United States, selling them the entire territory of Louisiana, which stretched from New Orleans to the Rocky Mountains, and in 1802 he made peace with Britain.

In 1803 the British made war on France again and this time they became quite ruthless at sea, confiscating any ship that traded with France and kidnapping foreign merchant seamen to replace casualties on their own warships. Many of these ships and sailors were American, an average of two per day being kidnapped, so naturally the United States government became extremely angry. To add to the grievances, the British refused to acknowledge the citizenship of naturalised Americans.

In 1811 the tribes of the North West Territory led by Tecumseh rose in revolt and were defeated at the Battle of Tippecanoe by an American force of regulars and militia. The Americans strongly suspected the British in Canada had been up to their old tricks of supplying the Indians with munitions and urging them to massacre Americans. Many Americans demanded an invasion of Canada to rid the continent of the British once and for all.

By 1812 President Madison and Congress realised that until the British shackles were removed the rest of the world would always regard the Americans as merely rebellious children of the British, undeserving of international respect in trade, diplomacy or social activity. The Americans did not see themselves as rebels any more, nor did they think the current British government was an example to be followed: two cabinet ministers Canning and Castlereagh fought duels, and Prime Minister Percival was assassinated. The Americans considered themselves and the modern British to be both offspring of seventeenth century English politics and philosophy. In other words, politically speaking Britain and the United States were not mother and son, but were brothers, and like all brothers they loved each other and fought each other at the same time.

As much to gain respect from the world as to settle current grievances the United States declared war on Britain.

The War: The British Army saw the American declaration as a stab in the back while they were in a desperate life or death struggle with Napoleon's forces in Spain. The British Army in Spain led by the Duke of Wellington relied on American grain shipments for their sustenance.

However, the British soon changed their demeanour from anger to merriment when the Americans failed miserably to liberate the Canadians from British rule. The American blue uniformed regulars were few in number and poorly trained and their grey uniformed militia were simply farmhands and shopkeepers in disguise. Within two months the British had repelled an American invasion of Canada, captured Detroit and occupied Fort Dearborn (Chicago). The most telling point was that the Canadians did not want to be liberated and their militia fought willingly alongside British regulars.

The war did have its darker side. The British saw the American burning of the Canadian city of York as an act of pure vandalism.

In April 1814 Napoleon surrendered and the naval cause of the Anglo-American War ceased to be, but the Americans refused to call off the war. This really angered the British and they made plans for a series of raids to hurt the Americans and thus force them to seek peace.

The greatest asset of the British was their Royal Navy, and a plan was created by their naval and army staff, including the Duke of Wellington, to make seaborne raids on the American coast. Wellington recommended several officers for this duty including Major General Robert Ross, like him a Protestant Irishman, and he offered some of his veterans from Spain, the 4th, 44th and 85th Regiments.

In August 1814 the fleet arrived in Chesapeake Bay, sailed up the Patuxent River and disembarked the troops at Benedict, Maryland on the 19th. They occupied Nottingham next day and seemed poised to take the city of Washington District of Columbia, the new capital of the United States.

On the 24th they met the American army at Bladensburg and in minutes they had the American militia on the run, and minutes later drove off the regulars, and really only had trouble with a body of sailors and marines. With only 2,600 men Ross had defeated over 5,000 Americans, taken ten guns and 120 prisoners and inflicted 150 casualties for 250 of his own killed and wounded. The veterans of Spain were not impressed by American fighting ability.

British sailors, marines and the 21st Regiment entered Washington and burned down several government buildings. British troops also captured Fort Washington and Alexandria. It was a shabby episode in American military history.

Despite being forced to govern his country from the back of a horse, President Madison refused to surrender. The British wondered what they could do next to bring the Americans to their knees.

In September Ross raided Baltimore, but his army suffered 300 casualties and he himself was killed. The British withdrew without doing further damage.

Grand Strategy: The Royal Navy now came up with another plan. They would hurt the United States economically. The city of New Orleans, in American hands for just twelve years, was a major commercial centre, a great port and was the terminal for all traffic between the Mississippi River and the open sea. The capture of this strategic point, its harbour, docks, warehouses full of cotton and sugar, and countless merchant ships and barges should hold the Americans to ransom until Madison sued for peace. It was a good plan.

The Duke of Wellington was asked to recommend a replacement for Ross as ground commander to work with Admiral Sir Alexander Cochrane the naval commander. The Duke recommended his brother-in-law, Major General Edward Pakenham.

The Approach: On 10 December 1814 Cochrane's fleet of 50 vessels anchored off Ship Island, which was to be used as an advanced base. Major General John Lambert went ashore with his troops to stretch their legs. Cochrane's plan was to use shallow draught warships and barges to enter Lake Borgne, which was a bay, then sail up Bayou Bienvenu and land the troops just ten miles or so from New Orleans, thereby bypassing the forts that guarded the sea entrance to the Mississippi River some 80 miles downstream of the city. This was a good plan.

Cochrane believed in good intelligence and he sent scouts and spies to learn as much as possible. He found that New Orleans was poorly defended, though reinforcements were expected, and that Lake Borgne was protected by a flotilla of five gunboats.

Armed with this knowledge, on the 14th Cochrane sent his shallow draught warships into the bay and in a short fight they captured the American vessels.

The British fleet sailed in as close as they dared – some vessels ran aground – then began to embark the troops into small boats and sailed on, until Major General John Keane picked out a campsite.

The navy had done its job well, but the army was showing signs of sheer arrogance. Keane, another Protestant Irishman, knew Pakenham would soon arrive to take command, so he determined to do as little work as possible. His unloading of troops and supplies was so leisurely as to be torpid, and in any event he was still not on the mainland, but on marshy Pea Island.

The Battlefield: These British soldiers who had fought in Spanish deserts, the tropics of the West Indies and 90°F heat in Maryland, found Louisiana in winter to be cold, foggy and damp. The terrain was unlike anything they had ever seen – weirdly shaped stunted trees poking out of foul smelling water, a cypress swamp with islets of soggy ground, pine trees and ground littered with dried pine cones and needles. The wildlife was abundant: a variety of noisy birds, raccoons and armadillos, resembling pigs in armour. Within a day some of the men had seen snakes and alligators. No one was worried, though, for the one thing no one saw was an American soldier.

The Army: The expedition included the 4th, 7th, 21st, 43rd, 44th and 85th Regiments wearing red tail coats, white trousers and black leather shakos. Also present were the 95th Regiment wearing short dark green coats and grey trousers and the 93rd Highlanders, who opted for a red coat and tartan trousers. There were also some red-coated light companies from other regiments, which like the entire 95th were armed with the lightweight 30inch barrel .625 calibre Baker rifle. These troops were to be joined by marines, in a similar red coat uniform, and the Negro 1st and 5th West Indies Regiments, in red coats and blue trousers. The army had artillery and a fleet behind them. Above all they had defeated the Americans in Maryland and had stood up to the best Napoleon could offer. The word invincible came to mind.

After a few days some Americans were captured, who talked freely, saying that New Orleans was defended by Andrew Jackson, a politically appointed general, and the local militia. It seemed too good to be true. Surely, New Orleans was theirs for the taking. However, according to a couple of American doctors Jackson had 20,000 men. Keane accepted their account rather than the others'.

On the night of the 22nd he led the troops onto the mainland, capturing Brigadier General Jacques Villere at his plantation.

The Enemy: Only when one of the captives, Major Gabriel Villere, escaped and reached New Orleans were the Americans alerted as to the close proximity of the British. The city panicked and many fled into the countryside. Coming towards them were the very same troops who had burned Washington, the very same who had raped and massacred innocent civilians at Badajoz in Spain, and with every retelling of these barbarous deeds the inhabitants of New Orleans became more fearful.

In command was Andrew Jackson, a Tennessee politician, who held a major general's commission of federal volunteers. A tall hawk-faced man with a full head of sweeping grey hair, he was a pensive but fiery individual who on this occasion was determined to act calm and methodical, unlike everyone around him.

The city's defences were in the hands of a militia regiment of the French-speaking bourgeoisie, known as the City Guard, and another regiment of the lower classes, who spoke English, German, French or Spanish. Few had the required grey militia uniforms. He also had the 44th Regiment of federal volunteers (issued grey uniforms to their dismay). Just days earlier he had been reinforced by blue-uniformed regulars, the 1st, 2nd, 6th and 7th Regiments. Expected any day were dragoons of the Tennessee and Mississippi militias and infantry of the Tennessee and Kentucky militias. Jackson knew the Kentuckians as he had led them against Indians, but how would they fare against Wellington's veterans he wondered?

He was so desperate for fighting men that he authorised the use of Cherokee, Choctaw and Creek Indians in the front line and accepted two hastily recruited regiments of local French-speaking Negroes. He even accepted the offer of pirates from their leader Jean Lafitte, if he released them from prison.

Jackson's first overt act was to send a schooner, the USS *Carolina*, downriver to shell the British camp, while he placed his men in position.

Preliminary Moves: At 7.30pm on 23 December the schooner's shells began to fall haphazardly among the British encampment. Keane could not reply, because he had yet to disembark the artillery, despite being ashore over a week. Therefore, he sent riflemen to slip, slide and wade through the soggy swampy ground to the north bank of the Mississippi River to snipe at the schooner. This caused little damage for the river was 800 yards wide and the schooner had a good deal of water in which to manoeuvre.

Throughout the night British pickets on the west of the encampment came under fire from American snipers and horse mounted dragoons.

Come dawn British pickets could see Americans in the blue uniform of regulars lining up about 1,200 yards to the west between them and the city. Under the cover of the cacophony of sound from the *Carolina*'s guns Jackson had approached with his army.

The Commander: It was this day that Pakenham arrived. Sir Edward Pakenham had entered the army as a boy through purchase and by the age of sixteen had bought a major's commission. In 1798 he had distinguished himself in battle against Irish Catholic rebels – he was a Protestant Irishman – and later he fought the French in the West Indies and the Danes at Copenhagen. In 1806 his sister married Arthur Wellesley (the Duke of Wellington) and that officer pleased his young bride by taking Pakenham under his wing. When Wellington went to Spain to command the army he made Pakenham his adjutant and by 1811 Pakenham was a major general. Thus when Pakenham was recommended for command in America he had never before commanded a battle of his own and it must be remembered he was not Wellington's first choice.

Pakenham was determined not to let down his brother-in-law. Additionally, as Napoleon had been defeated and this coming battle would more than likely bring the Americans to heel, it would be the last battle fought by a British army in a period of 22 years of warfare, and as such would be remembered out of all proportion. To be the victor of such a crowning glory was the sort of thing that comes to only one man in a nation and only once in a century. The pressure on Pakenham, still only 36 years old, was enormous.

It was all the more frustrating, therefore, to see the state of the army when he arrived. As he and his deputy, Major General Sir Samuel Gibbs, inspected the troops and surveyed the terrain they became ever more disappointed. Keane had made a hash of things. On his left flank (south) was the wide Mississippi River; on his right (north) an impenetrable swamp; to his rear (east) was the bayou, too shallow for warships to approach and give covering fire; to the front (west) was the enemy, fully alerted and waiting. Furthermore, his men were under artillery fire from the schooner to the south and from American field guns to the west and their gunnery was surprisingly accurate. Yet, Keane had not unloaded the artillery and many of the provisions were still aboard ship too.

Pakenham made three arrangements: the artillery and other stores were to be unloaded at once; the bayou was to be widened and deepened by his engineers so that boats could come in closer; and the navy was to invent a method of putting gunboats on the river. He also sent out scouts to study the enemy's intentions.

Causes of Arrogance: It is understandable why Pakenham was extremely confident, despite the results of his inspection. He was a British Army general, trained and trusted by Wellington, the greatest British soldier since Wolfe. Whereas Jackson was a politician. Pakenham's men were veterans who had bested Napoleon's finest and had overcome Americans in Maryland. Jackson on the other hand had shopkeepers, merchants, dock thieves, Negroes, farm boys, backwoodsmen and pirates and but a handful of so-called regulars.

The Bombardment: At last things began to move at feverish pace and the guns were disembarked, unpacked, and dragged, pushed and shoved to the river bank and to the west flank. They began to take the *Carolina* under fire.

On the 26th, as the normal winter fog thinned out in mid-morning, Pakenham unleashed his artillery on the American army. He trusted that such a bombardment would break the morale of Jackson's militia. American militia, he was informed, could not take more than a few minutes of cannon fire.

If deserted by his militia Jackson would have but two choices, to retreat eight miles to the city or to attack. Wellington's favourite tactic had been to goad the enemy into attacking and then mow them down with volley fire by two ranks of redcoats. Pakenham evidently attempted to mimic Wellington.

However, the American artillery continued to reply and accurately too. The British soon learned that if they lit a campfire the smoke drew gunfire. No doubt Pakenham assumed Jackson's guns were manned by veteran regulars.

By dusk the American fire had not slackened and Pakenham called off the duel to save ammunition. The Americans ceased fire too, though when British troops lit campfires American cannonballs came screaming in. The British had to eat cold rations that night and British pickets were subjected to sniping.

On the 27th the artillery began anew and the *Carolina* was struck, set afire and then blew up. Pakenham prepared to receive the American attack, but it did not come. Jackson, he realised was either extremely cautious or could not induce his men to leave their ramparts. Evidently the British assumed that the American militia had long since fled.

On the 28th American artillery played hell with Pakenham's camp and it was obvious Jackson still had his artillerymen if no one else. Moreover, a new annoyance appeared, the USS *Louisiana*, a replacement for the *Carolina*, which began to shell the British left flank.

By the 31st the Americans had fallen back to within three miles of the city and Pakenham's men had followed cautiously. American cavalry did not allow them to take a good look at the new line, but it was assumed Jackson would have some form of rampart and perhaps a ditch. To date the British had suffered 275 killed and wounded.

The navy had come up with a new invention. While ordinary soldiers working under engineer officers were dredging the bayou to the river, naval officers had created canoe gunboats each consisting of one large canoe fitted with a cannon firing forward. For days sailors and soldiers dragged and heaved the canoe gunboats through brackish water and reedy swamp. The work was excruciatingly painful and exhausting with bugs for company, the fear of stepping into quicksand and the constant terror of snakes and alligators. The newcomers did not know that their splashing and shouting scared the wild creatures away. With every exertion they cursed their officers for having placed them in surely the worst battlefield any British army had had the displeasure of fighting upon.

It was the early hours of New Year's Day 1815 before the canoe gunboats were in position and the gunners tensely expected the order to fire. Pakenham had to await the lifting of the morning fog and it was 9.00am before his artillery spotters could see their targets. The canoe gunboats opened fire from the river flank while the field artillery spoke with a roar from the landward flank. Within minutes Jackson's guns replied.

Some of the British guns were behind hogsheads of sugar for protection, but the Americans flung heated cannon balls at them, which knocked askew the parapets and burned them. However, it did look as if Pakenham's plan was working for some American companies came out to do battle. He was goading them into attacking and he was ready. Suddenly the Americans withdrew in good order.

After six hours of ear-splitting bombardment Pakenham called for a ceasefire. The Americans had neither broken nor attacked. Minutes later the Americans ceased fire too.

The noise had been so terrific that the following serenity was positively eerie, especially as music began to waft through the trees and over the tufts of swamp grass. Jackson had ordered his musicians to play 'Yankee Doodle'. The old British insult song had been adopted by the Americans almost as a national anthem. The British soldiers knew it was Jackson's way of saying he was still there. The day had cost Pakenham 55 killed and wounded.

The Assault: Pakenham probably suspected that Jackson's music had been a partial ruse and that he had lost many men from desertion and was close to collapsing. Pakenham decided, therefore, not to await an American attack, but to launch his own, though he had no intention of making a frontal assault until he had turned Jackson's flank.

He arranged for 1,400 men to be transported to the south bank of the river: the 85th Regiment, 200 sailors, 400 marines, the light companies of the 7th, 43rd and 93rd Regiments, part of the newly arrived 5th West Indies Regiment and fourteen cannon all under Colonel Thornton. Their purpose was to overcome any Americans on the south bank then reach a point opposite Jackson's main line and pour flanking fire with cannon and long-range rifles into the Americans while he himself led the remainder of the army, 5,900 men, in a frontal assault.

Pakenham and his staff were in fact very wrong in their appreciation of the situation in Jackson's camp. Jackson's militia had not run and his desertions were few. His artillerymen were extremely well trained and some of the guns were aimed by pirates, who were used to firing from a pitching vessel at a moving target, and for whom firing from a stationary platform at a stationary target was child's play. So far the American loss in sailors and troops was only 264.

Moreover, Jackson's army had grown in size as the expected reinforcements arrived and by 4 January he had 4,500 infantry, which with artillery, cavalry and engineers gave him 6,200 men. On the south bank to prevent such an outflanking move as Pakenham was planning, Jackson had placed a company each from his 1st, 2nd and 6th Regiments of regulars and about 900 Louisiana and Kentucky militia.

He put the remainder of his men on the west bank of the Rodriguez Canal where it led northwards at a right angle to the Mississippi River. Dry at the moment it was in effect a four foot deep ditch. As well Jackson had stood his men on a line of cotton bales and then placed cotton bales in front of them, so that British infantry would have to jump into the ditch and clamber up a parapet twelve feet or more under fire. Furthermore, only the heads and shoulders of Jackson's troops would be vulnerable to British musket fire.

By the early hours of 8 January Pakenham was ready to attack, or so he believed, but on the south bank only 500 men were in position.

Fog enshrouded everyone. Pakenham knew it would not lift until late morning but felt this was in his favour as it would prevent the Americans from seeing his men and therefore make it impossible for them to judge the range and take aim until the British were within 200 yards or so. That would put British muskets within range and by virtue of a stand up volley followed by a swift bayonet charge before the Americans could reload he hoped to overcome their defences.

Jackson had shown good sense and had not been enticed to leave his lines and evidently many of his men had shown courage in bearing up to Pakenham's gunfire. Needing a victory after almost a month in America Pakenham decided to assault at once.

Pakenham hoped that the last vestiges of bravery extant in the American ranks would be shattered by his artillery, suddenly barking in the middle of the night, his Congreve rockets, that would scream out of the fog into Jackson's men like a witch on a burning broomstick, and the sound of a British army with full bands playing approaching them invisibly in the fog. By the time his redcoats reached the enemy parapets there should be but few Americans left.

On the south bank Thornton led his men forward quietly and warily, tripping over vines and mounds of grass and suddenly they were upon the Americans. Both sides lined up for a volley, and both sides fired, their balls leaving their muskets and rifles like a crack of thunder. Thick smoke blended with the fog. Thornton was down, wounded, but the British charged with the bayonet, though those with rifles had to make do without a bayonet (not issued to riflemen). The American militia ran in terror and seconds later the regulars followed, only a few stopping to reload and let go a parting shot.

Over-running a small parapet and some guns the British continued on, but in the fog they could not see across the wide river to identify Jackson's main line. Their victory in fact came too late to have any effect on the course of the fight on the north bank. They had suffered six killed and 76 wounded, had killed one American and wounded three, and taken 30 prisoners.

Meanwhile on the north bank the artillery boomed and the Congreve rockets swooshed overhead erratically, while Pakenham's infantry officers mounted their horses and took up their positions in front of their men who were in parade formation. The gunners had judged the range to the American lines before the fog

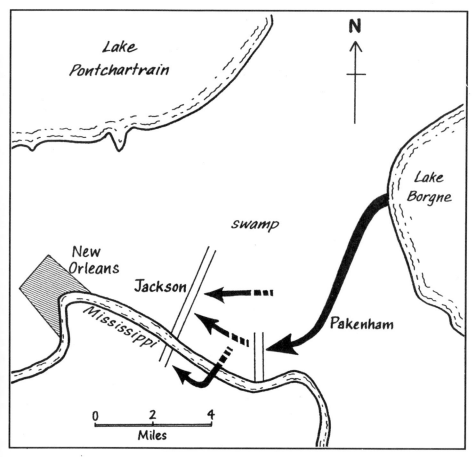

fell and believed their cannonballs were striking home. As the musicians began to play, the 5,300 infantry marched off, proud and confident. Major General Gibbs led the right brigade of the 4th, 21st and 44th Regiments, three companies of the 95th, some light companies, and Negro soldiers advancing in skirmishing order along the edge of the swamp to the north.

A hundred yards to the south, barely visible in the fog, Major General Keane led the left brigade of the 93rd Highlanders, two companies of the 95th, the 1st West Indies Regiment and some light companies.

A further 150 yards behind them and practically invisible followed Major General Lambert with the 7th, 43rd and 5th West Indian Regiments, the remaining light companies and dismounted dragoons.

The troops marched past six large cannon that had been lined up 800 yards from the enemy line and this meant the infantry were now between the lines in the killing zone. It was a chilly night and the damp fog made for an uncomfortable march especially as the fog rendered most of the army invisible. The men shouldered their muskets for the first few hundred yards and many carried short scaling ladders, with which to climb parapets, and fascines – tied bundles of sticks with which to fill in ditches. However, the 44th Regiment had forgotten their ladders and fascines.

Suddenly American cannon balls came glowing through the fog to meet them. A solid shot bouncing along the soggy ground could take off a man's leg, or smash his head to pulp or cave in his chest or knock a horse dead. Some balls struck one man and careered onwards to cause further mayhem. Ignoring them the redcoats marched on, stepping over the bodies or pieces of bodies of their friends, those in the rear rushing up to fill in the gaps in the front rank.

The American lines were not yet in sight, not even muzzle flashes from their guns. Some Britons must have begun wondering how, if they could not see the Americans, the Americans could get their range. It was so lonely in the fog that men probably wondered if the army had halted and their regiment was blindly attacking the enemy on its own through some error of communication. Yet they continued, their officers and sergeants calming them with firm but kind words.

Musket and rifle balls began spinning men to the ground. Many Britons would have been wondering by now how the Americans could have the range. Their ranks were thinning, but they had yet to fire back.

The beginning of the artillery bombardment, followed by the music of the British bands had announced to Jackson that they were attacking. Incredibly Jackson had already alerted his men that this would be 'the night'.

It has been suggested that he set up trip wire parties of Indians at fixed ranges, who fired burning arrows into the air when the British first wave was almost upon them, and that observers had climbed tall trees near his lines to sit above the fog and scan for burning arrows shooting up out of the fog, then had called down to their compatriots, naming the range for Jackson's gunners.

Apocryphal or not, Jackson's artillery bellowed continuously, and some infantry against orders blazed away, each man at his own rate, as if the fog was the target. It is possible that knowing where the British infantry had started from and knowing by their music when they had started and knowing their standard speed of march (30 inches a pace, 75 paces per minute) Jackson and his officers could mathematically calculate where the British would be at any given moment. As the British troops were in three brigades 250 yards from front to rear, even a wildly aimed shot might have hit someone.

Eventually the most forward British officers could see muzzle flashes. Advancing slightly they could soon see the enemy, and were happy they were going to give the Americans a taste of their own medicine. At 200 yards they fired a volley. Firing felt good, emotionally, even if physically it bruised the shoulder. They could not know that their musket and rifle balls thudded straight into bales of cotton. Those who fired on their own had a tendency to fire high, over the heads of the Americans. However, as the leading British infantry finally approached within view of Jackson's troops, fully exposed, they were met by a fusillade from rifles, muskets, shotguns, pistols and cannon. They offered a scarlet target five and a half feet high and so wide that their ranks stretched into the fog on either side. It was impossible for the British to hide from the continuous fire as some of them ran forward, reaching the ditch and jumping into it.

As the 93rd Regiment came within sight of the American lines they realised they had been marching obliquely, so that they presented their left closer to the enemy than their right. Unable to open volley fire they awaited their officers' orders, but with every wasted second another man spun to the ground in agony.

The British officers could not look back and count the bodies of the fallen because of the fog mixed with gunsmoke that rendered most of the battlefield invisible, but that was never their practice in any case. However, they did notice the thinning ranks. Pakenham rode up and down pointing his cocked hat towards the enemy and shouting encouraging phrases, despite having been slightly wounded twice. He sent a messenger to hurry up Lambert, then suddenly he was cut down by two balls at once, softly thudding into the waterlogged earth. His aide Major MacDougal rode up to him, dismounted and found the general was already breathing his last.

Gibbs keeled over off his horse at the slam of a musket ball. His aides carried him away, mortally wounded. Keane was also shot from his horse and was led away in pain. Some companies stopped dead in their tracks, while others slowed their forward pace to a crawl. Few carried on as before. A few members of the 21st Regiment tried to climb the parapet, trading shots with the Americans at arm's length. Perhaps 40 or so Britons entered the enemy lines: none of them survived.

Then the fire slackened and died. Apart from red-coated men writhing on the ground the Americans could see no targets. The British had backed up into the fog. The shooting ceased.

Deep inside the fog the British army stood motionless in utter confusion. It was just 25 minutes since they had marched off proud and confident.

Then Major General Lambert, deciding he was now the highest ranking officer, ordered a retreat. Stepping over the bodies of countless pals, here and there aiding a wounded friend to limp along with them, they retraced their steps. Once they reached the British cannon Lambert ordered the men to prepare to receive Jackson's counter-attack. There was no more music and the moans of the wounded through the fog were eerie and spine tingling.

Jackson did not counter-attack and in mid-morning the fog lifted. Now eyes on both sides widened in disbelief as they stared upon a scarlet coverlet draped across the 800 yards between them. No less than 2,036 British soldiers had been shot down. American and British doctors moved among them and began to treat over 1,700 wounded.

Jackson's losses on this side of the river were six killed and seven wounded.

Aftermath: Over the next days Lambert had his men bury their dead, difficult work as two feet down the spades hit water. The corpses of officers, including Pakenham, were pickled in barrels for shipment home to England.

Lambert knew that as long as Jackson exercised his marvellous discipline and did not leave his lines, there would be no chance of a British victory. On the 27th he began to evacuate.

Appraisal: When the news reached Wellington he consoled his wife by blaming Cochrane, but as has been seen Cochrane and his naval officers had done a very good job. So had Pakenham, up to the 7th, and he had begun with the handicap of having to salvage the army from Keane's mistakes and not having been able to approve or alter Cochrane's initial efforts.

All the same, Pakenham had made errors in three major categories: pace, reconnaissance and tactics.

Keane and then Pakenham had wasted too much time, allowing Jackson two weeks to train his raw militia and receive reinforcements. Had the British attacked on, say, 17 December, it might have been a totally different story.

Pakenham had failed to adequately reconnoitre the sort of line Jackson was holding.

His tactics were flawed. His use of bombardment only for two weeks was based on the assumption that his enemy of shopkeepers, merchants, pirates, Negroes and farmers would run away. It is always a dangerous belief to underestimate the enemy's courage. Choosing to make an assault, he had launched a flanking attack, but too far away to do any good, and had then attacked under the cover of fog, in itself a fine idea, but with his bombardment and music he warned the enemy he was coming. This destroyed the element of surprise and reduced the benefit of the fog to one of invisibility for aimed weapons, but he forgot that fog is far more disorienting to he who is moving than to he who is standing still.

An Alternative: If instead of using his canoes and small boats to transfer men across the river, Pakenham had sailed them upriver under the cover of fog and landed them on the north bank behind Jackson and had timed their assault to that of canoe gunboats firing from the river and a frontal assault along the river's edge at, say, 9.00am or earlier if the fog lifted – music could have been used to signal – and also launched a feint by a few widely scattered riflemen running in skirmish order towards Jackson's parapet, it is possible the triple envelopment might have turned Jackson's river edge flank and if so the British would then have rolled up the American cotton bale line pushing Jackson's men northwards into the swamp.

As for the Americans on the south bank, they could have been ignored.

If this manoeuvre had failed it would still not have cost as many men as Pakenham's blind frontal assault.

The Battle's Place in History: The battle of New Orleans had no effect on the war whatsoever, because the war had in fact been over since Christmas Eve. However, the communications of the day were such that no one in the field knew this and it was March 1815 before all contending armies and fleets gained such knowledge.

Ironically, because many Americans learned of Jackson's unbelievably one-sided victory before they heard of the peace treaty, they assumed the former had something to do with the latter. As a result almost 200 years later most Americans think they won this war.

The British never renounced their right to board American ships or kidnap sailors and continued to aid Indians against the Americans. Also, the American attempt to annex Canada was a complete fiasco. Therefore, in truth the Americans lost the war.

Jackson, apart from Winfield Scott, the only lasting American hero to emerge from the war, went back to fighting Indians, invaded Spanish Florida in 1818 and hanged two Englishmen for aiding and abetting Indian massacres of Americans. These were the last Englishmen killed in the long running Anglo-American dispute that had begun in earnest on Lexington Common 43 years earlier.

Jackson's heroics eventually took him all the way to the White House.

1861

Bull Run

Background: Notwithstanding the fact that state militia had rarely performed well in the Anglo–American War, in 1815 the federal regular army was whittled down to an almost harmless size, so that the militia remained the main reserve if war came.

Continued settler immigration into the west provoked new wars with the Sac, Fox, Kickapoo, Winnebago and others, which were fought predominantly by militia and armed civilians. In fact the regular army was given the mission of marching ahead of the frontier to pacify the vast territories that had come to the United States by the 1802 Louisiana Purchase and the treaty with Spain in 1818, effectively preparing the path for future immigration.

Such duty was generally a peaceful affair and the army did far more good than harm to the Indians, especially in their protection of peaceful tribes like the Wichita and Caddo from the outrages of warlike tribes, such as the Commanche and Kiowa.

However, the army did have to enforce President Andrew Jackson's policy of forced removal of some Indians hundreds of miles out of the path of immigration so that they could resume their tribal lifestyle. The chiefs argued against this to no avail, but only one tribe, the Seminoles of Florida, chose to fight. As Florida was in advance of the frontier, the duty of fighting the Seminoles fell on the regular army, assisted by some southern states militia. In 1842 after seven years of frustrating struggle the federal government claimed victory, though they knew a few Seminoles were still holding out.

In 1846 the federal government launched an aggressive war on Mexico and over the next two years conquered a vast territory all the way to the Pacific coast. However, this move was not popular with everyone. There was a notable lack of war fever in the north. Each state was asked to send militia volunteers to aid the army: most provided just two regiments, some only one and some none.

Northern anti-war activists blamed the conflict on the young hotheads among the southern aristocracy, plantation owners who lived the life of medieval barons with poor white tenants and black slaves forced to obey humiliating rules.

Northerners shared a Protestant work ethic, believing it sinful to benefit from another man's labour, and they welcomed European immigrants who were willing to work, whereas the closest the southern aristocrats came to hard work was watching their slaves toil in the cotton fields.

By the 1850s, the northerners, living in a landscape of railroads, steam operated factories, machinery, the telegraph and huge cities growing out of nothing in less than a decade, looked upon the southern aristocracy as a civilisation trapped in the past. The northerners used machines as slaves: the southerners used Negroes.

Of course the vast majority of southerners were too poor to own slaves and worked the land as tenant farmers living on the edge of starvation. Life was rough, but they were terrified of becoming like the north, where children worked fourteen-hour days in factories and coal mines.

In fact ninety per cent of northerners were farmers, identical to the southerners. Stereotyping is rarely accurate.

Within these not so United States each state in turn threatened to leave the union if it did not get what it was currently yelling for. This had happened so often that when several southern states threatened to secede if Abraham Lincoln was elected president no one really took it seriously: that is until 17 December 1860, when South Carolina voted to leave the union, in response to Lincoln's recent election by an overwhelmingly northern electorate.

The South Carolinans felt very lonesome after 73 years' membership and they began looking around for like-minded southerners. They proposed setting up a Confederate States of America based upon the Articles of Confederation idea, in which the rights of each state would prevail and a federal government regulated but did not rule.

Their courtship campaign was successful: Mississippi seceded on 9 January 1861, Florida next day, Alabama a day later, Georgia on the 19th and Louisiana on the 26th. On 1 March Texas, an independent nation which had joined the union in 1845, seceded.

Grand Strategy: Each of these states mobilised its own militia for self-defence and demanded the evacuation of federal troops from its soil. In April the garrison of Fort Sumter, an island in Charleston Bay, refused and gunners on the South Carolina shore opened fire. Two days later the garrison, none the worse for their experience, surrendered and left.

That would have been that, but President 'Honest Abe' Lincoln now declared that no state had the right to leave the union and that those that had seceded were in armed rebellion against the United States. His regular army at 16,000 men was far too small to tackle even one state's militia, so he called on the remaining loyal states to mobilise 75,000 of their militiamen to defeat the confederate states' militias.

The response was terrific as the issue of states' rights reached fever pitch, but not all of it pro-union. Virginia seceded on 17 April, Arkansas on 6 May, North Carolina on 20 May. Kentucky claimed neutrality and Missouri broke apart in its own civil war.

Lincoln was quick to point out the war was not north versus south: the southern states of Delaware and Maryland remained loyal; he believed he could woo the southern state of Kentucky; and his capital Washington DC was a southern city. Lincoln's wife was a southerner. Nor was it, he maintained, a war against slavery. Many a slave owner had volunteered to serve the union cause.

Causes of Arrogance: Most northerners were fully behind Lincoln. Their politicians and newspaper editors were exceedingly confident that the armed struggle would be over in one big glorious battle in which their militias trounced the effete aristocrats of the south. The loyal states had far more manpower, more horses, more cattle and more equipment than the confederates. They had the backbone of the regular army and the navy. They had industry and armaments factories that could outproduce the confederates in weapons 30 to one, and with their international banking systems, ships and the navy for protection they could import as many weapons as they needed.

The navy's warships were ironclad steamships, invulnerable to all but the heaviest cannonballs, which could sail up any coastal river in the confederacy. The regular army had the telegraph that could send a message 200 miles in seconds that would take a horse mounted messenger two days. Military goods could be sent by rail 100 miles in two hours, which would take a horse-drawn wagon a week or more.

The 'rebels' on the other hand were at a decided disadvantage. With no central leadership daring to overrule a state's vote, with no industry to speak of, with only three cities, Atlanta, New Orleans and Charleston, and not one sewing machine in the entire confederacy, no foreign credit and no navy to prevent a union blockade, they were doomed from the start. Moreover, there was considerable union support in parts of Mississippi, Arkansas, Texas, western Virginia and eastern Tennessee. Last but not least the Negro slaves would not be all that anxious to preserve their masters' land.

Lincoln and his cabinet were as convinced as anyone it would be a short war: he initially asked for militia for only 90 days' service!

All this is evidence of extreme arrogance on the part of the pro-union politicians, industrialists, bankers and newspaper editors, because the truth of the matter was that the union army being created at several depots throughout the north and at Washington DC was far below the standard proclaimed by the vociferous speech makers and inflammatory editors.

The Army: The regular officers, who were veterans of Indian conflicts and the Mexican War, inspected the militia volunteers as they arrived in Washington DC and shook their heads in disapproval. Yet they knew they needed them. Already a third of the regular army had resigned or deserted, some to opt for the confederacy, others to join their home state militias. A lieutenant in the regulars could wangle a major's commission in a state regiment. The federal government was also creating war volunteer regiments, and many an officer resigned his regular commission for a higher volunteer rank.

Normally militiamen received training one weekend a month or thereabouts and otherwise held civilian jobs, but most of the militia arriving in Washington DC were new recruits who had not even had the benefit of meetings. Their officers were political appointees who knew no more about military affairs than did their lowliest private. A regiment was supposed to arrive with 781 men: some came with more, most with fewer. Asian Americans and Indians were allowed to enlist, but as yet no Negroes were accepted.

The regulars wore a dark blue coat, dark blue forage cap or black broad-brimmed hat and sky blue trousers. The federal US Volunteers were fitted out in like manner. The states were told to provide similar uniforms for their troops, and most complied, though each regiment contrived to have some slight deviation such as extra buttons, a different cut of cloth, gold braid etc. The 39th New

York wore an Italian bersaglieri feathered hat; the 79th New York showed up in kilts. Some regiments arrived in zouave style: dark blue coat, red cap and red baggy pants. A Wisconsin regiment insisted on arriving in its traditional grey militia uniform, and the 2nd New Hampshire wore a grey tail coat.

Weapons varied from the Enfield, weighing 9½ pounds with a 39½inch barrel and firing a .702 calibre bullet to the Springfield at 8½ pounds with a 32½ inch barrel firing a .58 calibre bullet to the light Enfield which shot a .527 calibre bullet. All three were muzzle-loading percussion cap rifles.

Cavalry carried carbines: the Sharps with a 21½inch barrel firing a .577 calibre bullet, the slightly longer Richards firing a .476 calibre bullet and the Spencer with a 26inch barrel firing seven .56 calibre bullets held in a magazine.

Officers and all cavalrymen carried six-shot revolvers, usually Colts from .36 to .45 calibre. Officers, sergeants and cavalrymen were issued with swords.

A few men were issued other makes of weapon including muskets, some of clearly oddball nature. One Pennsylvania regiment arrived without weapons!

Some of the regiments were mobilised for 90 days, others for nine months and most of the New York units had agreed to serve for two years if necessary.

Lincoln had already begun to suspect the war would last longer than 90 days, despite what he read in the newspapers, and he soon asked for 42,000 more state soldiers to be enlisted for three years. He also authorised the regular army to be expanded by another 22,000 and the navy by 18,000, recruiting men on three year hitches.

By June those regular officers, whose job it was to inspect newly arrived units, had rejected a few and had accepted one cavalry and 39 infantry state regiments.

The Commander: Irvin McDowell was a 43-year-old Ohioan, who had been a regular officer since graduating from the Military Academy at West Point in 1838. He had distinguished himself in action against the Mexicans and on his own merits had risen to the rank of major, so in 23 years of service he had been promoted three times. A teetotaller, his only vice seemed to be an excessive fondness for food.

He chose to remain in the regulars, while his fellow officers were exchanging their regular commissions for state or volunteer ones, and this paid off for him, because on 14 May he was promoted three times to brigadier general!

Even the most humble of men would be momentarily inflated by such a turn of events and as the days passed and colonels and generals of militia began to ask him for advice on the most rudimentary of military subjects, his ego must have been given a boost.

Just two weeks later he received another accolade: he was promoted to major general and was given command of the Department of the Potomac, Lincoln's main field force.

After receiving congratulatory telegrams, pats on the back and a few cigars, he set up his headquarters on confederate Virginian soil in the home of Robert E. Lee, a regular officer who had chosen the confederacy.

Actually this 'invasion' of Virginia was merely symbolic, for the house was but a few hundred yards across the Potomac River from Washington DC.

McDowell must have been disappointed when he inspected his new command, especially as he knew these were the best regiments available. Yet Major

General Winfield Scott, hero of the Anglo-American War and now commander of the army, urged McDowell to drive on Richmond to force the confederates to risk all in one large battle. This was Napoleonic strategy, which all regular officers had studied, and it had considerable merit. Every officer dreamed of winning his own Austerlitz.

Despite the front line stretching 2,500 miles (the same distance between London and Baghdad), the union and confederate capitals, Washington and Richmond, were only one day's fast horse ride apart.

The War: There were skirmishes at once from Missouri to Virginia, for example the 3rd New Jersey Regiment fought a confederate regiment at Vienna Virginia losing one man. None of these skirmishes were of importance to McDowell until he heard news of Benjamin Butler's amphibious invasion of Virginia at Newport News on 9 June.

Advancing towards Big Bethel, Butler's 7th New York had fired into the enemy only to learn the 'enemy' was the 3rd New York. When they both met the real enemy they were quickly defeated with a hundred casualties. The confederates lost eight men.

McDowell and his staff took note of this affair, but were not disheartened. They knew that though Butler was the same age and rank as McDowell, he only had two months of soldiering under his belt. He was a Massachusetts politician, who was given a federal major general's commission by his cronies in Washington. His deputy, Brigadier General Pierce, held a Massachusetts state commission, also the gift of political friends, whereas their opponent, Virginia Colonel John Magruder was a West Point man who had resigned from the regular army just weeks before. The fate of Butler reinforced the regular army's belief that their officers were superior to 'amateur' soldiers.

Meanwhile McDowell was under serious pressure to advance, receiving official despatches from Secretary of War Cameron and General Scott, plus unofficial visits by Congressmen and letters from editors, well intentioned armchair generals, wives who wanted their husbands home for the harvest and mothers who just wanted their sons home. He also had one eye on the calendar, for in mid-July he would begin losing his 90-day men (known as 90-day wonders).

On 17 June his intelligence gatherers informed him of a confederate movement towards Vienna and at once he sent Brigadier General Schenck and the 1st Ohio to dislodge them, and to steal a march on the enemy he sent them by train. This was the first time American soldiers had gone into battle by locomotive and the confederates were taken by surprise. For five killed and six wounded Schenck repelled a South Carolina brigade.

McDowell had shown considerable speed, initiative and nerve to gain this minor victory, which provided him with more time to train and equip his army, because for the moment the confederates were willing to wait and see what else he had up his sleeve.

The Approach: By 1 July there were 73,000 union troops in the Washington environs, but only 15,766 had passed inspection. McDowell's spies told him the confederate field force had at least 25,000. McDowell dare not strike out with so few troops. A defeat similar to Butler's would not only give heart to the enemy, but would probably lose him his job.

Yet the pressure was on for McDowell to advance or resign. Under this constant pressure he sent out scouts to study the best route of advance. He could turn north following the Potomac and link up with the smaller union force of Major General Patterson, who faced a confederate enemy of his own, J. E. Johnston, or he could sail downriver and make an amphibious attack, or he could push right through the centre for Richmond and take the enemy army head on.

At last on 8 July he gave orders to advance. He would take the enemy head on.

McDowell divided his army into five divisions commanded by Colonel D. Hunter, Colonel S. P. Heintzelman and Colonel Dixon Miles, all regular officers, and T. Runyon, commissioned a brigadier general by New Jersey, and D. Tyler, who held a Connecticut brigadier general's commission.

At once the lack of experience and poor training was evident. Of the 35,000 men he proposed taking with him, only 1,000 of his infantry were regulars and they were all in one regiment. For political reasons Scott and Cameron had not deemed it necessary to assign regular corporals and sergeants to state regiments as cadre. The wagons jammed together, infantry companies marched to the wrong rendezvous, officers absented themselves and went to Washington to get drunk one last time, men wandered about without orders and it was in fact eight days before the first troops broke camp and began marching south-westwards into Virginia.

Yet, so confident were the politicians, businessmen, lawyers, and society folk that they accompanied the army, many bringing their wives with them, riding in carriages driven by liveried coachmen and taking picnic hampers and tents. They came along to see 'Johnny Reb' get his comeuppance.

As a result McDowell was still not free from political pressure. He would be fighting this battle quite literally under the eyes of his government. Of course they constantly offered advice.

The first day the men made seven miles then flopped down exhausted, some sleeping where they lay. They learned that military marching defied the laws of mathematics: the leading men in a column marched at normal pace, those in the middle marched swiftly and those in the rear had to run to keep up and in temperatures of 90°F this was an effort.

The Enemy: Awaiting them near Manassas was the confederate field force, the Army of Virginia, commanded by Pierre Toussaint Beauregard, a French-speaker from New Orleans, not yet born at the time of Jackson's victory there, who was a West Point classmate of McDowell. Entering the regular army he had risen faster than McDowell and in early 1861 had been offered the post of commandant of West Point, but he chose to resign and take a state commission.

However, there were few ex-regulars in the confederate forces. The army consisted of state regiments mustered for one year's service. They arrived at the various depots in their all-grey militia uniforms, but many regiments were newly recruited and wore their own uniforms, such as: grey coat with sky blue trousers; a bluish grey uniform; grey uniform with black trim; uniforms of butternut, i.e. a mustard colour; the Maryland Guards with red cap, dark blue uniform worn open to show a red shirt; the New Orleans 'Washington Artillery' in dark blue with red cap; and the Louisiana Tigers in pants of vertical red, white and blue stripes, brown jacket and straw skimmer (flat hat). Officers were even more flamboyant in their attire, with gaudy sashes and hat plumes of red or gold.

Their weaponry matched the union army, though a few recruits arrived with their own hunting rifles and shotguns.

Few of the officers had ever worked for a living, though some were teachers or engineers, but the ordinary soldiers were for the most part illiterate farmers who spoke of the union soldiers as Yankees or Dutchmen. Some thought all northerners spoke German. Few of them had been to the other side of the 'river' or the 'valley' before, let alone hundreds of miles distant. Even some of the Virginians had walked 400 miles to reach Manassas.

Yet whenever their pickets yelled to union pickets at night they were surprised to find they were much alike. They decided this was a rich man's war and a poor man's fight.

Beauregard divided his 25,000 men into seven brigades of infantry and one of cavalry all from Virginia, two brigades from South Carolina, and smaller groups from North Carolina, Florida, Georgia and Louisiana.

The Battlefield: Tyler's Division entered Centreville where the road divides into the Warrenton Turnpike heading north-west that crossed the Bull Run (i.e. Bull stream) by Stone Bridge and the Richmond road that headed due west and crossed the run by Blackburn's Ford. The terrain was hilly, green and well cultivated with small farms, but broken by narrow ravines and thickly wooded in places.

Without waiting for instructions Tyler led his men to the ford, which he found guarded by confederates. He tried to organise his 12th New York for an assault, but after 83 casualties he withdrew.

Strategy: McDowell was angry, for Tyler's impetuosity had wrecked a regiment and alerted the confederates. Leaving Runyon's Division seven miles to the east of Centreville to protect his line of supply, McDowell urged his other three divisions to make Centreville by nightfall. But his men did not march as quickly as he had hoped, nor did his officers show that much concern and it was another 48 hours before the last men were in bivouac in the town. He must have known Beauregard could have amassed his army by now, yet he did not call up Runyon, obviously feeling his 28,000 men could defeat Beauregard's 25,000.

Studying the landscape he decided to pin Beauregard at Blackburn's Ford with one of Tyler's brigades, make a feint at Stone Bridge with the remainder of Tyler's Division, and send Hunter and Heintzelman two miles north of Stone Bridge to cross the run and sweep down on Beauregard's left (north) flank. He told Miles to remain in Centreville. Therefore, only 21,000 of his men would be going into action.

He was confident at the council of war on the night of the 20th that he would outmanoeuvre Beauregard. He had arranged with Patterson that, at the first sign of Johnston coming to help Beauregard, Patterson would telegraph him. Patterson was a cautious officer who had first seen action in the war against the British.

According to him Johnston was still several days' march from Bull Run that evening and therefore could not interfere on the morrow.

There was a minor ruckus. The 4th Pennsylvania and an artillery battery of the 8th New York refused to go on, saying their 90 days were up. They were shunned by the other regiments.

As the two lead divisions had a nine-mile march ahead of them before they would reach the run, McDowell ordered them to begin at 2.00am, which would put them across the run at sunrise and into the enemy north flank by about 7.00am.

The Battle: Unfortunately McDowell failed to take into account the turtle-like pace of his troops. It was 6.00am before they even broke camp and 10.00am in full view of confederate scouts when they reached the run. They then stopped to fill canteens and it was many precious minutes before they resumed the march southwards into Beauregard's flank.

Ambrose Burnside, known for his facial whiskers (soon to be called 'side burns'), was a 37-year-old businessman, who had graduated from West Point. Now a Rhode Island brigadier general he led the lead brigade of Hunter's Division over the run and reached a point immediately north-west of Stone Bridge at noon. Because Beauregard had been given plenty of time to place reserves on this flank, Burnside's Rhode Islanders found themselves making a frontal assault across an open plain.

Virginian cannon and rifles poured volleys of fire into the blue-coated men and they fell back, dazed, into the cover of a small wood.

Brigadier General Porter brought up the other brigade of Hunter's Division, which included the regiment of regulars, and they attacked with such élan and force that they drove back one line of confederates. This uncovered the stone bridge and now Tyler sent his brigades under Sherman and Keyes across it to join Hunter.

Therefore by 1.00pm four union brigades were facing Beauregard's north flank, Schenck's Brigade protected Stone Bridge, and Richardson's Brigade of Tyler's Division was making noises at Blackburn's Ford. Heintzelman's Division was still to the north in reserve.

McDowell was confident: he had crossed the run, outflanked Beauregard, forced him to use his reserves, and had already pushed some of the Johnny Rebs back. However, Beauregard's army was in a tight little group, most of his 25,000 men occupying a one-mile line stretching west from Stone Bridge, whereas McDowell had less than 18,000 along this line, plus Beauregard had received some reinforcements brought by Johnston in person by rail.

Beauregard chose to counter-attack Richardson's Brigade at Blackburn's Ford, then swerve north to cut off Tyler, Hunter and Heintzelman from their line of supply. At best he would trap three divisions. At worst they would flee across the run abandoning their wagons and guns. Fortunately for McDowell, Beauregard had trouble with inexperienced officers too and the orders were never carried out.

McDowell ordered a continuation of the attack southward by bringing up most of Heintzelman's Division. There were bloody moments and gunsmoke blinded everyone, but, though exhausted from lack of sleep and the long march, the union boys steadily forced back the confederates, who were willing to trade space for time. Trying to get a better look, Hunter was wounded. Heintzelman fell with a wound.

As the gunsmoke cleared the union troops realised the confederates had fallen back several hundred yards, but instead of following they stopped to rest. Their officers seized the occasion to reform ranks, assist the wounded and acquire ammunition. This was a mistake, for it gave the confederates time to regroup.

McDowell was pleased by 2.30pm: 'All were certain the day was ours,' he later said.

Then Porter's union soldiers on their extreme right (west) saw a cloud of dust. The ground was green, but all roads were dirt and the summer sun made them dusty. The cloud was evidence that a body of troops was marching their way. Some surmised it was Patterson's men.

Only when the new arrivals formed in ranks and opened up volley fire did the union troops realise the truth. Their flank had been turned. The arrivals were Elzey's Brigade of Kirby Smith's component of Johnston's army, who had just leapt from their train at Manassas station.

The union men on the end of the line began to run northwards to the rear or eastwards pressing against the army. Only the regular regiment stood its ground along a stream called Young's Branch. Seeing the potential disaster Heintzelman threw in his last reserve brigade, that of Howard, and by 3.30pm the situation was saved.

However, from the confederate main line Early's Louisiana-Virginia Brigade struck the regulars on the south. Within minutes this caused a ripple effect of considerable confusion. Troops all along the union line began to fall back, some uncertain, others scared, and some completely terrified out of their wits. The panic spread like a flood. Porter noted: 'Soon the slopes were swarming with our retreating and disorganised forces, while riderless horses and artillery teams ran ferociously through the flying crowd.'

Within fifteen minutes the first men were seen running into the run, splashing and wading across and it was now that McDowell realised he had lost control.

The pride of Washington society in their fancy bonnets and top hats, who had braved heat, flies and dust to see a great victory stared from their carriages in stupefied awe as they witnessed men by the thousands running towards them, some without weapons. Then the crack of confederate artillery shells broke their trance and they turned their carriage horses around and bolted at racing speed towards Washington. Picnic baskets and tenting were tossed aside.

Aftermath: In Centreville civilian carriages jammed with military wagons and horse-drawn ambulances as the union soldiers enfolded them in a human flood. Miles' Division tried to trap the panic-stricken soldiers, and calmed most of them down, but some broke through and ran all the way to Washington.

McDowell reassembled his whipped army around Miles' and Runyon's Divisions, but next day he ordered a retreat. The men finally reached Washington 36 hours later on the evening of the 23rd, their shoulders sagging in exhaustion, shame and embarrassment.

McDowell had been soundly broken: 1,011 of his troops were wounded and 1,700 were dead or missing, and 23 of his 55 cannon were lost.

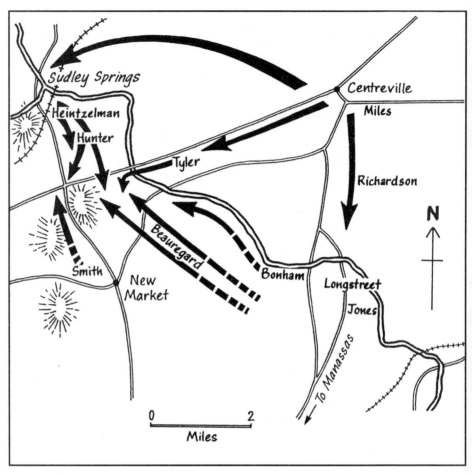

Cameron, Scott and Lincoln took alarm that not only had they lost a battle, but they might have to abandon Washington. At best it would take another year to put a field force together. At worst they may have to seek terms. To add to his depression Cameron learned his brother had died on the battlefield.

Appraisal: The union troops had given a good account of themselves until 3.00pm, inflicting 378 killed upon the confederates, including two generals, which with wounded meant a man for man trade. However, as a percentage this was a far higher loss for the union troops, as much of the time they faced odds of two to one against.

It was McDowell's misfortune that certain confederate officers, Kirby Smith, Early, Johnston and Beauregard recognised the moment of balance and tipped the scales, though they were in the thick of action themselves, Kirby Smith being wounded and Beauregard losing a horse. It was McDowell's fortune that Beauregard and Johnston refused Brigadier General Jackson's request to chase after the Yankees all the way to Washington.

The errors of the union forces were many and they were caused by the arrogance and naivety of politicians, civil servants, Scott and his staff, McDowell and his staff, editors and industrialists and anyone else who influenced the army to fight before it was ready.

Errors can be identified in ten major categories: training, timing, strategy, pace, dispersal, reserves, tactics, ground, reconnaissance and intelligence.

The training was abysmal. The structure that sent into battle entire regiments of civilians in uniform with nothing but a regulation manual to refer to, and not so much as one regular corporal to show them how things were done, was a farce. Such a method of instruction was barely adequate and brigade and divisional exercises were non-existent. McDowell had no part in this failing: the nation was at fault.

The timing of the advance to Bull Run was critical, for it was weeks too soon in terms of preparedness. McDowell and Scott were wrong to let the civilians pressure them to the point that their timetable was dictated by the expectations of newspaper editors and politicians who had one eye on the next election.

The strategy of trying to win the war in one fell swoop was the correct one, but in advancing directly on Richmond McDowell gave the enemy no discomfort and no need for long marches to meet him. Beauregard was allowed to choose the battlefield.

The pace of McDowell's army was languid. Beauregard moved slowly too, but he had no plans to go anywhere. It took McDowell's men some five days to reach Centreville, but they retreated the same distance in 36 hours. Confederate bayonets provided the motivation for the retreat. Nothing as dramatic provided the motivation for the advance. One wonders how fast the men would have marched if their officers knew they might lose their commissions if the men arrived late?

McDowell's dispersal of his forces was criminal. To challenge an enemy of 25,000 with less then 20,000 when you have 35,000 is ludicrous. His cavalry could have protected his short line of supply with Washington, but instead he chose to use an entire division of infantry. Thus he divided his army into six parts: Runyon's Division on supply duty; Miles' Division in Centreville; Heintzelman's Division in reserve; Tyler's Division waiting to cross the run through Stone Bridge; Richardson's Brigade demonstrating at Blackburn's Ford; and Hunter attacking alone for almost an hour with only about 5,000 men.

Possession of reserves is essential, but if too far away they are no longer reserves. Miles was a half day's march away and Runyon a full day's march.

As for tactics, for all McDowell's fancy manoeuvres his men ended up making a frontal assault. He must have known his men's marching speed by this date. Trying to catch the enemy at dawn on an open flank is tricky with élite troops. With the human material McDowell had available it was impossible. Yet, once committed he refused to back off.

His use of ground was poor. Bull Run was shallow in the summer heat and at just about any place it could be crossed. His men certainly had no problems getting across it in retreat. If McDowell and his generals had realised this they could have attacked as if the stream did not exist, stretching Beauregard's army up to four miles in length with feints and then striking a weak spot.

McDowell had taken Scott's advice to leave behind all cavalry bar his few regulars and he assigned them to inconsequential duties. He placed no reconnaissance trip wire cavalry to his west which, stationed just west of Manassas station along the railroad line, might have delayed or even derailed the confederate reinforcement trains. At the very least these horsemen could have alerted McDowell in time to place a blocking position on his west flank.

McDowell had not anticipated Johnston's sudden arrival on the battlefield by rail, and yet he himself had been the first to use troops in this manner. Did he and his intelligence team really think no one else would show the same initiative? Obviously Patterson also made a serious intelligence mistake in not noticing the absence of Johnston's army.

There is no doubt that McDowell was outgeneralled. To mitigate this indictment it must be remembered that two months earlier he had been a major, trained at most to lead 350 men not 35,000.

He remained in the army and kept his rank, but was soon shunted off to the rear.

Alternatives: Training should have been done by regulars to create training units, who in turn would train others, and the offensive should have been timed to await this training, at least until September. Part of the training should have been an emphasis on speed.

Once ready the last thing that should have been done was a direct advance on Richmond. The enemy's field force was the target not their capital, and with Patterson's army in the north and naval control of the Virginia coast, enough feints could have been made to make Beauregard and Johnston positively dizzy, until they dispersed, then the union forces could have struck with a full 60% of their troops and 40% in immediate reserve. Sufficient cavalry scouting teams would have given McDowell complete knowledge of where the enemy was and possibly his intentions.

This strategy was in fact used eventually and was victorious.

The Battle's Place in History: Psychologically this was a terrible defeat, comparable to Bladensburg fought on the other side of Washington 47 years earlier. Scott never thought he would live to see his capital threatened a second time. What made it worse was the thought that of the 4,000 or so killed and maimed in a few short hours all had been Americans.

The defeat put the union forces in Virginia on the defensive for the next eight months, while the government turned from a Napoleonic strategy of one big battle to a British-style strangulation programme, the Anaconda Plan, which blockaded the confederacy at sea, then sliced up the territory into workable chunks and then by attrition bled southern manhood dry.

Thus the war which Lincoln initially expected to fight with 90-day volunteers was to last 1,500 days and the casualties mounted so that by 1863 the loss of a few hundred men in a day was hardly worth a newspaper entry. By June 1865 when the guns at last fell silent 618,000 Americans had fallen in this heartbreaking fratricidal struggle.

1876

Little Big Horn

Background: Before, during and after the Civil War, beyond the frontier the regular army never set out to make aggressive war on the Indians, but the encroachment on Indian land of settlers, prospectors, miners, hunters, railroad builders, stagecoaches and telegraph linesmen constantly ensured that some tribe was retaliating with violence, and the army had to step in.

Reservations were created, in theory to keep whites out not to keep Indians in, and reservation Indians were allowed to leave on hunting expeditions and to visit friends. Unfortunately, inter-tribal wars continued and some reservation Indians left in war parties to raid other reservations. Some tribes were so warlike they could not adapt to peace.

What complicated matters was that the white man thought in terms of tiered government: city, county, state, federal. The Indian did not, and a sub-chief of a band might ignore the orders of the tribal chief with complete impunity, or he might periodically obey when the mood took him. This made treaties ineffective. In any case newly elected politicians in Washington often revoked previous treaties.

From 1846 the army was forced to wage long wars with the Paiute, Bannock, Shoshone, Jicarilla, Mescalero, Lipan, Commanche, Kiowa, Plains Apache, Mimbreno and Mogollon, with further wars beginning in the 1860s against the San Carlos, Coyotero, White Mountain, Tonto and Cibecue. In 1862 the Mdekakanton-Dakota attacked settlers in Minnesota and within weeks other members of the Dakota had joined the war. While chasing them the army came into conflict with the Lakota and the Nakota.

In 1864 the Cheyenne and Arapaho began to fight white encroachment and in 1866 the Yavapai and Hualapai rose in 'rebellion'.

The Army: In 1865, as had happened every time the United States finished a war, the accountants stepped in with their cost savings analysis and overcame the pleas of the generals. By 1869 they had reduced the regular army to a total strength of 36,774 and by 1876 to 26,312.

Obviously the army was too small to patrol the wild west, man coastal garrisons at strategic sites and provide from a quarter to a third of its strength to occupy the ex-confederate states to ensure the rebels remained defeated.

Furthermore, the army was almost never able to draw upon state militia for aid in the Indian conflicts, because the vast territory of the west had not really been settled in sufficient numbers to create an effective militia.

Having said this, life in the army on the western plains was not one of dodging arrows. Army life was tedious, with long hours in hot sun or freezing snow just moving from one location to another or day after day of boring training inside forts, which resembled small towns not the stockades of popular imagination.

Most of the troops were infantry and they walked everywhere, even when chasing Indians. Their lack of speed really did not matter, for over a period of days cavalry did not travel any faster. Casualties were insignificant, perhaps five per year per 1,000 men. After 1865 losses of three killed in one engagement made headline news in the newspapers back east. A soldier stood a much greater chance of dying in a drunken brawl or dying of fever than he did in combat.

The Commander: Of all officers engaged in the west in the post-Civil War years the name of George Armstrong Custer is the most remembered – which is exactly how Custer would have liked it.

Graduating from West Point in June 1861 at the bottom of his class he went straight into the regular army and performed bravely at Bull Run. He gained a captaincy under the wing of a popular general, Phil Kearny, only to lose it when the general's popularity waned. Always on the lookout for a way to get noticed, Custer became one of the army's first aviators – flying in an observation balloon at 1000 feet. In 1863 he convinced his superiors to pin the stars of a brigadier general of cavalry on his shoulders and began to earn considerable praise and publicity at Gettysburg, Yellow Tavern, Trevillian Station, Winchester, Fisher's Hill, Brock's Gap, Tom's Brook, Cedar Creek, Waynesboro, Five Forks and other battlefields. A by-product of all this glory was that his brigade suffered higher casualties than any other Union cavalry brigade. By the end of the war he was a division commander and still only 24.

When the regular army was reduced in size and good officers were discarded like so many used tools, Custer pleaded for some form of duty even at lower rank – though he drew the line at commanding Negroes. When rebuffed he considered joining the Mexican Army. It was over a year before he was offered field command (but not overall command) of the 7th Cavalry Regiment currently fighting Indians in Kansas.

When he arrived to take up his new command in July 1866 he made quite an impression on the men. Wearing a privately tailored blue uniform, outlandish red scarf and sporting long golden hair and a moustache and goatee to partially cover his bony face and knife-like nose and wearing the double stars of a major general, despite his new rank of lieutenant-colonel, he gave the appearance of a showman not a warrior.

A cavalryman's authorised uniform was a shirt of either white, blue and white check or pink and white check, a dark blue shell coat, sky blue trousers with a yellow stripe, and black broad-brimmed hat, armed with carbine, revolver and sword. Custer found his men lounging around the fort coatless in civilian shirts, wearing scarves of various colours and wide-brimmed civilian hats. On patrol they dressed even more casually and never took swords. They often carried extra revolvers.

The make up of the men was probably a surprise to Custer. They came from all parts of the country and from many backgrounds. Hardly any were experienced horsemen. Some were ex-Confederates and a good portion were foreigners, predominantly Irish, British, Italian and German. Some were obviously ex-convicts and the guardhouse was never empty. There were no Negroes, as Negroes had their own units.

Custer's first job, he determined, was to make soldiers out of these fellows, but his methods were not popular. He seemed heartless: during the Civil War he had executed prisoners of war; and he now introduced the death penalty for desertion.

In one episode Custer led the regiment after a Cheyenne band for two months: the troopers wore out their horses and contracted cholera, whereupon half the regiment deserted.

To a man like Custer who had led thousands in one charge this duty was humiliating. To his men he was not just cruel, but a hypocrite. Though married he kept mistresses, of which one was a Negress and another a Cheyenne, and in 1867 when he took a patrol to visit his sick wife without permission, effectively deserting his post, even his superiors were shocked. He was suspended for a year, the final insult he believed. The resulting inactivity almost drove him mad.

Once back on duty, despite his regiment's poor discipline, he spread the word that his regiment was the finest, bragging that the 7th Cavalry alone could whip 'all the Indians on the plains'. He was so good at this public relations campaign that a century later some still believe in the efficiency of the 7th. In truth his regiment was no better than the other ten cavalry regiments on the plains and considerably worse than the 9th and 10th, both Negro units.

He was soon given a chance to back up his words with deeds on a search for hostile Indians in western Oklahoma in November 1868. His Osage scouts informed him they had located a solitary village on the Washita River. Custer desperately needed a victory, not just to cure his own depression, but to put his name back in the newspapers. He knew that many an officer had 'faded away' on the plains. He had no intention of remaining out of the limelight for long. The result was his charge against Black Kettle's village of Sutaio Cheyenne. His men whooped and hollered and rode around the lodges shooting: three of the soldiers were killed and fourteen wounded in the 'battle', the regiment's highest casualties to date. They killed eleven warriors and 92 old men, women and children. Ceasing fire they then arrested 53 women and children.

Custer had not yet reconnoitred further down river, an area hidden by a few trees, and he now sent a patrol of eighteen men to do so.

Custer basked in the glory this skirmish gave him: not surprisingly he inflated the enemy casualties to over a hundred dead warriors. However, the affair caused deep divisions within the regiment, for the patrol never returned and Custer never bothered to find out what had happened to them.

By 1875 Custer was playing politics, or more accurately certain ambitious politicians were playing him like a fiddle. They induced him to speak out against corruption in army circles, land deals, railroad contracts and the like. In Washington in front of a public committee he named his own commander, Colonel Sturgis, and Orville Grant, the brother of the President of the United States, as examples of corruption. None of this endeared him to his superiors and he was lucky not to have been dismissed from the service.

Grand Strategy: Having returned to his regiment, in 1876 he was informed that there was to be a major campaign to round up certain tribes of the Lakota Indians who had left their assigned homeland and invaded the land of the Crow. The Crow were naturally anxious for aid to repel them. The fact that these Lakota planned to spend the summer on Crow land was really of no concern to the government, but it was the impudence of the Lakota that the government did not like. The politicians wanted to be seen to be in control of the plains.

Ironically Custer had a good deal of sympathy for the Lakota, but he obeyed orders. Moreover, another victory similar to the Washita would give him a political boost. He knew that in June the various parties would be picking candidates for the November elections.

Strategy: General Philip Sheridan's plan was for Brigadier General George Crook to advance with his column northwards from Fort Laramie, Wyoming; Colonel John Gibbon to lead his column eastwards from Helena, Montana; and Brigadier General Alfred Terry to advance westwards from Fort Lincoln, South Dakota. Their destination was the Big Horn River, which they were to reach on 27 June.

Terry sent Major Marcus Reno of the 7th with a patrol to reconnoitre the region and on the 22nd Reno saw signs of a large number of Indians. Terry, obviously a cautious man, sent another troop of the 7th westwards along the Yellowstone River to verify this.

Terry was visited by Gibbon, whose column of 409 soldiers and some Crows was still approaching from the west along the Yellowstone. Gibbon was ordered to turn his column southwards along the Big Horn River, then turn eastwards along the Little Big Horn River. Terry planned to take his own column, of four and a half companies of infantry, four Gatling guns and two cannon, plus some Arikarees, westwards along the Yellowstone then southwards along the Rosebud River to its headwaters, then westwards across the Tongue River, thence on to the Little Big Horn. He ordered Custer to take his regiment further westwards along the Yellowstone then southwards along the Tongue to its headwaters then west to the Little Big Horn.

The campaign map resembled a washing line, the Yellowstone, and hanging from it from left to right the Gibbon column, the Custer column and the Terry column. Crook would be approaching from the south. In this manner they hoped to trap as many of the hostiles as possible: two or perhaps three tribes. The manoeuvre was to take five days and each column's safety relied on interaction with the others.

Custer was offered four Gatling guns, weapons that could have mown down charging warriors like a scythe, but he refused, saying they would slow him down, despite knowing they could be dismantled and carried on pack mules. This is evidence that he wanted to move fast and had no intention of waiting for the other columns. However, Custer did want to take his regimental band with him to play such tunes as '*Garry Owen*', the regimental marching song, but Terry forbade this ostentatious display.

Gibbon knew Custer, for he had taught him at West Point, and he knew his reputation for rashness, so he yelled to Custer as he rode out to join the 7th Cavalry: 'Now Custer, don't be greedy. Wait for us!' Whereupon Custer replied with a grin: 'No. I won't.' A retort that can be taken two ways.

The Officers: A major problem was that the 7th Cavalry's officers were divided into pro-Custer and anti-Custer factions. Major Marcus Reno led the anti-Custer faction, and Custer knew this. In fact Custer had insulted Reno by refusing to give him a job on this expedition. Reno had come along as nothing more than a tourist.

In Reno's faction was Captain Frederick Benteen, now in his forties, who was a southerner who had opted for the Union cause in the Civil War and though having no formal military education had risen to the rank of colonel. Reno on the other hand had graduated from West Point four years before Custer, but had only reached captain during that great conflict. Benteen and Reno had not forgotten Custer's abandonment of those eighteen men on the Washita and wondered if Custer would repeat this cowardly deed. Another member of the Reno faction was Lieutenant Sturgis, because Custer had publicly insulted his father.

In Custer's faction were men who addressed him as 'General': Captains Tom Weir and George Yates, both of whom had served with him in the Civil War; Captain Tom Custer, his brother; Lieutenant James Calhoun, husband of his sister Maggie; Lieutenant William Cooke, a Canadian immigrant; Captain Miles Keogh, an Irishman who had left the Pope's army to fight for the Union in the Civil War, after which he had traded his lieutenant-colonel's oak leaves for a captain's bars to serve in the 7th. It had been he who introduced '*Garry Owen*' (i.e. Garden of Owen) to Custer.

Causes of Arrogance: As the 7th Cavalry rode they resembled civilians on an outing rather than a trim military column. Owing to the terrible heat they had taken off their coats and exposed shirts of a considerable variety. Many had bought skimmers for 25 cents each just before they left camp, for the flat white straw hats were cool to the head.

Custer wore a long frilled buckskin coat and a white wide-brimmed hat, but he had recently cut his hair, as had most of the men, owing to new rules. He carried a pair of Webley revolvers and a sporting rifle.

Almost a third of the men were recruits, whose training had been cut short. They were uncertain how to act in a skirmish and many could not keep straight in the saddle. They became skittish the further they rode from their base and the old-timers constantly had to reassure them. The heat – over 100˚F – made the ride unbearable and many men had headaches so bad they could hardly open their eyes and definitely did not care to strain their eyes scanning the horizon. They left that duty to the scouts.

The recruits' horses wandered pretty much where they wanted and on occasion a recruit fell off.

However, Custer and his veterans were highly confident. They knew this area well, for they had campaigned here in 1873 and 1875, losing no more than a dozen killed and wounded in total. They were certainly not worried now that they were part of a 2,500-man expedition, the largest seen in the Wyoming-Montana area.

Furthermore, their opponents, the Lakota, were a rag tag bunch of tribes that rarely spoke to each other let alone made a joint decision. They were skirmishers, who had been known to run at the sound of a cannon. A Lakota tribe could not muster more than about 200 warriors, and in summer many would be off hunting or visiting. Leaving out those who protected the women and children, this meant a tribe could probably field no more than 100 warriors if that.

The 7th had twelve troops of 40 troopers each, and every man carried 100 rounds for his '1873' Springfield .45 calibre breech-loading single shot carbine and 24 rounds for his Colt .45 six-shot revolver, enough ammunition to fight off an entire tribe.

Additionally they had veteran civilian scouts with them, who would ensure they were not ambushed: Isaiah Dorman, a Negro, who had earned a reputation as a trustworthy scout and interpreter; two white scouts; a mixed blood; six Crows and 24 Arikarees. Both these tribes disliked the Lakota, and the Crow were invaluable in that they knew this region well.

The scouts continually brought Custer much information. News also came from solitary friendly Indians and cowboys met en route. The scouts estimated the number of hostiles gathering to the west at 6,000, which if correct could mean as many as 1,000 or more warriors.

The recruits were alarmed at this news, but the veterans laughed, for if true it would indicate as many as seven or eight tribes, and that would make this the largest gathering of Plains Indians in known history! The veterans explained to the recruits that Indian scouts had a tendency to exaggerate, and told them that a Plains Indian warrior moved by riding a horse and leading two or three other horses. His wife and perhaps mother and mother-in-law and several children walked slightly to the rear and aside. Their tepee and 'household' belongings were placed on a travois, a wheelless cart, which was dragged by another horse. Thus the little entourage scarred and flattened the grass for several yards on either side. Fifty such families, travelling side by side, which was common, could leave a scar on the landscape a half mile wide, giving the impression that thousands had passed by.

Custer was so confident that he had brought along family members to witness the great victory: Boston Custer his brother, whom Custer listed as a civilian employee, and Autie Reed, his seventeen-year-old nephew. Another brother and a brother-in-law were fellow officers in the 7th. Perhaps of lasting benefit as far as Custer was concerned was Mark Kellogg a writer whom Custer had brought along to get material for a book.

The Approach: On the second day of the march the Crows did indeed find a scar half a mile wide leading to the west. None of the veterans were alarmed until Custer gave the order to turn west after them, against his original orders. It appeared Custer intended to fight before the other columns converged.

This became obvious on the night of the 24th when Custer ordered the march resumed at 11.00 that night. By stealing a march on the other columns Custer would arrive at the rendezvous a full day ahead of schedule. The men were surprised and concerned. Already exhausted from the day's ride they were soon riding again in pitch darkness, their horses tripping into prairie dog holes, which were common in this territory. Some men rode into dead end gullies and had to retrace their steps. However, getting lost from the column was not a problem, for the regiment made considerable noise. The recruits hoped the veterans knew what they were doing, and the veterans hoped Custer knew where he was going. They had no ambition to ride straight into a hostile camp.

Custer had sent off the Indian scouts again, this time with a white officer, who would, he hoped, deliver a more realistic report. At dawn while the regiment halted for breakfast a party of scouts rode in. They had found the rendezvous of the hostiles along the Little Big Horn River and they indicated it was the biggest they had ever seen. They recounted seeing the ground dark with horses. Several had misgivings about attacking such a large camp and they urged Custer to wait for the other columns.

At 8.00am Custer ordered a resumption of the march. It was already hot and the heat, coupled with the exhaustion and tedium of riding and walking, made many of the men drowsy.

A trooper rode in to say he had startled some Indians. That did it, as far as Custer was concerned. The enemy had been alerted of his approach. Again the scouts decided this was reason for caution. Custer saw it differently. He ordered a resumption of the march and began to formulate a plan of battle in his mind, but did not consult his officers.

It was standard practice for a cavalry column to divide in two at the beginning of a battle, one part to guard the pack horses. Captain Tom McDougal was dismayed that he drew this duty. His men may not have been so dismayed.

However, Custer had chosen to divide his column into four! His officers were taken aback by this, especially when he ordered Benteen to take three troops towards the south-west, that is away from the enemy camp. Custer now called up Reno and gave him a command: he was to take three troops and cross the Little Big Horn River, then charge the south edge of the enemy camp. Custer stated: 'I will support you.'

Much has been made of this last remark, but that is Custer's fault for it was an ambiguous statement (like his reply to Gibbon). 'I will support you' could mean 'I'll be right behind you', or 'I'll be here if you need me' or 'I'll attack the enemy elsewhere and take some of the pressure off you'.

If Reno asked for an explanation, he did not get one. In a hurry now, Custer rode off to the north with the remaining five troops of the regiment.

The Enemy: The word Sioux is an Ojibway word meaning enemy and was adopted by the white man for a group of languages spoken by a large number of American Indians whose original homes stretched from the Atlantic coast to the Rocky Mountains. These languages are Lakota, Dakota, Nakota, Dhegiha, Gros Ventre, Eastern Woodland, Chiewere, Assiniboine, Staitan, Mandan, Sewee, Nahyssan and Crow.

All of the 7th's troopers had met Sioux Indians of some description. Many hung around the forts looking for handouts or casual work. The 7th had used Osage Dhegiha scouts in Oklahoma. Some troopers had taken women of these tribes as mistresses and it is possible that one or two of the soldiers were themselves part Sioux.

On this current expedition one of the Arikaree scouts with them was half Oglala Lakota and had relatives among the hostiles. The mixed blood scout Mitch Bouyer was half French and half Santee Dakota and also had relatives among the hostiles. The Crow scouts were themselves Sioux, but did not consider themselves related to the Lakota, anymore than an Englishman considers himself related to a Dutchman because both speak a Germanic language.

Politically and organisationally, therefore, there was no such thing as the Sioux. Each tribe had its own chief and invariably he listened to a council before making a decision on even the most common rulings, such as where to camp that night.

Custer's men did not know which of the seven tribes of Lakota were in front of them on the Little Big Horn: it could be the Two Kettle, Sihasapa Blackfoot, Brule, Hunkpapa, Oglala, Sans Arc or Minneconjou. They would have been astonished to learn that the entire Lakota had assembled, but for the Two Kettle. In addition the river camp contained Northern Cheyenne, Northern Arapaho, Santee of the Dakota and Yankton of the Nakota. It was the largest rendezvous of Plains tribes in history.

No one chief was in charge. An inter-tribal council had been set up, which met in an oversized tepee, consisting of tribal chiefs, elders, medicine men, war leaders and notables including: Sitting (Buffalo) Bull, a respected medicine man of the Hunkpapa, who as his name suggested was middle-aged, i.e. sitting not running; Gall, the Hunkpapa war leader; and such noted warriors as Hump, Crow King, Young Black Moon and Crazy Horse.

Crazy Horse was an Oglala in his early thirties, a short wiry light-skinned man, born of an Oglala father and a Brule mother, who had the appearance of a savage warrior, but he was known as a thinker. For example even as a teenage boy he would not shoot from his horse, but would dismount and take careful aim. He was unassuming and never boasted.

Inside the dark council tepee the discussion revolved around Crazy Horse's recent victory. Just a week earlier he had led a mixed-tribe war party against Crook's column of Crows, Shoshones and cavalry in the valley of the Rosebud and had killed nine bluecoats and a Shoshone and scared Crook so much he had retreated. Neither Terry, Gibbon nor Custer knew of this encounter.

The young warriors were eager to face the enemy again, but wiser heads were arguing that Crazy Horse should not have inflicted such a defeat on the bluecoats, for it would only make them angry and harder to negotiate with. Some elders suggested they all move to Canada until the white man's anger cooled off and the bluecoats became tired of searching and went home. The redcoats in Canada had always treated the Plains Indians well.

Everyone was aware that Custer's column and others were coming towards them, but they did not expect an attack. They were after all in greater strength than anyone could ever remember and it would be sheer lunacy for the bluecoats to attack.

The Battlefield: Rarely did all the bands of a tribe camp together, and almost never did two entire tribes share a camp. A band would have twenty or so tepees and its camp would cover an area about 40 yards wide and 200 yards in length. Cavalry troopers had rarely seen a larger camp. The rendezvous camp on the Little Big Horn on the morning of 25 June was half a mile in width and almost three miles long stretching north to south along the west bank of the river. It covered a greater acreage than the towns of the American west.

West of the camp the valley extended a few miles and this is where the various tribes put their horses out to graze. The ground did indeed look dark with horses as several thousand stood together.

East of the river the ground sloped upwards into the hills so steeply that a man could not run up, but scarred into the hillsides were several gullies which were not nearly as steep and would allow a man or horse to move up slowly. There were trees along the water's edge and a few stunted trees in the gullies, otherwise the only vegetation was grass about eighteen inches high and some tiny bushes. One could see for miles from the hilltop, but with no distinguishing features to a stranger's eye it was like staring at an ocean and distance was hard to judge. The steepness of the hillside meant that the horse herd could easily be seen by a scout on the hilltop, but the village, which was closer in, could not be seen in its entirety.

The Indians did not wander up the hillside. They knew it was crawling with rattlesnakes!

The Battle: Just past 3.00pm Reno led his three troops down a gully to splash across the shallow narrow river and then they swung around to face north. Spreading out they drew carbines and approached the camp at a trot. They could only see the southern narrow edge of the camp, but even this gave them food for thought. They were obviously attacking a very big camp indeed.

Indian dogs and boys saw the approaching troopers and alerted the camp. Women began gathering their children and the older men ordered them to run westwards towards the horse herd. The warriors ran to their tepees and without time for prayers or to daub war paint they grabbed their individual weapons: bows, lances, clubs, steel axes and rifles of a variety of models and calibres.

Already the troopers could see some Indians falling from their long distance fire. Two of the victims were a wife and child of Gall.

Two troopers charged ahead of the others – possibly recruits unable to rein in their horses – and they rode into a small ravine and found the warriors of the Hunkpapa and Sans Arcs hiding there. Gall had organised this. The two were instantly killed. Seeing this Reno's men halted and now the Indians opened up a terrific fire towards them. The Arikarees with Reno turned and rode off. Reno ordered his men to dismount and fight kneeling.

After several minutes, Reno, deciding he was outnumbered about three to one and under fire from Indians who were working around his flanks, ordered a series of withdrawals, eventually choosing to re-cross the river.

Running and riding Reno's men made it to the river and waded across, the Indians afoot hard on their heels, and as the troopers began to clamber up the steep far bank the Indians shot at them. Men who slid down fell into the waiting Indians and were stabbed and clubbed to death. Amongst the thickets many troopers fought back wildly until rushed by several warriors at once.

Gaining the top of a bluff Reno ordered his men to set up a perimeter defence. Many were without horses and they hid behind small tufts of grass and a couple of trees to shoot any Indian who popped his head above the bluff edge.

Reno counted 80 men, of whom several were wounded, which meant that 46 were missing. After a few minutes the soldiers came under sniper fire from Indians who had seized higher ground. Trapped, with only the water in their canteens and the sun glaring down at them the men were in a hell of a fix.

The Indians on the other hand could walk down to the river and get a drink when they wanted. Their casualties had been light, though one of them was Young Black Moon who was sadly mourned.

Meanwhile Custer had ridden northwards, but his Arikaree and Crow scouts baulked at this. They claimed they had been hired to find not fight, which was true. These were brave men, and the Crow were fighting for their own land, but they were not fools. Custer told them to join Reno. Only a few stayed with him. This must have really unnerved Custer's troopers.

About 3.20pm Custer sent a messenger to Benteen: 'Come on. Big village. Be quick. Bring packs. PS bring packs', the words actually written by Lieutenant Cooke.

Custer led his men another mile, believing he would now be north of the camp and about 4.10pm he ordered Calhoun and Keogh to go down a gully to make sure. They did so and as they reached level ground and began to cross the river they found themselves literally in the midst of a forest of tepees. Warriors here were as surprised as the troopers and a short but fierce fight developed until the cavalrymen could turn around and ride back up the gully. Informed of the startling discovery that the camp was perhaps two miles in length or more, Custer ordered his five troops to proceed further northwards.

It was obvious to Benteen when he received Custer's message that he was to reinforce Custer, that the enemy was bigger than expected, and he was to bring the packs (i.e. extra ammunition) but Benteen did not have the packs, McDougal did, and Benteen would have to send a message to him. Moreover, Reno was far closer to Custer than Benteen, so Benteen may have assumed Custer had sent a similar message to Reno. Benteen was not informed where Custer was, only where the messenger, who spoke better Italian than English, had last seen him.

On his way to join Custer, Benteen came within earshot of Reno's stand and he diverted to join him – understandably, for he did not know Custer was not there. His first words when he arrived were 'Where's Custer?' However, he deferred to Reno when the latter thanked him for arriving in the nick of time and proceeded to give him orders to share some of his ammunition and help defend his perimeter.

Captain Weir became disgusted as he heard Reno and Benteen discussing their own defences rather than planning to aid Custer, so in violation of Reno's orders he remounted his own troop and led them northwards. Benteen thought about Custer for several minutes, then decided to follow Weir.

However, Weir did not get far before he was charged by scores of Indians on horseback. When Benteen caught up with him they held their ground, but after an hour they reluctantly fell back towards Reno, who was in fact approaching with three troops. They all returned to 'Reno's Hill' which had been reinforced by McDougal.

About 5.00pm Custer halted his column as he spied Two Moons' Cheyennes on horseback far to the north. Looking around he saw he was on the side of a hill as it sloped down westwards before dropping off above the river. He now made a most unusual decision. Ignoring the crown of the hill just yards to his right (east) he ordered his troopers to dismount and set up a perimeter defence, though the terrain was so open that it afforded no natural cover whatsoever. Furthermore, he dispersed the five troops to the point that they were not able to assist each other. Lieutenant Smith's troop was to send their horses to the crown of the hill while they knelt in firing position as close to the western drop off as possible, though Smith himself was to stay with Custer. Custer set up his own headquarters with Yates' troop about 300 yards to the north-east of Smith's troop. To Custer's south-east he placed Keogh's troop, and further south-east Lieutenant J. J. Crittenden's troop and then Calhoun's troop.

With 215 men he intended to defend a line a mile and a half long, and as every fourth man had to hold the reins of four horses, only three-quarters of his troopers would be firing.

Yet the horse-mounted Indians did not come on. Instead, Indians from the camp, Cheyenne, Arapahos, Oglalas, Blackfoot, Santees, Minneconjous, Brules and Yanktons all under Gall's command began running up the gullies – the only way they could gain the hilltop, and when they ran into the open atop the gullies they came upon the 28 men of Smith's troop. Lying down in the gullies the Indians began shooting arrows into the air in order to fall down on the troopers. Within minutes Smith's men were sorely wounded by these projectiles, though not killed, and in anger, frustration and pain they crawled to the edge of the gullies or stood up to fire back and, exposing themselves in this way, they were shot down and killed by the full force of arrows and rifle bullets. It is feasible that one or more soldiers knew they were helpless from bloody wounds and fearing being taken alive and tortured they shot themselves. In pairs, which is how they were trained to fight, Smith's troop died.

The Indians then charged on foot towards the other troops. Already some soldiers holding the reins of horses decided they had better mount up and ride off, but they were quickly shot or dragged from their horses and beaten to death.

Kneeling, the troopers fired steadily, but many found their carbines jamming. They took out knives to pry out the jammed cartridge, but seeing a group of Indians jump up out of the grass and charge them, they threw away the carbines and drew revolvers. After six shots, aimed wildly, they needed to reload, but by then the Indians were upon them.

After about 15 minutes Crazy Horse appeared. He had gathered together a band of warriors and they had mounted and ridden far to the north, then east, then south and come up the north side of the hill, which slopes much more gently. Reaching the crown of the hill they could quite easily see every single soldier and Indian before them. They charged a gathering of cavalry horses first and dispersed those, easily killing the troopers who were trying to hold the reins of four nervous horses and take aim with a revolver at the same time. Cavalry horses began to fall rapidly. The Indians may have been told by their war leaders not to waste time trying to capture a horse, but to kill the horses if necessary to keep the cavalry troopers afoot. However, the Plains Indians took pride in their horses and they viewed the heavy, awkward forage-fed cavalry horses as poor quality compared to their grass-fed ponies. They may simply not have cared if they killed the troopers' horses. It is also possible that bad aim killed many a horse. With little spare ammunition the Indians could never practise and were notori-

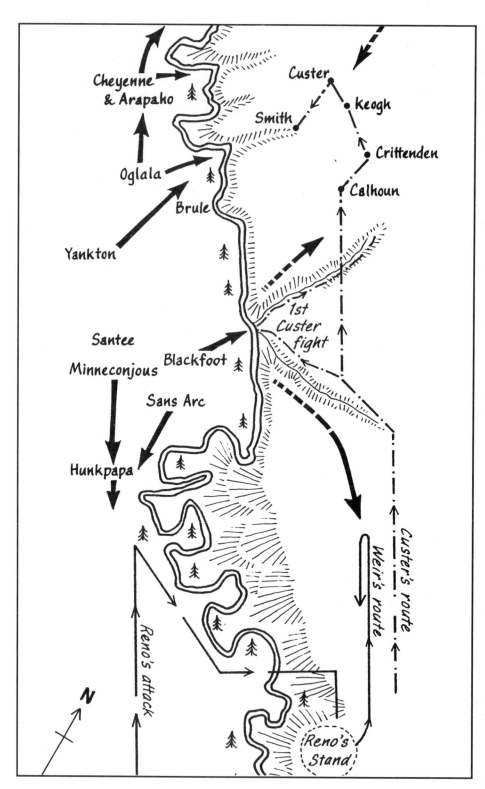

Cheyenne & Arapaho

Custer

Keogh

Smith

Crittenden

Oglala

Calhoun

Brule

Yankton

1st Custer fight

Santee

Minneconjous

Blackfoot

Sans Arc

Hunkpapa

Weir's route

Custer's route

Reno's attack

N

Reno's Stand

ously poor shots. It is also probable that many a soldier shot his horse to prevent it falling into enemy hands and to use its carcass as a barricade.

Then the horse-mounted warriors charged down on the Custer–Yates and Keogh troops. No doubt the Indians did not recognise Custer – he no longer had his long golden locks – and in any case why should they have known who he was? The soldiers did not know who Crazy Horse was. How Custer fell is not known. Probably a bullet in the head, which implies, but does not prove, suicide. Autie Reed and Boston Custer who had come to see a battle died almost shoulder to shoulder.

Certainly some of the troopers saw that all was lost and they ran. After all, many were fresh recruits. They did not get far because the fleet-footed Indians could outrun them especially in this stifling heat.

Only twenty minutes after Custer and his five troops had dismounted, they were all dead.

During the night, which remained oppressively hot, some of Reno's and Benteen's men braved capture by attempting to sneak down to the river to fill canteens. In the dark some missing men who had been hiding since early afternoon crawled in to safety.

On the following morning Reno and Benteen exchanged a few shots with snipers, but by early afternoon no more activity was heard and the soldiers realised the Indians had gone. At last after 26 hours they could rush down to the river and drink frantically of the cool water.

Reno and Benteen had suffered 53 killed and 52 seriously wounded.

Aftermath: The Indians were amazed at their victory, having suffered less than a hundred killed, but they were alarmed, like a mob of striking workers who find they have killed a policeman. The council ordered the tribes to disperse and make their way to Canada to escape the wrath of the bluecoats, which must now surely descend upon them.

Appraisal: Many errors contributed to Custer's defeat. The shrinkage of the army to hopelessly inadequate numbers meant that hostile tribes were allowed to come and go as they pleased for years despite their land having been officially reshaped in favour of white immigration.

Soldiers were often outnumbered by hostiles.

Generally the quality of recruits was poor, because military life did not offer much. Ex-soldiers of foreign armies such as British, German and French found discipline to be harsher and conditions worse in the United States Army.

Officers were not rotated to civilisation periodically, therefore they became bored to the point of alcoholism or insanity. Their promotion chances were practically non-existent. New graduates of West Point did not even receive commissions until there was room for them.

The carbines issued to the cavalry were worn out and usually single shot. Yet excellent models like the Winchester fifteen-shot repeater were on the market. In any case troopers were only allowed an average of one cartridge every four days for practice.

These were inherent flaws that Custer had to work with, but he created his own errors too, which fall into sixteen major categories: morale, training, firepower, intelligence, disobedience, timing, reconnaissance, command structure, communications, counsel, tactics, dispersal, ground, manpower, reserves, command ability.

His attitude towards his men was offhand and he did little to foster a sense of regimental élan that could cut down on desertion and crime. It could be done even in the rough conditions of frontier life: the Negro regiments' desertion rate was one tenth that of Custer's 7th. In early 1876 many of Custer's men had run off to dig for gold.

To make up numbers Custer took with him recruits, who should have been completing their training, not matching their wits against warriors who had been skilled in hand-to-hand combat since boyhood.

His refusal to take Gatling guns with him remains an academic argument. Never had Gatlings made a difference, but a couple of them sitting on the crown of 'Custer's Hill' might have made all the difference in the world.

Few commanders have gone into battle knowing as much about the enemy as did Custer. His scouts were good and had friends and relatives among the hostiles. They knew how the enemy thought, what he wanted and how he would react. Yet Custer seems not to have listened to this plethora of valuable intelligence.

His deliberate disobedience in reaching the rendezvous a day ahead of schedule was suicidal. Had he waited, the Indians might not even have resisted seeing the odds were against them. His soldiers probably knew he had disobeyed orders, and this damaged their morale even more.

By timing his march the way he did he ensured he attacked with exhausted men and horses, while the enemy's men and horses were rested.

He sent Benteen and three whole troops to reconnoitre for more Indians, a job that two scouts could have done, yet sent no one to judge accurately the size of the enemy camp and as a result he blundered into the middle of the village on one occasion.

His command structure reflected his arrogance. Not only did he intend to tell his senior officers only what he thought they needed to know (Reno was after all his deputy by virtue of rank), but he didn't tell them that much. Benteen and Reno went into action knowing nothing. Custer probably explained more to his nephew Autie and to his biographer Mark Kellogg.

Another reflection of his arrogance was his poor communications. His orders to Benteen in the midst of battle were badly written and a solitary message to Benteen was insufficient. However, it is possible he sent other messengers who failed to get through.

He sought no counsel from his fellow officers and scouts in formulating his battle plan, yet they were as experienced as he.

His tactics were fundamentally flawed. If victorious in his two-pronged attack he would have dispersed the Indians, but that is exactly what he was not supposed to do. The whole purpose of the expedition was to round up the hostiles, not scatter them as far as Canada.

His dispersal of forces was laughable. Convinced, as he must have been, that he was facing at least several hundred warriors, odds of 1:1, he divided his assault force into three, sent one out of the way, leaving him only with two, odds of 1½:1 against.

When he realised his own battalion was about to come under heavy counter-attack he divided them into five separate troops that would give him, after the horse holders were taken out of the equation, an average of one man standing in the open every 40 feet. As troopers paired up and tried to maintain troop integrity this placed some troops hundreds of yards from support and facing odds of 5:1 against. In fact the Indians by their own count numbered between 1,500 and 3,000 combatants (some women and boys fought): placing Custer at disadvantageous odds of 2½:1 before he dispersed.

He did not choose the site of his final stand until minutes before he was under attack. He had come over broken ground to get here and could have withdrawn to that natural cover. Instead without hesitation he chose to fight on a hillside that resembled a sloping billiard table.

He could have had more manpower if he had asked, but it appears he wanted this to be an 'all 7th' show, hence he would rather use recruits than veterans from other regiments.

Because of Benteen's orders, putting him out of the picture, one cannot call his three troops Custer's reserve, which means Custer attacked an enemy of unknown force without a reserve.

Overall Custer's command ability comes down to one word, luck. Custer's Luck had become a saying in the army. It is ironic that he had gained glory leading 60 cavalry charges in the Civil War, but he died fighting on foot in defence. He had run out of luck.

The army needed a scapegoat and Reno was court martialled. Had Custer survived he would most certainly have been court martialled. He disobeyed orders and paid the price.

An Alternative: The best alternative for Custer would have been to obey orders and play his part in what was a good plan, which may have succeeded despite the defeat of Crook.

However, having disobeyed orders he could still have found a good defensive site and holed up. If he had suspected the Indians were about to scatter at his approach, he had another alternative. The Indians had placed their horse herd on the west in the open, making it a perfect target for Custer to charge from the south-east, forcing the horses to run away from the Indians. Those horses that were tethered could have been shot down. Seeing their wealth and mode of transportation at risk the Indians would have counter-charged on foot towards Custer, but being horsed his men could have withdrawn slowly, keeping the Indians under fire and then ridden off if ammunition ran low. Such tactics were successfully used by Boers in southern Africa. A shortage of horses in this terrain would have placed the Indians in the bag once the other columns arrived.

Consequences: When the other columns converged and rescued Reno and Benteen, they sent the news to the four corners of the world. In many nations the news was greeted with astonishment. Savages who had no written language had overcome a major military expedition.

The American newspapers took up the cry that the Indians had a 'general', another Pontiac, another Little Turtle. Some editors went further, deciding he must be half white, which caused others to speculate he was all white, perhaps an ex-Confederate general, a foreign general, a disgraced West Point cadet. The more racist one was, the more fanciful a story one would believe.

Eventually, the mantle of 'general' fell on the holy man Sitting Bull, though he had spent the entire battle in his tepee praying and was no more a general than the Bishop of Chicago.

Crazy Horse was the white man's second choice for 'general', an opinion that had some logic at least. No one chose Gall, who had as much right to the title as any one. The white man could not understand that the Indians had no general and that Custer was so arrogant he would have been outmanoeuvred if he had tried to round-up cattle.

Of course for a drink of whiskey some Indians would tell a newspaper reporter anything he wanted to hear.

The respectable Indians, those who had actually fought in the battle, had to come to terms with their victory. All participants in a battle only see one side and a limited view at that. Thus the Indians thought the two cavalrymen who rushed the ravine were brave. They also praised the courage of Reno's men, whom they failed to defeat, but told stories of cowardice about Custer's men, whom they had defeated. It is illogical to assume the troopers under Reno were more brave than those under Custer, thus it seems the Indians were making excuses for their victory over Custer or were genuinely misled. They said many a soldier threw away his carbine in panic, but had they in fact seen someone discard a jammed weapon. They saw soldiers run in panic, but had they in fact seen someone react to a sergeant's order. They thought it despicable that some wounded soldiers shot themselves, but they considered the white man as just another tribe, whereas the white man saw the Indian as godless and therefore devil-like. Raised on Bible-thumping Christianity and a Victorian sense of guilt and good versus evil, some soldiers would have thought that to fall into the hands of Indians was to risk one's soul as well as one's life.

Over the next years the Indians in exile in Canada drifted back into the USA and when Sitting Bull returned, expecting to be imprisoned or executed, he was instead turned into a circus star!

The Battle's Place in History: More books and motion pictures have been made about this affair than any other oneday battle in history. Custer's wife lived long enough to see Hollywood immortalise her. In terms of tactics, the battle deserves none of this publicity, for Custer's tactics were terrible and the Indians did not show all that much tactical skill in that they ran up gullies, the only route available – a herd of sheep would have done the same – and they were caught completely unprepared by Reno's charge. Having corralled Reno and Benteen they then did not know what to do with them. Despite Custer's death it must be remembered that the bluecoats not the hostile Indians were left in command of the battlefield and the hostiles are the ones who retreated. The land was returned to the Crow, who have it still.

Isandhlwana

Background: In the nineteenth century there were more similarities between South Africa and the wild west of the United States, than between the Canadian west and the United States' west.

The British had entered southern Africa by capturing the coastal settlement of Cape Colony from the Dutch in the early part of the century and had inherited the Dutchman's war against native tribes, whom the Dutch called Kaffir (an Arabic word meaning unbeliever). This was a direct parallel with the British conquest of New Amsterdam from the Dutch in 1664, whereby the British inherited Dutch troubles with native American Indians.

The South African tribes, speaking many languages, were dominated by a handful of warlike tribes, who eked a living by raising huge herds of cattle, and tribal wars were invariably waged over grazing or water rights.

As the tribe nearest the British-Dutch settlement came under attack from its northern warlike neighbour, the British aided them and defeated the warmonger and gained rule over their lands, but in so doing inherited their war with a war-like tribe still further north. In this manner the British regular army was involved in a series of wars, which inevitably they won by the use of massed volleys against spear-wielding natives. British rule spread northwards hundreds of miles over the next three generations.

Settlers moved north too: Dutch Boers (farmers), who moved to escape British laws; British farmers, who sought their own land; and several nationalities of gamblers, confidence tricksters, prospectors, botanists, missionaries, engineers and miners. The native Africans were enslaved or employed as cheap labour. White women were few and far between.

Wearing a slouch hat, a shirt and trousers of rough material for warm weather hard work, a revolver or rifle and mounted on a horse, there was little to distinguish the British or Boer cattle worker from the American cowboy. The former placed their cattle in a kraal. The cowboy put his in a corral.

There were some very important differences too. The warrior tribes never adopted the horse in large numbers, thus remaining at a disadvantage when fighting mounted Boers or Britons or regular British cavalry.

Another difference was that within the Boer communities the posse was an efficient method of law enforcement and within British areas a police force was soon set up, which could call upon the regular army. As a result the outlaws of the African south were not as numerous or as effective as those of the American west.

In August 1877 Sir Bartle Frere, a professional civil servant and newly appointed Governor of Cape Colony, was informed that the 'natives were restless', but this did not worry him. He knew of the long string of victories called the Kaffir Wars. For example, in 1873 the British had invaded the lands of the Hlubi and

Putuni, repelled them with a couple of volleys fired by regular infantry, then counter-attacked and shot them down by the hundreds, stolen their cattle and enslaved thousands (despite slavery supposedly being illegal).

Inquiring who was causing trouble currently, he was informed it was the Gcalekes. He urged Prime Minister John Molteno of Cape Colony to make war upon them, but this and other problems caused considerable friction between the two. In January 1878 Frere took the unheard of step of dismissing Molteno from his position. Though legal, this dismissal of an elected official caused ripples of discontent throughout South Africa, and Frere made it worse by replacing him with an obvious puppet. For Frere to show such unbelievable arrogance as to become a dictator was scandalous in the extreme. Yet the British government of Prime Minister Benjamin Disraeli supported him.

The Commander: In March 1878 Frederic Augustus Thesiger arrived to take command of the army, and Frere directed him to hunt down the Gcalekes and the Ngquikas.

Thesiger was at the pinnacle of his career and he dived into the mission with vigour. Born in 1827 to a modest family, he had purchased a commission at the age of seventeen and quickly proved to be an adept, diplomatic, teetotal, disciplined staff officer. He purchased a captaincy in 1852 and soon achieved a choice position for a staff minded officer: aide to the Viceroy of Ireland.

During Britain's war with Russia 1854-56 he earned a promotion to major for his staff work and in 1858 he earned another promotion to lieutenant-colonel during the great revolt in India.

That year his father was created the 1st Baron Chelmsford. Thesiger liked India and remained there for years, and at the age of 39 married a general's daughter. In 1868 he took part in the British invasion of Ethiopia and then was promoted to the greatest staff position in the empire: personal aide to Queen Victoria herself. This gained him the rank of major general.

Now here he was in Africa in command and he took the opportunity to lead the expedition against the Gcalekes and Ngquikas himself; not really his job, but as he had never led troops into battle he wanted to have the experience.

Usually wearing a dark blue uniform, with short hair parted in the middle and a full beard, he looked every bit the Victorian general and he directed his troops well and looked after their needs: always the staff officer first.

The hostile natives were overcome with a couple of volleys fired by the regular infantry of the 24th Regiment after which mounted local volunteers chased after them. The local volunteers looked indisciplined and they were: they murdered hundreds of prisoners.

With his first victory under his belt, Thesiger felt confident, and then his father died, elevating him to the peerage as the 2nd Baron Chelmsford.

Grand Strategy: Frere was pleased with Thesiger-Chelmsford's victory and he now decided the army was ready to challenge the greatest of all tribes, the Zulu. Zululand stood to the north of Natal Province, the home of 16,000 British and Boer settlers, and the east of Transvaal, a Boer republic that Britain had taken over recently through diplomatic means.

Frere's main purpose in destroying the Zulus was not just to remove the threat to Natal and Transvaal, or even just to take their land, but to show the black man in South Africa who was boss: for after all if the Zulu could not stand up to the British then no one could. The British government had not directed Frere to become warmonger, any more than they had directed him to become dictator, but he took advantage of the fact that communication between Cape Town and London was by long sea journey. More often than not London had to accept deeds done in their name.

In July Frere ordered Chelmsford to prepare an invasion force, while he sought out a pretext for war to satisfy London.

Seizing upon a Natal–Zulu boundary dispute he appointed a committee of Anthony Durnford, Michael Galwey and John Shepstone to decide the issue. It appeared he had rigged the vote, for Galwey was Attorney General for Natal. Durnford was an officer who had received a crippled arm fighting natives and had settled in Natal, where he was currently organising his own troops to take part in the invasion, and Shepstone was the brother of Theophilus Shepstone, whom Frere had made administrator of Transvaal.

Frere was flabbergasted when the committee voted in favour of the Zulu! He had not counted on the honesty of the three men.

Disregarding the result, Frere sent Theophilus Shepstone to King Cetshwayo of the Zulu with an ultimatum, and on 11 January 1879 without waiting for an answer he published a declaration of war.

The Army: The regular army was not, as might be expected, seen as a method of escaping the poverty and unhealthy living and working conditions of the filthy, overcrowded, insanitary cities of nineteenth century Britain. Emigration provided the escape. In fact the soldiers of 1879 were not as low class or illiterate as later generations assumed. However, they were not all fine physical specimens, either. Army life was rough and recruitment was difficult and when Irish recruitment dried up because so many Irish died of starvation in the 1840s the army was forced to lower its physical standards to maintain even the small force that it had become.

The men Chelmsford led were the products of the 1868–1871 reforms of Secretary for War Edward Cardwell: reforms such as a new minimum enlistment of just seven years; regionalism, so that most men of one regiment came from the same district; and the abolition of purchased commissions.

The 24th Regiment was the backbone of Chelmsford's central column: the 1st Battalion made up of long service men, mostly veterans in their 30s and 40s; and the 2nd battalion, made up of short service men, mostly in their 20s, though some of their sergeants were long service men. This was an English Midlands regiment, but had a high proportion of Welshmen. Both battalions were seasoned and had made short work of the natives in the recent conflict.

In his white helmet, red coat and dark blue trousers, each infantryman carried a Martini-Henry 8½-pound, 33½-inch barrel, lever action breech-loading rifle, which fired a .45 calibre metallic cartridge bullet at 1,350fps. A trained regular could fire one shot every few seconds and knock down a charging warrior at 1,000 yards' range, and each soldier carried 70 rounds.

Each company of about 100 men was led by a lieutenant, who had a colour sergeant to aid him, and the company was divided into four sections, each led by a sergeant and a corporal.

Besides infantry Chelmsford had regular artillery, engineers and commissary, and he temporarily mounted some of his regular infantry into the Imperial Mounted Infantry.

In addition to full-time regulars Chelmsford had amassed in his central column: the black uniformed Natal Mounted Police, temporarily taken off their law enforcement duty; the Buffalo Border Guard, the Newcastle Mounted Rifles and the Royal Natal Carbineers, all settler volunteer colonial horsemen wearing khaki uniforms and slouch hats; and native volunteers organised into the Natal Native Contingent (NNC), the Natal Pioneer Corps and the Natal Native Horse (NNH).

Most of the native troops were either Zulus in exile or tribes conquered by the British and who owed no loyalty towards the white man. Some were Hlubis, who had survived the slaughter inflicted on them just five years before. The pioneers were simply manual labourers and porters. The NNC were infantry, but only one native in ten was issued with a rifle, the others carried an assegai (spear) and/or knobkerrie (club) and shield. Their uniform was a red rag around the head. Every twenty natives had a sandy-uniformed white sergeant, recruited from itinerant labourers, smallholder farmers, miners and adventurers, many of whom were as illiterate as the natives. Almost none of them spoke the language of their men and made do with hand signals. The officers were little better than the sergeants.

The NNH was a good unit, whose natives were fully uniformed and well armed and who could rise to sergeant-major. The officers were gentlemen.

Causes of Arrogance: Chelmsford was supremely confident. There was no thought of the Little Big Horn in Chelmsford's army. It had been 30 months since the Custer massacre and the suggestion that such a calamity could befall a British army was laughable. Chelmsford had no less than 16,000 troops, with which to face the Zulus who could muster probably 20,000 warriors. His rifles and artillery would cut them down like wheat, he envisaged.

Chelmsford's only experience of fighting Africans had been his recent encounter with the Gcalekes and Ngquikas, and that had flavoured his opinion of their war-making capabilities to think they were all equally weak. He had plenty of men around to tell him different, but they were either Boers, whom he felt he could not trust, or British settlers, who appeared extremely uncivilised in their attire and mannerisms. He certainly had no intention of taking advice from natives.

Frere had deliberately launched the war in January for it was harvest time, and most of the Zulu warriors would be on their farms. Cetshwayo would only be able to mobilise some nearby warriors to defend his 'capital', the village of Ulundi, and Chelmsford intended to defeat them rapidly and take prisoner the fat, tyrannical chief.

To the Victorian mind, therefore, the army had superior numbers, superior firepower, superior training (the regulars at least), superior generalship (for one could hardly compare a native chief to the Queen's aide) and superior morality – the superiority of the white man over the black man, the civilised Christian over the pagan savage.

Strategy: Chelmsford had organised five separate columns: Colonel Pearson's, which would cross the Tugela at Lower Drift (ford); Colonel Durnford's, which would cross at Middle Drift; the central column under Lieutenant Colonel Glyn crossing the Buffalo, a tributary of the Tugela, at Rorke's Drift; Colonel Wood's column coming from Utrecht, Transvaal; and Colonel Rowlands' column coming from Derby, Transvaal. Chelmsford hoped to entice the Zulus into attacking at least one of these columns, each of which had enough firepower to crush the hastily mobilised warriors.

The Battlefield: The terrain was open rolling grassland, scarred by ravines and gullies (dongas) that were only visible when one was upon them. A few rocky out-croppings created sufficient distinguishing features that could be navigated easily. Trees were sparse and often stunted. Apart from the outcroppings the area resembled that of the Little Big Horn.

The Approach: Not all supplies reached the columns in time, forcing Chelmsford to order Durnford and Rowlands to remain where they were. He would invade with the remaining three columns.

He decided to accompany Glyn's column, for it had the shortest route to travel to Ulundi, and on 11 January, the first day of the war, Chelmsford watched as Glyn's men crossed the fast-flowing, deep Buffalo. Horsemen had little problem crossing, and the regulars used rafts and wagons, while the natives rushed the river arm-in-arm and several were knocked loose by the force of water and drowned. Chelmsford inquired as to how many were lost, but Major Rupert Lonsdale commander of the 3rd Regiment NNC had never bothered to count how many natives he had to start with so he did not know.

The colonial horsemen rode on to capture a Zulu farm.

On the following day scouts discovered a native kraal and Chelmsford ordered an attack at once by a battalion of the NNC and four companies of the 1/24th together with the cavalry. This should have been Glyn's decision, but Chelmsford did not consult him. The Zulus put up a show of force, some with old rifles, but within minutes 32 Zulus were shot down or assegaied and the NNC lost two killed and twenty wounded, of whom three were white men. To impress Frere, Chelmsford wrote to him of 'the storming of (Chief) Sirayo's stronghold'. With this 'victory' under their belts the column marched deeper into Zululand.

Colonel Durnford obeyed new orders to bring to Rorke's Drift three companies (450 men) of the NNC and five troops (250 men) of the NNH, and on the 17th he rode on with a small escort to report to Chelmsford. He found Chelmsford with Glyn's column in camp at Mount Isandhlwana. In other words in a week the column had advanced ten miles as the crow flies.

On the 21st Chelmsford ordered Major Dartnell to take 150 colonial horsemen to seek the Zulus and Major Lonsdale to follow him with most of his NNC. It was little risk to put cavalry in danger of a Zulu ambush for they could outrun the Zulus, but to put poorly armed NNC in their path was suicidal, and the NNC knew it. This would not have helped their morale, which was already bad from mistreatment by ignorant and racist sergeants and officers. Perhaps some natives suspected Chelmsford was using them as bait.

Ten miles east of the camp Dartnell's men sighted several hundred Zulu warriors in fighting kit. Dartnell sent a horse courier to Chelmsford, who responded by ordering Dartnell and his horsemen and the NNC to attack the next morning.

Elsewhere that day Lieutenant E. S. Browne and 100 red-coated Imperial Mounted Infantry clashed with 40 Zulus.

Chelmsford was so eager he rode off with a small escort to see for himself. He intercepted a second courier from Dartnell, who was asking for regulars before he attacked. Chelmsford agreed and ordered the regulars up: but only the 2/24th, four guns and some cavalry. Thus by now he had divided his central column in the face of the enemy into Browne, Dartnell, Lonsdale, Glyn and the 2/24th, and Lieutenant-Colonel Pulleine and the 1/24th still in the camp at Isandhlwana. He then sent orders for Durnford to join Pulleine, which meant he had eight separate formations near or inside Zululand, counting the base camp at Helpmakaar and the supply camp at Rorke's Drift. If the Zulus chose they could have attacked either one of these on its own. Yet Chelmsford was so confident he rode in the dark almost alone to find Dartnell!

However at dawn Dartnell could no longer locate the Zulus, but Chelmsford did not change anyone's orders. Dartnell continued to advance and eventually found the Zulus lined up for battle. They charged and he sent his horsemen against them. Shooting and retiring, shooting and retiring, the horsemen accounted for 80 Zulus for no loss, until the Zulus retreated.

Well pleased with this news Chelmsford ordered his officers to join him for breakfast at 9.30am.

Durnford, after receiving Chelmsford's message delivered by Lieutenant Horace Smith-Dorrien, gathered his men together and assigned a company of the NNC and a troop of the NNH to bring up his slow baggage wagons, while he rode on towards Isandhlwana with 200 NNH, 300 NNC and a rocket detachment manned by regulars. Rorke's Drift was left in the hands of a company of the 2/24th and 300 NNC.

That morning at Isandhlwana Pulleine breathed easier. He had been overshadowed too long by Chelmsford and Glyn. A brevet lieutenant-colonel (substantive major) he had in the camp 100 colonial horsemen, two guns manned by regulars, five companies of the 1/24th and one company of the 2/24th, four companies of the NNC, several native labourers and porters, some commissary and medical troops and some sick: all told about 1,300 men.

Soon, though, scouts sighted many Zulus to the north and Pulleine sent a message at 8.05am to Chelmsford: 'Zulus are advancing in force from left front of camp.'

Chelmsford received this message an hour and a half later, but as it did not conform to his expectations, that Cetshwayo and his Zulus were really up front (eastwards), he replied by ordering only one battalion of NNC to retrace their steps and reinforce Pulleine.

Durnford arrived at Isandhlwana at 10.00am and saw that Pulleine had made hopelessly inadequate dispositions: the wagons were not laagered into a barricade; F Company 1/24th was placed on the south flank; the remainder of the 1/24th was spread out in one rank almost a mile long to the east of the camp about 800 yards; two guns protected the north-east corner; the horsemen were spread out on the north flank; and the NNC was inside the camp. To the west was Isandhlwana itself, sticking up like a sand-coloured iceberg, too steep for anyone to climb. At this point there were now about 1,800 men under Durnford and Pulleine in the camp.

This was a delicate moment for the two men. Durnford in his rough khaki uniform could not have been more different than Pulleine in his red infantry coat. At the moment Durnford was a colonial volunteer, but he had served several years as a regular army engineer. A 48-year-old balding Irishman with bushy greying moustache and joining sideburns he had chosen to settle in Natal and had come to respect the natives, despite losing the use of an arm in a fight with Hlubis. Some of his NNH were Hlubis, who reciprocated this respect. Some had converted to Christianity. Durnford knew Africa and he knew the native mentality. Pulleine did not. Durnford was a physical worker and a fighter. Pulleine was a staff officer.

As he entered Pulleine's tent Durnford may have had other things than Zulus on his mind. He had just become engaged to a settler half his age.

They discussed the situation, but did not argue, at least not loud enough for anyone to hear. Durnford, a brevet colonel (substantive lieutenant-colonel) outranked Pulleine, but Pulleine held a regular commission in a regular unit, and Durnford was a mere 'colonial'. Pulleine was infantry, whereas Durnford had never been other than an engineer. Most embarrassingly for both, neither knew Chelmsford's wishes on who should command.

Durnford asked Pulleine for help to go after the Zulus before they attacked, but the best Pulleine could offer was to support him if he got into trouble. Durnford suggested Pulleine let his men finish breakfast while he sent some NNH to scout the area.

At 10.30am the NNH scouts sighted Zulus retiring to the east. At Durnford's suggestion Pulleine sent his infantry back into line and placed one company and 150 NNC on the north flank, while Durnford decided to harass the retiring Zulus and rode out of camp with his NNH, the rockets and 100 NNC.

Four miles north-east of the camp Lieutenant Raw and some NNH scouts saw some Zulus and followed them into a ravine, stumbling straight into thousands of Zulus. Both sides were surprised and Raw and his men were able to open fire, back out and ride hell bent for leather towards the camp. They had found Cetshwayo's army.

The Enemy: Cetshwayo was no savage. He was the king of a nation of a quarter of a million souls, whose society was as complex as any white nation. Based upon a core ethnicity of Mtetwa, the Zulu were not a tribe but a military empire started by Dingishwayo just 70 years earlier. Eventually the empire incorporated scores of tribes, clans and ethnicities. The name Zulu, the nGuni word for 'Heavens', was adopted from the name of an historical warrior.

The Zulu Army of 1879 consisted of reservists, who were only mobilised during wartime or ceremonial occasions, and had seen little action in the last twenty years, giving the lie to Frere's claims they were a threat. When mobilised they exhibited a discipline any British general would have been proud of.

Unknown to Chelmsford many Zulus had mobilised for a ceremony and were with Cetshwayo at his capital when the news arrived of the British invasion.

This army was not a mob, but was administered in regiments recruited regionally, each with its own traditions and élan. The shield decoration identified the regiment. The warriors fought with shield, knobkerrie and iKlwa (a very short spear used like a sword). There were also a few riflemen.

Within the ravine discovered by Lieutenant Raw were twelve regiments: the umKhulutshane, uDududu and the isaNgqu containing the oldest warriors placed into the Nodwengu Brigade. Warriors were not allowed to marry until they had distinguished themselves in battle, thus many of these men in their thirties and forties were still bachelors. The umKhulutshane were in their sixties!

The uThulwana and the inDlu-yengwe Regiments made up the Undi Brigade. The other regiments were unbrigaded: the umHlanga, umCijo, uNokenke, uVe, inGobamakhosi, uMbonambi and uDloko. The uVe were the youngest warriors, willing to do anything to prove their courage.

Each regiment was commanded by an inDuna and the army was led by a council rather than a general, the most influential members being: Mnyamana, the 60-year-old 'prime minister'; Mavumengwana, a 40-year-old veteran inDuna; Tshingwayo, 70-year-old veteran inDuna; and Dabulamanzi, commander of the Undi Brigade and Cetshwayo's brother.

So far the only Zulus encountered by the British had been cattle herders, stragglers and scouts, though Dartnell had on the previous day sighted a corner of the army. The council had planned to wait an extra day before attacking. Now suddenly they had been discovered.

At once Qetuka, deputy commander of the Undi Brigade, ordered his men to charge out of the ravine after the horsemen. Within minutes the other ten regiments followed them. The council members shouted to their troops, but were only able to recall the Undi Brigade and the uDloko. The others continued on, temporarily out of control.

The Battle: Captain George Shepstone, one of Durnford's staff officers, saw the mass of Zulus running towards the camp and he sent a messenger to warn Durnford while he rode for the camp.

Thus warned Pulleine now had the chance to pull in his men to form a solid wall of Martini-Henrys, while sending a message for Chelmsford to come quick. After all, each individual Zulu regiment outnumbered his and Durnford's men combined. Instead he ordered F Company to his north flank and sent a message to Chelmsford: 'Heavy firing to left of our camp. Cannot move camp at present.'

He was attempting to hold a line 2,000 yards in length with less than 600 regular riflemen. He did have 500,000 rounds of ammunition in the camp, but he had not ordered them to be unboxed yet. By the time Captain Mostyn's F Company reached the north flank in a sweat to reinforce Captain Cavaye's A Company, they could see Raw's NNH approaching 600 yards away and the Zulus (uNokenke and uDududu) behind them moving towards the undefended west flank on the left.

As their sergeants instilled a measure of calm, the regulars began to fire volleys at the Zulus' flank. It was impossible to miss the large force and scores of Zulus fell, but the two regiments ran on oblivious. Seeing the NNC fall back further into the centre of the camp Mostyn and Cavaye decided to do likewise and Raw's horsemen now rode up and covered their withdrawal.

Pulleine reinforced Mostyn and Cavaye with Younghusband's C Company and together they set up a new defence line about 200 yards to the north of Pulleine's tent, each man about four feet from his neighbour. The east flank, still 800 yards from Pulleine's tent was held by three companies, E, H and G, and there were 200 yards between companies. Pulleine sent some NNC and spare artillerymen to hold the corner hinge between the north and east flanks.

Pulleine also put his mounted men 500 yards behind the east line, too far to the rear to give covering fire or be ready to charge, so his purpose is unknown. The remainder of the NNC and the rear-echelon troops were among the wagons.

Meanwhile Hamilton-Browne was leading his battalion of the NNC back to camp to reinforce Pulleine as per Chelmsford's instructions, when one of his scouts came riding in reportedly having seen a battle at the camp. Hamilton-Browne sent a message to Chelmsford: 'For God's sake, come back. The camp is surrounded.'

Durnford was warned by Shepstone's messenger and he ordered a withdrawal to the camp at once. During this move he could see the terrain to the north was black with Zulus. The rocket detachment became separated and was overrun by the entire umCijo with no more thought than that for the grass they were trampling.

At noon the Nodwengu Brigade arrived a mile north of Pulleine's defenders, the umCijo and umHlanga a mile to the north-east, the uVe a mile to the east and the inGobamakhosi and uMbonambi two miles to the south-east.

To the south of the uMbonambi Durnford's men ran and rode past the Zulus and he swerved his NNH to enter a four-foot deep donga between the Zulus and the camp 500 yards in front and slightly to the south of Pulleine's east flank. They dismounted and began to fire rapidly at the oncoming uMbonambi and inGobamakhosi, who suddenly flattened themselves on the ground. For the moment Durnford had stopped them in the nick of time.

Thirty horsemen of the Newcastle Mounted Rifles rode out to join Durnford, while the regulars began firing upon the other Zulu regiments as they approached. The warriors charged, ignoring the continuous volleys, which cut fearful chunks out of the mass of Zulu manhood, until they, too, suddenly went to ground as if operating on one brain. Lying there just 200 yards from the redcoats, pitifully trying to protect themselves with hide-clad shields, they individually offered as small a target as possible, but as a regiment they could easily be discerned in the bright heat of the day and they continued to take casualties as British bullets thudded into them. Having run five miles they lay there exhausted and scared.

It appeared that the volleys had been too much for the Zulus and many a redcoat must have thought the warriors were whipped, for this is how previous Kaffir wars had gone, yet the Zulus did not break and run, but lay there motionless. The British did not know that the inDunas were counting the British rifles, searching for weak spots and judging the rate of fire.

As British troops began to run low on ammunition, because many had not brought their full issue of 70 rounds with them, the sergeants sent runners to get more ammunition, but some runners had to cover as much as a mile to reach the ammunition wagons and then had to line up behind runners from other sections. The supply officers were snapping the copper bands on the wooden ammunition

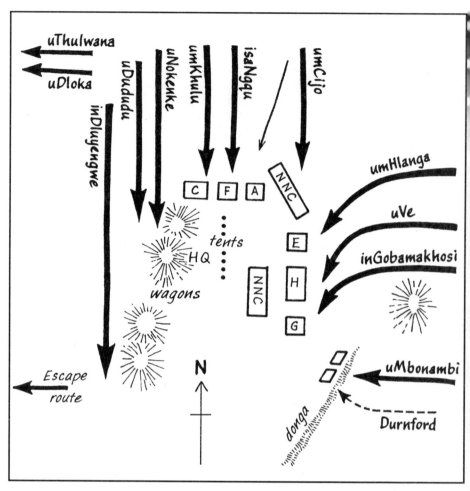

boxes, unscrewing the six often rusty screws, sliding off the grooved lid and awkwardly extracting tightly fitted packets of bullets. Then the runner had to retrace the mile, reach his section, tear open the packet and dole out bullets evenly to each of the 25 men. The whole operation took about 20 to 30 minutes and the regulars slowed down their rate of fire to preserve ammunition.

Durnford was angered when his runners told him the supply officers had refused to issue ammunition to them for his Westley-Richards carbines without proper authorisation.

The inDunas noticed the slackening rate of fire and assumed the British were low on ammunition. The umCijo and umHlanga inDunas saw that the north-east corner of the British line was held by the NNC, and the fire here was sporadic indeed. With only the sergeants and officers and one native soldier in ten armed with rifles this was the weakest part of the line. Without 30 artillerymen armed with rifles standing among them they would have been unable to pin down any charging Zulus in front of their 300-yard line.

After an hour of firing and almost out of ammunition Durnford ordered his men to withdraw, and they now remounted and rode out of the donga. At once the inGobamakhosi and the uMbonambi jumped up and charged after them, chanting 'uSuthu, uSuthu'.

When Durnford's men rode into the camp, the Zulus were not far behind, running swiftly. Seeing this, Lieutenant Pope, whose G Company was the southernmost regular unit, turned to face south-east and shoot into the mass of charging warriors as fast as possible.

At this moment the umCijo rose to charge the NNC and artillery riflemen at the north-east corner. The NNC natives fled at once. The white riflemen tried to reload for one more shot, but many were overrun by iKlwa-stabbing Zulus before they had a chance. The NNC inside the camp also turned and fled towards the open south-west, and the gunners with the two cannon also limbered up and followed them.

The umCijo did not follow, but swerved due south and began to run behind E, H and G Companies, who were facing east. The umHlanga then flooded through the open gap and swerved due west running behind Younghusband's, Mostyn's and Cavaye's companies, who were facing north. As the Zulus ran past the backs of the redcoats, a few left the main body to stab or club British soldiers from behind. Many of the regulars standing as much as eighteen feet apart were so mesmerised by the Zulus in front they did not see or hear those behind them.

The isaNgqu charged through the gap too, while the umKhulutshane charged the British north flank head on. The uVe then rose and charged the British east flank head on.

Younghusband on the north-west of the line ordered his men to fix bayonets and run for Mount Isandhlwana. Sixty of them managed to outrun the charging Zulus to ascend part way up the steep slope.

As they halted they surveyed the scene below them, which must have been heartstopping. The red uniforms of their comrades were swamped by a sea of black flesh. Zulus were everywhere, and among the regulars only a handful could still be seen fending off with their bayonets as many as six iKlwa-jabbing warriors at once. The noise of the chanting Zulus was deafening.

At the foot of the mount among the wagons, between boulders and standing on a couple of low mounds to the south were Durnford's native horsemen, the white horsemen, some rear echelon people and a pitiable remnant of red-coated regulars, firing into the charging inGobamakhosi with rifles, carbines and revolvers. Durnford, Pope and George Shepstone tried to create order. There was no sign of Pulleine. The inGobamakhosi were so stunned by this wildcat defence they withdrew a hundred yards.

Some soldiers seized their chance and ran to the south-west and a few mounted up and rode out.

Then the uMbonambi charged the mob of defenders and ignoring the consequences of running straight into gunfire and clambering over their own dead they slammed into this intrepid band, over-running each defender with a bloody stabbing and slashing motion: Pope, Shepstone, Durnford and all the others.

Now one by one Younghusband's men were overrun by climbing Zulus. He scrambled down into a wagon and sniped at passing Zulus for several minutes, perhaps the last lone defender of the camp.

Those soldiers who were running and riding towards the south-west found themselves dodging warriors in twos and threes. These were members of the uNokenke and uDududu, who had marched to the west of Isandhlwana and had taken no major part in the battle. These Zulus, some of whom had the stamina to outrun a horse-mounted soldier over distance, followed the fleeing invaders.

The Zulus heard the last shots on the battlefield at 4.00pm (possibly Younghusband), fully four hours after the first shots.

Of the 913 white men at Isandhlwana 55 survived by escaping on horseback: one of them, Lieutenant Raw, who had fired the first shot. Of the 900 natives (NNC, NNH, pioneers and civilian workers) about 300 survived. The Zulus knew that the regulars were the backbone of the British forces and it is interesting that not one man wearing a red coat survived.

Roughly 2,000 Zulus had been killed on the battlefield and about 1,000 of those who were carried away with hideous wounds would have died over the next few days. Thus Zulu fatalities were about 20% versus the British 81%.

Chelmsford had received Pulleine's second message and had heard the sound of the battle, but when his own scouts saw nothing from a distance and as the sound of firing died out in the afternoon, he continued with his plans to search for the enemy.

That afternoon he received Hamilton-Browne's message and a scout's report of the battle, both of which he refused to believe. At 3.30pm Lonsdale arrived to say he had ridden into the camp and had found himself surrounded by Zulus. As startled as he was, they left him alone and he escaped. Only now did Chelmsford react by ordering his forces to go to Pulleine's aid.

It took fully two and a half hours for his forces to reassemble, so scattered were they, and it was dark when they marched into the Isandhlwana camp to find the Zulus gone and the wagons and corpses looted. Chelmsford and his men were horrified. They all had friends among the dead and some had brothers.

Appraisal: The parallels with Custer's defeat were striking: similar terrain; a white army versus a native-led confederacy of tribes; a multi-column invasion; only one column finding the enemy main force; that column dispersing in the face of the enemy; one element forced to fight defensively and wiped out; a small rescue force halted by the sight of overwhelming force; while the other elements refuse to attempt a rescue until it is too late.

The conduct of Chelmsford was appalling. He was in command of an invasion of enemy territory, not a parade through flower-strewn streets, yet his conduct suited the latter more then the former.

The errors of this expedition can be divided into sixteen categories: timing, psyops, supply, intelligence, strategy, tactics, pace, reconnaissance, counsel, dispersal, misuse of specialists, morale, command structure, communications, misuse of reserves and command ability.

The invasion was launched at harvest time so the warriors would be busy at home, but this choice of timing was bungled, for the warriors were currently assembled for a ceremony.

Facing an empire of tribes, some of whom had been forced into swearing allegiance to the Zulu king, Chelmsford could have at least made an attempt to woo one or more chiefs away from Cetshwayo. Whether this psychological operation would have succeeded is academic, for it was never tried. Other colonial generals have done this most successfully.

Supplies were insufficient for Chelmsford's strategy, hence one column was immobilised and another ordered to join Glyn's column. When first alerted, Pulleine did not order the supply officers to open ammunition boxes; his regulars were allowed to enter the line without their full complement of ammunition; and the native riflemen of the NNC were only issued five rounds each!

Chelmsford had an incredible amount of intelligence about his enemy if he had bothered to ask for it. Many colonials such as George Shepstone knew the Zulu intimately, and Boers who had fought and defeated Zulus were available. They could have told him the Zulus had already mobilised. It appears that Chelmsford took little or no notice of any of this wealth of information.

His strategy of goading the enemy to attack was sound but one wonders why he needed five columns. Surely three could have done the job and as it turned out, he could only supply three, thus, having called up Durnford, one column was completely wasted.

His tactics were minimal to say the least: when the enemy charged, his rifle-men would shoot them and that would constitute victory. His regulars were well trained, thoughtful fellows, who could have performed a more intricate manoeu-vre than this, but apparently Chelmsford was incapable of creating a plan of more substance. Having set up bases at Rorke's Drift and Isandhlwana he could have at least afforded them protection. Regulations suggested parapets, laagered wagons and trenches. Chelmsford chose thin lines of infantry standing in the open.

The pace of his march left much to be desired. 2,500 yards a day is not forg-ing ahead, but is dithering to the point of immobility. Thus he gave the Zulus ten days to mobilise, plan and counter-attack.

Chelmsford did have excellent reconnaissance teams and he used them. His horsemen sighted just about every body of Zulus in the area, from cattle herders, scouts and stragglers to Cetshwayo's army itself, but all of this information was useless because Chelmsford seemed only willing to react to information that fit-ted his plan. At any time he could have asked for counsel from his officers. There was certainly no shortage of officers. Several heads may have concluded that the Zulu army had outflanked him. They may have offered him different tactics. Instead Chelmsford listened to no one.

His dispersal of his army is incomprehensible. He certainly had to have a base at Helpmakaar and one can argue that his Rorke's Drift element was protecting the nearby bridge his engineers were building but, these units aside, he at one time had his men scattered into eight components: Durnford, Durnford's bag-gage, Pulleine, Hamilton-Browne, Glyn, E. S. Browne, Lonsdale and Dartnell, none of whom was capable of assisting the other, except for Durnford and Pulleine. The fact that it took him two and a half hours to assemble before retreating to Isandhlwana shows how far flung they were. If the Zulus had chosen they could have massacred Hamilton-Browne's and Lonsdale's men at a very minimal cost.

Chelmsford totally misused his specialists. Cavalry could avoid the enemy. Regulars could fire massed volleys and defend themselves. The NNC could do nei-ther. These specialists were on hand to charge a broken enemy as on the 12th. For them to be ordered to march alone through enemy territory as in Lonsdale's and Hamilton-Browne's commands was inviting disaster. When he responded to Pulleine's message he did not send cavalry who could cover ground quickly in emergency, but sent a battalion of NNC.

This brings us to morale. The NNC were not very pro-British to start with and their inhuman treatment at the hands of ignorant whites who had a slave-driver mentality must have lowered their morale considerably. The fact that only one man in ten was issued with a rifle, often an old model, and only five rounds of ammunition, while their white sergeants were issued with new Martini-Henrys and plenty of ammunition, suggested the British did not trust them. White men should not have blamed the disaster at Isandhlwana on the NNC, which some did loud and clear, but should have praised the NNC for standing bravely in front of a Zulu army for over an hour. It is noticeable how courageously the NNH fought under the humane leadership of Durnford.

Chelmsford's poor command structure was responsible for the fact that no one knew what the hell he was supposed to do. Durnford knew he was to come forward, but exactly where to and why and under whose authority he was not told. Pulleine was ordered to hold the camp until later in the day, but not told what to do with Durnford. Lonsdale and Dartnell were ordered to attack an enemy who had already flown. It was coincidence that Dartnell found a few Zulus. Why Chelmsford had not left the camp in the hands of Glyn is not known. Glyn was unpopular, but he was an experienced infantryman. Chelmsford certainly had no need of Glyn with him for he had yet to allow Glyn to exercise command of the column. Pulleine may have been 1/24th commander, but he was obviously not the man for the job. His performance under attack was unbelievable.

Chelmsford's use of communications was inept. Hamilton-Browne's message was obviously a cry for help, but Chelmsford ignored it. Yet, he believed Lonsdale's unlikely (but probably true) story. Chelmsford set the tone of all messages and Pulleine imitated him: his calls for help to Chelmsford were muted, almost fatalistic.

The entire battle is an example of a misuse of reserves. Firstly it must be remembered that the Zulus never launched a major assault against any of Chelmsford's front line. They attacked Pulleine, Chelmsford's reserve. Secondly Pulleine mishandled his reserves, that is his cavalry, placing them too far away to prevent the regular infantry from being surrounded.

Despite the above errors someone with excellent command ability might have salvaged something, but Chelmsford exhibited a complete lack of it. He behaved as if he was invisible to the Zulus, riding alone in the dark, setting up breakfast tables in the open and giving off not an air of invincibility but one of extreme naivety. At no time did he react rapidly. True, Pulleine made his dispositions then abdicated command, but Chelmsford must bear the responsibility for the manner in which Pulleine fought his battle. Chelmsford set the tone of complacency, which Pulleine imitated.

An Alternative: There are usually alternatives as to how to fight a battle and Lieutenants Bromhead and Chard proved this. They were in charge of Rorke's Drift, which was attacked on the same afternoon as the massacre at Isandhlwana. Their

NNC and cavalry having fled, the two officers retained only their 100 regulars, but they built parapets out of biscuit boxes and wagons and fortified two buildings meeting the uThulwana, uDloko and inDlu-yengwe regiments with massed volleys fired by men standing shoulder to shoulder. Into and throughout the night and into the next morning past dawn they held off the charging warriors, slaughtering over 500 and mortally wounding others, for the loss of only 17 killed, and most of them from Zulu riflemen. The Zulus retreated.

Pulleine and Durnford had faced odds of 8½:1 against and had killed Zulus at the rate of 2:1 for. Chard and Bromhead faced odds of 60:1 against and killed Zulus at the rate of 35:1 for.

Consequences: When the news reached London there was a major political backlash. Disraeli's government almost fell, for he had been unable to control a mere civil servant and as a result 1,450 'Britons' lay dead.

Disraeli could do little in response except order the war to continue: honour demanded that much. Of course, Chelmsford had been shown to be incompetent and Disraeli asked General Sir Garnet Wolseley to take reinforcements out to Africa and tidy up the situation.

The reinforcements reached Africa before Wolseley did and Chelmsford seized the opportunity to use them to reinvade Zululand. Now respecting the Zulus as if they were a European army, Chelmsford kept his men in squares with artillery and Gatling guns on the corners and when they met the Zulus in a series of fights they slaughtered them in heaps for little loss.

By the time Wolseley arrived he found victory already accomplished and a few more square miles of grassland added to the British Empire.

Chelmsford won the war, but could never escape the humiliation of Isandhlwana. His friendship with Queen Victoria saved him, at least to the point that he was given a series of ceremonial posts. He was never allowed to command troops again.

Frere was recalled, a discredited and broken man. He died five years later.

The Battle's Place in History: For the Zulus the battle's place in history is a landmark. Their greatest victory, it nonetheless signalled the beginning of the war that was to smash them as a military power. From 1879 onwards they had to take their luck as they could get it along with every other native in white-dominated South Africa.

As for the British, they could always recall the defenders of Rorke's Drift, to whom they awarded eleven Victoria Crosses. Without belittling the bravery of the defenders it is obvious the awards were an attempt to disguise the fiasco at Isandhlwana, just like the 25 awards of the Medal of Honor for Little Big Horn. Throughout the next century in Britain Rorke's Drift was remembered, while the massacre of Pulleine's camp was lost in the fog of the past.

1896

Adowa

Background: For well over 2,000 years non-Africans have been trying to colonise some part of Africa: Phoenicians, Greeks, Romans, Arabs, Turks, Portuguese, French, British, Spanish. However, in the latter half of the nineteenth century there was suddenly a scramble for new colonies, as if a shortage of unconquered territory had just been recognised.

Three of the scrambling nations had themselves only just been unified into sovereign states: Belgium, Italy and Germany. They were eager to attain colonies, knowing that the older nations such as France and Britain had a head start.

As a result the three new nations had to take what was left, which was not always choice land. Belgium seized most of the fever-ridden Congo. Germany took among others the colony of South West Africa, much of it worthless desert. Italy, through a private venture gained the colony of Asmara in Eritrea. The Italian dream was to control the ports of the Horn of Africa and therefore the sea passage into the Red Sea which, once the Suez Canal was built, would be a counterweight to Britain's control of Aden on the Asian side of the sea. In 1882 the Italian government formally took over the colony and began a modest expansion throughout Eritrea.

In 1868 the British had invaded Ethiopia (Abyssinia) to rescue hostages – Thesiger was a member of the expedition – and when 5,000 British and Indian troops defeated the Ethiopian hordes, Theodore the Ethiopian Emperor shot himself in disgrace. The British took one look at the barren, harsh landscape and decided not to remain. Their departure caused a vacuum, which led to Ethiopian civil war, following which Ras (Lord) Kassa of Tigre emerged as the Negus (Emperor) Yohannes. Feeling his oats he challenged the Egyptians in 1875 for control of the great Eritrean city of Massawa. At Gura a swarm of 60,000 Ethiopians overwhelmed 6,000 Egyptians, of which only 2,000 survived to reach the coast.

In January 1881 a few Italian officers and 500 locally-raised native troops entered the lands of Yohannes and for their impertinence were attacked at Dogali by a very large force of Ethiopians. Only 100 of the small force survived to retreat to Italian territory. Coming only two years after Isandhlwana this was another indication that native Africans could outfight European officers. The Italians consoled themselves with the knowledge that some of their troops had been illiterate natives.

The Italians now tried psychological operations and succeeded in convincing King Menelik of Shoa to repudiate his support for Yohannes.

Now another pressure came from the west. In Sudan a fanatic religious sect, the Dervishes, overwhelmed two Egyptian armies and repelled a British invasion and in 1889 they invaded Ethiopia. Yohannes met them on 9 March at Gallabat, a border village, and the Dervishes were completely victorious. Yohannes was killed and his army dispersed.

Though the Italians did not like the result they took advantage of it by suggesting Menelik seize the imperial throne. He needed no urging.

In return for their support, by the Treaty of Wichale, the new emperor gave northern Tigre province to the Italians. It was no loss to him, for this area was under the suzerainty of Mangasha, Yohannes' son.

The Italians should have been grateful, but became greedy. Occupying villages up to 50 miles south of the new border, they claimed that Emperor Menelik was 'their man' and his empire was an Italian Protectorate, a move aimed at the British and French. The British accepted this, but France began supplying Menelik with provisions and modern rifles through their colony of Djibouti on the Red Sea coast.

The Commander: Oreste Baratieri, like other Italians of his age (born 1841) had watched with eager anticipation as a series of wars unified Italy. A northerner, he hoped some day to lead an expedition to free the remaining Italian towns in the north-east, which were still under Austrian occupation. Following a short war with Austria in 1866, training for further wars with Austria was the prime purpose of Italian officers such as Baratieri.

However, the years of his military service were years of peace and though loyal to the newly established monarchy of King Umberto, in practice this meant the army served whichever political faction was in parliament. Gaining a promotion in the Italian Army came through political favours or through family connections with nobility. Merit was not a reliable way of getting anywhere. Thus when Baratieri was ordered to Eritrea at the age of 50 as military governor, he knew he was being given a rare chance among his fellow officers, for military action would surely result and he could at last show merit and perhaps even be rewarded for it.

In 1894 the Dervishes invaded Italian Eritrea and under Baratieri's overall command the Italian-trained native soldiers defeated the invader at Kassala. Victorious, where the British, Egyptians and Ethiopians had failed, the Italians were in their element. Never known to be reticent about accomplishments, they thrived on this solitary affair for months.

Then Bahto Hagos led a revolt in Tigre. Mobilising 4,000 troops, mostly Eritrean-Tigreans, Baratieri overcame the rebel and killed him.

With support from Prime Minister Francesco Crispi, Baratieri then led an expedition southwards into the territory given to Italy by Menelik, but still jealously guarded by Mangasha. Within weeks Baratieri occupied Adigrat and Makalle, two of Mangasha's major towns.

The Italians, who had only been united just over a generation, whose north-east was still under Austrian occupation, and whose people were emigrating to the Americas by the thousands, desperately needed something to be proud of. They chose Baratieri, deciding that his victories had brought them an empire, something they had not had of their own for 1,500 years. It was not so much the size of the victories that made them great, but their timing.

As a result Baratieri was hailed as a hero in the newspapers in Italy and when he returned to Rome in July 1895 he was lauded in the same manner as another Italian general, Scipio, had been for his African victories 2,200 years before. There is no doubt that this sort of praise – being likened to a great Roman general – went to Baratieri's head slightly. This was more than he had ever expected.

Grand Strategy: While in Rome Baratieri came up with a proposition. He wanted to conquer Ethiopia. Naturally there were some misgivings among the government, but Crispi figured Baratieri was on a roll, and he authorised the invasion and gave Baratieri everything he asked for, which was primarily money and regular army troops. Crispi also instituted a campaign to recruit colonists who would civilise Ethiopia once Baratieri had dispersed Menelik's horde. Baratieri promised he would bring Menelik to Rome in a cage, in the same manner that ancient Roman victors had returned with their prisoners.

The Catholic church had always supported colonisation of heathen lands by Catholics because this helped spread the gospel and naturally the church gave its support to Baratieri's proposal. As the Pope was an Italian, resident in Rome, this gave Baratieri powerful backing.

The Italians wanted to recreate the ancient Roman Empire and tried to mimic it in every way during these heady days as the troops were mobilised and marched to the ports. One thing they forgot, though, was that whenever a Roman general was praised in the streets of Rome a servant accompanied him everywhere, whispering 'Sic transit gloria' (remember glory is temporary). Baratieri had no such servant.

The Army: Despite such setbacks as Little Big Horn, Isandhlwana and Dogali, in the latter half of the nineteenth century the white nations were forging ahead with the conquest of non-white people at an unbelievable rate. The map makers in Washington, London, Paris and Berlin could not keep up, such was the rapid change, as areas hitherto marked 'unknown' were redrawn with straight administrative boundaries – always a sign that someone was being cheated out of something. Baratieri and the Italians were not alone in their jingoism, the street-level propaganda that led to ever more conquests.

One of the reasons for this was the jump in military technology since the Battle of Bull Run: magazines for rifles, so that a soldier could fire four rounds in five seconds; machine-guns that sprayed lethality at a hideous rate scything down dark-skinned bodies; better telegraph systems so that news could travel the breadth of a continent in the twinkling of an eye, and therefore government approval or disapproval gained instantly. Native armies invariably had nothing to compare. Colonial battles were inevitably a clash of modern armies versus eighteenth century armies.

The Italians had recruited native troops, but unlike the past in which natives had fought as allies under loose control, the white powers had begun to introduce the ascari system. Ascaris of the Italian Army were in effect clones of Italian soldiers recruited from Eritrean-Tigreans, Sudanese, Somalis and Arabs. Of visible difference, apart from skin colour, was that ascaris fought either barefoot or in sandals and wore a fez rather than a helmet, but otherwise they were attired in a sandy coloured uniform similar to Italian soldiers, were equipped the same and were trained to fight European-style. Allowed to operate machine-guns and artillery and to rise to the rank of sergeant major, their status was far higher than that of native civilians. Good Italian officers attracted an impressive loyalty from their ascaris. If the officers were poor: well, the ascaris were professional soldiers and they obeyed orders, no matter who gave them.

Some natives served the Italians as bande: fighting in traditional garb, but with Italian equipment and obeying an Italian officer. The bande were good, but had the habit of taking leave when the mood took them.

The standard issue rifle was the '1870' bolt action Vetterli weighing 8½ pounds with a 33inch barrel and four 10.4mm rounds in a magazine. Each infantryman was issued 112 rounds. Officers carried a sword and revolver.

Causes of Arrogance: The first cause of Baratieri's arrogance must have been his reception in Rome. He had been hailed the conquering hero and nothing was refused him. A rise from obscurity to such giddy heights would have an impact upon the most modest person. Baratieri seems to have been carried away by it all.

His enemy, apart from Mangasha's few hundred warriors, was Menelik, but though that fellow may have called himself Negus and ruled with all the trappings of an ancient monarch, the Italians remembered him when he was 'their man'. They saw him as an ungrateful upstart and were half convinced no Ethiopian would fight for him.

In any case, the Italians believed, the 25,000 warriors of his own fiefdom, Shoa, were ill-armed uncultured savages and the white man's weapons of magazine rifle, machine-gun and artillery had always proved superior to human wave assaults by natives. Baratieri would soon have 20,000 men in the field, the largest European army ever sent against African natives in one body. Nothing could go wrong.

The War: Returning to Eritrea Baratieri launched an expedition southwards in September with 8,500 ascaris and an Italian cavalry battalion without waiting for the promised Italian reinforcements. On 9 October he met Mangasha's 1,300 warriors in the field at Debra Haila and completely defeated them. Baratieri sent glowing reports of the victory to Crispi.

Receiving reinforcements continually, he now ordered Brigadier General Giuseppe Arimondi southwards with 7,500 ascaris to fortify the border region.

Once done, he ordered Major Toselli and 20 Italian officers to take 1,850 ascaris and 300 bande southwards 36 miles inside Menelik's territory to build a camp in the Amba Alagi mountain range. Arimondi was to follow soon with part of his force and then take command. By November Baratieri was able to report to Crispi that all was going according to plan.

On 7 December, with Arimondi and 1,500 ascaris approaching within a few miles of Amba Alagi, Toselli's camp was attacked by thousands of Ethiopian warriors under Lord Makonnen. Toselli evidently directed a spirited defence which held for four and a half hours, but then collapsed. Toselli and his officers went down under a hail of bullets and sword slashes, while some of his men managed to break out.

Only 850 ascaris and bande reached Arimondi, who himself had to beat off an attack. He then withdrew.

Baratieri was stunned. With only 5,000 men left under his own command he retreated northwards, abandoning Lieutenant-Colonel Galliano and his 1,200 strong garrison of Makalle.

Makalle was a formidable fortification and the Ethiopians who began to besiege it on 6 January 1896 realised this at once. After 45 days of siege Menelik made a shrewd move. He offered Galliano's men safe passage. Galliano accepted and Menelik kept his word. The ascaris marched north to join Baratieri.

Obviously Menelik was no bloodthirsty savage and he had outgeneralled Baratieri. The Italian press, ever fickle, began asking if Baratieri was the right man for the job. Some even questioned the wisdom of the war.

Crispi sent more money to Baratieri, but said he could do little else as the political opposition was making great capital out of his humiliation.

Humiliation was not Baratieri's goal and he felt he had to do something spectacular to regain the confidence of his countrymen. Yet, his intelligence people suggested that he was in fact winning if he only held out longer. Both Menelik and he had large forces in the field, stationed in areas of sparse vegetation and rocky soil, and both were quickly running out of food. If Baratieri could outlast Menelik he might find his enemy dispersed to their villages, which would make conquest of Ethiopia much simpler. Therefore, he began a campaign of waiting.

The Enemy: Ethiopia is one of the oldest civilisations on the planet. A thousand years before Christ Ethiopia was a great empire with ambassadors at the Egyptian and Israeli courts. Indeed such was the close connection with Israel that Jewish evangelists went to Ethiopia and converted the people to the Judaic faith.

According to Ethiopian belief an Israeli king of the sixth century BC turned against Judaism, so the priests of the Temple of Solomon took the Ark of the Covenant to Ethiopia for safe keeping, as it was the only other Jewish nation, and there it remains to this day.

In the fourth century AD Christian evangelists spread the gospel throughout Ethiopia, creating a deep and lasting division between the new converts and the Jews, known as Falashas. As late as the thirteenth century Jewish and Christian kings were still warring with each other and it is quite possible that at least one Christian victory was brought about by the intervention of the European Knights of the Temple of Solomon (the leading warrior/monk society in Christendom). The impressive architecture of thirteenth century Ethiopian churches points to Templar involvement.

During the late middle ages the Ethiopian kings, known as Prester John, were deemed by successive Popes to be the saviours of Christianity in the eastern world, fending off not only Judaism but Islam.

In the fifteenth century Portuguese intellectuals visited Ethiopia and in the eighteenth century British scientists made the pilgrimage of knowledge to such holy sites as Adowa and Axum.

By the nineteenth century the Amhara were the leading ethnicity of the empire and Menelik controlled a score of ethnic nations ruled by kings and lords. The state religion was a Christian sect (erroneously thought by westerners to be Coptic), which retained much of early Judaism, and which had created both an episcopal and a monastic clergy. Some sections of the empire had been converted to Islam and in the south along the Kenya border many tribes held animist beliefs.

Now the Italians were coming to 'civilise' the Ethiopians.

When Menelik called for a holy war to repel the invader at the end of 1895 he knew he could command for sure only his own 25,000-man Army of Shoa. For extra warriors he was at the mercy of the imperial nobility to provide their own retinues. As they arrived in his capital, Addis Ababa, to pay homage and offer their services they resembled a cross-section of eastern Africa: tribes resembling the Zulu, carrying shields and spears; white-robed Amharics and Gallas brandishing wide-bladed swords and small round shields; horsemen looking like medieval European knights with lances and metal helmets and armour; Tigreans wearing multi-coloured robes with bracelets, beads, feathers and fur shoulder wraps. There were Christians, Jews, Moslems and animists.

Many warriors arrived with a bewildering variety of firearms from ancient flintlocks to modern magazine rifles. From his days of Italian support Menelik had a few thousand Vetterli rifles and he had recently been gaining shipments of modern French rifles. He had also gained some heavy Maxim water-cooled machineguns and six Hotchkiss cannon that some Russians had taught his men to use.

Leaving the Army of Kaffa to put down a revolt in Aussa, he marched north with the armies of Shoa, Semien, Wollo-Galla, Lasta, Guraghe, Atikim, Goggiam, Iejjiu, Hamasen and Tigre to join Lord Makonnen's Army of Harar at Adowa. All told this gave him about 110,000 warriors. Then he too began the waiting game.

The Battlefield: The opposing armies were about fifteen miles from each other near Adowa. Between them was a harsh landscape of scrub brush and flat rocky soil punctuated by several small cone-shaped hillocks. Some were quite high and steep, others not much more than a mound with gentle slopes.

The hillocks provided scouts with a good view, but those on the level could not see far. To the newcomer the land was repetitive with no major distinguishing features.

The Battle: When Baratieri was informed on 28 February 1896 that his army had only ten days' food left, he had three choices: retreat to the arable coastal plain; remain and hope to outlast Menelik whose larger army required more food; advance and force Menelik to fight.

Something else created a sense of urgency. Baratieri suspected that Crispi might succumb to pressure and relieve him. (Indeed he already had and a relief general was on the way by sea.)

Calling a council of war, he asked his generals if they wanted to retreat. 'Retreat? Never!' replied Brigadier General Dabormida. The others responded in similar tone. Baratieri then presented his plan. He would steal a march on the enemy by advancing the following night in three columns plus one in reserve and surprise Menelik at dawn. This was agreed.

At dusk on the 29th the army set off marching in the dark. Night marches are difficult and in this terrain the men were easily led to take wrong turns past one of the conical hillocks.

Menelik's scouts notified him at 4.00am of the approach of the Italians. He had been ready to order a retreat that day as his men were critically low on food, but now the Italians had played into his hands.

By 5.00am Brigadier General Albertone's left column had reached a point one mile north-east of Enda Hill. With him were 376 bande in the lead, four ascari battalions and fourteen guns, six of them manned by ascaris, for a total of about 4,400 men. However, as the dawn brightened it was apparent that

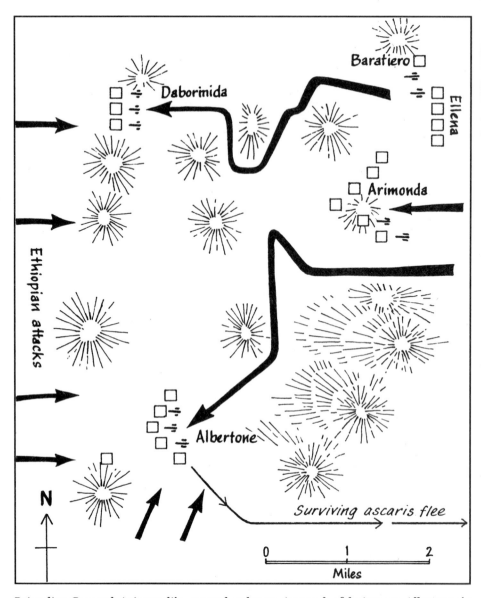

Brigadier General Arimondi's central column, instead of being on Albertone's immediate right flank, was three miles to the right rear (north-east).

With Arimondi were two battalions of the 1st Bersaglieri (recognisable by the black plumes on their helmets), three battalions of the 2nd Regiment, a company of ascaris and twelve guns: about 3,000 troops.

Brigadier General Ellena had the reserve column 3,000 yards behind (eastwards of) Arimondi, with the 4th and 5th Regiments, a battalion of ascaris, an engineer company and twelve guns: around 4,500 soldiers. There was no sign of Brigadier General Dabormida and the 4,500 men of the right column.

Neither general was exactly sure of his location and they had not brought their heliograph signalling equipment with them, thus they relied on mounted messengers. Baratieri was with Ellena and was unaware of the poor disposition of his columns. The ascaris were familiar with this type of terrain and warfare as were about a thousand of the Italians, but the rest of the Italians were new to Africa, had never fought and in fact many had recently joined the army or transferred to be part of this expedition.

At 6.00am the bande of Lieutenant Spelli in front of Albertone saw the Ethiopians charging towards them. At once they fell back to a line of guns protected by most of Major Turitto's ascari battalion and together they prepared to meet the onslaught in a kneeling position to fire massed volleys. They caught the full force of the attack by the armies of Harar, Iejjiu and Wollo-Galla led by Lords Makonnen, Olie and Mikael, fully 35,000 warriors.

Within minutes elements of the swarm, seemingly oblivious to the gunfire, passed around the bande and ascaris and charged Albertone's column, which he tried to place into an arc with Major Valli's battalion facing south-west, Captain Cesarini's company of Turitto's battalion facing west, Major Cossu's battalion facing north-west and Major Gamerra's battalion in reserve. Gunners hauled their pieces to the tops of small hillocks for safety and better observation. Soon their shells were tearing fearful gaps in the ranks of the enemy. Ethiopian guns were shelling too, but were inaccurate.

The Ethiopians now lay down and began steadily to shoot at Albertone's men.

Baratieri and his staff had heard the fighting almost at once, but the general gave no orders or asked any questions and stood silently, staring at his inaccurate maps.

At 6.50am Albertone sent a messenger to find Baratieri to ask for support.

At 8.00am after holding off the enemy for two hours the bande and Turitto's ascaris were overwhelmed by thousands of screaming warriors.

At 9.00am Baratieri received Albertone's message. His response was ineffective and he returned to his maps. Albertone was still holding, but he espied a massive enemy reinforcement. Menelik's Empress had insisted he throw in his own Army of Shoa at this juncture and he agreed. The 25,000 warriors charged towards Albertone's column and joined by the others already in the battle they began to pressure the ranks of ascaris, who knelt shoulder to shoulder. The ascaris were naturally wondering where the other columns were.

Just after 10.00am the line collapsed and the ascaris ran for it, many falling under the blows and stabs of swords and spears. Horsemen ran them down with lances and swords. Major Gamerra was wounded and captured as was Albertone. The artillery gunners died to a man defending their pieces.

Seeing the remnants of ascaris running past them to the south-east, Arimondi's column spread out in a long straight line to meet the onrush of the enemy, while Ellena (probably on his own authority rather than Baratieri's orders) brought his column up to assist, interspersing his own units with Arimondi's.

Baratieri only seemed to come alive at 10.45am, when he personally saw the Ethiopians attack this line. He ordered a couple of Bersaglieri companies to advance in the centre – a feeble and suicidal move, for the poor Bersaglieri were sticking out like sore thumbs on a mound and were soon massacred.

Arimondi, Colonel Brusati with two battalions of his 2nd Regiment, Lieutenant-Colonel Galliano and his ascari battalion and Colonel Nava and part of his 5th Regiment and 24 guns tried to hold the left of the line, but by 11.00am these

3,270 soldiers (1,900 Italians and 1,370 ascaris) were completely crushed by the unstoppable momentum of 50,000 Ethiopians. Within minutes Arimondi was cut down revolver in hand. Galliano was wounded and captured.

The blood-crazed Ethiopians now swerved northwards to roll up the remainder of the line, manned by 2,100 Italians, one unit at a time, first the remnants of Colonel Stevani's Bersaglieri Regiment, then the Alpini Battalion and 15th Battalion of the 5th Regiment, and lastly they surrounded Major De Amicis' 4th Battalion of the 2nd Regiment. At noon Baratieri, who still had the 4th Regiment of 1,380 Italians in reserve, ordered a retreat. It was his first comprehensible order since the battle had begun six hours earlier.

He backed away from the debacle, revolver in hand, yelling: 'Viva L'Italia', as if he could not believe his eyes. The Italians with him withdrew too, at first in good order, but as they came under sniping from Ethiopians they began to panic. Throughout this time Dabormida, who did not know of the fate of the army, had his hands full. Having gone down the wrong valley, the Mariam Shoaita, instead of the Mai Agam to his left, his column encountered sniping. Scrambling over rocks and high boulders and hiding behind scrub bushes the 3rd and 6th Regiments (2,190 Italians) and 1,160 ascaris plus eighteen guns kept up a good return fire and advanced slowly. The Ethiopians here were disciplined and gave ground only after light counter-attacks, sucking the column deeper into the valley.

However, in the afternoon the Ethiopians increased in number significantly and began to pour a withering fire down upon the column and to counter-attack from the valley's west end. Dabormida did not know it, but his men were under assault now from the armies of Wollo Galla, Lasta, Guraghe, Atikim, Iejjiu and Hamasen, possibly as many as 50,000 warriors.

Furthermore Major Rayneri's 450 Italians holding the eastern entrance to the valley in Dabormida's rear came under attack from the victorious armies of Shoa and Harar after they had surrounded Major De Amicis' battalion.

Only at about 4.00pm did Dabormida realise Baratieri's plan had gone seriously wrong and that he was in danger of being trapped in the valley, so he ordered his men to begin a fighting withdrawal in good order, hoping that De Amicis and Rayneri could hold open his escape route.

Over the next few minutes as the reality dawned on everyone the units began to lose their integrity and jumble together. Fear gripped every man and they fought tooth and nail against suicidal warriors and pushed and shoved against each other to flee the valley of death.

At dark they broke through and met up with elements of the other columns, but there was not one moment of peace. Continually charged by Ethiopians the officers grabbed anyone they could to form temporary rearguards. In one of these Dabormida went down, his revolver blazing fire in the darkness. Individual Ethiopian horsemen charged into the mob and lanced to death some poor wretch, then disappeared into the blackness. All night long the mob fled.

The following day there were further rearguard actions and it was only the day after that the first survivors reached relative safety at Adi Caieh having run 60 miles in 36 hours. Others did not drift in until two days later.

Only then was Baratieri able to take roll call. Of his 9,914 Italians and 6,624 ascaris, 4,924 Italians and 4,000 ascaris had survived, of which 1,428 were wounded. Probably none of the 376 bande survived. Thus his casualties were 57 per cent.

Aftermath: More embarrassing news was to reach Rome: Menelik had prisoners. Not all of Baratieri's men had been mown down. About 700 Italians and perhaps 1,800 ascaris had been taken alive, many of them badly wounded.

Each prisoner watched in horror as one by one they were taken away to be publicly tortured to death. About 70 Italians and 230 ascaris died in this manner (probably including Lieutenant-Colonel Galliano) before Menelik put a stop to the sport.

Menelik decided that the Christian Tigreans among the prisoners were traitors to him and he punished them according to custom: each had his right hand and left foot chopped off.

About 15 per cent of Menelik's army were casualties, about 7,000 killed and 10,000 wounded, thus his losses were less than twice that of Baratieri: remarkable considering the disparity in weaponry. However, his army was still out of food so they retreated.

Appraisal: Baratieri had made errors in seven major categories: strategy, timing, reconnaissance, pacing, tactics, communications, command ability.

His military intelligence was fairly good and he took note of it, yet still chose the strategy of advancing into the range of an army outnumbering him (as he thought) 4:1, an extremely dangerous move.

His timing of the march – during the night – ensured that when the battle began his troops would be exhausted from having been awake for 24 hours and having made a rough march, but the enemy would be refreshed after a good night's sleep.

Moving large units is always tricky, and doing it in the dark compounds the problem and calls for a knowledge of the terrain from previous reconnaissance, but his guides had inadequate knowledge of the terrain, hence Dabormida taking the wrong turn. With no cavalry to reconnoitre the region, Baratieri was stumbling like a blind man.

Indeed he was fortunate that his lack of reconnaissance did not destroy him. He knew the importance of his artillery, machine-guns and rifles and they required visibility to be effective. So he surely had no intention of fighting at night, only of moving at night. However, what if the enemy had been waiting for him in the dark? He may not have escaped if they had.

He ignored the pace of his troops. Baratieri had been marching ascaris and Italians long enough to know that over rough ground natives could move at a faster pace than Italians, thus it should have come as no surprise that after eight hours of marching Albertone's ascaris were three miles ahead of Arimondi's Italians. Thus he achieved exactly what he did not want, a dispersal of his army.

His tactical plan was simple: to move, then wait; but he had issued no contingency plans if the columns became separated. As a result his army fought three battles not one. It would have been four, but Ellena took the initiative to reinforce Arimondi. Thus he gave the Ethiopians the opportunity to swallow his army in three bite-sized chunks one at a time. Some of his troops were outnumbered as much as 20:1 in hand-to-hand combat!

Good communications would have kept Arimondi's and Albertone's columns level and Dabormida's on course, and would have alerted Baratieri to the danger as it unfolded. Evidently his generals deliberately left their heliographic equipment behind so as not to receive interfering orders from Baratieri. If true, this indicts all four column commanders with the crime of arrogance.

This brings us to Baratieri's own performance on the day. He seems to have panicked early on, not giving orders, not wishing to know what was happening up front, not responding to Albertone's plea for aid, not realising Dabormida was lost, not attempting to recall Dabormida and in the end only issuing one meaningful order: retreat. In effect he abdicated his command from the moment his men marched off the night before, and he had no command structure to replace him.

Alternatives: The immediate alternative that comes to mind is not to have fought at all. Baratieri was winning the battle of supply if he had only realised it. Then again he may have known this, but he also knew, or strongly suspected, his days of command were numbered. In other words it seems he risked the lives of his soldiers to save his career.

Furthermore, what could he possibly have gained by arriving in front of Menelik in the morning? If he had rested his men on the night of the 29th and approached in daylight, his columns would be fresher, would have retained cohesion and would have reached Menelik at 2.00pm. (In fact he might have caught Menelik's army in retreat.)

Consequences: The defeat of an Italian army of 17,000 by a 'mob of savages' was a catastrophe. Crispi could not survive such an unimaginable humiliation or the street riots it caused. He stepped down and the new government recalled Baratieri to Rome. There would be no laurels this time.

Deciding that the whole venture was flawed, the new government negotiated with Menelik as an equal and acknowledged the sovereignty of his empire. Before the year was out Menelik released 1,705 prisoners, a third of them Italians.

The Battle's Place in History: Adowa was played down by Italians abroad, and soon Italy's colonial rivals had other things to worry about. In foreign lands the story of the battle was soon forgotten and that's what the Italians wanted.

However, the Italian Army did not forget. Adowa became a bone of contention for a generation of officers and only with their outstanding feats of bravery and endurance during World War I did they regain their full measure of respect.

Italy had retained its Eritrean colony and expanded in Somalia, thereby maintaining a border with Ethiopia. In diplomacy they tried the carrot first: Mussolini, Italian dictator from 1922, sponsored Ethiopia's admission to the League of Nations, the first 'third world' nation to be treated equally.

This policy did not accomplish much, though, and in 1935 Mussolini discarded the carrot and picked up the stick; he launched an invasion of Ethiopia to wipe the stain of Adowa from memory once and for all. With the benefit of aeroplanes, tanks and poison gas the Italians massacred the waves of Ethiopians, who had not changed their weaponry.

PART 2

Something happened with the 1914-18 engagement known as World War I to change warfare forever, from the 'over in a day' Napoleonic one big battle to the continual bloodletting of Ypres, the Somme, the Isonzo. Yet this was not a result, as has been suggested, of a change in weaponry. Submarines, iron warships, automatic weapons, magazine firearms, aerial reconnaissance and trenches had been used in the American Civil War a half century earlier and in many other conflicts. The only significant weapon making its debut in World War I was the tank, and that was a response to the new style of warfare, not the cause of it.

The change was brought about by the new modes of transportation. For the first time most battlefields could be reached by rail, trucks, troop and cargo planes and large steamships. A fleet could disembark 10,000 men a day. Trucks could move 100,000 to a battlefield and keep them supplied indefinitely. As long as someone was willing to expose his (or her) bare skin to bullets, the battle would go on.

Long battles had taken place before, namely city sieges. Some had been extremely long, such as at Troy, which supposedly lasted ten years. Soldiers always hated sieges because of this, and generals hated them because invariably the army with the most food won, which was not a manly way of winning.

World War I introduced the concept of a siege without a city, siege for the sake of siege, one line pitted against another for months if not years.

Naturally with life in the twentieth century becoming more complicated, wars also became more complicated to the point that they required specialists, who would never have gained a uniform a generation earlier such as public relations officers, rail transportation officers, entertainment officers, etc.

Part Two of this book attempts to look at the errors caused by arrogance and compare them to those of the 'simpler' days. In other words we wish to know if our errors have become as complicated as our accomplishments.

1939

Poland

Background: Poland was reborn in the twentieth century. An ancient people the Poles had fallen under the conquests of the Germans, Austrians and Russians in the late eighteenth century, and by 1914 when Russia went to war against the other two there were Polish towns inside all three empires. The tragedy was that Poles were conscripted into the three armies to fight each other.

By 1915, when the war had reached a bloody stalemate, the Germans, Austrians and Russians each approached their own Poles with an offer of some sort of autonomy if they managed to recruit the enemy's Poles. This soon became a farce as German Poles, Austrian Poles and Russian Poles wooed each other to fight for Poland.

The French, long the friend of Polish nationalism, suggested that Poles currently behind Russian lines (Russian Poles and defectors from the Austrian and German armies) be allowed to fight in France against the Germans. This was agreed and the Polish Legion was born: only just in time, for in February 1917 Russia exploded into civil war.

In November 1918 World War I ended when Austria and Germany surrendered.

With British and French support the Poles declared independence and demanded all armies leave their soil. Unfortunately, there was considerable confusion as to what constituted Polish soil. Ethnic Poland was where Poles lived in the greatest majority and this was good enough for most Poles, but some fanatics demanded a Greater Poland, consisting of those parts of the collapsed empires of Germany, Austria and Russia where Poles lived in the minority.

The fanatics won the argument and within a month of the ending of the war, new wars broke out as Poles invaded the lands of the Lithuanians, Byelorussians, Ukrainians, Czechoslovaks and Germans.

In October 1919 German troops counter-attacked the Poles in Silesia and in 1920 a Russian Communist (Soviet) army invaded from the east. The Lithuanians, Byelorussians and Ukrainians made peace with the Poles in order to fight the Soviets, and with the aid of French advisers the Poles launched a counter-attack on the Vistula River with armoured cars and outflanked the Soviets. Days later the Soviets were fleeing.

By 1921 the Poles had gained control over large tracts of Lithuania, Ukraine and Byelorussia, but in an international plebiscite the residents of Upper Silesia opted to remain German citizens. Responding angrily the Poles invaded the territory, but were repulsed by the Germans on 23 May at the Battle of Annaberg on the Oder River.

Following further plebiscites in 1923 the Poles were at last at peace. Their new nation, really a Polish empire, contained 24,385,000 Poles, 4,850,000 Ukrainians, 1,100,000 Byelorussians, 800,000 Germans and Austrians and 200,000 Lithuanians, almost all living in their own towns. Also the 100,000 Kashubians (a type of Pole) were illogically discriminated against as a separate ethnicity. With better logic the 2,880,000 Jews in the nation were held as a separate ethnicity because they spoke Yiddish and maintained an individual culture, though some Jews learned Polish and became de facto Poles, even converting to Roman Catholicism, the Polish religion. About 36,000 Gypsies wandered around the nation unwanted by anyone.

Yet 1,000,000 Poles still lived under German rule and 75,000 under Czech rule.

At peace at last the Poles turned on each other and the next decade was one of virtual dictatorships and cosmetic democracy.

The Commander: Edward Rydz had been 28 years old when World War I began and he spent the war years fighting, as he saw it, for Polish independence and helped organise the Polish Legion. During this time, as he still had relatives under German occupation, he took the code-name Smigly (lightning).

After Poland achieved nationhood he achieved distinction fighting the Ukrainians and Soviets. A general a decade later, he became a member of a cabal and achieved considerable power, far more than his rank would imply, and in 1935 he was appointed armed forces inspector general.

Through the cabal, which was becoming ever more public, he effectively became the dictator of Poland by 1938.

His style of government was to rule through a puppet parliament and military clique, which was unashamedly racist. For example, when the Germans, now led by Adolf Hitler, deported Polish-born Jews back to Poland, Smigly-Rydz ordered them arrested at the border and imprisoned.

In 1938 when Germany crushed Czechoslovakia, he rushed in and grabbed Teschen, the home of 75,000 Poles, which was also the home of 20,000 Austrians and 133,000 Czechs.

He was also a man of culture, enjoying society life in Warsaw, and was himself an accomplished painter.

Life in Poland seemed to be good, but there was a dark cloud hanging over the nation and everyone knew it. On the north-east border Lithuania stood menacingly, longing for the return of her lands and people; in the south-east the Ukrainians wanted independence; in the east Stalin the dictator of the Soviet Union wanted to recreate the Russian Empire and that would mean occupation of Polish Ukraine and Polish Byelorussia; Hitler in Germany to the west and north was demanding the liberation of the German-speaking people of Poland (in West Prussia, eastern Pomerania and Lower Silesia).

As a result Smigly-Rydz maintained a large standing army and a massive body of reservists.

In March 1939 the British issued a guarantee of Polish sovereignty, an act which took the Poles totally by surprise. Smigly-Rydz knew this was aimed at Hitler, not at Stalin, and indeed the British began to negotiate with Stalin and asked Smigly-Rydz to do the same. Smigly-Rydz, who knew that occupation by Hitler would be brutal, nonetheless thought that Stalin's godless communism would be even worse. He refused to have anything to do with Stalin making the public statement: 'With the Germans we may lose our freedom, with the Russians we should lose our soul.'

The Armed Forces: In 1939 the Polish Air Force manned 266 bombers, mostly PZL P-37s, and 159 fighters, mostly PZL P-24s, (numbers serviceable in August) and there were also 1,600 planes performing reconnaissance, transport and training duties or undergoing maintenance. The small navy was based in ports taken from the Germans two decades earlier.

The regular army stood at 280,000 men, divided into 38 infantry and two mountain divisions and eleven cavalry, a tank, three mountain and two mechanised brigades, which with corps and army headquarters units should have come to over 1,000,000 men. Obviously many regulars were simply cadre for units which would be filled with recalled reservists in time of war. There were almost 3,000,000 reservists, some of them old enough to have fought in World War I. Those who were not called upon to fill out existing units would be called into the defensive militia.

The 475 tanks assigned to the tank brigade, mechanised brigades and a few scattered among the army were to be kept in reserve until the situation demanded their use. The best of them was the R-35, a French-built vehicle weighing 10.1-tons, standing 6 feet 10 inches high and 13 feet 2 inches long and manned by two men, one to drive and use a machine-gun and the other to fire the 37mm gun, which could knock out any current German tank at 250 yards. It had thick armour for its time and could cover 87 miles before refuelling. There were also some Vickers E 7.4-ton tanks carrying a 47mm gun and 7TPjw 10-ton tanks with a 37mm gun. The cavalry and infantry had some TKS tankettes, a vehicle smaller than a passenger car, with a two-man crew, poorly armoured and carrying a fixed forward firing machine-gun.

The infantry divisions were powerful bodies, containing: a cavalry squadron (horse-mounted troops carrying carbines, with some armed with swords and lances too); an anti-tank company armed with the 7.62mm anti-tank rifle; a company of anti-aircraft machine-gunners; a company of anti-infantry machine-gunners; an engineer battalion; a signals (radio and telephone) company; an artillery regiment and detachment armed with 24 75mm guns, twelve 100mm guns, three 105mm guns and three 155mm guns; three anti-tank companies (each with twelve 37mm guns); three armoured car companies; and nine infantry battalions, each of which had a company of machine-guns and mortars and three companies of 230 riflemen each, armed with the Mauser 7.92mm bolt action rifle. All told each division constituted 16,492 soldiers. A few motor vehicles were attached and others were available, but normal transportation was by wagons drawn by 6,940 horses.

In total the Poles were ready to receive an attack with 774 anti-tank guns and 2,065 artillery pieces.

Strategy: Marshal Smigly-Rydz adopted Plan Z for the defence of Poland in case of a German assault. This called for the defence of every square inch of Greater Poland, rather than holding only the ethnic Polish core of the nation centred on Warsaw. Furthermore, the defence was based upon region, that is on administrative boundaries, rather than boundaries that a soldier could see such as rivers and mountain ranges: the Narew Group would hold the ground between the Narew River and East Prussia to cover the north-east approach to Warsaw; the Modlin Army would protect the north-west approach between Warsaw and East Prussia;

the Pomorze Army would defend West Prussia and eastern Pomerania (lands which separated German-held East Prussia from the rest of Germany); the Poznan Army would hold the Poznan region in the west on both banks of the Warta River; the Lodz Army would protect the Lodz area and the lower Warta River; the Krakow Army would protect the south-west border in Silesia between Krakow and Gleiwitz; the Karpathy Army would defend the Carpathian Mountains in the south between Tarnow and Boryslaw; and the Prosy Army was to hold a reserve position between Radom and Lodz. Along the border were trip wire units.

Some argued against this strategy for it placed the Polish Army in a semicircle bowing towards the west and German troops attacking from East Prussia might outflank the extreme right of the Polish line, while German troops attacking from Czechoslovakia might outflank the extreme left of the Polish line.

Causes of Arrogance: During the summer of 1939 Hitler ranted and raved on the radio about the 'poor oppressed German-speakers in Poland' and began to mobilise troops on the border, but Smigly-Rydz was exceedingly confident for the following reasons.

His plan was to hold on to as much land as possible and if he had to trade space he would be trading villages of German-speakers not Poles.

This tactic would draw in the Germans and bog them down until the British and French could honour their words and invade western Germany.

As East Prussia was connected with Germany only by air and sea they might not have too much military strength in East Prussia and would remain on the defensive there.

The Germans in Czechoslovakia could only reach Poland through high narrow mountain passes, where a handful of Poles could hold off an army.

He believed Stalin's Soviet Union, which was currently negotiating with the British, would keep out of the conflict as long as Poles were killing Germans. Stalin and Hitler were mortal enemies: their troops had been fighting each other in Spain as recently as March. Stalin would be more concerned about the Japanese, who had invaded the Soviet Union in May.

The Polish Army had already begun to mobilise and did not have as far to march as the Germans.

Most of Poland's roads were dirt and these dusty avenues would soon turn to mud at the first drop of rain. September was known for its rainy days and October was a rainy month. The Germans, who bragged about their tanks, would not be bragging when their tanks became stuck in mud, but the Poles who relied on horse-drawn wagons and had eleven brigades of horse cavalry would find the rain to their liking – horses needed water – and they would be able to outflank the mud-bound Germans.

Many of the Poles were veterans of the German Army and they knew the inherent weaknesses of that system. The Poles had been victorious against all comers since 1918, apart from the minor affair at Annaberg.

The French, who had whipped the Germans soundly in 1918, had aided the Poles to create a modern fighting formation.

Between them the Poles and French could mobilise 150 divisions, the Germans only 89, and the French had more tanks than the Germans. Hitler could not afford to leave less than half his army facing the French, meaning the Poles would meet a German invasion at odds of 1:1. This would be bad for the Germans for an attacker always likes to have a 3:1 superiority.

Last but not least the Poles would be morally right in this conflict, defending their nation. Surely that would count for something?

The Enemy: Until 1935 the German Army had been limited to a strength of 100,000 men and poor weaponry. In that year Hitler had repudiated Allied restrictions dating from 1919 and had expanded his army through conscription and rearmament.

The vast majority of his soldiers were recruits and reservists aged 19–45, who had by August 1939 only just been mobilised, so their training was limited.

On the face of it a German division at 17,734 men was essentially similar to a Polish one at 16,492, but there were some key differences.

In weapons: the German division possessed 54 mortars of 81mm compared to the Polish 20; 527 machine-guns compared to 320; 39 anti-tank guns of 75mm compared to none for the Poles; fourteen field guns of 150mm compared to three of 155mm. In communications the German divisions had a battalion of signallers, the Poles a quarter of that.

The Polish division relied on horses and a mere handful of cars and trucks, whereas the German division required only 1,133 horses as it had 942 motorised vehicles, including a few score of the excellent rough country half-tracks.

Only two Polish brigades were fully motorised, whereas seven divisions and two brigades of the Germans were motorised. Compared to the one Polish tank brigade the Germans had created five tank (panzer) divisions and one tank brigade, each division running 312 tanks, 48 armoured cars, two motorised infantry battalions and numerous other heavy weapons.

In total for his invasion of Poland Hitler had amassed 2,511 tanks, 4,019 anti-tank guns, 5,805 field guns, 219 dive bombers, 648 bombers and 426 fighters.

Moreover, the command structure of the Germans was different. They had divided their invasion forces into two sub-headquarters called army groups, one in the north under General von Bock with two armies and one in the south under General von Runstedt with three armies. Each army was sub-divided into two or more corps headquarters, with an average of 3.1 divisions per corps. The Polish armies had corps too, with an average of 4.4 divisions and two brigades each.

Put another way, Hitler's headquarters had two generals to control, one of whom had two and the other three generals to control, while one German army commander had five assault unit subordinates to control, and three army commanders had four to control, whereas Smigly-Rydz intended to direct eight subordinates, and two of his army commanders had six assault units to control, and two army commanders had five.

Not only could each German general spend more time per day on each of his subordinates, but each general had a chief of staff who was more like a deputy who took part in strategy and tactics discussions – based on the premise that two heads were better than one.

Furthermore the Germans intended their motorised formations to be used en masse; for example two corps were fully motorised, one corps was half motorised, and one was two-thirds motorised. Not one Polish corps was even partially motorised.

Of greatest importance was the reason why the Germans had chosen to distribute their units and weapons in this manner. *Blitzkrieg* (lightning war) tactics had been created by a few farsighted officers working independently following the butchery of World War I. The leading exponent was Basil H. Liddell-Hart, but his British colleagues ignored him. The Germans did not and General Heinz Guderian tried out Liddell-Hart's theories in small-scale actions in the Spanish Civil War, which ended in March 1939

Basically the tactics consisted of the following: a reconnaissance unit of armoured cars, motor cycles or half-tracks would invade until they came up against serious opposition, then would withdraw and radio for artillery and air support, following which they would try again. If they still encountered resistance they would radio for reinforcements of tanks and infantry riding in trucks and/or half-tracks, who would attack the defender. Meanwhile the reconnaissance unit would look elsewhere for a weak point in the enemy line. Once they found one the tanks and motorised infantry would be replaced by normal infantry so that they could follow the reconnaissance unit. The operation would be repeated continuously. Like water seeping through a dam, they would continuously search for the weakest spot.

The defender would have two choices: remain and battle the normal infantry while they were being outflanked by motorised infantry and tanks; or retreat and hope to outrun the attacker. To put it simply, while the Poles intended to rely upon artillery, machine-guns and rifles, the Germans would rely on the radio and the internal combustion engine.

The fact that the German tanks were small and ill-armed was irrelevant in this new type of warfare. Almost half were Mark Is, only 5.4-tons, two-man crew, 5 feet 7 inches high and armed with a machine-gun, and most of the others were Mark IIs at 9.5-tons and armed with a 20mm cannon and a machine-gun. Only 30 of the German tanks were the 38t or Mark III armed with a 37mm or 50mm gun, and 36 were Mark IVs armed with a short 75mm gun.

Countdown: Smigly-Rydz would have loved to have mobilised all his reservists as soon as Hitler had begun his warmongering speeches, but reservists hold down civilian jobs, have wives and children, are the very fabric of cultural, commercial and industrial life, and to call them up damages that fabric accordingly. Therefore, he delayed some call ups. Still he planned to have about 40per cent of his reservists in barracks by the end of August.

On 23 August Hitler and Stalin signed a non-aggression pact. The world was stunned. Communism and Fascism had climbed into bed together. Actually this did not affect Smigly-Rydz in the least. He had never had any intention of calling upon Stalin for assistance any more than he had thought of asking Hitler for aid against Stalin. However, this news did shock the French and British into becoming more reticent to the point of indecision.

The Battlefield: The Polish–German border was 920 miles long. Facing westwards Poland's front wall was the Warta River, which meandered along the border and up to 50 miles inside Poland. The left flank (south wall) was the great natural barrier of the Carpathian Mountains as far west as Krakow and the Silesian Plateau to the north of Krakow. The right flank (north wall) was the Narew River, in Warsaw's right rear; and the Vistula River, which ran through Warsaw then meandered north-westwards to the sea. Other than a few smaller rivers, much of Poland was bereft of natural obstacles to an invader. Parts of the country were flat with large agricultural fields, small plots and narrow dirt lanes – a tank commander's dream.

The Battle: There had been some light skirmishes along the border, which both sides wished to keep secret, but in the early morning hours of 1 September a bridge over the lower Vistula was bombed and the Polish naval base at Wester-platte was shelled by a German warship. At 4.45am crossroads and installations up to five miles inside Poland came under German artillery fire. Minutes later border guards were machine-gunned as German reconnaissance vehicles smashed through the frontier, followed by the marching infantry in their green tunics, grey trousers and 'coal bucket' helmets. The invasion had come.

Throughout the morning countless reports reached Smigly-Rydz and General Stachiewicz his Chief of Staff about air raids, border crossings, shelling and a plethora of activity, most of which turned out to be spurious. It would take a day for the shock to wear off and at the moment everything was believed. Smigly-Rydz did not make a full report to President Mosciecki because of this and perhaps because he had already bypassed him on so many issues.

However, the Poles knew where the enemy was concentrating through spies and radio interception and they sent their planes towards them. Taking off in the haze of a hot morning Polish bombers struck these concentration areas, while Polish fighters challenged German aircraft that were already causing destruction in Warsaw and at Polish assembly areas.

Polish pilots returning to Puck and Krakow airfields found unbelievable wreck-age. German bombers had just visited them and had crippled aircraft undergoing maintenance, cratered runways, burned barracks, flattened hangars, destroyed spare parts, set fire to fuel and blown up ammunition.

On day two, the border trip wire units having been overrun, the main Polish infantry in their brown uniforms and round helmets came under air raids, artillery fire and ground assault. Polish cavalry in their French-style helmets waited with lances to counter-attack.

Major General Czeslaw Mlot-Fijalkowski's Narew Group, which held the north-east wall between the Narew River and East Prussia with two divisions and two cavalry brigades supported by a large body of non-divisional artillery, was under light probing attacks.

North-west of Warsaw General Emil Przedrzymirski-Krukowicz's Modlin Army centred on Mlawa, which held the north-west wall with two divisions and two cavalry brigades up front and three divisions in reserve, was under assault by the German Third Army of seven divisions, two brigades and a panzer (tank) brigade. The Modlin Army's non-divisional artillery had yet to arrive.

Still further north-west on the opposite bank of the Vistula General Bortnowski's Pomorze Army of five divisions and a cavalry brigade had orders to hold West Prussia north of Bydgoszcz, but was under attack by the German Fourth Army of seven divisions, a brigade, and the powerful XIX Corps of two motorised divisions and a panzer division. In one day the Polish 9th Division was badly beaten on the Brda Line and Bortnowski's left (south) flank was already being turned.

Surprisingly General Tadeusz Kutrzeb's Poznan Army of four divisions and two cavalry brigades and two divisions in reserve, which held the northern part of the west wall along the Warta River, reported they were not under attack.

On the southern part of the west wall along the Warta General Juliusz Rommel's Lodz Army of four divisions, a mountain division and two cavalry brigades was holding back the German Eighth Army of six divisions and a regiment.

General Antoni Szylling's Krakow Army was centred upon Krakow city, holding the hinge between the west wall and south wall with four divisions, a mountain division, a mountain brigade, a mechanised brigade and a cavalry brigade. Two other divisions had yet to arrive. He reported that formations of the German Fourteenth Army were slipping past both his flanks and were 50 miles inside Poland already.

General Kazimierz Fabrycy's Karpathy Army was watching the mountain passes of the south wall with his two mountain brigades and a mechanised brigade, and in Tarnow he had two divisions in reserve. So far so good, but at day's end Rommel reported some elements at Wielun were surrounded.

Polish anti-tank gunners found that they could knock out any of the German tanks at 250 yards' range, but tanks that sat back at 400 yards could machine-gun them with impunity. Often the tanks could sneak up quite close, almost invisible because of their extremely low height, 5 feet 7 inches for the Mark I, and unheard in the general noise of battle, to overrun the gun positions. One miss by an anti-tank gunner was fatal: the gunners never got a second chance.

There was another problem. Some members of minority groups were dodging their call up, especially German-speakers. Indeed Polish troops had reported a hostile reception in the German-speaking areas, including sniping and sabotage. A few Poles overreacted and murdered German-speaking men in front of their families!

On day three General Przedrzymirski-Krukowicz ordered General Stanislaw Skwarczynski to bring up the three reserve divisions, but they soon found that movement along the roads was difficult as the troops had to move against the flow of refugees who had begun to mass upon the roads, their pitiful belongings crammed into baby carriages and on horse-drawn carts. Every hour or so they would scramble into ditches as German planes strafed the roads. It was much easier to go with the flow.

Realising no reinforcements could reach him and that he had been outflanked, Przedrzymirski-Krukowicz ordered his Modlin Army to retreat.

On that day Britain and France declared war on Germany. Throughout Poland this was cause for rejoicing for the Poles believed the Germans would now have to withdraw divisions from Poland to defend the Franco-German border.

On the same day Kutrzeb asked Smigly-Rydz for permission to counter-attack southwards against the northern flank of the German Eighth Army. He believed he was in an excellent position to do so and his troops were in fighting trim. Smigly-Rydz refused and instead authorised a withdrawal eastwards.

This same day Lodz Army began to retreat. Prosy Army in reserve under General Stefan Dab-Biernacki with six divisions, a cavalry brigade and a tank brigade had not yet been attacked, but had to evacuate Radom district to make room for the retreating Lodz Army. Another two of Dab-Biernacki's divisions had not yet arrived.

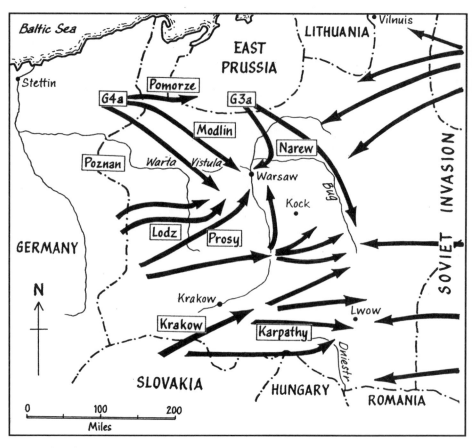

On day four Smigly-Rydz ordered newly recalled reservists to create the new Lublin Army by assembling at that city.

On day five General Bortnowski reported that the German XIX Corps had outflanked him to the south and reached East Prussia. His Pomorze Army was cut off.

This day Szylling reported that he was under attack in Krakow City by five divisions and a regiment, while the German XVIII Corps of a panzer, a light motorised and a mountain division had outflanked him to the south.

Also this day elements of the Karpathy Army were surrounded by German mountain troops at Tymbark on the Dunajec River, while Slovakian troops invaded Poland through the Dukla Pass.

So far the Lodz Army had retreated 75 miles under air attack and was utterly exhausted, and one element had been caught and surrounded at Piotrkow 40 miles east of the Warta by the German XVI Panzer Corps. General Stefan Dab-Biernacki ordered a tank counter-thrust to rescue this element, but poor communications, air raids and too many calls for aid from elsewhere doomed the venture from the start.

Because of poor communications, Smigly-Rydz was having trouble ascertaining exact strengths of his own units: his radios were jammed, telephone lines cut, messengers strafed by planes or lost among the mass of refugees, and he had no real information of the enemy. Few Polish reconnaissance planes were flying by now so he was fighting the war blind. Whenever his generals managed to report they demanded air cover, reinforcements and resupply, none of which he could deliver.

On the sixth day he surprised everyone by ordering a complete retreat to the Narew, Vistula and San Rivers, thus abandoning the entire western half of the nation. Warsaw on the west bank of the Vistula was to be turned into a fortress – it already had a garrison of over 50,000 – and behind the Narew he placed the new Wyszkow Group of three divisions (though only two were currently available).

Obedient to this order: the Karpathy Army (renamed Malopolska) began to retreat eastwards towards Lwow; the Prosy Army towards Deblin on the Vistula south of Warsaw; the Lodz Army towards the Vistula north of Warsaw; and the Modlin Army south-eastwards towards the rear (east) of Warsaw. Bortnowski replied he could not break out of his encirclement and Szylling said he could not break out of Krakow. Kutrzeb's Poznan Army was still moving eastwards trying to reach the war zone.

On day seven General Zajac reported his fighters had shot down hundreds of German planes (actually 105) for only 63 lost in the air, but because his airfields were being overrun he had ordered all units to move to Lublin and anything that could not be taken was to be destroyed. Effectively Poland no longer had an air force. That day Fabrycy's two divisions at Tarnow were surrounded.

Despite Warsaw having been declared a fortress Smigly-Rydz ordered his headquarters and government to be removed. They were to set up a new capital at Brzesc on the Bug River, far to the rear.

On day eight, to defend Warsaw, General Rommel was ordered to combine his Lodz Army with the city garrison. As this order was being drawn up the garrison repelled a lightning-like thrust by the German 4th Panzer Division of the XVI Panzer Corps. The attempted *coup de main* failed, but it alarmed the Poles to think the Germans had come this close.

On day nine General Tadeusz Kutrzeb again asked for permission to counter-attack. He claimed his Poznan Army was in excellent shape and was approaching the rear of the German Eighth Army on the Bzura River. Smigly-Rydz agreed.

Kutrzeb's troops charged down upon the German 28th and 30th Divisions taking them completely by surprise. The fighting was bitter to the extreme.

However, the German response was astonishingly quick and soon most of the Poznan Army was surrounded.

Meantime elements of the Prosy Army were trapped along the Bzura River.

On day ten, much of the Prosy Army was destroyed. This day the Modlin Army coming into the rear of Warsaw at Siedlce and Praga was incorporated into the Warsaw defences.

Smigly-Rydz now came to the conclusion that he should divide his command in two, a southern force and a northern force, to match the invaders, but his first order for the northern force's Narew and new Wyszkow Groups shocked several of his staff: they were to hold the line Kock-Brzesc, i.e. south-east of Warsaw. This was tantamount to abandoning the Warsaw defenders.

He also came up with another stunning order. All other units were to retreat east of the Bug and southwards towards the Dniestr, placing their backs on the border of neutral Romania and the Soviet Union. This order abandoned ethnic Poland!

Most of the troops realised they would not be able to march that far owing to air attacks, long range artillery fire, and assaults by armour and infantry against their flanks and rear. They felt abandoned by their commander.

On day eleven Major General von Briessen personally led his German 30th Division to counter-attack the Poznan Army, losing half an arm in the process, such was the fanaticism of Kutrzeb's attack. (Hitler personally visited von Briessen with a medal). On day twelve the garrisons of Kock and Bialystok were overcome, and three divisions of the Prosy Army surrendered at Radom west of the Vistula. On day fourteen the Modlin Army protecting Warsaw's rear was all but surrounded at Siedlce. On day fifteen the great fortress city of Przemysl on the San River fell, along with much of the Malopolska Army.

This day Praga on the east bank opposite Warsaw was attacked by much of the German Third Army.

On day sixteen all elements of the Krakow Army that had managed to escape were absorbed into the new Lublin Army, but they were in danger of being cut off at the very moment of assembling. On day seventeen Stalin's Red Army invaded eastern Poland with fifteen divisions, nineteen cavalry divisions, a motorised brigade and ten tank brigades. Fewer than 200,000 Polish troops including rear-echelon units were in the path of these 250,000 Soviet assault troops, and they had nothing to thwart the advance of the 650 Soviet tanks. Their 37mm anti-tank shells just bounced right off the heavy Soviet vehicles which shot back with a 76.2mm gun.

The Poles, already depressed by the constant bad news, were utterly dejected by this latest report. One officer committed suicide. Smigly-Rydz ordered all personnel to retreat into Romania, where they would ask to be transported to France. It was an admission that the campaign, if not the war, was over. The French and British had yet to make any attack on the Germans. On the same day the newly formed Kutno Group of two divisions was surrounded at Kutno and the rearguard left behind at Brzesc by Smigly-Rydz's headquarters was overcome.

On day twenty the remnants of the Malopolska and Lublin Armies surrendered in the Piskor area, and the Poznan and Prosy Armies surrendered on the Bzura. Scattered resistance lasted another day. The Krakow Army also surrendered.

Next day Soviet troops arrived at German-occupied Bialystok, and Fascists and Communists shook hands. Now the Poles realised that Stalin's invasion had been planned as part of the Stalin-Hitler non-aggression pact.

On day twenty-three the Warsaw garrison (plus remnants of the Lodz and Modlin Armies), a total of 150,000 men, came under a fierce air, artillery, tank and infantry assault. Casualties were high among soldiers and civilians. On day twenty-seven the Warsaw garrison surrendered rather than see the city destroyed. On day twenty-nine 25,000 troops holding out in the city of Modlin just north of Warsaw surrendered.

Smigly-Rydz with about 90,000 troops of several units reached the Romanian border and were allowed to enter. Romania, which had good relations with France, agreed that these men could be transported to France to continue the war.

For another week there were clashes throughout Poland and some Poles took to the mountains to wage guerrilla war against the Soviets and Germans, but for the nation the war was over.

In trying to stem the German tide the Poles had inflicted casualties of 16,000 killed and 32,000 wounded, but had suffered 66,300 killed, 133,700 hospitalised with wounds and 607,000 taken prisoner.

The Poles killed or wounded 2,600 Soviets, but at a cost of 5,000 killed, about 10,000 wounded and 180,000 captured.

During September an estimated 25,000 civilians had been killed, about half within Warsaw.

Appraisal: Smigly-Rydz's errors can be divided into twelve crucial categories: intelligence, timing, strategy, dispersal, communications, command structure, reserves, firepower, specialists, tactics, supply and command ability.

Smigly-Rydz had excellent intelligence reports coming from Germany from spies, recent visitors, defecting anti-Fascists, foreign agents and much from Hitler's own pronouncements. These did not point to German strategy, but they did point to intentions. Hitler could hardly let the year go by without attacking and could not wait for the October rains. Therefore, he had to attack in September at the latest (Hitler originally planned it for August). Yet Smigly-Rydz ignored or misinterpreted this intelligence. What his intelligence could not tell him, but his intuition should have, was that the French and British would not fight for Poland. Poland was on her own.

The result of Smigly-Rydz's misinterpretation of intelligence was that he got his timing totally wrong: by invasion day he had only mobilised about 40 per cent of his reservists and was not able to gather many more.

He knew he was facing a semi-mobile army that encircled him on three sides, yet he chose a strategy of covering all bases. He intended to defend the homes of German-speaking Poles from the Germans, the very people who did not want defending. Or was it perhaps Polish honour he was defending? Honour seems to be the only logical motive when one risks one's home in order to defend one's conquests.

This strategy of defending Poland in an arc bowing towards the west meant that the Germans only needed to break through in one location to place themselves inside the arc, deep inside the Polish rear. The most damaging breakthrough came from the German Third Army out of East Prussia against the Polish north-west wall less than 72 hours after the first shots were fired.

As Smigly-Rydz did not have enough troops to defend 920 miles of front line, the adoption of this strategy forced him to disperse his forces. The Pomorze Army was stuck out on a limb, unable to take part in the main defence: a total waste of an eighth of his army. The Poznan Army was stuck out 75 miles in front of the Lodz and Krakow Armies, and thus was unable to man the main defence line. The Germans proved that this was a waste of a tenth of his army, when they did not even bother to attack it. Thus before the battle began he had denuded himself of almost a quarter of his fighting strength.

Swift reaction depended on reliable communications, which Smigly-Rydz did not have. Enemy planes bombed telephone exchanges and headquarters and strafed messengers. Enemy radio interception units jammed his radios and/or sent false messages. However, some of the problems were of his own making. Each division had only a company of signallers and each corps and army headquarters was likewise short changed. Radio operators, telephone linesmen, motor cycle couriers and carrier pigeon units in abundance were essential in modern war. He failed to realise this.

This leads us to his command structure. It was to say the least unwieldy. He attempted to personally control eleven army and group commanders, plus dealing with rear-echelon functions, through an inadequate communications system, while his own headquarters moved three times under air raids.

His chain of command structure seemed jumbled, in which each army commander was required to communicate directly with one or two corps commanders plus a divisional commander and a couple of brigade commanders, instead of the normal system whereby army talks to the corps, each of which talks to its divisions, each of which talks to its brigades/regiments.

Smigly-Rydz had to have a powerful centrally placed reserve army to deal with any breakthrough, and it had to be mobile, but he chose the Prosy Army of eight footslogging infantry divisions and one cavalry brigade, the least mobile of his armies!

Reserves belonging to armies were placed too far away: no less than five divisions (12 per cent of the infantry) and two artillery regiments were not able to reach their assigned positions, whereas during the campaign the Germans were able to advance with 47 divisions and reinforce with fifteen!

Only in 1938, seemingly, had Smigly-Rydz realised he needed more tanks, and he never gained them in time, but what he really needed was not more firepower in the conventional sense, but more mobility for his firepower.

Of course Smigly-Rydz did have some mobility (tanks, armoured cars and horse cavalry), but he completely misused these specialists. He thought in terms of linear defence by infantry and chasing a broken enemy with cavalry. He wasted his cavalry by using them in defence, or worse: on one occasion Polish horse cavalry charged tanks with lances!

His tactics leave a lot to be desired, for he looked upon German mobile breakthroughs as if they were cavalry and able to go on and on, but they were mechanised and would have soon run out of fuel: as early as the third day he was refusing the Poznan Army permission to counter-attack and ordering them to retreat; three days later he ordered everyone to retreat 150 miles eastwards; three days later he authorised one army counter-attack; hours later he ordered a retreat to a line 120 miles southwards abandoning 15 per cent of his men in Warsaw; hours later he ordered a retreat to a line 50 miles eastwards and 150 miles southwards; six days later he ordered everyone to escape to Romania, his last effective order.

The distance between the Polish front and the supply depots and the pace of Polish resupply were of paramount importance. The problem with horse-drawn wagons is that they are slow and the least bit of bombing can kill or incapacitate a horse and render the wagon immobile, whereas trucks are surprisingly durable. Moreover, trucks cannot panic: horses can. These factors, added to the packed refugees on the roads, made resupply all but impossible.

Smigly-Rydz exhibited a complete lack of command ability from the first moment, bearing in mind he was the first general to suffer a major blitzkrieg, and the Germans were themselves astonished by their speed of advance. But he did refuse the suggestion of a counter-attack early on that might have made some difference, and he never asked his reserve army to do anything but retreat. True, the

Soviet invasion signed Poland's death warrant, but it was really only the icing on Hitler's cake. The Poles fought bravely, but their commander in chief was a defeatist.

Alternative: There was little Smigly-Rydz could have done given his lack of motor vehicles, and especially given the Soviet stab in the back, but it does seem that accepting the loss of much of the German-speaking districts by leaving only trip wire and delaying units there would have given him a good 24 hours' breathing space before the Germans reached his infantry.

Furthermore, he could have made his west wall defence line more resistant by placing it along the Bzura manned by the Krakow, Lodz, Prosy, Pomorze and Poznan Armies, with a reserve force containing most of his cavalry, mechanised troops and tanks, so that the Poles attempted to block the 24 attacking German divisions with 27 of their own, instead of the fifteen under Smigly-Rydz's plan.

A second reserve force could have been made from the 50,000 men of the Warsaw garrison and the remainder of the mobile forces, with orders to act as an independent army not a town defence unit, in order to counter-attack any invasion from East Prussia.

The Narew Group was not hit hard and could have been ordered to invade East Prussia. Hitler would have had to respond to this occupation of German villages for prestige reasons, and may indeed have called off part or all of his northern offensive.

Consequences: The immediate consequences of the disappearance of Poland were the imposition of two equally evil horrors, Soviet Communism in the east and Hitlerian Fascism in the west. For every Polish soldier killed in the battle, a hundred civilians would soon die, giving Poland a higher percentage loss than any other nation in World War II.

Reaching France Smigly-Rydz found his officers had lost all confidence in him. They refused to acknowledge him as leader of the exiled government, so in a vain attempt to seek death or glory he returned to German-occupied Poland to join the guerrillas, where he died in 1943 at the hand of some unknown assailant: perhaps the Germans, perhaps one of his political rivals.

The Battle's Place in History: Considering Britain's war against Germany was to last another five and a half years, the overrunning of Poland appears with hindsight to have been extremely swift. Certainly in August 1939 it was thought impossible that a nation with a 3,000,000-man army could be overrun in 700 hours. The Germans were as surprised as anyone.

Blitzkrieg had come of age. Indeed the Germans were to perfect it in the coming months so that they made even greater conquests.

Thus the Battle for Poland has been pushed aside by historians and readers alike in an eagerness to come to grips with these greater conquests, and subsequent defeats.

However, had the war ended in October 1939, engagements such as Krakow, the Bzura, Warsaw, Kock and Kutno may have become internationally known household names.

1939–40

Finland

Background: In 1917 a revolution tore the fabric of the Russian Empire, and with the abdication of Tsar Nicholas, a new democratic government was created. However, in November a tiny group of revolutionaries led by Vladimir Ulyanov (code-name Lenin 'man of iron') seized Petrograd and Moscow and claimed to represent all Russia.

The chaotic situation in the empire now exploded into civil war as Lenin's followers, the Bolsheviks (Communists), created the Red Army and occupied village after village in bloody oppressive warfare, defeating anti-Communist Russians and units from a score of nations including Britain and the USA.

It was 1921 before the communists could cease fighting and survey that which they had conquered. They had taken all of ethnic Russia, and over a hundred other ethnic lands were consumed. Lenin had recreated the empire, with himself as de facto 'tsar'. Officially titled the Union of Soviet Socialist Republics, Lenin nicknamed it a prison of nations. The only lands that had successfully resisted the Red Army were Lithuania, Estonia, Finland, Latvia, Poland, Galicia, western Byelorussia, North Bukovina and Bessarabia.

The Commander: Lenin was not to see the fruits of his labour, dying somewhat mysteriously, to be succeeded by his long time supporter Iosef Djugashvili, who chose to rule by the name Stalin (man of steel). Thus began the largest most consistently evil regime of modern times.

Stalin, a Georgian peasant born in 1879, had adopted the Russian language and lifestyle and had become a petty crook and later a revolutionary like many in his family. Prison only hardened his resolve. Basically an evil man he adopted Communism only as a method. He was no more a Communist than the Pope.

From robbing banks at gunpoint and enforcing protection rackets he rose to Red Army political commissar and then to dictator of the empire by the age of 43.

Unlike Tsar Nicholas, Stalin made up the rules as he went along and this involved considerable hypocrisy. The Tsars and their nobility had flaunted their wealth: the Communist party bosses hid theirs.

The most serious problem facing Stalin was that communism was unworkable, but if anyone suggested an improvement could be made, that communism was not pure, that the Soviet Union was not paradise on earth, or that Stalin was not infallible, he risked arrest by Stalin's political police (the NKVD) and a sentence to a spell of 're-education' in a concentration camp.

The imposition of communism meant that property owners lost everything: landlords, shopkeepers, landowners, small plot farmers, businessmen, industrialists, small workshop proprietors. The state confiscated every business enterprise, project, farm, even every house. The state became the new god too, as religion was formally proscribed. Priests were arrested for performing the most insignificant of rites.

Despite the harshness of the régime on the Russian people it was even harder on non-Russians. Confiscation of farms in Ukraine and other states sentenced millions to starvation and the hungry who attempted to steal food were shot down by the NKVD. As a result there were full-scale revolts, which Stalin put down with his Red Army and Air Force: by the Yakuts in 1928, Ukrainians 1928-33, the Buryats in 1929, Tatars 1929-33, Kazakhs in 1931, Chechens, Ossetians, Kabardins, Kalmyks, Avars, Dargins, Laks and Lezhghins in 1935.

Stalin was a survivor, if nothing else, and survived by being the most paranoid of leaders. He murdered friends, relatives, trusted colleagues at the merest suggestion that they were disloyal. In protest his wife committed suicide. In 1937 he launched a series of purges and imprisoned or executed any of his industrial bosses who failed to meet production quotas. Then he massacred his civil servants.

Still not sated, the madman then murdered his own communist supporters: 98 of 179 members of the Central Committee, and 1,108 of 1,966 delegates to the 17th Party Congress.

Nor were communists abroad safe. His NKVD assassins murdered leading communists in Germany, Austria, Poland, Czechoslovakia, Yugoslavia and elsewhere.

Once done he ordered the NKVD to murder their own boss: this was done.

A rough estimate is that Stalin murdered by one method or another 20,000,000 of his own people by 1939 and had placed 8,000,000 in concentration camps.

The Army: The Red Army was on the face of it a classless society. Supposedly its officers were elected. Actually they were chosen by the Communist Party and did their duty under constant scrutiny from political commissars, who lived the life of a soldier, in the same manner as chaplains in other armies. In order to keep up this charade, officers did not wear insignia.

A hard core of regulars kept the army alive, but the vast majority of soldiers were conscripts brought in at nineteen for a couple of years. As they came from lands speaking a hundred different languages they had to be placed in their own ethnic units, but often their officers were Russians. Conscripts who failed to report for training were arrested as were their entire family up to cousins!

In such a police state Soviet soldiers obeyed orders without question and did not publicly complain, though their lifestyle was brutal and spartan. A pot of soup and an ounce of crusty black bread was considered a good meal. A spare uniform was a prize. Their pay was worthless. With Russia at war 1914-1921 and constant rebellions 1928-1935 it was quite feasible for a veteran regular of 40 years of age to have spent fifteen years in combat by 1935.

In 1937 Stalin decided that his officer corps needed pruning. He ordered the NKVD to arrest three-quarters of his general staff, thirteen of nineteen army commanders and 110 out of 135 divisional commanders, half the brigade commanders, 80 per cent of colonels and 43 per cent of other officers. Most were shot.

One of the few who survived Stalin's insanity during these dreadful years was Kirill Afanasievich Meretskov. Born in 1897 and brought up in Moscow in a working-class family, he barely made a living as a mechanic. Joining the communists he dodged conscription into the tsar's army and in 1917 joined the Red Army to help spread the revolution by the sword. Judged to be politically sound he was promoted to officer rank and fought anti-communists until 1920, then invaded Poland and was one of the Soviet soldiers defeated at the Battle of the Vistula. It was during this period he met Stalin, at the time an army commissar, and through Stalin's influence he was promoted to brigadier general at the age of 24.

Stalin trusted him enough to allow him to be trained in Germany and Czechoslovakia and to take 2,000 military advisers to Spain in 1936 to advise the Republicans in their war against the Nationalists, Italians and Germans. In 1937, at age 40, he was appointed deputy chief of the general staff. (There were few older officers still alive!) In 1938 he was appointed commander of the Volga Military District and in 1939 took a similar position in Leningrad (Petrograd).

The basic unit of the Red Army was the infantry division, which consisted of a reconnaissance battalion of mostly infantry and horse cavalry, a signals company, an engineer battalion, an artillery regiment of 24 76mm guns and twelve 122mm howitzers, and three infantry regiments, each possessing three battalions. Some divisions had as many as 180 motor vehicles, but most relied completely on horse-drawn wagons. At full strength a division possessed 9,619 personnel.

Each infantry battalion consisted of two 45mm anti-tank guns, nine 82mm mortars, six 50mm mortars, and about 650 men armed with rifles and machine-guns.

The new DShK air-cooled machine-gun weighed 78 pounds and fired a heavy 12.7mm bullet from a 50-round magazine, but the most common machine-gun was the 1910 model water-cooled Maxim, weighing 52½ pounds with tripod and 38 pounds with bipod, which fired a 7.62mm bullet from a 250-round belt. Usually these weapons were pulled along on wheeled trolleys.

A few shoulder-fired 7.62mm DP sub-machine-guns with a 47-round drum were issued.

The standard rifle was the 1891 model bolt action Moisin-Nagant, weighing 9.7 pounds and firing a 7.62mm bullet from a five-round magazine.

A tank brigade contained four 76.2mm anti-tank guns, six 82mm mortars, a signals company and 65 tanks. There were two basic tanks in 1939. The 13.8-ton BT-7M with a crew of four, armed with a 76.2mm gun and two 7.62mm machine-guns, and distinguished from most other tanks by being steered by a pair of front wheels, i.e. it was a half-track. The T-35 had no less than three turrets, one sitting forward housing a 45mm gun, another in the rear housing a 76.2mm gun that could fire over the forward turret, and a third turret housing a machine-gun. It weighed 45 tons and carried as many as ten crewmen. There were still a few T-26s left, a three-man 9.4-ton tank with a 45mm gun. There were also a few experimental tanks such as the 47-ton T-100 and the SMK, weighing 56 tons. Neither had a machine-gun turret, but otherwise were similar to the T-35. A special feature of Soviet tanks was a machine-gun that fired from the rear of the main turret.

In July 1938 the far east of the Soviet Union was invaded by a force of Japanese and anti-communist Russians, which was obviously testing Stalin's defences. At Chankufeng the Red Army repelled them.

Grand Strategy: The arch enemy of Communism was Fascism, because Leninist-Stalinist communism was in effect a form of fascism, and Stalin would brook no rivals. The most worrisome fascist leader was Adolf Hitler, who had taken control of Germany in 1933, rearmed that nation in 1935, militarised the Rhineland in 1936, sent troops to Spain in 1936, conquered Austria in 1938, occupied Memel in Lithuania in 1939 and conquered Czechoslovakia in March 1939, all in the face of Anglo-French complaints.

Seeing that diplomatic complaints were not going to stop Hitler, Stalin saw Hitler not just as an ideological rival but a military rival, and only Polish soil stood between Hitler's and Stalin's armies. (In Spain Germans and Soviets were in fact fighting each other on a small-scale until March 1939.)

The Japanese were also military rivals. In May 1939 a Japanese and anti-communist Russian force had invaded Mongolia, a Stalinist puppet state. Thus it was with extreme relief that Stalin accepted Hitler's offer of an alliance in August 1939.

Stalin learned that Hitler was going to crush Poland and in return for Stalin's passivity he could name any territory he chose. Stalin initially asked for Lithuania, but then opted for those portions of Byelorussia, Lithuania and Ukraine (Galicia) under Polish control, and a right to make later decisions regarding Lithuania, Latvia, North Bukovina, Bessarabia, Estonia and Finland, those nations that had escaped Lenin's empire-building. Stalin suddenly saw a way to finish what Lenin had begun.

On 23 August 1939 when the Stalinist-Hitler non-aggression pact was signed both communists and fascists the world over felt betrayed. However, this did not worry Hitler or Stalin in the least: they knew their people would do what they were told.

Stalin gave command of Mongolia to General Zhukov, who fortunately was able to stay clear of Stalin's interference long enough to win a resounding victory at Nomonhan on 30 August, inflicting 11,000 casualties and driving the Japanese back into China.

On 1 September Hitler invaded Poland. Seventeen days later Stalin unleashed General Semyon Timoshenko with fifteen infantry and nineteen cavalry divisions, a motorised brigade and ten tank brigades. In three days they brushed aside all opposition and occupied the homes of 5,300,000 Poles, 4,500,000 Ukrainians, 1,100,000 Byelorussians, 1,100,000 Jews, 200,000 Lithuanians and 134,000 German-speakers, for a cost of 2,600 killed and wounded.

The German-speakers were deported to Germany; 180,000 Polish soldiers were taken into a cruel captivity; and the NKVD was let loose on the helpless population, butchering and imprisoning hundreds of thousands of innocents.

Stalin now demanded the Finnish, Estonian, Latvian and Lithuanian governments allow him to place air and naval bases on their soil. He bribed the Lithuanians by offering them Polish Lithuania, which he had just conquered.

Causes of Arrogance: The prime cause of Stalin's arrogance in October 1939 was that no one had been able to stand up to him since his decision to aim at the leadership of the communists. He was no military leader, having had no influence on the battles of the Russian Civil War, though he always claimed he had captured one city practically single-handed and later ordered its name changed to Stalingrad.

Every revolt, every coup, every lone fanatic that aimed to overthrow him had failed. He was an arrogant man to begin with and by 1939 he had become like the ancient Roman emperors, who thought of themselves as gods.

The Red Army had been victorious in almost every war and had defeated Americans, French, Germans, British and Japanese. Only the Romanians (in Bukovina and Bessarabia), Lithuanians, Finns, Estonians, Latvians and Poles had defied the Red Army, and by 21 September 1939 the Poles had finally succumbed.

Stalin believed his army was invincible and came to the conclusion that his purges had been successful: a little massacre now and then was a good thing; it kept the survivors on their toes.

Of course, he did not look for other reasons for his victories, but they were plain to see. The revolts of 1928 to 1935 had been led by peasants waving pitch forks and shotguns and he had bombed them with his air force and shot them down with machine-guns.

Zhukov had defeated the Japanese because he was Zhukov. In his forties like all the senior Russian generals, Zhukov was a military genius. The distance between Stalin and the battlefield, 6,000 miles, was a help to Zhukov, not a hindrance.

Timoshenko had defeated the Poles because he was up against trip wire units, untrained reservists still in barracks and rear-echelon troops. In Poland the Red Army had not faced one combat-ready division.

Stalin's confidence that the nations he was now bullying would capitulate was also based on sheer arithmetic. Together the populations of Lithuania, Latvia, Estonia and Finland came to just over 9,000,000. The Red Army had over 4,000,000 soldiers!

By November they had all given in and his troops poured across the borders: except Finland that is. The Finns had not only refused, but had mobilised.

Stalin was actually impressed by the Finns: as all bullies are impressed by force; but he knew his army would make short work of them. Their army was small: their air force tiny; their navy had just 30 gunboats and five submarines; their handful of small tanks were no match for the Soviet mammoth tanks; and they had no war industries of their own. Last but not least the Finnish–Soviet border was over 900 miles long and thus indefensible with such a small force.

The Battlefield: To be more exact the border stretched from the sea in the south (Gulf of Finland) northwards across 88 miles of land – the Karelian Isthmus, sparsely populated flat irregular forests with a few small lakes and streams – to Lake Ladoga, 90 miles south to north; thence across a landscape that was essentially one vast forest dotted with lakes of all sizes, rivers and streams, a few hamlets, some low hills and a few mountains for fully 750 miles to the Barents Sea.

This immense border was intersected by only six roads and a handful of logging trails.

The climate of this region creates two landscapes, the one just described and the winter one. November brings freezing rain that saturates the ground into mush and December brings the full blast of winter, turning the landscape into a frozen mass of ice. The sea itself is known to freeze in February.

Come November each day is graced by only four hours of daylight, a cloudy grey twilight type of daylight, and the further north one moves the less daylight appears each day. In the northern third of the border inside the Arctic Circle there are only two hours of daylight. To complicate the situation storms and blizzards are common.

Strategy: Having given Zhukov and Timoshenko a chance for glory, Stalin now offered Meretskov a chance if the Finns continued to refuse him. However, Stalin took an integral part in the planning as did his political commissars, so that in no way could this be considered Meretskov's plan – but of course if it went wrong Meretskov would pay with his head.

Stalin was no strategist and Meretskov's timid suggestion that they wait for spring was ignored. The longer little Finland defied the might of the Soviet Union, making Stalin look weak, the greater the chance that Hitler might convince the French and British to make peace and join him in attacking Stalin.

The plan was that the Fourteenth Army would take the Arctic port of Petsamo; the Ninth Army would occupy Salla 200 miles to the south and a further 200 miles southwards would capture Suomussalmi and Kuhmo; 100 miles further south the Eighth Army would conquer Ilomantsi and Pilkaranta; while the Seventh Army would invade the Karelian Isthmus and aim for the cities of Viipuri and Vuossalmi and if necessary advance westwards to the capital Helsinki.

The Enemy: Once Finland's Prime Minister Cajander and his democratically elected government had chosen to resist Stalin they handed their military problem to Marshal Baron Carl Gustav Mannerheim. At 72 years of age Mannerheim, a Swedish-speaking Finn, was the grand old man of Finnish history. He had joined the Tsarist army when Finland had been part of the Russian Empire and by World War I was a general. (He was older at the beginning of that conflict, than Meretskov was now). Following the collapse of the Russian Empire he led Finnish armies to fight alongside the Germans and win Finnish independence from the Soviets.

He had been looking forward to a peaceful retirement, writing memoirs and offering young officers advice. Suddenly the fate of Finland was in his hands once again.

He called for a complete mobilisation of all able-bodied men up to the age of 60 and asked for women volunteers for combat units.

This gave him 127,800 regulars and reservists, 100,000 replacements (teenage boys and men in their forties) and 200,000 Civic Guards, of which about half were men in their fifties and the other half were female volunteers.

Thus he mobilised 11 per cent of the population, despite the pronouncements of military theoreticians that this would cripple the socio-economic fabric of the nation. Mannerheim realised this, but decided that either the Finns fought with their heart and soul and every fibre of their being or they died, not just as a nation, but individually in concentration camps or in front of NKVD firing squads. He declared there was no choice, therefore socio-economic considerations were simply irrelevant, despite protests by lobby groups, associations, industrialists and politicians.

Mannerheim planned to have ten divisions, each of 14,200 troops manning a signals company, engineer company, artillery regiment of 36 75mm guns and three regiments of three infantry battalions each. Riflemen used the 7.62mm Moisin-Nagant. Each division also possessed eighteen 81mm mortars.

The Civic Guard was organised into smaller formations.

The Finns also had a variety of hand-held weapons, but the only one for which they had an assured ammunition supply was their own invention, the Suomi machine pistol, and each division was issued with 250.

Mannerheim had only one tank battalion, which maintained vehicles of several makes. He also had only 110 anti-aircraft guns and 112 37mm anti-tank guns. There were not enough uniforms for everyone – grey-green with a World War I German helmet – and only enough white snow suits for the ski troops.

The navy's few gunboats were utterly outclassed by Soviet battleships and the 56 Fokker DXXI and Bulldog fighters and 51 Fokker CX and Blenheim bombers of the Air Force would be going up against odds of 30:1.

The Battle: On 13 November with the Finns refusing to take part in further talks, Stalin knew he had to use his army to gain his requirements.

Late in the morning of 30 November 1939 Soviet bombers struck the cities of Helsinki, Viipuri and Vuossalmi and the naval base at Hango. Finnish fighters rose to challenge them and gave a good account of themselves.

Soviet warships bombarded Hango and other installations. The Finnish Navy was unable to interfere.

Stalin publicly announced that a Communist government had been set up for Finland. He was obviously intending this 'government' to ask that Finland be annexed into the Soviet Union.

The Fourteenth Army advanced in total darkness through scattered forests and over Arctic tundra with the 52nd and 104th Divisions. Owing to the cold, the soldiers' brown uniforms were covered with a long grey overcoat and they wore grey high crown hats with ear flaps. Their destination was the port of Petsamo and the small town of Nautsi another 100 miles westwards.

The 88th and 132nd Divisions were marching along a narrow forest road in darkness towards the town of Salla.

The 163rd Division was marching along a similar road in darkness to approach Suomussalmi from the north-east: they found that the road soon petered out into a logging trail. To their south about 30 miles was the 44th Division approaching Suomussalmi from the east.

Another 40 miles south was the 54th Division following a logging trail towards Kuhmo. Though there were no hills, except around Salla, the roads had to curve around lakes and ponds, which were already frozen over. The march was made in almost perpetual darkness.

The Ninth Army controlled the above divisions.

Under Eighth Army's control the 155th Division was using logging trails and in places cutting its own roads hoping to reach the lake-splattered district of Ilomantsi.

About 50 miles to the south the 139th Division was marching south-west towards Tolvajarvi on the north shore of Lake Tolva and the 75th Division was advancing due west towards that town.

Just a few miles to their south the 56th Division was bypassing a Finnish village, Suojarvi, and was aiming to reach Kollaa, while to its south the 18th Division was marching directly on Kitela and the 168th Division was moving on Pilkaranta. The Eighth Army had shared out tanks of two tank brigades among their divisions.

On the Karelian Isthmus the Seventh Army was advancing smoothly with the 24th, 43rd, 49th, 70th, 90th, 123rd, 138th and 142nd Divisions, four tank and three motorised infantry brigades.

Almost at once the Soviets encountered restrictions, though not the type they had expected. The great size of the invasion was giving Soviet supply officers nightmares, as the units were strung out along narrow roads and logging trails that intersected the vast snow blanketed forests. The fact that everything had to be done in darkness and bitter cold made ordinary duties more difficult.

North of Lake Ladoga the Finns took advantage of this – it was after all their homeland and they knew its conditions – and they used delaying tactics: felling trees across the trails; halting the Soviets by rearguards, which would then immediately pull out; and raiding in the darkness with ski troops, who would swoosh in and out of the Soviet columns like ghosts spraying bullets from their machine pistols. Most Soviets could only reply with bolt action rifles, and many found their rifles frozen solid. By the time the machine-gunners set up their weapons the Finns had blended into the night. The Soviets cursed under their breath, because they had not been issued light automatic weapons.

On the Karelian Isthmus, things were different as Soviet reconnaissance troops peered at the Mannerheim Line, a Finnish defence position that they had to conquer. Meretskov was relieved when reconnaissance informed him that the line consisted merely of a network of trenches and a series of machine-gun positions, few of them concreted.

As a result on 5 December Seventh Army gave authorisation for a full-scale attack with massed waves of infantry. The battle was soon under way and the noise and fury of the assault was nerve shattering to all concerned, but the Finns held. Most of the fighting took place in darkness. Lakes and rivers channelled the Soviet infantry into restricted access avenues, where Finnish machine-gunners expected them, and their bodies tumbled over one another in death.

The Finns had placed five divisions of regulars and reservists on this line and therefore the Soviets could not reach a 2:1 superiority, let alone the normally required 3:1.

The Soviet infantry called for tanks, but that raised another problem. The massive Soviet tanks were so heavy they were mud bound and could not move. The lighter BT-7M could move, but found steering difficult in the mud.

The infantry also called for more artillery support, but the guns had to be dragged along muddy trails by horses, which sank their hoofs deep into the cold soggy soil. Only after three days of slaughter were the first trenches conquered.

Still, Stalin and Meretskov were pleased with the first week of operations: the Fourteenth Army managed to force a Finnish battalion out of Petsamo; the 132nd Division took the hamlet of Kemijarvi; the 44th and 163rd Divisions reached Suomussalmi; and the 54th Division made it to Kuhmo.

The divisions of the Eighth Army were halted several times by rearguards and had not achieved any of their targets yet, except for Tolvajarvi. They did not know it, but the Finns were reinforcing their two divisions in this region by another two, which were in fact their only reserve divisions!

On 10 December, while the battle for the Mannerheim Line continued, the Soviet supply officers got their way and every column was told to halt to await resupply. Already some men had been crippled with frostbite and respiratory ailments and the ground was getting harder as the weather turned colder. Harder ground meant tanks could move more easily, but now their engines froze and in some cases fires had to be lit underneath them just to start them.

The aiming mechanism on the guns also froze: entire divisions were almost without artillery support.

On the 12th the supply troops of the 139th Division were suddenly attacked in darkness by a major force and they called for aid at once. The Finns had crossed frozen Lake Tolva and struck the rear of the division and this manoeuvre also cut off the division from its neighbour the 75th. In places Soviet troops held their ground wonderfully and inflicted heavy casualties on the attacking Finns, and elsewhere Soviets counter-attacked and killed or drove off the Finns, but many other Soviets had had enough of this week-long frozen night and they turned and ran. Sergeants in the Red Army were not taught to think for themselves and they relied on officers, but the initiative of the Russian male had been destroyed by Stalin's NKVD and his political commissars. Everyone looked to the commissars, but they were among the first to run.

After 48 hours of night battle the men of the 139th Division fell back from Tolvajarvi in retreat. Men ran off in all directions, not having the faintest idea where they were going. The forests were too thick to navigate by the stars: every tree looked alike; the snow was waist deep in places; the night was almost continuous; and it was bitterly cold (probably −40˚F). Now and then a swishing sound and a burst of automatic fire told them that Finnish ski troops were upon them. They ran faster and stumbled through the snow.

The 75th Division was ordered to break through to the 139th, but they failed to make any headway, though their machine-guns cut down many Finns. Eventually they too had to retreat.

Therefore, the Eighth Army had been split into two, its 155th Division stopped at Ilomantsi on its own 75 miles from the nearest aid, while the 168th Division held Kitela, the 54th Division held Kuhmo and the 18th Division was stopped in the Pilkaranta area. The 75th Division reached Aittojoki and dug in. Soon the entire Eighth Army was under counter-attack.

In mid-December east of Suomussalmi the 44th and 163rd Divisions' lines of supply were attacked by large bodies of ski troops and conventional infantry:

then from both sides of the large lake in this area came major assaults by Finnish regulars, reservists and the women and old men of the Civic Guard.

Only by 24 December could the Eighth Army breathe easily as the Finns ceased to attack. The 139th Division had been destroyed.

Two days later Seventh Army called off its assault on the Mannerheim Line. Some tanks had broken through, but the Finns had simply sealed the line behind them and denied it to following Soviet infantry. The tanks were then either set afire by petrol bombs or they ran out of fuel.

On 29 December the 44th and 163rd Divisions began to retreat from Suomussalmi, abandoning much of their equipment. Rearguards were useless as the Finns moved in and out of the forest at will, unlike the fleeing Soviets who had to stick to the trails or become lost. After nine days of retreating the 44th and 163rd Divisions were practically wiped out.

On 6 January 1940 Eighth Army was attacked by four Finnish divisions in a major onslaught. From behind every tree Finns suddenly appeared shooting and yelling. Finnish light artillery seemed to work just fine, while many of the Soviet guns were frozen. The Soviet infantry held on to their holes in the snow and fought back with every ounce of strength.

Meretskov authorised four fresh divisions to be rushed up to the threatened sector, but they found movement hard going – they could not rush – and when they encountered Finnish opposition they were soon brought to a halt.

Meanwhile the 168th Division was trapped at Kitela with its back to Lake Ladoga, and the 18th Division was under serious pressure at Pilkaranta.

On 29 January Stalin began to negotiate with the Finns, which showed two things: they knew they could not win; he knew he could not win all that he wished to. Stalin's immediate bargaining position was to drop the idea of annexation and to abandon the Finnish communist 'government'.

As negotiations went on the soldiers continued to die: some Soviets were now dying from hypothermia; others were quite literally found frozen stiff as a statue; others were dying of starvation, their food supply cut off; and others got lost in the forest and went mad. Some units ate their horses, rendering the guns immobile.

However, Stalin still wanted to negotiate from strength, so he dismissed Meretskov and brought in Timoshenko. Meretskov must have thought his neck was in the noose, but Stalin had had second thoughts about his purge of 1937 and he simply gave Meretskov a different command.

Timoshenko demanded reinforcements and Stalin gave him no less than another 24 divisions, 1,000 more tanks and as many provisions as possible.

Timoshenko felt that with this force he could bulldoze his way through the Mannerheim Line and on 1 February he attacked. But even with 650 tanks it took the Soviets two weeks of mayhem before they broke through, and the Finns were still allowed an orderly withdraw to set up a new defence line.

This could not prevent the trapped 18th Division from surrendering on 18 February, nor a tank brigade from doing so on the 29th.

By now it was so cold the sea had frozen to the point that it could bear the weight of trucks and medium tanks. Timoshenko saw his chance and on 2 March outflanked the Finnish defences by this route.

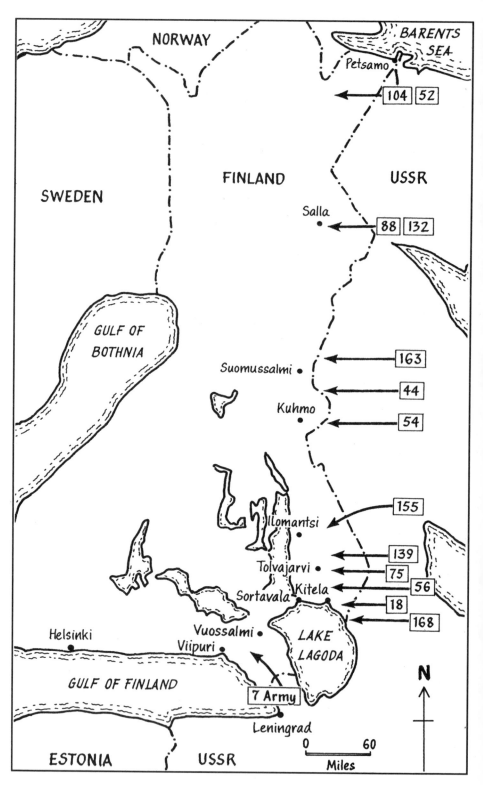

At last Stalin could negotiate from strength and on the 13th the Finns agreed to cease fire.

Aftermath: Stalin was satisfied with annexing the naval base at Hango, the Arctic port of Petsamo, the Karelian Isthmus and a sliver of forest along the border. His Red Army had inflicted extremely high casualties on the Finns: 25,000 killed and 43,500 wounded.

However, the cost to the Red Army was disastrous. Never one to admit a mistake, Stalin publicly announced his losses in Finland as 900 aircraft, 1,600 tanks, 48,000 killed and 158,000 wounded. His assessment of equipment losses was certainly accurate – it included planes crashing in bad weather – but he was almost definitely lying about his personnel losses. A later Soviet dictator, Nikita Kruschev, claimed Stalin lost a million casualties in Finland, and while this is surely an exaggeration, it does seem that Stalin's losses were probably between these two figures, say 200,000 wounded and 100,000 dead from battle, extreme cold and starvation.

The Finns released their prisoners at once: Stalin sent most of them to concentration camps for not having fought harder.

Appraisal: Meretskov cannot really be blamed for his performance, for he had been given an impossible task, an inefficient plan and an inadequate tool.

Stalin was responsible for the errors, which fall into seventeen major categories: command structure, counsel, training, timing, grand strategy, communications, morale, equipment, intelligence, psyops, dispersal, strategy, ground, tactics, reconnaissance, supply, firepower.

The command structure was ineffective, because no one commanded anything. The officers Stalin gave Meretskov were afraid to show initiative, through fear of being arrested by the NKVD. Additionally all local tactics had to be approved by the unit commissar. It was exceedingly difficult for a commander to command from company level upwards.

This and many other problems could have been pointed out to Stalin, but no one in the nation had the courage to offer him counsel. Dictators always cut themselves off from dissent and argument, rendering their decisions final without regard to facts.

Moreover, the purges had produced an army for 1939 in which senior generals were in their forties, junior generals in their thirties and some colonels in their twenties. What they made up in energy did not compensate for what they lacked in experience and in battle know-how, such as the ability to judge the balance of a battle. Men like Zhukov, who were natural born leaders, were one in a million.

Stalin's greatest failing was the timing of his attack. His planes could only fly four hours a day in the south and almost not at all in the north. His tanks were useless in the dark. The weather was as great an enemy as the Finns. This is a classic example of conflict between the right timing in a political sense and the right timing in a military sense. Stalin seems to have thought that like some ancient god he could melt the ice and part the forest.

His grand strategy was ridiculous, of course, to chose a land campaign when he could have invaded the Finnish capital in hours with a sea-borne landing.

The best commanders cannot function if they cannot communicate with their troops. Despite knowing that they were going into an area of limited access, where a divisional column would be strung out ten miles and more, there was no additional issue of radios and trained operators.

Many of the soldiers were from ethnic nations that had experienced NKVD massacres. Their morale was very low as a result and it is a wonder they fought at all. Only the presence of the NKVD in their home towns adequately explains this.

Much of the army's equipment was shown to be inferior. The tanks proved to be too bulky and complicated and were only of marginal value to the infantry. The Soviet Union had plenty of cold weather of its own during which to test equipment. There is no excuse that so many incidents of equipment failing to operate efficiently in sub-zero temperatures only showed up in combat.

The Soviet intelligence service was excellent, though it had taken a few knocks during the purges, and Stalin knew what the Finns were up to, yet he misread the Finnish will to resist: a calamitous error. Had he read the intelligence reports correctly he might have waited until winter was over before making his public claim to their soil, thereby enabling his army to attack in spring or summer.

His psyops were incredible. One day into the war he created an alternative government made up of Communist lackeys. He could hardly have expected to woo many Finns to his cause and all he did was strengthen their determination to resist.

His dispersal of his divisions was unnecessary. He totally wasted two divisions to secure Petsamo – Mannerheim only defended it with a battalion. His expedition of two divisions to take Salla was also a waste. Even had this force progressed all the way across Finland it could not have held its lines of supply over such a great distance. It was a dagger thrust into thin air.

The strategy of sending divisions down long narrow lanes of mud and ice was to send them into traps. There was justification in attacking along both sides of Lake Ladoga, thereby pinning the Finns in the isthmus and wheeling around from the north with six divisions, but Stalin was too impatient to allow this strategy to work.

Basically the ground offered two choices: ignore the forest or use it. The Soviets chose to ignore it, seeing it as a barrier, but the Finns used the forest as an ocean for travel and a fog for concealment.

Unfortunately, instead of waiting for the Eighth Army to advance, the Seventh Army wasted its manpower with the tactics of charging against the Mannerheim Line in human waves. They could hardly have done worse if they had allowed the Finns to give them orders.

Reconnaissance seems to have been negligible. Time and again large Finnish formations appeared where they were not supposed to be.

This brings us to Stalin's lines of supply. They were unguarded and open to every Finn with a shotgun. A reliance on horses in 1939 was an outmoded manner of warfare as the Germans had proven three months earlier. Moreover, in extreme cold horses freeze to death, rendering their cargo, be it wagon or gun, immobile. Some horses fell through frozen lakes and ponds and drowned.

There was no excuse for Stalin's failure to provide light automatic weapons for his infantry.

Alternative: The alternative that comes to mind immediately is not to have invaded at all. Finland posed no threat to Stalin and the additional bases he asked for were of no real value to him.

Once the political decision to attack had been made, however, he should have waited for good weather and then invaded by sea. He had a base just 60 miles across the sea from Helsinki. This would have outflanked the entire Finnish defences and given him their capital, which surely they would have been willing to trade for bases.

Consequences: The consequences of the Winter War, as the Finns called it, were twofold. The Red Army generals, Stalin included, were immensely depressed by the disastrous campaign, despite the fact they won. They reacted positively: instituting winter operations training; bringing in new equipment; scrapping their old tanks and inventing the excellent T-34; and issuing infantry with light machine-guns and sub-machine-guns.

Stalin's decision to keep Meretskov not only alive but useful took a great deal of pressure off officers who previously dared not make a decision lest it cost them their head. They saw that they were now allowed to think for themselves, perhaps even make mistakes.

The second consequence was that the Finns provided Hitler with all their intelligence of Soviet fighting capabilities giving the German Army an accurate picture of the state of the Red Army in December 1939, but one which would be drastically inaccurate by 22 June 1941, the day Hitler invaded the Soviet Union.

Most important for the Finns it gave them a false sense of power and they eagerly joined Hitler in his venture in 1941, and suffered as a result.

The Battle's Place in History: The Winter War is one of those conflicts that sits uneasily in the public mind. It was not part of World War II, or was it? Finland was surely the innocent party, but was also a friend of Nazi Germany.

One thing is certain. Had the Finns held out a month longer they might have been reinforced by a French and British expedition, which was currently preparing. That would have changed the picture of World War II completely.

1940

Greece

The Commander: Benito Mussolini was born in 1883 in Italy, the son of a revolutionary father and sedate schoolteacher mother. He inherited his father's rebellious tendencies – at the age of nine he was expelled for stabbing a pupil and he was suspended several times from another school.

Yet he also inherited his mother's intellectual qualities and studied hard, becoming a teacher at the age of eighteen. His wildness was soon channelled into radical politics and in 1902 he emigrated to Switzerland rather than be conscripted into the Italian Army. There he joined agricultural rebels known as Fascists and was in constant police trouble for his activities as a rabble rouser.

However, in 1904, tired of being hounded by Swiss police, he took advantage of a general amnesty for draft dodgers, returned to Italy and served as a private in the Bersaglieri light infantry. Despite his earlier indiscipline he was reported to be a 'good soldier'. Following demobilisation he submerged himself into political journalism in Italy, and in 1909 the Socialist Party offered him a job in Trento, an Italian city still under Austrian occupation. He did not last long. The Austrians deported him when he called for the liberation of Trento.

In 1911 when Italy made war on Turkey in order to conquer Libya, he became an anti-war activist, achieving fame when he was imprisoned for his activities.

In 1914 he took part in the unsuccessful Socialist rebellion and in August that year when Austria went to war against Serbia, he argued through his own newspaper that Italy should declare war on Austria to liberate those Italian towns still under Austrian oppression. Italian nationalism swayed the government and in May 1915 Italy declared war on Austria.

Mussolini, still a reservist in the Bersaglieri, demanded he be mobilised, but the army did not want a rabble rouser in their ranks, and it took months of arguing before they relented. He served as a private, but wrote a regular newspaper column from the trenches. Actually he proved to be a good soldier, popular with all ranks and was made sergeant in early 1917. Shortly afterwards he was wounded testing a new mortar and was invalided out with a pension.

Rejoining the world of political journalism he broke with the Socialists and created his own style of nationalist socialism under the Fascist Party banner.

Following World War I Italy's streets were scenes of brawls and gunfights between fascists and communists and both against the police. Mussolini organised his streetfighters as the Blackshirts of the Squadristi.

In one sense this was his worst move, for everybody loathed the Blackshirts and their bully-boy methods, but on the other hand they came in useful on occasion, and on 30 October 1922 when the Blackshirts on their own initiative decided to march on Rome to seize power, King Vittorio Emmanuele asked Mussolini to be his prime minister with the sole purpose of calling off the Blackshirts.

Mussolini accepted, forced the Blackshirts to back down and alleviated the fears of other political parties by asking mostly non-fascists to help him govern.

This was a brilliant move for he was then able to seize dictatorial power methodically bit by bit. With the end of World War I Italian troops were still in action in Libya where Senussi Arabs refused to give up. This was a forgotten war, which involved few troops and it was used as a training and experimentation ground; for example, here tanks were used in the desert for the first time. It was 1932 before the Senussi gave up.

In October 1935 Mussolini launched a full-scale invasion of Ethiopia using tanks, planes, poison gas and a ground force of eighteen divisions. His army completed the conquest by May 1936, but Ethiopian guerrillas continued to operate.

In December 1936 Mussolini agreed to provide combat troops to aid General Franco's fascist-nationalist army fighting a civil war in Spain, and he dispatched one army and three Blackshirt divisions, later expanding this force with another twenty army and Blackshirt battalions.

With Italian, Portuguese and German help Franco won in March 1939.

A few days later, on Good Friday, Mussolini invaded Albania with four divisions. The nation's tiny army was destroyed over the holiday weekend.

Finally, apart from some guerrilla incidents in Ethiopia, the Italian armed forces settled down to a period of peace.

When Hitler's Germany went to war against Poland, Britain and France in September 1939, Mussolini was determined to remain outside this major conflict, for he did not think Hitler could possibly win.

However, the Germans smashed Poland in weeks, conquered Norway and Denmark in April 1940 and overran the Netherlands and Belgium in May. By 4 June the Germans had thrown the British Army into the sea at Dunkirk and by the 9th they were overrunning France.

Ever the opportunist, Mussolini called in the British and French ambassadors on the 9th and declared war! This appeared to be a very good move for on 20 June under Mussolini's direction General the Prince of Piedmont invaded France with the First and Fourth Armies. Four days later the French surrendered.

In July General the Duke d'Aosta with forces based in Ethiopia and Eritrea put the British on the defensive in Sudan and Kenya. In August d'Aosta conquered British Somaliland. In September Marshal Graziani with forces based in Libya invaded British-held Egypt.

The Armed Forces: The armed forces seemed to outsiders to be in very good shape. With so many conflicts under their belt by 1940 they were obviously experienced. Drawing from a population of 43,800,000 Mussolini only needed to mobilise his reservists on a selective basis, choosing from the age classes 21 to 55, and taking in volunteers from the age of 18. By September 1940 he had recruited an army of 1,630,000, a large air force and the fifth largest navy afloat (below France, Britain, USA and Japan).

Mussolini took considerable interest in his army and was always experimenting and altering. In 1939 he restructured his divisions from tricary to binary, giving them two infantry regiments instead of three, but left the remainder of the division alone, which automatically increased the ratio of artillery guns per infantry battalion.

The new division consisted of two regiments of three infantry battalions each, an engineer battalion, a battalion of eighteen 81mm mortars, a company of eight 47mm anti-tank guns, a company of eight pack mule 47mm guns, a reconnaissance battalion of 45 L3 tanks and 71 motorcycles, and an artillery regiment with twelve 75mm howitzers, twelve 75mm guns, twelve 100mm guns and eighteen 20mm anti-aircraft cannon.

The infantry battalion consisted of riflemen supported by 54 45mm mortars, six 81mm mortars, eight 47mm anti-tank guns and four 65mm guns.

Rifle companies were armed with a 7.35mm bolt action rifle and liberally supplied with the Moschetto-Beretta automatic carbine firing 9mm bullets from either a 10-, 25- or 40-round magazine, the Breda 6.5mm shoulder-fired (or bipod used) automatic rifle with a 20-round clip, the Breda 8mm tripod machine gun weighing 42 pounds using 20-round reusable strips, and a 7.35mm tripod belt-fed machine-gun. From guns and mortars to automatic weapons Italian infantry were, therefore, supported by a greater allotment and variety of firepower than in most armies.

In 1940 most tank units were still provided with the L3, a three-ton, two-man, turretless vehicle mounting twin 8mm machine-guns. The larger M11 carried a 37mm gun in the hull and machine-guns in a turret. Only a handful of M13s had yet reached the troops: a 14-ton tank with a 47mm gun in a turret.

In addition to the army there were the Blackshirts, who raised their own units, though in March 1940 Mussolini came up with a new rule: all Blackshirts on combat duty would become members of the army too! This dashed the hopes of the blackshirts of creating an army to rival the army, such as the SS was doing in Germany. Normally in an all-black uniform, when on duty with the army their uniform was the same grey-green coat and trousers as the army, but their insignia was black and they wore black shirts.

There were blackshirt divisions, but most fought in legions, each consisting of two infantry battalions, a machine-gun company and a mortar company.

The air force had been the envy of the world throughout the 1930s and Italian pilots were known for their courage and stamina.

The SM79 twin engine bomber was very good for light work: dropping 2,700 pounds of bombs on troops or ships; but the other bombers were getting old by 1940. Fighter pilots flew the CR32 and CR42 open cockpit biplanes – much better than they looked – and a few were receiving the impressive Macchi 200 closed cockpit monoplane.

However, a nation can fight too many wars for too few reasons. Every nation has a percentage of would-be warriors, who willingly fight anyone the government designates and Italy had provided her sons with somewhere to fight for 29 out of the last 30 years. Thus all the young firebrands had been more than sated. By 1940 there were few left who still wanted to pursue the excitement of war.

This put the onus on the ordinary Italian soldiers, most of whom were 21-year-old conscripts or older reservists recalled in spring 1940, men who had families, careers and expectations far removed from the battlefield. These fellows were poorly trained and a high ratio of privates to sergeants put many of them on their own in combat situations.

Officers were generally reservists of the same poor martial material as the soldiers, and the few professional officers were more concerned with the comforts of life than its risks. Dedicated warriors were few and far between.

Morale was poor, because all these wars were of Mussolini's making. Furthermore, to have kicked France when she was down was seen as a despicable act, and the soldiers did not like the idea of fighting the British on behalf of the Germans. Many wished it was the other way around.

Mussolini personally damaged the morale of the Slovenian and Croatian troops in the Julia Division by suggesting these non-Italians were not trustworthy.

Even among the Blackshirts morale was low. Indeed many Blackshirts had been sent home from Spain after being judged to be poor fighters. Their battlefield performance did not live up to their bravado on the sidewalks of Italian cities. The Blackshirts may not have questioned Mussolini's foreign policy, but they were angry about the recent decision that they had to obey army rules. A democratic bunch, the Blackshirts did not like taking orders from Italian army officers, whose sole qualification for rank was their links with nobility. They would obey most reluctantly.

In Spain Italian troops had become embarrassed whenever their equipment was compared with that of the Germans. Their 75mm anti-aircraft gun was good, but just about everything else from boots to tanks was shown to be shoddy, unreliable and ineffective. Many an adventure was curtailed through inoperative equipment. The invasion of France in June 1940 was evidence of the lack of tactical knowledge within the higher echelons. The Italian infantry had been thrown into frontal assaults without planning. The result was 1,247 killed, 2,631 wounded, and 3,878 captured including many wounded versus French losses of 37 killed, 42 wounded and 150 prisoners!

Moreover, the men wondered if they would have to put up with cold weather again without adequate clothing. In France in four days 2,151 men had been permanently maimed by frostbite: and that had been in summer!

Grand Strategy: It has been suggested that Mussolini had long had his eye on Greece, but that is not necessarily so. True, in 1940 he launched a diatribe of anti-Greek propaganda, but his writers were overworking their fertile imaginations about many countries at this time.

Certainly since beginning his war with Britain Mussolini had given the impression that he wanted to goad Greece into war: his planes and submarines sank 40 Greek merchant vessels between 10 June and 28 October and his warships confiscated twelve. The most publicised incident was the torpedoing by an Italian submarine of the *Helle* on 15 August, for she was a Greek warship and was publicly transporting a religious icon in time for a sacred holiday.

It is possible that the submarine captain usurped his authority or he thought the *Helle* was British. Either way, Mussolini knew the truth when he lied to the world that no Italian submarine had done the foul deed. Surely, had he meant to push Greece into overt action he would not have denied it, but would have bragged about it.

On 4 October Mussolini met Hitler in the Brenner Pass, ostensibly to discuss their joint war on Britain, in which Italy was bearing the brunt, but instead he had to listen for hours to Hitler boasting about his conquests and how he would restructure the post-war world. Mussolini, a bear of a man who enjoyed rough and tumble play, became embarrassed and finally angry as this weedy, sickly looking Austrian upstaged him.

A week later Mussolini along with his public heard that Hitler had gained control of Romania's oilfields. Mussolini went into a rage at the news: first of all, Hitler must have known of his intended move on the 4th and had not mentioned it to Mussolini: secondly, Italy took most of her oil from Romania and now Hitler controlled the tap!

Mussolini saw this as a personal insult. Yet he could not admit that Hitler, his ally, had gone behind his back, but he could hardly admit he had agreed to such a move. This placed him in an extremely embarrassing position and he wondered how he could regain his self-respect, the fear of the world, the tolerance of his people and the adulation of his fascists. He chose to do something spectacular: he would conquer Greece and he would time the invasion for his next scheduled meeting with Hitler.

King Vittorio Emanuele was the nominal commander in chief of the armed forces, but in reality Mussolini was the commander as chief of Commando Supremo, the high command. His chief of staff was Marshal Pietro Badoglio and below him were the Ministers of War (army), Navy and Air (air force). However, Mussolini held all three positions!

The senior man in the army was General Ugo Cavalero. The senior sailor was Admiral Domenico Cavagnari and top airman was General Pricolo. On 18 October when Mussolini gave the order to invade Greece his entire staff was astonished – not only by the choice of target, but by the timing. They explained that such an event would normally require months of painstaking planning and training. He was giving them days. Knowing Bulgarian hatred of Greeks, Mussolini asked Tsar Boris if he wanted to participate. The Tsar politely declined.

Mussolini agreed to Badoglio's suggestion of General Mario Roatta as commander of the air, land and sea expedition. He was a good leader with experience in Spain and had once been chief of military intelligence. However, Mussolini chose the ground commander, Lieutenant General Sebastiano Visconti-Prasca.

These appointments were not surprises, because there were two political factions at the top of Italy's military tree, the Mussolini supporters and the Badoglioists. Among the latter were Generals Geloso, Vercellino and Roatta. Among Mussolini's sycophants were Generals Visconti-Prasca, Soddu and Cavalero.

Roatta accepted the appointment, but immediately began to argue against the whole plan, stating that through his contacts at military intelligence he had concluded that the Greeks were not only capable of resistance but would fight fanatically. This would be no Albanian weekend. Others expressed their fears, including Emanuele Crazzi the ambassador to Greece, who urged Mussolini to think again, saying the Greeks were strong and would resist.

Badoglio explained that if the decision was irreversible then a very large expedition would be required, far larger than the suggested eight divisions.

Of course, these were not the sorts of thing Mussolini wanted to hear. He was much more pleased with Visconti-Prasca's reaction. That general, who at the age of 53 had never led a major force into battle, was such a yes man that he habitually used the latest sayings of Mussolini in his conversation. One of his favourites was to declare that anything could be done if one had iron will.

When asked what he envisaged in the forthcoming campaign, Visconti-Prasca replied: 'A series of rounding up operations against the Greek forces – estimated to number about 30,000 men.' As for length of operations he anticipated a ten- to fifteen-day operation to occupy the Epirus Mountains, after which the Greeks would surrender. Echoing Mussolini he stated: 'Greeks . . . were not people who liked fighting'.

Mussolini did not want to use more than eight or so divisions as a larger expedition would give the impression the Italians were afraid of the Greeks.

Visconti-Prasca was also eager to keep the force small, for he knew that a larger force would require a commander of higher rank than he, and he saw this as his one chance for glory and did not want to share it: he had already made up his mind not to listen to Roatta.

After hearing the pros and cons, Mussolini made his decision. He ordered Visconti-Prasca to 'attack with the greatest determination and violence'.

Causes of Arrogance: It is obvious that Mussolini was an unbelievably arrogant man to believe that his armed forces could pull off such an accomplishment within days. There are several reasons for his arrogance and top of the list must be his history of survival. Though he cannot be compared to most dictators, for his police state at this time was relatively easy going, he did have enemies and had survived plots and assassination attempts. Eighteen years of this breeds arrogance.

His rise also contributed to his arrogance. He, a peasant, now had a king in his pocket. He, a sergeant, gave orders to generals. He, who had been imprisoned, now ruled an empire. Another cause of arrogance was his military success rate. His navy was holding up well against the much vaunted British navy. His air force was currently bombing Britain. His army had conquered the Libyan desert, the first to do so in a thousand years. He had conquered Ethiopia and wiped out the shame of Adowa. He had conquered Albania, won a major war in Spain, and had forced the British onto the defensive on two fronts, conquered one of their colonies and was invading British-held Egypt.

The Battlefield: The Albanian–Greek border is one of the most mountainous in Europe. The mountains dominate the landscape right from the coast where they shoot up to 5,500 feet and then climb up to 7,500 feet inland.

The four passes through these mountains are the Saranda-Konispol coast road, Dhrin Valley through Kakavi to Kalpaki in the Epirus Mountains, Vijose Valley to Konitsa in the Pindus Mountains, and Devoll Valley from Korce through Bilisht on the edge of the Macedonian Mountains.

The terrain is steep and craggy, with Alpine grasses nearer the coast and forests in the Bilisht area. October brings cold autumn rains that quickly turn into freezing rains in November. Snow blankets the slopes from late November onwards and the temperature falls to –20˚F in mid-December.

Strategy: The plan called for a four-pronged invasion from Albania into Greece by the Tsamouria Corps, Julia Division and XXVI Corps.

The Tsamouria Corps of Lieutenant General Carlo Rossi would advance down the coast road with the Siena Division (9,200 men) and into the Epirus Mountains with the Ferrara Division (12,785 men including a Blackshirt legion). Both would be followed by horse cavalry. In reserve Rossi had the Centauro Armoured Division, consisting of a tank regiment with 163 tanks, the 5th Bersaglieri Regiment of two battalions, a support battalion, an artillery regiment, a mortar company and an engineer company: a total of 4,037 men. Following the corps would be an infantry regiment, a horse cavalry regiment and eighteen artillery batteries.

Advancing through the Pindus Mountains, reporting directly to Visconti-Prasca, would be the Julia Mountain Division containing two regiments of three infantry battalions each, a machine-gun battalion, an artillery regiment of 24 pack mule 75mm howitzers, an engineer battalion, and an anti-tank gun platoon, for a total of 10,800 men and 5,400 mules.

Entering the Macedonian Mountains would be the XXVIth Corps of Lieutenant General Gabriele Nasci, who would advance initially with the Parma Division (12,000 men) and the Piedmont Division (9,300 men), followed by an Albanian battalion, a machine-gun battalion, a tank regiment and fourteen artillery batteries. In reserve Nasci had the Arezzo Division (12,000 men including two Albanian battalions) and Venezia Division (10,000 men).

The San Marco Brigade of marines was standing by to make an amphibious invasion ahead of the Siena Division. Each division would be assigned from 85 to 135 supply trucks depending on size, about one for every hundred men, but the lines of supply would rely primarily on horse-drawn wagons and mules.

The air force agreed to provide 188 fighters, 222 bombers and 52 reconnaissance planes flying from bases in Albania, south-east Italy and the Dodecanese Islands (south-east of Greece).

The navy agreed to protect the 70-mile sea supply line between Italy and Albania, bombard coastal positions and land the marines.

Mussolini had more at stake than his reputation. Edda his daughter chose to serve as a nurse on a hospital ship. His son-in-law and foreign minister, Galeazzo Ciano, chose to serve as a bomber pilot in the same unit as Mussolini's two sons Bruno and Vittorio.

Countdown: The scene was one of frenzied activity at fever pitch 24 hours a day as supply planes flew into Albania: trains filled with soldiers and equipment whizzed past non-stop to the Italian ports; troopships were convoyed across the short stretch of water to Durres and Vlore; and from there a never ending line of trucks, horse-drawn wagons and pack mules snaked their way up mountain roads. Every element of the entire armed forces worked at breaking point, rushing madly to meet the deadline. Though the army failed to be ready by the 28th, this was in truth an outstanding feat of logistics.

Major General Rodolfo Nagli of the Piedmont Division urged his men on towards the Macedonian Mountains, though the weather was cold and some men were already falling ill with respiratory ailments. Over their greenish grey uniforms they wore a knee-length overcoat of similar colour and their round grey helmets glistened in the rain. Nagli was aware his men had the farthest to march.

Colonel Luigi Zacco hurried his 84th Regiment of the Venezia Division into the Macedonian Mountains to be on time to follow the division's 83rd Regiment. Colonel Felice Trizio leader of the Ferrara's 47th Regiment and his battalion commanders such as Lieutenant Colonel Udalgiso Ferucci pushed their men to accomplish the fast marching orders they had been given: to reach the Epirus Mountains in time for the assault. Lieutenant Franco Sampietro led his platoon down the Vijose Valley along with the rest of the Julia Division. He wondered how he would behave under fire and hoped his men would not suspect his fear.

The other officers of the Julia from lieutenant all the way up to Major General Mario Girotti the divisional commander were thinking the same thing. None of them wanted this to be another debacle as they had experienced in France four months earlier.

Major General Gualtiero Gabutti's Siena Division had the shortest distance to cover once they disembarked, which pleased Colonel Giannini of the 32nd Regiment just fine. His men were nervous enough without having to leave the comfort of the fleet's guns. He recognised the tension among his men and knew he would have to lead them from the front.

At 5.30am 28 October Italian planes struck airfields and the transportation network in Greece. That morning Mussolini welcomed Hitler at the rail station with the words: 'Führer, we are on the march.' Hitler was visibly angered. It was a magnificent moment for Mussolini.

The Enemy: Greece is one of the oldest continuous civilisations and the world owes much to these mountain and island people, but in the last few hundred years they have fallen on hard times and by 1940 were a nation that had been pushed around by the British, French and Turks.

Though they had a king, few took this British-imposed dynasty seriously, and 69-year-old General Ioannes Metaxas was the real ruler.

Unfortunately for his people he suspected Mussolini's troop movements were a bluff, another attempt to goad him into doing something rash. Even if it was real, he did not think the Italians could attack so quickly. Therefore, the air raids took him by surprise.

The air force was alerted, but with only 38 serviceable PZL P-24 and Bloch MB151 fighters and 85 Blenheim, Battle and Potez bombers and only two all-weather airfields they could do little and with models from five different countries spare parts would soon be a problem. It was decided that training planes would have to be used in combat. Ironically, Greece was not at war with Germany so German airliners continued to use the same runways as Greek bombers!

Metaxas had three regular divisions, the 8th in the Pindus Mountains, the 9th in the Macedonian Mountains and another watching the Bulgarians. He authorised the call up of his 350,000 reservists into twelve divisions plus smaller units. With a population of only 7,460,000 this would severely damage the nation's socio-economic fabric, but he felt he had little choice.

He reminded the commander of the army, 57-year-old General Alexandros Papagos, that he would receive no large concentrations of artillery, no tank force and would have to rely on the 8th and 9th Divisions, horse cavalry and the élite Evzone Guards to slow down the Italians until the reservists were assembled.

The Battle: Rough seas prevented the Italian navy from landing the marines, but the rain and winds of the border region did not prevent the Greeks from mobilising, as they did so far to the south in a milder climate zone.

By the morning of 30 October two days of advancing in the rain had brought the XXVIth Corps to the east of Bilisht just two miles inside Greece; the Julia Division as far as Konitsa about six miles inside Greece; the Ferrara Division six miles inside at the headwaters of the Dhrin in the Epirus Mountains; and the Siena was also only six miles inside enemy territory and closing upon the Kalamos River, which, reconnaissance reported, was full and fast flowing owing to the rains.

That day the Venezia was ordered to begin following the XXVI Corps.

On the 31st the Ferrara Division meandering its way along the Dhrin Valley was suddenly caught in a very well prepared artillery ambush. The shells were not high calibre , but fired from mountain pack howitzers, though landing on rocky soil they did fearful damage. The ground was poor for digging foxholes, so the Italians could only grin and bear it, their better officers like Colonels Trizio and Ferucci ordering the lieutenants to calm the men.

On 1 November in the Macedonian Mountains the 83rd Regiment of the Venezia, which was supposedly in the rear was struck by elements of the Greek 9th Division, running down the mountainside in their green uniforms and round helmets. Colonel Zacco of the 84th Regiment was alarmed at this news and he led his men to the rescue. Only after a rough fight were the Greeks driven off.

On 2 November the lead battalion of the Julia encountered a rearguard of Evzones, horse cavalry and small mountain guns and immediately attacked it. Girotti allowed two more battalions to reinforce the spearhead unit.

On 3 November the full force of the Julia was in action now as the Greek rearguard held up the division. Girotti brought every available man up front.

On 4 November on the coast the Siena Division was attacked by the Greek 8th Division. Colonel Giannini's 32nd Regiment bore the brunt of the assault, but he led from the front and defeated the enemy: then he organised a crossing of the swollen Kalamos River, where the engineers performed wonders. The 32nd gained the south bank for just 98 casualties, but Giannini was one of their fatalities.

In the Pindus Mountains in freezing rain Greek infantry, dismounted cavalry and Evzones poured down from the mountain slopes 1,500 feet to the valley below on all sides and slammed straight into the lines of supply of the Julia Division. Within minutes Italian mule handlers, clerks, truck drivers, engineers, gunners, teamsters were battling the Greeks with rifles.

Alerted by radio, Girotti radioed Visconti-Prasca for immediate aid, while he ordered some of his infantry to attack to the rear, while others were told to hold in case of an enemy counter-attack from the front. Visconti-Prasca authorised the 5th Bersaglieri Regiment to drive in trucks into the Vijose Valley through Permet.

On 5 November the Bersaglieri entered the valley and made contact with Julia rear-echelon troops, who were fighting for their lives. Many lightly armed or unarmed men had been taken prisoner. This day Papagos received five divisions of reservists, enabling him to organise his front into three corps. His V Corps was ordered to bypass Bilisht and seize the high ground overlooking Korce.

On 6 November General Ubaldo Soddu, Badoglio's deputy, ordered the ground forces to be divided in two: Lieutenant General Vercellino would take command of the new Ninth Army, consisting of the XXVI Corps and the Julia and newly arrived Bari Divisions.

As a sop to Mussolini, Visconti-Prasca was kept on: he would have the Eleventh Army, though his only troops would be Rossi's Tsamouria Corps. Though this was ostensibly Soddu's decision it was made with Badoglio's approval and possibly his wishes. Soddu was in fact a Mussolini puppet, who preferred composing music to soldiering!

On this tenth day of the offensive, Major General Girotti radioed that his Julia could not hold the head of the column and attack to the rear as well, so he was ordering his lead battalions to fall back through Konitsa. Vercellino ordered the Bari Division to take the same route as the Julia and join with that division.

On the 7th the Bersaglieri and the Julia infantry linked up and momentarily celebrated, while the officers took roll call. Girotti was informed his division had suffered 20 per cent killed, wounded and missing.

This same day the Ferrara came under a severe attack in the Epirus Mountains. Again Greeks appeared out of nowhere charging down the slopes. Lieutenant Colonel Ferucci tried to organise a counter-attack to squeeze the Greeks from both ends of the Dhrin Valley, but was killed in the attempt.

Accompanying the Ferrara was the Albanian Tomor Battalion which scattered in all directions: some to surrender to the Greeks, some to join the Greeks, and some to flee: only 120 returned to duty. With the Bersaglieri of the Centauro Division busy aiding the Julia, Rossi had no reserves to draw upon to help the Ferrara and in desperation he ordered a unit of military police to counter-attack.

On the 8th the Julia began to advance again, assisted by the Bari Division, and the Bersaglieri returned to the Centauro. This evening seven supply ships on their way to Albania were intercepted by British warships and sunk.

Mussolini was angry at his navy's failure to protect the convoy, but he was more angry at his army. International public opinion was beginning to ask why had the Italians not won yet?

In a surprise move, and perhaps to save his own neck, Badoglio dismissed Visconti-Prasca on the 11th and replaced him with Lieutenant General Carlo Geloso, giving him care of the Julia and Bari as well as the Tsamouria Corps. In fact Visconti-Prasca was forced into retirement. On the evening of the 11th there was further bad news for the Italian people: thirteen bombers were shot down over Britain, by far the highest loss in a single raid; four supply vessels on their way to Albania were intercepted by the British navy and sunk; and British carrier planes made a night raid on the naval base at Taranto and sank two battleships and damaged a third battleship, a cruiser and a destroyer.

On 14 November the Parma, Piedmont, Arezzo and Venezia Divisions were counter-attacked by the Greek V Corps, which appeared along their lines of communication. Total and utter confusion reigned as Vercellino ordered all units to attack to the rear! The supply columns became jumbled as trucks, horse-drawn wagons and mules were jammed together in freezing rain under artillery fire. Shells blew apart the bodies of horses, mules and men in a bloody tangled mass, while rear-echelon troops armed with rifles made some effort to fend off the hordes of Greeks armed with machine-guns and mortars.

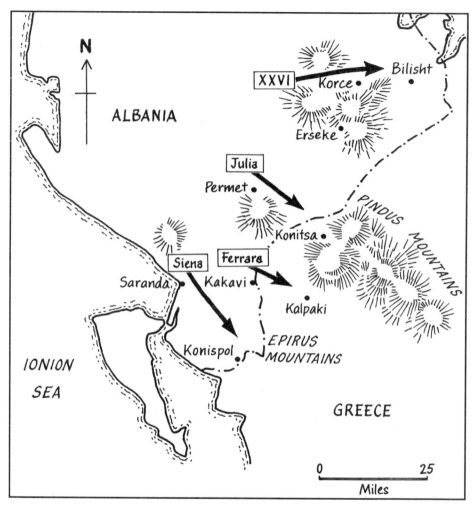

Attacking backwards along the route they had travelled, engineers fought as infantry and were soon joined by artillerymen, who had to abandon their guns. Many of their horses were casualties and the guns rendered immobile.

Of these four divisions the Venezia performed the best, always managing to maintain some sort of cohesion. Only after several hours of madness did the infantry begin to rescue their rear echelons, but always in penny packets. Several times Colonel Zacco personally led his 84th Regiment in bayonet assaults.

On 17 November the Siena was counter-attacked in front by the Greek 8th Division, while the Ferrara was counter-attacked up front and in the rear by the Greek I Corps, and the Bari and Julia Divisions were both assaulted in the front and rear by the II Corps. The Greek tactics were exactly like that of previous battles.

Geloso authorised the Centauro to try to break through to the Ferrara, but when Major General d'Havet of the Bari Division also demanded rescue, there were no further reserves to hand. Geloso reluctantly ordered a unit of customs police to try to reach the Bari!

Lieutenant Sampietro ran around collecting panicky and dazed soldiers of the Julia Division from various units and formed them into an *ad hoc* infantry unit and then led them into a counter-attack. In his part of the battlefield his swift and courageous action saved the day.

This day Lieutenant General Bancale arrived with his VIII Corps staff to take over the Bari and Julia Divisions, reporting to Geloso, and after a brief radio conference he ordered a complete retreat. D'Havet agreed, but Girotti did not want to take part in a second retreat. He flatfooted the order and when Geloso became involved he stood by Girotti: the Julia would hold its ground. Meanwhile Vercellino ordered the Arezzo to attack against Greeks who were almost encircling Korce, an Albanian village in the Ninth Army rear. Within hours Vercellino learned that Greeks had reached Erseke in Albania between Ninth Army and VIII Corps.

Meanwhile Mussolini was receiving constant reports from Roatta and possibly from others who jumped the chain of command, and he knew he had to regroup his expeditionary force. He authorised a complete withdrawal from Greece in order to repair his shattered divisions. Badoglio reminded him he had always asked for a larger expedition: Mussolini now concurred and ordered the nine divisions to be reinforced by twelve divisions!

However, giving an order to retreat was easier than accomplishing it as the divisions now had to reverse everything and advance northwards tail first! Girotti obeyed this order and his Julia launched short ,sharp attacks towards their rear and thereby succeeded in breaking through.

Each day and night the combat was fierce as the temperature dropped steadily. Medical teams did their best, but ran out of supplies in their efforts to combat pneumonia, bandage awesome wounds and treat limbs maimed by the dreaded frostbite. Much of their work was under fire. In enabling his fellow soldiers of the Venezia to escape Colonel Zacco led one bayonet charge too many and was killed.

Breaking through was only solving one problem: all divisions still had to fight off Greek counter-attacks on the head (now the tail) of the columns. Every day each division had to sacrifice a rearguard so that the remainder could survive. Time and again Girotti reported that he could hold, but was ordered to continue the retreat.

On the 21st Vercellino led his four divisions into Albania and that night they slept in the Korce area. Next day they moved out and abandoned the town.

On the 29th a month after they had begun their invasion, the Italians were all back inside Albania and attempting to dig a defence line in the frozen earth. They had little time to reflect on their survival, because the Greeks were constantly shelling them with mountain guns and captured Italian artillery and launching brief attacks. In one such fight the Ferrara Division lost Colonel Trizio.

The Julia had been torn apart: one regiment had only 500 men left out of 3,000 and the other had 1,000. Many others in the division were missing, dead, wounded or maimed by frostbite. On 3 December the Bari and Julia were forced into yet another heartbreaking retreat, northwards from Permet. Next day the Siena lost Saranda and would not stop retreating for another two weeks.

Aftermath: On 6 December the Italians were astonished when Mussolini dismissed Badoglio, replacing him with General Cavallero. Roatta was brought to Rome to head the army and the ground operation was given to Soddu.

Other officers were brought home in disgrace over the next few weeks, including Bancale and Vercellino – and Soddu, who took only two weeks to prove his incompetence.

The Italians continued to attempt to re-enter Greece, but it was only in April following a German invasion of Greece over the Yugoslav border that the Greeks surrendered. Italian troops then occupied most of Greece, the remainder going to Germans and Bulgarians.

Mussolini's Greek adventure cost the Italians almost 100,000 men: 13,755 killed, 12,368 maimed by frostbite, 50,870 wounded and 20,000 taken prisoner and sent to British territory.

Appraisal: The Greek campaign errors of self-styled armed forces commander 'Il Duce' Mussolini were obvious to many, though which could be directly attributable to him the soldiers did not know. The answer is of course all of them, for he assumed responsibility for all when he continually interfered with his subordinates.

His errors basically fall into nineteen categories: intelligence, grand strategy, strategy, ground, manpower, timing, morale, command structure, unit structure, training, equipment, reconnaissance, tactics, pace, specialists, reserves, psyops, counsel and supply.

His intelligence staff knew what the Greeks were capable of, but he refused to listen to anything that did not coincide with his dreams of glory.

Since June 1940 he had been handcuffed to Hitler in a war against Britain, a war which he was winning, but Britain was able to acquire oil from the world at large, whereas both Germany and Italy were highly dependent on the Romanian oilfields, which were beyond the range of British bombers. Mussolini's grand strategy to invade Greece caused the Greek government to invite British bombers to use Greek airfields, which put them within range of the oilfields.

Moreover, his reason for invasion – to gain 30 seconds of one-up-manship over Hitler – was possibly the most ridiculous reason for fighting a war ever thought up, outdoing Swift.

His strategy to invade across a land border, rather than use his powerful navy to land on the Greek coast to seize Athens is incomprehensible. The sea routes would not have been any longer than his current sea routes to Libya, and he already outflanked Greece from the south-east by his possession of the Dodecanese. Politically Mussolini thought big, but militarily he thought too small.

His choice of ground, i.e. mountains, rather than seeking the coastal plain only emphasizes his bad strategy.

His insistence on using less than an eighth of his army, thereby providing insufficient manpower to do the job, was lunacy.

His choice of timing was the worst he could make. By not allowing adequate time for preparation he ensured his army was unprepared. By going into a campaign at this time of year: he forced his navy to take a back seat, owing to rough seas in the region; lost many men through seasonal ailments and frostbite; immobilised his artillery in mud; froze his weapons; and neutralised his air superiority through bad flying weather.

His troops certainly had no trust in their generals, all of whom assigned to this expedition were political favourites of one faction or another. It was Mussolini's job to know that the morale of his troops was poor, but Mussolini the dictator never bothered with such things, unlike Mussolini the sergeant.

The expedition's command structure was slipshod: expedition headquarters above ground headquarters above two corps and a division; switching after nine days to expedition above two armies (one of a single corps and the other of one corps and two divisions); switching after five days to expedition above two armies (one of two corps and one of a corps and two divisions); switching after three days to expedition above two armies (each of two corps). With every change new codes had to be enciphered, new radio links created, new documents written, new supply authorisations established.

Furthermore, Mussolini's tolerance of the political infighting that riddled his high command was nonsensical – his own man was fired twice in two weeks! It destroyed any chance of continuity.

In the year that the United States Army chose tricary divisions as the best structure, Mussolini abandoned ttricary for binary. True this increased his guns per infantry battalion ratio, but he still expected each division with six battalions to accomplish the mission of a ttricary division with nine.

His reservists were poorly trained. As a combat veteran he should have known that good training was essential. One strong division such as the Julia could not prevent a weak neighbour like the Bari from coming apart at the seams.

The poor quality of equipment was also his fault. Having read 'after action reports' from Ethiopia in 1935, he knew that much equipment needed replacing. Experience in Spain only confirmed this. Yet little had been remedied.

Reconnaissance was obviously non-existent. For entire Greek divisions to appear in the Italian rear is shameful and there is no excuse. The Italians simply did not send out adequate scouting teams or aerial reconnaissance.

The tactics of the generals were bad, but again Mussolini knew what they were doing and could have overruled them. They sent divisions down long thin corridors between mountain ranges, just as Stalin had sent his divisions along logging trails. There are many parallels between the Finland and the Greek campaigns and as the latter came just months after the former, and Mussolini could have studied Finnish tactics through his connections with German intelligence, it highlights how ignorant Mussolini was when it came to tactics. He should have remained a sergeant.

His unwillingness to provide sufficient motorised transport for his divisions sentenced them to the pace of a Sunday stroll: giving the Greeks plenty of time to mobilise and counter-attack.

As for Mussolini's use of specialist troops one can only wonder why he sent only one mountain division to a mountain war when he had six available.

His refusal to provide infantry reserves is unbelievable. For an army the size of Italy's to resort to attacking with military police and customs police is a joke.

Mussolini's psyops was self-defeating. Undoubtedly one reason why the Greeks fought so fiercely was that Mussolini had insulted them every day for months, including a sacrilegious insult. He had no real demands for them to satisfy, thus giving them no choice but to fight.

His encouragement of sycophants, meant that he rarely received advice and most of that was bad. By cutting himself off from counsel he denied himself access to the brains of an entire nation.

He had to rely on a sea supply route, but his failure to protect that route was inexcusable. Much of the equipment and provisions his brave men desperately required went to the bottom of the Adriatic.

Furthermore, because of the mad rush to meet the invasion deadline, Italian ships destined for Albania were not combat loaded; instead of placing first needed items into the vessel last, things were simply thrown in willy nilly! This resulted in immediate shortages of necessary equipment such as radio batteries and cooking utensils, which either were not loaded by the supply officers in Italy or were overlooked by supply officers in Albania.

It is easy for infantry to run out of ammunition in a fierce fight, so a constant supply of ammunition is paramount, but because Italian infantry weapons used four different calibres, supply was irregular, for example a shipment of 8mm bullets was of no use to a rifleman with his 7.35mm.

Alternative: The immediate alternative that comes to mind is not to have invaded at all: Greece represented no threat to Italy.

However, once the political decision had been made, militarily two things should have happened: first the invasion should have been put off until spring or early summer; secondly it should have taken the form of several simultaneous amphibious assaults at key points. Greek mobilisation would have been impossible if key areas were quickly seized, and Athens as the political, administrative, cultural, industrial and social centre of the nation should have been the main target.

Hitler had used this strategy to take Norway six months before Mussolini struck Greece, and Hitler's navy was quite inferior to Mussolini's.

Consequences: The Italians gained no glory in Greece and their retreat reinforced the poor opinion many nations had of the Italians as a martial race, an opinion only established in 1917. The British government and press were especially vitriolic in their ridicule of Italian military capability even to the point of publicly stating, as if it were fact, that all Italians were natural born cowards.

In Italian-occupied France French boys wrote graffiti saying: 'Greeks! Stop here!'

The Italian defeat at the hands of the British in Egypt in December 1940 added fuel to the flames of prejudice.

The Battle's Place in History: In fact for two generations afterwards the Italian defeat in Greece was cited as evidence that Italians were and are cowards.

For a generation it was also cited as evidence that Greeks were efficient warriors, though a lack of any other evidence has failed to sustain this belief.

Prejudice never has a firm foundation. The Greeks were not supermen, and the Italians were not cowards. In fact the one constant that comes from a serious study of the Greek campaign is the fatalistic courage shown by the ordinary Italian soldier. He deserved better.

Pearl Harbor

The Battlefield: The largest campaign battlefield ever chosen was that picked by Japan in 1941. It stretched from Hawaii to Malaya, Japan to Australia.

The time difference was an added complication as the sun only shines on one place at a time and this difference had to be kept in focus. Washington DC was five and a half hours ahead of Hawaii, London five hours ahead of Washington, Singapore another eight hours ahead, Tokyo another one hour ahead, and Hawaii another four and a half hours (but minus a day). So if it was 7 December 7.30am in Hawaii it would be 1.00pm in Washington, 6.00pm in London, 8 December 2.00am in Singapore and 8 December 3.00am in Tokyo. (For the following narrative all dates and times are Hawaiian.)

Hawaii consists of several islands of which Oahu was the most useful to the American navy. A rough rectangle with sides approximately 15 by 25 miles it contained the finest natural harbour in the eastern Pacific, Pearl Harbor, which was really several bays with Ford Island as the centrepiece. By 1941 Oahu contained no less than seven army bases and seven airfields in addition to the Pearl Harbor naval base, which was home to the US Pacific Fleet. The island also contained the capital city, Honolulu.

The British chose Singapore as a home for the Far Eastern Fleet, their equivalent of the Pacific Fleet. An island similar in size to Oahu, with several military bases and four airfields, Singapore had the added advantage of being at the end of the Malay peninsula, a British colony.

By October 1941 the one great difference between Pearl Harbor and Singapore was that the British had yet to assign any large warships to their Far Eastern Fleet.

Background: The Japanese invaded China in 1931, but it was not until 1937 when the Japanese conquered the city of Shanghai, which had an international business settlement protected by British and American troops, that the Americans and British could see at first hand the violent destruction waged upon the Chinese by the Japanese, and when American and British warships on Chinese rivers were bombed by Japanese aircraft, the British and American governments seriously denounced the Japanese.

Inquiring as to the ability of the British Empire to fight Japan if the Japanese got too big for their boots, the British government was informed by their admirals that Singapore would have to hold for 70 days before any fleet could come to its rescue, because the naval base had no navy!

However, when Britain declared war on Germany on 3 September 1939 both Britain and the USA turned their attention towards Germany not Japan.

As Germany had a decent sized navy, the British admirals changed their estimate that Singapore would now have to hold out six months before a fleet could come to its rescue.

Looking into the matter more deeply, Winston Churchill, the First Lord of the Admiralty (British political navy chief), declared that Singapore with its heavy coastal guns and 20,000 strong garrison should be able to hold out against 50,000 Japanese for four or five months. Though this was less than the six months required, he stated that Singapore was a 'fortress'.

This estimate of the time required to rescue Singapore lengthened again on 10 June 1940 when Italy, which had a powerful navy, declared war on Britain, and it lengthened again on 22 June when the French surrendered, thus removing their fleet from Britain's arsenal, and it lengthened again on 3 July when the British under Churchill's orders – he was now Prime Minister - attacked the French, thereby putting the French fleet on the list of Britain's enemies.

The British navy certainly had its hands full now and could not hope to rescue Singapore.

Britain's impotency as a Pacific naval power made the American navy more precious as a counter to Japanese expansion, and in July 1940 Franklin D. Roosevelt, the American President, declared an embargo on aviation fuel destined for Japan. The British followed suit, at once. This hurt the Japanese, because the United States was Japan's biggest provider of materials for her war industries.

Roosevelt was still concerned about Germany, though he had not declared war, and in August 1940 he transferred 50 old destroyers to the British in return for access to British islands in the Caribbean. These islands were then turned into American bases to enable American planes and ships to search for German submarines, so that they could report their position to the British. For all intents and purposes the American armed forces had become a reconnaissance arm of the British: obviously an act of war against Germany.

American warships were soon escorting British shipping in American coastal waters, and over the next few months they extended their escort service to the mid-Atlantic. American sailors in the Atlantic were effectively at war.

On 16 September 1940 Roosevelt signed the Selective Service Act, enabling him to conscript young Americans to enlarge the armed forces. The American public was made aware that war might be just around the corner.

A week later the Japanese invaded French Indo-China, and this alerted the Americans and British to the fact that the Japanese were no longer satisfied with conquering Chinese villages. However, at that moment Britain was under German air attack and possibly facing an invasion, so the only reaction from the Anglo-Americans was an American embargo on scrap iron shipments to Japan. In November the embargo was extended to all iron and steel, and the British followed suit.

It was now that US intelligence began to inform Roosevelt quite regularly that the Japanese were planning to attack the USA!

In early 1941 the Americans began training British personnel in the USA, assigning American 'observers' to British ships and planes, and on 29 January senior British officers arrived in Washington for permanent talks on war planning.

Meanwhile Roosevelt was alerted by Joseph Grew, ambassador to Tokyo, that there were rumours in Japan that the Japanese navy was studying the feasibility of an attack on Hawaii!

Additionally, intelligence kept Roosevelt informed of considerable disturbing evidence and his code breakers began to decode Japanese 'war' messages. As a result Roosevelt froze all Japanese assets in the United States on 25 July 1941.

Three days later the Japanese increased their garrison in Indo-China. The Americans replied with an embargo on oil. Roosevelt knew this would force the Japanese to a timetable, for they only had enough oil stocks to last a few months, so they must attack soon or not at all. Yet, he could hardly be expected to continue to supply them.

However, the British were still exporting rice to Japan from Burma.

Roosevelt also authorised a 'civilian' fighter plane squadron to go to China to fight the Japanese.

On 4 September 1941 Roosevelt and his commanders were distracted by the Germans again when the US destroyer *Greer*, using sonar to guide a British plane towards a German submarine, was fired upon by the submarine. The torpedo missed, whereupon the *Greer* dropped depth charges, alsomissing. This was the first known 'fight' between the Americans and Germans.

A week later Roosevelt took the gloves off: he ordered American ships and planes to shoot at German submarines on sight: as close as he could get to a declaration of war on Germany without asking Congress.

This order was meant for the entire armed forces, including those in the Pacific where German raiders were known to be operating.

There were several incidents as American warships escorted British convoys, but the first casualties came on 17 October when the destroyer USS *Kearny* was torpedoed and eleven sailors were killed.

On the 30th the destroyer USS *Reuben James* escorting a British convoy was torpedoed and sunk, only 45 of her 160 crew surviving.

On 13 November Congress authorised the arming of all American merchant ships and opened all war zones to them. While the Americans were sliding into war against Germany, the British were sliding into war against Japan. Hoping to deter the Japanese from any further expansion, they set aside the aircraft carrier *Indomitable*, the battleship *Prince of Wales* and the battle cruiser *Repulse*, which were to unite with the destroyers at Singapore to become Force Z, the teeth that the Far Eastern fleet had so far lacked.

Though three capital ships were not much to stop the Japanese navy, the British hoped that the despatch of these vessels, which were obviously sorely needed to fight Germany, France and Italy, would be seen as an indication of how strongly the British felt.

Unfortunately, the *Indomitable* ran aground and the British decided they could not spare another carrier, so the other vessels sailed on alone in November 1941.

British officers in Singapore had begun to suspect that the Japanese might try a takeover of Thailand as a prelude to an invasion of Malaya and Singapore, so they came up with Plan Matador: if the Japanese invaded Thailand the British would also, to fight them there before they had overrun the Thais and were in a position to invade Malaya.

The Navy: By the early twentieth century the pride of any large navy was the battleship, because gun power was the dominant factor. Since 1775 American warships had performed exceedingly well against the British, French, Confederates, Germans, and in countless skirmishes at sea against pirates and on far away shores against intemperate tribal leaders, but only once, against the Spanish in 1898, had American battleships mastered an enemy fleet. This sole success influenced Congress to spend the money for a whole new generation of battleships.

Following World War I, in which the United States Navy fought only small actions, the British and Americans gathered together the leading naval powers to limit fleets, as a way of maintaining Anglo-American supremacy. The result was the Washington Naval Treaty of 1922, which allowed Britain to sail twenty battleships and battle cruisers, the Americans eighteen, the Japanese ten, the French seven and Italy six. Moreover, none should weigh more than 35,000 tons or have guns bigger than 16-inch, and the total capital tonnage should maintain a ratio of Britain 5: USA 5: Japan 3: France 2: Italy 2.

Battleships were massive vessels that required several years to build, a year or more to fit out and much money to maintain: hence there were fewer than 70 in the world and this included museum pieces.

In 1930 the Japanese argued for a change and the result was the London Naval Treaty, which altered the tonnage rate to Britain 10: USA 10: Japan 7: and limited these restrictions to 1936. For the Japanese to be so bothered to acquire an extra 10per cent tonnage, shows how valuable battleships were perceived to be.

American admirals were so battleship focused that by 1941 they were building twelve new battleships.

The Americans required a large navy for they had two shores, the Atlantic and the Pacific, and kept a colony, the Philippines, at the opposite end of the Pacific. Therefore, two fleets had been created, the Atlantic and the Pacific, and the warships were more or less equally divided between them.

Pearl Harbor was the home of the Pacific Fleet, which in December 1941 contained the following battleships:

California 35,200 tons, 1,480 crew, twelve 14-inch guns;

Maryland 39,100 tons, 1,916 crew, twelve 16-inch guns;

West Virginia 40,300 tons, 2,182 crew, twelve 16-inch guns;

Nevada 34,000 tons, 1,301 crew, ten 14-inch guns;

Oklahoma 34,000 tons, 1,301 crew, ten 14-inch guns;

Pennsylvania 36,500 tons, 2,290 crew, twelve 14-inch guns (currently in dry dock);

Arizona 36,500 tons, 2,290 crew, twelve 14-inch guns;

Tennessee 35,200 tons, 1,480 crew, ten 14-inch guns.

A 14-inch gun could fire a shell weighing 1,400 pounds up to eighteen miles, and a 16-inch gun could fire a 2,100-pound shell the same distance. All crew members had to go inside during firing, for the aerodynamics of these massive shells could suck a man overboard.

No other warship could open fire at more than twelve miles, so a battleship could plaster a smaller vessel with impunity. One shell from a battleship could explode a destroyer or sink a merchant ship, but a battleship could suffer serious punishment from enemy shells and still fight.

Up to seventeen miles inland no column of tanks or body of troops in the open could stand up to a battleship, and cities such as New York, London and Tokyo were at the mercy of a battleship, which could shell them from over the horizon.

Yet as early as 1919 supporters of air power had claimed that aircraft could bomb or torpedo a battleship to the bottom of the sea. When an American, Billy Mitchell, proved this, by sinking an unmanned captured battleship, he was court martialled on a trumped up charge! Admirals liked battleships and if reality proved them vulnerable then reality would have to be ignored!

On 11 November 1940 a handful of British biplanes from a carrier attacked the Italian naval base at Taranto at night and sank two battleships and damaged another. The British press might see this as an example of Italian ineptitude, but British admirals shook their heads in disbelief, realising that battleships really were vulnerable to air attack. American admirals, notwithstanding their boasting, in 1939 had authorised a refitting of battleship anti-aircraft artillery (AAA), so that by 1941 each vessel had ten or twelve 5-inch guns, which could fire six explosive shells a minute up to 30,000 feet, a height which few bombers could reach and which precluded accurate bombing. All warships were liberally fitted with 40mm guns, that could fire at a rate of 150 rounds per minute up to 17,000 feet. Additionally .50in calibre machine-guns were fitted.

Carriers were assigned to protect battleships in daylight, but at sundown the roles were reversed, for few carrier pilots could land at night.

Inside Pearl Harbor the eight battleships had the added protection of shore based AAA and the AAA of any other warship in port, which on 7 December 1941 included: the old battleship *Utah*, a 23,400 ton vessel with 519 crewmen used as an AAA trainer; the heavy cruisers *San Francisco* and *New Orleans*; the light cruisers *Detroit, Helena, Honolulu, Raleigh* and *St Louis*; 22 destroyers plus three in dry dock; a gunboat; nine minesweepers; a command ship; a support ship; seven minelayers; two oil tankers; three seaplane tenders; three repair ships; a dredger; four submarines; three tenders and an auxiliary ship.

Of the navy's seven aircraft carriers three were assigned to the Pacific Fleet, but on 7 December the *Saratoga* was refitting at San Diego, the *Lexington* was delivering planes to Midway, and the *Enterprise* was on her way to Pearl Harbor. Also at sea were several cruisers and destroyers.

The Commanders: While Winston Churchill was Prime Minister of an empire engaged in total war in Europe and Africa, he could not pay as much attention to Japanese sabre rattling as he would have liked.

In November 1940 he chose 62-year-old Sir Robert Brooke-Popham to control the defences of all British possessions in the far east: Burma, Malaya-Singapore, Brunei, Sarawak and Hong Kong. The low priority that he gave to these colonies is exemplified by this choice, because Brooke-Popham was brought out of retirement for the job. Surely, had he been judged to be a valuable leader, he would not have been left in retirement during fourteen months of war with Germany. Furthermore, he was an air force officer, not a navy man, though the only manner in which all these places could be reinforced and defended was by sea.

It seemed to Brooke-Popham that his was to be a backwater administrative job, especially as he was informed he would only be required until December 1941. To add to the offhand method of his appointment he was told he would not have the authority to directly control his air, ground and naval commanders.

The British naval commander in the far east, Rear Admiral Sir Geoffrey Layton, was instructed in November 1941 that when Force Z arrived he would not command it, but would continue in his capacity of caretaker of naval bases and coastal defence.

The man Churchill chose to command Force Z, Rear Admiral Tom Phillips, was Nelsonian in his planning and also in appearance, being only 5 feet 2 inches. Strictly a staff officer, he had risen to become a deputy chief of staff and had never commanded a flotilla, so his appointment raised quite a few eyebrows, especially as he had argued against sending the force to Singapore.

His appointment can only be understood in light of the fact that the best sea commanders were needed to lead flotillas against the French, Italians and Germans.

Unlike Churchill, Roosevelt had the time to take a long look at the global situation and divide his attention equally between the existing German threat and the potential Japanese threat. Having been elected President in 1932 and 1936 he had to win another election in 1940 before he could move forward towards his war aims.

Following his 1940 electoral victory he began to wage war against Germany as much as the law allowed without asking Congress. His style of leadership was to pick a few knowledgeable subordinates and use their energy and expertise, rarely acquiring a consensus and often not even a compromise, but that was what he wanted: he would not tolerate sycophants.

His army commander, General George Marshall, was considered the grand old man of the army, and was treated with the utmost reverence by all officers including generals such as Patton and Eisenhower. One reason he was popular was that he did not interfere in how a general ran his command.

Roosevelt's air leader, General 'Hap' Arnold, was more of an unmilitary fly boy, who wanted to be up in the clouds not behind a desk, and who believed the long range bomber could win a war by itself if applied correctly. In December 1941 Arnold ordered B-17s, currently the world's finest bomber, to the Philippines, in hopes they would sink a Japanese invasion fleet before it reached that American colony.

Roosevelt took special pride in the navy – he had been Under Secretary of the Navy during World War I – and in 1939 he had promoted 59-year-old Admiral Harold Stark to command it. Stark proved to be an excellent administrator with just enough quirks of character to make him acceptable to Roosevelt.

Immediately below Stark were Admirals Ernest King, Commander in the Atlantic, and Husband E. Kimmel, who wore two hats, Commander in the Pacific (CincPac) and Commander of the Fleet (CincUs [pronounced 'sink us']). While the fleet was in Pearl Harbor, CincPac headquarters, this was no problem, but if it put to sea this soft spoken 59-year-old Kentuckian was expected to be in two places at once. Kimmel was not a sociable person, but a tough workaholic, who had risen as a cruiser and battleship commander, though he had seen no action. He had not brought his wife out to 'Pearl', so that he could concentrate on his assignment.

The army commander of Hawaii was 61-year-old Lieutenant General Walter Short, who had seen infantry combat against Mexicans in 1916 and had trained machine-gunners in World War I. He was responsible for the 24th and 25th Divisions and the Hawaii National Guard, plus rear-echelon forces and the air force.

Short's air commander was Major General Frederick Martin, who had become a pilot at the age of 39. Now twenty years later he was the most experienced pilot in the air force. In September he had startled everyone by suggesting they run exercises based upon a Japanese carrier raid on Hawaii!

Wearing his CincPac hat Kimmel was expected to designate someone to meet regularly with Short to coordinate Hawaii's defence, but the army and navy had a long tradition of non-cooperation and often one service chose a course of action simply because it went against the wishes of the other service.

Short and Kimmel were less service blinkered than most and they ironed out any difficulties on the golf course.

Causes of Arrogance: The British navy was the finest afloat and the American navy the second finest, and as they were now allies it is understandable that their admirals had begun to think of themselves as unbeatable. In battleship actions the British had bested the Italians and Germans.

Kimmel could not help but think his fleet was invulnerable in Pearl Harbor for the simple reason it was 2,000 miles from the nearest Japanese-held island and 3,400 miles from the main base of the Japanese fleet. As carrier planes only had a range of 300 miles or so, it would take a Japanese fleet ten days of fast sailing just to get within range and by then he would have been alerted.

If by some fluke Japanese carrier torpedo bombers made it to Pearl Harbor, their torpedoes would explode as soon as they struck the sea bed – the navy ordnance department had assured him that aerial torpedoes dived more than 60 feet down before levelling off and thus the water in Pearl Harbor was too shallow for them. As a result Kimmel had not bothered to install anti-torpedo nets around his ships.

One thing did concern Kimmel. He had not received enough long range reconnaissance planes to patrol continuously in all directions. Therefore, he chose to patrol only towards the south-west.

On Oahu Martin's Army Air Force had plenty of bombers for anti-shipping work and possessed the excellent P-40 Warhawk fighter, which could fly at 335mph, could stay aloft two hours and could climb to 10,000 feet in just four and a half minutes to use its six .50in calibre machine-guns against Japanese bombers. The navy fighter, the Wildcat, was as good as the Warhawk.

In fact Martin, under Short's direction, was so confident he had recently spared some of his fighters to reinforce Wake and Midway.

In Singapore Air Chief Marshal Sir Robert Brooke-Popham and his staff knew November was the beginning of the Malaya-Singapore monsoon season and surely the Japanese would not start a campaign at this time! In other words they decided that it was a case of 'probably not now', and 'if now, only Thailand', and 'if Thailand and Malaya, then only northern Malaya until the monsoon ends'.

Brooke-Popham was also highly confident, because he had a poor opinion of the Japanese, calling them 'sub-human'. Many of his officers thought along similar lines and were angry that they might have to fight the Japanese, as they considered them an unworthy enemy, unlike the Germans or Italians.

While most Americans and British did not consider the Japanese to be sub-human, nonetheless the Japanese at this time were a joke in the English-speaking world. The Mr. Moto series of films made in Hollywood that featured a Japanese detective were popular because of the stories and because of the funny situation pretending that a Japanese could really be intelligent enough to be a detective. Mr. Moto was played by an immigrant Jew, Peter Lorre, not by a racial Japanese, thousands of whom Hollywood (in Los Angeles) had access to.

The British and American press actually claimed that Japanese pilots could not aim bombs well owing to their slant eyes!

While the Americans did not belittle Japanese battleships, they did belittle the ability of Japanese admirals to use them correctly. Indeed some wished the Japanese would 'try something'. Then the army, marine and navy AAA could knock Japanese planes out of the sky by the hundred and the excellent army fighters pursue the remnants and shoot them down. At the same time, the army and navy bombers would sink their small craft and destroyers and the carriers could send planes to damage their battleships and carriers. Then the American battleships would sail out to deliver the *coup de grace*. 'Just let them try' was the cocky attitude of the Americans.

Countdown: On 27 November 1941 Marshall and Stark issued a war warning to all commands, and named those bases at risk. Hawaii was not mentioned. Moreover, Roosevelt was on vacation in Georgia.

Nonetheless Short decided that, because there was a large Japanese immigrant community on Oahu, spies and saboteurs might blend into that community, therefore he ordered all aircraft to be bunched together, so that they could be easily protected from saboteurs, and they were to be kept without ammunition or fuel to cut down on the risk of explosions. He also ordered an increase of sentries on all airfields and bases.

Normally the island's radar station was shut down at 4.00am. Short ordered it to be manned until 7.00am.

Kimmel thought that the Japanese might try a diversionary raid on Hawaii using submarines, so he made sure there would always be a duty destroyer at the entrance to Pearl Harbor. Just in case of attack by planes or saboteurs he ordered a quarter of all the .50in calibre machine-guns aboard ship to be manned at all times.

Tom Phillips flew into Singapore on the 29th (30th local time) and met with Brooke-Popham and his staff. Orders had come from London that Brooke-Popham and Phillips were to be jointly responsible for strategy in the Far East, despite the fact that Phillips had only just arrived and Brooke-Popham was scheduled to leave in a few days. Layton informed Phillips that in the far east area the British, Netherlands and Australian navies had eight cruisers, ten destroyers and some submarines and gunboats, and that the *Repulse* and *Prince of Wales* were due to arrive at Singapore within hours.

Intelligence informed them that there was solid evidence from spies, radio interception, and sightings that a Japanese naval task force was forming in Cam

Right: Monongahela. At the time of the Monongahela the purpose of ornate uniforms, as worn by this British Grenadier, and line soldier to the right, was to instil enough pride in troops that they would march into the enemy's guns. (2648 P. J. Haythornthwaite Collection)

Left: At Saratoga British troops were easy targets for Patriot riflemen. (Print after P. W. Reynolds. 2983 P. J. Haythornthwaite Collection)

Left: New Orleans. Well dressed, like this soldier of the line, British infantry marched without hesitation into Jackson's guns. (Print by Gentry. 2005 P.J. Haythornthwaite Collection)

Below: With blue and grey uniforms on both sides, the Battle of Bull Run was as confusing as this correspondent's drawing suggests. (Mansell Collection)

Above: Little Big Horn. 'Buried where they fell': The original graves of the 7th Cavalry, looking southwest from 'Custer Hill'. The tree line marks the Little Big Horn River: The black tombstone is Custer's. Note the lack of natural cover. This photo was taken on the anniversary of the battle. (Author's collection)

Below: Isandhlwana. Artist's impression of the last moments of organised resistance. (Print by G. Durand. 2902 Mansell Collection)

Left: Poland. The thousands of Polish lancers may have impressed illiterate Polish villagers, but they failed to impress German machine gunners. (HU40880, by permission of the Trustees of the Imperial War Museum, London)

Below: Poland. Shattered by air attacks and bewildered by the speed of the German advance, this Polish unit is then ordered to surrender. (HU5311, by permission of the Trustees of the Imperial War Museum, London)

Above: Finland. Two snow suited Finnish soldiers pass one of the countless piles of Soviet dead. The ground was too frozen to dig graves. (HU52939, by permission of the Trustees of the Imperial War Museum, London)

Below: Pearl Harbor. Left to right, the burning and sinking *West Virginia*, the trapped and damaged *Tennessee*, the smoking and sunken *Arizona* and Ford Island on the extreme right. It was almost impossible for the Japanese flyers to miss as the ships were so close together. (MYF22545, by permission of the Trustees of the Imperial War Museum, London)

Above: Malaya. Japanese tanks in Malaya were first hurt by an Australian ambush. (MH33566, by permission of the Trustees of the Imperial War Museum, London)

Below: Kasserine. The high silhouette of the American Lee is evident as it leads a British truck past a knocked out German Mark III in Tunisia. (NA190 by permission of the Trustees of the Imperial War Museum, London)

bove: Korea. When the
ommunists advanced,
illions of South Koreans
ed, blocking the roads.
3F166, by permission of the
rustees of the Imperial War
Iuseum, London)

ight: The mountainous
errain of Korea in which
ntire armies hid. (MH32763,
y permission of the Trustees
f the Imperial War Museum,
ondon)

Above: Korea. British Marines in borrowed US clothing during the retreat from the Changjin Reservoir, Korea. (KOR/V3 by permission of the Trustees of the Imperial War Museum, London)

Left: Kuwait. Saddam Hussein's arrogance resulted in his vehicles being destroyed, his soldiers killed and his enemy hovering proudly overhead. (GLF590 by Permission of the Trustees of the Imperial War Museum, London)

Ranh Bay, Indo-China, which they suspected was destined for Thailand or Malaya. They speculated whether or not a Japanese attack would be preceded by a declaration of war.

However, there was no sense of urgency in Singapore and it was decided to ask the Netherlands Navy to send a couple of submarines to Indo-China to take a look.

Meanwhile Brooke-Popham asked Churchill for permission to launch Matador, his pre-emptive strike into Thailand, but next day Churchill refused on the grounds that this might precipitate a war with Japan and if Britain was seen to be the aggressor it would alienate the Americans.

Churchill did not know that some American intelligence officers in Washington thought the Japanese might attack this very day as it was a Sunday! When no attack materialised, they concluded it would be the following Sunday, 7 December.

Seeing no urgency, Major General Sir Arthur Percival, Malaya–Singapore ground commander, flew off to Sarawak 450 miles across the sea on an inspection.

When he received more alarming intelligence data Brooke-Popham issued a state of emergency in Malaya–Singapore calling up all reservists and part time soldiers. Naturally, colonists and natives alike were alarmed: this was the first indication something was wrong. Brooke-Popham thought better of Percival's trip and radioed him to return.

Meanwhile the British government informed the Americans of the Japanese task force, but emphasised it was probably destined for Thailand.

On Monday 1 December there were great cheers along the quayside at Singapore naval base as the *Prince of Wales* and *Repulse* arrived. The officers of the *Prince of Wales* held a reception for dignitaries while the crewmen hit the fleshpots.

That day Japanese submarines were seen south of Indo-China.

On the Tuesday an American submarine counted 21 transports in Cam Ranh Bay. Kimmel in Pearl Harbor was more concerned over the main Japanese battle fleet, and he asked his intelligence staff for its latest known position and they replied they did not know where it was. Somewhat surprised, he asked, half jokingly: 'Do you mean to say, they could be rounding Diamond Head (twelve miles distant) and you wouldn't know it?' They sheepishly grinned.

Phillips was becoming concerned and he took the unusual step of asking Churchill for four more battleships. He of all people knew the state of the navy at this time and that Churchill could not possibly acquiesce.

However, he too felt no sense of urgency and flew off to the Philippines, 1,400 miles away, to confer with the Americans.

On Wednesday Phillips met with Admiral Thomas Hart, commander of the American Asiatic Squadron, who by coincidence was the same height, and then they talked with General Douglas MacArthur, commander of all forces in the Philippines. MacArthur was polite, but let the navy men get on with it. He knew nothing of naval affairs. Despite Phillips's request for four battleships not being approved yet, he talked to the Americans as if he would soon have them.

However, Churchill's reply reached him while he was still with the Americans: not only would Churchill not send them, but he suggested Force Z sail to Australia or Ceylon!

This must have been embarrassing for Phillips. He took the hint and ordered the *Repulse* to Australia. The *Prince of Wales* would follow as soon as her boilers were cleaned in Singapore.

The same day Churchill mentioned the idea of Matador to Roosevelt, and was surprised that the President approved the concept. On the Thursday Churchill telegraphed Brooke-Popham that he could initiate Matador if he saw fit.

On Friday an American submarine reported that Cam Ranh Bay was empty.

Hours later an Australian reconnaissance plane sighted the task force heading in the direction of Thailand and Malaya.

Brooke-Popham discussed Matador with Percival, telling him to alert his troops, then telegraphed Phillips about Churchill's decision. Phillips told Hart, who at once offered four destroyers for the operation, without checking to see if Roosevelt really did approve. Phillips ordered the *Repulse* to return.

Meanwhile on Oahu, as it was Friday and no alert orders having been received, many men began a weekend pass, the officers hoping to spend the time in the cooler mountains, the enlisted men hitting the bars of Honolulu. Married men hoped to spend some quality time with their families.

Fifty-six minutes into Saturday (Hawaii time) 60 miles off Malaya a British Blenheim reconnaissance aircraft sighted the Japanese task force, but was fired upon by AAA and flew out of range.

Forty-nine minutes later American naval intelligence intercepted a message from Tokyo to the Japanese embassy in Washington alerting embassy staff to get ready to decode a fourteen-part message answering Roosevelt's demands.

Fifteen minutes later Brooke-Popham was informed that the Blenheim had been fired upon. He did not issue an alert, nor did he inform Churchill.

Thirty minutes later American intelligence began to decode the long message to the embassy.

At 5:10am that morning the American government was informed of the Australian sighting.

The same morning Phillips returned to Singapore and ordered the *Prince of Wales* to prepare to sail.

After breakfast Kimmel's staff learned there was bad weather to the north-west of Oahu. Kimmel's order to fly reconnaissance only to the south-west seemed to be appropriate on this day at least, for surely no fleet would deliberately sail into such rough weather. If the Japanese were out there, they would not be to the north-west.

After cleaning up from his air trip Phillips met with Brooke-Popham, who had decided it was too late for Matador to be implemented. They then went to a previously scheduled meeting with British, American, Netherlands and Australian liaison officers.

At 3.15pm Roosevelt received the decoded message to the Japanese embassy, minus the last part.

Five minutes later a British PBY reconnaissance aircraft shadowing the task force was shot down by a Zero fighter!

At 6.16pm thirteen B-17 bombers left California for Oahu on their way to the Philippines, as per Arnold's orders. As there was no alert they did not carry ammunition for their machine-guns.

On Oahu that Saturday evening sailors, soldiers and airmen not on duty hit the night spots of Honolulu. Only a few stayed aboard or in barracks to write letters or read or listen to KGMB Radio. There was a dance at each of the several officers' clubs.

Short's evening was interrupted by the FBI, who played for him a recording of a telephone call between someone in Tokyo and the Japanese wife of a Honolulu dentist. It sounded highly suspicious.

At 10.00pm a Norwegian merchant ship was stopped by the Japanese task force off Malaya, her crew was taken off and she was sunk. She was not able to radio for help.

The Enemy: The Japanese had suffered the humiliation of British and American interference in the mid-nineteenth century and this sparked their determination to become a nation too strong to be pushed around. Recognising their geographic position to be similar to that of the British: an island nation with a large population, but no natural resources; they imitated the British by creating a powerful navy. Like the British they would exploit colonies for raw materials, turn them into manufactured products at home, then sell them back at exorbitant prices to the colonies. Their navy would gain the colonies and protect the sea lanes.

They also adopted 'Copenhagen-ing', named for the British surprise attacks on Copenhagen in 1801 and 1807. With a navy modelled on the British, the adoption of Copenhagen-ing and a trust in torpedoes they defeated the Chinese in 1894 to acquire Formosa and the Russians in 1904-05 to gain Korea. They even sank a Russian fleet in open battle at Tsushima Straits.

Unlike the British, however, they did not match imperialism with democracy at home and by the 1930s an army clique had gained control of the government. The navy argued against them, but were grudgingly dragged into their schemes bit by bit. Then in early 1941 the army asked for a navy plan to 'get the Americans off their back'.

Ironically this duty fell on one of the leaders of the anti-army faction, Admiral Isoroku Takano-Yamamoto. Wounded at Tsushima Straits at the age of 21 in 1905, he had been one of the leading thinkers in the navy, becoming a proponent of air power as early as 1915. He knew carriers. He also knew the Americans and British: he had attended Harvard University for two years, spent three years in Washington and several months in London. In 1934 as Vice-Minister of the Navy he was vociferously opposed to an alliance with Hitler and as a result was somewhat demoted to command of the Combined Fleet in 1939.

The plan he came up with was to knock out the Pacific Fleet in Pearl Harbor with carrier planes. Studying the British raid on Taranto he found that aerial torpedoes could be modified to dive only a few feet before levelling off. With currently ten carriers to choose from, he picked the *Akagi*, *Kaga*, *Hiryu*, *Soryu*, *Shokaku* and *Zuikako*, which would be escorted by two battleships, three cruisers, eleven destroyers and auxiliary vessels. They would sail in radio silence, able to hear but not talk back. In this manner they would simply disappear into the vast Pacific.

At the same moment as other Japanese task forces would be attacking Thailand, Malaya, the Philippines and Hong Kong, Yamamoto would unleash his planes 230 miles north-west of Oahu: 49 Nakajima B5N2s carrying bombs and 40 carrying torpedoes; 51 Aicni D3A2 dive bombers; and 43 Mitsubishi Zero fighters. The Zeros would keep American fighters at bay, while the torpedo bombers would aim at the battleships and carriers. The dive bombers would target ships and specific buildings. The bombers would flatten warehouses, hangars and parked aircraft. Once each plane had dropped its ordnance it would pick out targets of opportunity and strafe them until out of ammunition. If no fighters were encountered the Zeros would strafe AAA positions.

These would be followed by a second wave of 54 bombers, 78 dive bombers and 36 fighters concentrating on any capital ships that had escaped destruction, then on smaller warships. If no fighters were met the Zeros would shoot up parked aircraft.

The first wave would return to the carriers, refuel and pick up bombs in order to destroy Pearl Harbor's fuel tanks and repair facilities.

Meanwhile sixteen submarines and five midget two-man submarines would approach Pearl Harbor. The midgets would enter the harbour and try to sink something in the entrance, thereby bottling up the American fleet. The submarines would hover outside the entrance like a pack of wolves waiting for any vessel that escaped the harbour.

However, his plan was rebuffed by admirals and generals as too optimistic. On 20 October he threatened to resign if his plan was not accepted. The army would have eagerly let him go, had he not had a considerable following among junior naval officers. He pleaded they would have one shot only. He hoped not just to destroy the capability of the Americans to fight in the Pacific, but the Americans will to do so, for if the Japanese failed to do that they would rue the day they challenged the United States. Reluctantly the plan was accepted.

Yamamoto could not choose the carrier force commander. 54-four-year old Chuichi Nagumo would not have been his first choice. A destroyer torpedo man, he had no combat experience and had only been in carriers since April. Fortunately, the airborne commander was the highly respected Mitsuo Fuchida.

On 25 November Nagumo sailed, but it was another week before he got the green light to attack. During this time he had been sailing inside a storm, hoping to escape detection, riding it all the way across the Pacific. Some men were swept overboard.

On Friday night, 5 December, a Japanese submarine reconnoitred the Hawaiian islands looking for American vessels.

On Saturday evening a spy in Pearl Harbor informed Tokyo, who informed Nagumo, which ships were in port and where.

Very early on Sunday morning five midget submarines began their journey towards the entrance to Pearl Harbor.

At 5.15am Nagumo launched a seaplane to reconnoitre Oahu. His first wave was supposed to take off fifteen minutes later, but the seas were so rough he delayed twenty minutes. When they did take off one Zero crashed into the sea.

The Battle: At 3.42am on Sunday morning 7 December the minesweeper USS *Condor* off the entrance to Pearl Harbor reported a periscope sighting to the duty destroyer, USS *Ward*, which began a search.

Eighteen minutes later American intelligence decoded instructions to the Japanese embassy in Washington that the long message was to be delivered to Secretary of State Cordell Hull promptly at 1.00pm (7.30am Hawaii). Obviously this represented some sort of deadline, Stark and Marshall realised, but they did not think of informing base commanders such as Short and Kimmel.

At 6.00am at sunrise a few miles to the west of Oahu eighteen fighters took off from the USS *Enterprise* headed towards Oahu.

Fifteen minutes later (00.45am 8 December Singapore time) Japanese troops began invading Malaya!

At 6.30am the unarmed supply ship USS *Antares* off Oahu sighted an object and informed the USS *Ward*. Seven minutes later the *Ward* sighted a midget submarine and opened fire. She dived and the *Ward* dropped depth charges.

About ten minutes later Oahu radar operators sighted a blip to the north-west (the Japanese seaplane) and reported it.

At 6.50am a PBY reconnaissance aircraft sighted the midget submarine and dropped depth charges.

At 7.00am General Marshall alerted Philippines, California and Panama with a war warning, but atmospherics interfered with the radio signal to Hawaii so the army sent it by civilian telegram!

Meanwhile Kimmel and Short prepared for their Sunday morning golf game.

At 7.02am, working on their own time, the Oahu radar operators saw large numbers of blips to the north-west. They telephoned their duty officer, a pilot who had not been trained for this position, and he, knowing a flight of B-17s was expected, replied: 'Don't worry about it'.

At 7.10am Kimmel was informed of the *Ward*'s action, but he was not told of the PBY's action. The USS *Monaghan* was ordered to get up steam to aid the *Ward*.

At 7.33am Marshall's war warning telegram reached Oahu, but as it was not marked urgent it was laid aside!

At 7:48am twenty Zeros, seeing no fighter patrol over Oahu, began strafing Kanoeha Naval Air Station, twelve miles north-east of Pearl Harbor. There were no AAA guns here and the astonished ground crews ran for their .50in calibre machine-guns, but these were locked up, so they had to wait for the officer who had the keys. Meanwhile a hundred marines grabbed bolt action rifles and began shooting back.

At this moment a Zero shot down a civilian single-engine plane.

Five minutes later six Zeros began strafing Ewa Marine Air Station, four miles west of Pearl Harbor.

Japanese planes were flying over several bases, but no one noticed, until at 7.54am a dive bomber struck Ford Island Naval Air Station. The explosion alerted some ships' duty officers, but not all.

Thirty seconds later a whole flight of dive bombers began bombing Ford Island.

On the outside of Battleship Row on Ford Island's eastern shore, the first that the crew of the *West Virginia* knew of the raid was when three torpedoes exploded deep inside her.

Immediately south of the *West Virginia* was the *Oklahoma*, whose crew was also awoken from a sound sleep by three exploding torpedoes. Some crewmen were killed in their sleep. The mighty ship at once began to list as water poured in.

To the west of Ford Island the first that the *Utah's* crew knew of the attack was when a torpedo slammed into her. She immediately began to list. The *Raleigh*, next to the *Utah*, was only alerted when a torpedo rammed into her.

Within seconds the *West Virginia* was burning brightly and smoke drifted across Ford Island.

At 7.56am dive bombers hit Hickam Field, on the south east shore of Pearl Harbor. There were no AAA positions operative, so the sentries shot back with pistols!

Only now were gunners running to their AAA positions aboard ship and on land as alarms sounded. Many of the men first thought it was a drill, especially those with hangovers from the night before. The crews of the .50in calibre machine-guns already on duty could not fire back, for they had been given no ammunition. They had to await arms officers who would issue it.

Throughout the entire harbour area AAA ammunition bearers rushed to the ammunition lockers and waited for officers to bring the keys.

At 7.57am a torpedo ran into the minelayer *Oglala*, south of the *Oklahoma*, another struck the *Helena* on the east shore of the harbour, and one hit the *Arizona*, which was sandwiched between Ford Island's eastern shore and the repair vessel *Vestal* – obviously the torpedo had run under the *Vestal* – men running to their battle stations were flung off their feet. The *Vestal* was damaged by pressure and began to take in water.

The *Arizona* was burning as Captain Valkenburgh tried to gain control, asking for damage estimates and ordering fire fighting teams to tackle the blaze. Rear Admiral Kidd was on board and he too gave out emergency orders.

At Hickam some airmen grabbed rifles and fired back, while sentries at nearby Fort Kamehameha opened fire with rifles. At the naval dockyards around Pearl Harbor marine sentries were also shooting at the planes. Individual riflemen soon found themselves being strafed.

At 7.58am dive bombers attacked Wheeler Field, six miles north-west of Pearl Harbor. There were no AAA positions.

At this moment naval headquarters at Signal Hill, overlooking Pearl Harbor, sent out the signal: 'Attack – this is no drill!'.

At this very instant the three torpedoes bored their way into the *West Virginia*: the explosions ripped out her guts. She slowly started to sink trapping the *Tennessee* against Ford island.

At last some ships managed to get their .50s into action and the *Hulburt* claimed a Zero almost at once. Two minutes later the *Selfridge* claimed two.

It was now 8.00am and the ship and shore AAA positions at last began firing. Soon the noise was deafening. From now on the Japanese planes were vulnerable.

Dive bombers now began a strike on Schofield Barracks, near to Wheeler field. Elsewhere on Oahu sentries at Camp Malakole, Fort Ruger and Fort Weaver began firing at any planes that flew over.

Yet it was only now that Fort Shafter and Fort de Russy received the alert. Surprised soldiers ran to their arms rooms and then began shooting at passing planes with rifles from barracks windows.

In the harbour small craft began taking men from shore to their ships and bringing back wounded. Smoke drifted across the water and visibility was poor, but whenever it cleared Japanese planes strafed the ships.

At 8.01am the *Nevada* on her own at the north end of Battleship Row watched as a torpedo bomber lazily approached and dropped a torpedo which spun right into her. Machine-gunners blasted away with their .50s and saw the plane lurch and then crash. Officers ordered the engine room to get up steam: they intended to escape this savagery. At this moment explosions shattered the buildings and streets of Fort Shafter and the city of Honolulu: naturally those on the ground thought they were being bombed, but it was in fact defective AAA shells falling to earth and exploding on contact.

Amidst this carnage the KGMB Radio announcer calmly read a message ordering all military personnel to duty, then returned to normal programming.

On board the *California* at the south end of Battleship Row no one was listening to KGMB as two torpedo bombers neatly put their ordnance straight through her hull. The explosions set fire to oil and wiring and she took on a list.

At 8.04am west of Ford Island the crew of the *Raleigh* realised she was listing badly, but those on deck were distracted by the sight of the *Utah* turning completely over: 58 of her crew died and several were trapped below.

The *Vestal* was shattered by two bombs and the survivors ran to aid the casualties, choking from smoke coming from the *Arizona*. Wounded had to be lifted onto the *Arizona* or lowered into passing small craft.

The service hospitals were already receiving wounded, many of them badly burned, and they asked the island's civilian hospitals to assist. The response was exemplary: even a mental asylum opened its doors.

At 8.05am Roosevelt was informed of the attack.

At 8:08am another torpedo gouged its way into the *Oklahoma*, which suddenly and violently jerked and then rolled completely over: 415 men were killed, drowned or suffocated inside her. Upside down, much of her hull above water, she trapped the *Maryland* against Ford Island.

Short and Kimmel had driven to their respective headquarters as soon as they heard the explosions and at 8.10am Short ordered everyone to prepare to meet an invasion and then busied himself with this duty.

Kimmel could only stare from his window down at the harbour and the burning and sinking ships, the pride of the navy. He had been entrusted with a powerful fleet and it was disappearing before his very eyes. Suddenly a spent American machine-gun bullet crashed through the window onto his chest then fell to the floor, momentarily startling his aides. He mumbled: 'It would have been merciful had it killed me.'

Down amongst the hell in the harbour smoke was strangling everyone: the sea was aflame with burning oil; the stench of oil, burned wiring and burning flesh almost choked the men and women who tried to fight the flames, tend the wounded, pass AAA ammunition and give and obey orders.

At 8.20am a bomb ploughed through the *Arizona* into her forward magazine and she exploded in an horrific spectacle, snapping in half and collapsing: a thousand dismembered bodies were flung into the air along with wreckage and burning fuel. Pieces of human and material debris fell onto Ford Island and nearby ships like

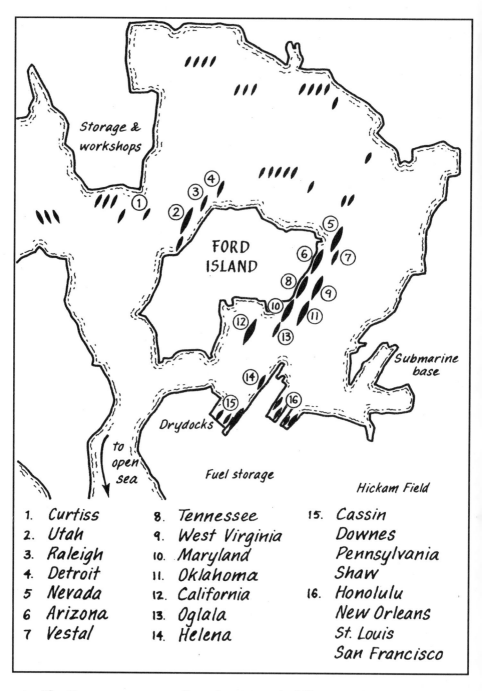

Storage & workshops

FORD ISLAND

Submarine base

to open sea

Drydocks

Fuel storage

Hickam Field

1. Curtiss
2. Utah
3. Raleigh
4. Detroit
5. Nevada
6. Arizona
7. Vestal
8. Tennessee
9. West Virginia
10. Maryland
11. Oklahoma
12. California
13. Oglala
14. Helena
15. Cassin
Downes
Pennsylvania
Shaw
16. Honolulu
New Orleans
St. Louis
San Francisco

rain. The *Tennessee* was set aflame by *Arizona*'s falling wreckage. Among those killed were Rear Admiral Kidd and Captain Valkenburgh. The force of the blast blew a hundred of *Vestal*'s sailors overboard, stripping some men of their clothing.

The destroyer *Helm* was attempting to escape the harbour when she sighted a midget submarine and at once opened fire: other ships soon joined the fight.

In the air the unarmed B-17s arrived, one being shot down by a Zero, and two crash landed in flames. The eighteen *Enterprise* fighters also arrived, too low on fuel to fight, and only twelve of them managed to land safely.

The *Arizona* had lost 1,177 of her crew, but miraculously others were still alive on board and trying to save their comrades as she settled on the sea bed.

At 8.23am two bombs fell on the burning *Tennessee*, wrenching her insides.

By now the *West Virginia*'s crew had been fighting back flames and incoming water for 25 minutes, but suddenly she was holed by three torpedoes, which blew out her bottom. By now 105 of her crew were dead or dying and over 200 were badly burned or sliced with shrapnel.

Two minutes later two bombs hit the *Maryland*. She burst into flames. That instant at least four bombs struck the *California*.

Meanwhile fifteen miles east of Pearl Harbor Bellows Field came under air attack. There were no AAA positions.

At 8.30am two P-40s took off from Wheeler Field, the first to do so. Five minutes later two P-40s took off from Haleiwa Field eighteen miles north-west of Pearl Harbor. However, the Japanese planes were now leaving: the air raid was over.

In the shallow waters of the harbour several ships were fighting midget submarines, and the *Monaghan* rammed one.

At 8.50am (2.20pm Washington) Cordell Hull received Ambassador Nomura, who began to read the fourteen part message. Unknown to Nomura Roosevelt was already releasing the news to the press.

At 8.53am the second wave arrived over Oahu. At once AAA from every location opened fire.

Any ship was now a target, and bombs landed near many vessels. A near miss could structurally damage a ship and throw shrapnel through her bulkheads. The *Helena* was damaged as was the *California*, which was sinking with 98 of her crew killed, and also the *Nevada*, which was now sailing towards the entrance. The *Nevada* proceeded on her slow journey, despite continually taking bomb hits and near misses.

Haleiwa Field launched P-40s and Bellows Field tried to, but three were destroyed by strafing Zeros as they attempted to take off. The first pair of P-40s to take off had landed to refuel and then taken off from Wheeler again, narrowly dodging a flight of strafing Zeros. Hickam and Kanoeha were also attacked again.

Within five minutes the pair of P-40s had claimed three Zeros.

At 9.05am a dive bomber crashed into the tender *Curtis*, spewing flame and destruction.

At 9:07am the Japanese turned their attention to the dry docks, planting bombs directly onto the *Pennsylvania* and destroyers *Shaw*, *Cassin* and *Downes*, setting fire to them. These vessels had only skeleton crews aboard, nonetheless the *Pennsylvania* lost 15 killed, 14 'disappeared in flames' and 38 badly wounded. Sixty seconds later the *Shaw* blew up in an explosion seen by everyone at Pearl Harbor. The crew of the *Nevada* could see nothing as so many bombs were landing near that they threw blinding geysers of water over her. Realising she was too badly damaged to remain afloat, the crew decided to run her aground. Already 50 of the crew had been killed and many wounded.

The ships in the extreme east of the harbour now caught the attention of the Japanese; bombs landing just a few feet from the *San Francisco*, *St Louis*, *Honolulu* and *New Orleans*. This did not stop the *St Louis* from moving away from her berth to escape the harbour, shooting down a plane as she did so.

In the air the pair of P-40s claimed another four Japanese planes, and Haleiwa's P-40s claimed four, but lost a P-40.

Despite complete devastation aboard the *Curtis* her machine-gunners continued to fight, unflinching amid the falling bombs, claiming two planes.

At 9.26am the Japanese turned for home. Four minutes later the *Cassin* blew up.

Aftermath: At 10.40am, despite there not being one enemy plane in the sky, some AAA gunners opened fire again, and within a minute everyone in Pearl Harbor was firing. Defective shells fell like bombs and for an hour the Americans fought themselves!

Throughout the day jittery AAA gunners fired on friendly aircraft.

As ships escaped into the open sea they made sonar contact and threw out depth charges, and continued to do so well into the night.

Still further out to sea the cruiser *Northampton* fired on a Japanese reconnaissance aircraft, and dive bombers from the *Enterprise* got into the act by attacking the cruiser USS *Portland*: fortunately they missed.

Within the harbour after dark AAA gunners shot down four planes, which turned out to be from the *Enterprise*. Defective shells caused three casualties.

All through the night warships depth-charged sonar contacts and on Oahu AAA gunners fired at mythical bombers, and sentries, told to expect an invasion, shot at each other.

Come morning American P-40s strafed friendly fishing boats and killed six fishermen.

Aboard the crippled vessels fire fighters continued courageously to tackle blazes, while others used cutting torches to enter the *Utah* and *Oklahoma* to look for survivors.

2,467 people were killed in the air raid, of whom 64 were civilians and about 2,000 were aboard ship. Hospitalised wounded numbered 1,178. During the raid and aftermath fourteen American planes were shot down and 153 were destroyed on the ground, with another 200 or so damaged. Warehouses, workshops, barracks, tool sheds, hangars and mess halls were demolished and countless items of equipment were destroyed.

The *California*, *West Virginia* and *Arizona* had sunk, the *Utah* and *Oklahoma* capsized, the *Nevada* had beached, the *Maryland* and *Tennessee* were seriously damaged and trapped, and the *Pennsylvania* was badly damaged. The *Raleigh* and *Helena* were seriously damaged and the *San Francisco*, *St Louis*, *Honolulu* and *New Orleans* were lightly damaged. The destroyers *Cassin*, *Downes* and *Shaw* had blown up. The minelayer *Oglala* had capsized, the tender *Curtis* had burned out and the repair vessel *Vestal* had beached. Scores of other ships were damaged. At sea a merchant ship was sunk.

Japanese casualties were five midget submarines sunk, 30 planes shot down and five written off after returning with damage, 79 fliers and submariners killed and one submariner taken prisoner.

Appraisal: So what had gone wrong with America's defences? The most obvious answer is that American and British arrogance blinded them to the worst case scenario. If they had planned for the worst case and reacted accordingly things might have gone differently. The failures were in thirteen categories: intelligence, command ability, timing, equipment, training, reconnaissance, communications, firepower, reserves, tactics, supply, dispersal and morale.

Allied intelligence sources were excellent: spies, radio interceptors, decoders and collectors of peripheral information had all done their job extremely well. The Allies knew the Japanese were planning to attack. Yet, owing to a misguided policy of retaining secrets, little of this knowledge filtered down to the people responsible for forward defence. The Americans only had two vulnerable naval commanders, Hart and Kimmel, but neither was informed of the intelligence picture that was building up. The Americans also held back some of their knowledge from the British: and the British did the same. Ultimately these were the faults of Roosevelt and Churchill.

Marshall's and Stark's command ability was flawed, because they did not put Hawaii on the 'at risk list' on 27 November. Indeed why have such a list? Surely all bases were at some risk? Brooke-Popham failed in not notifying Churchill of the incidents in which a British plane was fired upon and another was missing.

Time is the most precious commodity and the Americans were given plenty of time. Kimmel's fleet had assembled at Pearl Harbor with the express purpose of preparing for war with Japan. Yet Short and Kimmel kept their personnel on peacetime duty. However, as has been seen, the American navy was not at peace and had not been for some time. German raiders were known to be in the Pacific. Why, therefore, were the defenders of Oahu allowed to behave as if on holiday?

The misuse of equipment is all the more damning for a nation of such abundant wealth. A year after Taranto Kimmel still thought anti-torpedo nets were unnecessary. Had he installed them only the *Arizona* would have been sunk. Oahu desperately lacked air raid shelters, airplane revetments and an anti-submarine net at the mouth of Pearl Harbor.

The training of the Americans was shown to be a farce. Why were there not enough trained radar operators to man the screens full-time? Why was the radar duty officer untrained for the job? Despite the existence of training schools, many servicemen had only been given on the job training, and in some cases not even that, but were simply expected to muddle through. AAA gunners had been trained to fire at targets flying half the speed of modern aircraft, hence only 29 planes were shot down over Oahu, seven by fighters and the rest by small arms or machine-guns. AAA guns did not kill any Japanese, but with their defective shells and inaccurate settings probably killed over a hundred Americans.

Aircraft recognition was non-existent. At least four American planes were shot down by their own side, and some AAA gunners were still firing twelve hours after the enemy had left. The raid on the *Portland* proved two things: American pilots could neither recognise an American ship nor hit one.

Allied reconnaissance was excellent. They watched a Japanese task force build up in Indo-China: they knew when it left and its probable destination; they knew the main Japanese battle fleet had left port; they knew of other suspicious movements; but reading these reconnaissance reports the British concentrated on

Malaya and the Americans on the Philippines, and both failed to see the big picture. It is disturbing to realise: that the Japanese had fired on an Allied aircraft fully 31 hours before the attack on Pearl Harbor; twelve hours before the attack an Allied plane was declared missing from its mission to watch the Japanese; four hours before the attack the USS *Condor* sighted a possible submarine just outside Pearl Harbor; 90 minutes before the attack the Japanese invaded Malaya; an hour before the attack the *Ward* opened fire on a submarine; 50 minutes before the attack an American plane opened fire within sight of Pearl Harbor; 46 minutes before the attack radar operators saw the Japanese air armada approaching; yet the Americans were caught completely by surprise.

The British and Americans had the best communications of any forces in history, so the fault does not lie with the equipment. In truth the advance in communications technology had far outstripped the ability of men born and raised in the nineteenth century to use it correctly. Twenty minutes after a PBY went into action off Pearl Harbor, Kimmel had still not been informed. Poor communications handling was evident all the way to the top. When Marshall's staff sent their war warning through a civilian telegraph company rather than through the navy, because of inter-service rivalry, and did not bother to mark it 'urgent', it was one of the most remarkable communications failures in history.

Most airfields on Oahu were devoid of any AAA firepower, and for the United States to have to fall back on sentries with pistols for anti-aircraft protection is astonishing.

Kimmel, Martin and Short completely mishandled their reserves. Although American ships had been dodging German submarines for two years, Kimmel did not have any anti-submarine vessels with warm boilers ready to aid the duty destroyer immediately. When the *Monaghan* was ordered to lend a hand it took her almost an hour to heat her boilers in order to move.

A year after the highly publicised Battle of Britain, on Oahu there were neither fighter pilots on standby nor fighters fuelled and armed ready to go. The first two fighter pilots to take off had driven to the airfield in a car after they heard explosions!

Short's, Martin's and Kimmel's tactics were abysmal. Only one warship patrolled outside the harbour and there were no fighters patrolling the skies. The best fighter in the world is useless on the ground.

Within the previous 27 months no less than fourteen neutral nations had suffered surprise attacks, but Short and Kimmel kept their AAA ammunition supply under lock and key.

Dispersal of ground forces is a flaw, but for ships and planes it is a requirement. To have six battleships so close together they almost touched is stupid. The explosion of the *Arizona* damaged the *Tennessee*. The capsizing of the *Oklahoma* and sinking of the *West Virginia* trapped the *Maryland* and *Tennessee*. The bunching together of aircraft made it easy for one bomb to damage several machines.

Prior to the raid American morale was extremely high and completely based on ignorance. As often happens such morale did not survive the first shot. There was considerable panic and fumbling, alongside courage and initiative.

Consequences: The crippling of the Pacific Fleet forced the Americans to rely on cruisers and carriers and placed them on the defensive and as a result the admirals would not risk a rescue convoy to the Philippines, thereby abandoning that colony and its 130,000-man garrison to the Japanese.

Naturally the public and Congress wanted to blame someone and their wrath fell on Short and Kimmel. They were both retired, though an appeal in 1944 found Kimmel not derelict of duty. Kimmel became an embittered man blaming Roosevelt. The loss of a son in the war only made him more bitter. To be sure Short and Kimmel had warranted their dismissal, but they were scapegoats all the same.

Martin was temporarily relieved. Stark was replaced by Admiral King and given a liaison job in Europe. Neither Marshall nor Arnold were affected. Roosevelt became more popular than ever.

The Battle's Place in History: The Americans of 1941 were a naive people, who thought the common folk of other lands loved Americans: a belief possibly fuelled by the fact that almost every foreigner they met had entered the USA in order to become an 'American'. Thus they took the attack on Pearl Harbor more personally than other nations would have. One psychological factor was the navy habit of naming battleships after states and cruisers after cities, so when the people of Oklahoma heard 'their ship' had capsized, everyone in the state felt affronted. Roosevelt called it a date in 'infamy'. Everyone agreed, though few knew what the word meant. It sounded right, because they did not know how to describe how they felt.

Recruitment offices were besieged night and day with mile long lines of men and women. Every citizen wanted to pay back the Japs. Yamamoto had warned his government this would happen. The wrath of the Americans was even worse than he anticipated as they began to wage a war bordering on genocide.

Americans whose Japanese ancestors had immigrated in the nineteenth century were not immune: they were arrested and sent to camps and their property confiscated. A quarter of Americans had German ancestors and a twelfth were of Italian ethnicity, too many to be arrested, but had there been only a handful nothing would have happened to them, for they were white and the Japanese-Americans were so easily recognizable in this white dominated society. The attack on Pearl Harbor unleashed the greatest and most deep-seated fear in American whites: namely terrifying 'memories' of Indian massacres and negro slave revolts.

America's post war obsession with 'invasions from outer space' and the nuclear arms race can be explained by 'December 7 1941'.

1941-42

Malaya and Singapore

The Battlefield: Malaya in 1941 had a population of 4,500,000: 50per cent indigenous Malays, 38per cent Chinese and 11per cent Tamils. Stretching 515 miles south from the Thailand border and up to 220 miles wide, the colony was surrounded by water on three sides. Mostly cultivated into small plots and rice paddies, there was a forest covered mountainous spine with some jungle in the east.

November brought the monsoon, almost continual downpours, but the temperature rarely fell below 70˚F.

Malaya was a valuable British colony, for it possessed 43per cent of the world's rubber and 33per cent of its tin.

The 25- by 15-mile island of Singapore lies off the southern tip of Malaya and in 1941 was inhabited by 585,000 Chinese, 48,000 Tamils and 48,000 Malays.

By December 1941 there were still about 20,000 British colonists in Malaya and Singapore. A third of the Chinese in Malaya and Singapore were local born, but the remainder maintained Chinese citizenship and already considered themselves to be enemies of Japan.

The Tamils were mostly migrant workers from India and Ceylon. Other Indians had immigrated, many to serve in the police.

The War: The Japanese invasion of Malaya began 45 minutes past midnight on 8 December at Kota Bharu on the north-east coast. (See previous chapter.) The allied commanders had been watching the Japanese task force, guessing as to its destination, and had not considered the possibility that it would divide into several amphibious landing forces, in fact six landings on the Thailand coast in addition to Kota Bharu.

Once alerted, Air Vice-Marshal Sir Robert Brooke-Popham, Commander Far East, ordered a council of war for 2.30am at Singapore naval base.

At 4.10am during the meeting the alarms sounded and almost at once bombs fell. It was an inglorious beginning to the campaign as Brooke-Popham, Rear Admiral Sir Geoffrey Layton the naval commander, Air Vice-Marshal Pulford the air commander, Lieutenant General Sir Arthur Percival the ground commander, and Rear Admiral Tom Phillips commander of Force Z, and their staff officers crawled under a large table. They heard the *Prince of Wales* still in dry dock open fire with her sixteen 5.2-inch guns and eight four-barrelled 40mm guns.

The civilian colonial administration had not built any public air raid shelters or created an adequate civil defence organisation. Not surprisingly there was considerable panic in Singapore city: civilian casualties were 61 killed.

Brooke-Popham agreed with Phillips that Force Z should sail as soon as possible.

That afternoon Pulford told Phillips that his ability to protect Force Z might be affected by enemy air raids.

That evening Force Z sailed. The battleship *Prince of Wales*, Phillips' flagship, had already made a name for herself though only seven months old: she had fought the German battleship *Bismarck* and had been the scene of a conference between Roosevelt and Churchill. In addition to her AAA, she carried ten fourteen-inch guns.

The 32,000 ton *Repulse* (technically a battle cruiser not a battleship) had seen sterling duty in World War I. In addition to her six fifteen-inch guns she carried an AAA armament of twenty 4.2-inch guns and six four-barrelled 40mm guns.

Accompanying the two capital ships were four destroyers.

During 9 December Force Z sailed towards Kota Bharu. Phillips had only sketchy information as to what was happening there and in the evening he found that he was being shadowed by enemy reconnaissance planes. Playing safe he decided to return to Singapore.

However, he received a message that the enemy had landed at Kuantan, just 200 miles north of Singapore, and he changed his mind, ordering a course for that coastal village.

At dawn on the 10th he reached Kuantan, but saw nothing. It had been a false report. Frustrated, he ordered a new course, which would put him about 150 miles offshore, but did not inform anyone at Singapore where he was going. When he later gave orders to return to Singapore, he still did not inform anyone. Even after being told an enemy reconnaissance aircraft was watching him he did not report his position or ask for air cover. A squadron of Buffalo fighters would take an hour to reach him, he knew.

The *Prince of Wales*'s own radar was 'down', but the *Repulse*'s radar saw planes approaching. Phillips did not radio for air support.

At 11.18am in a fairly clear sky Japanese bombers began their attack: all the ships swerved this way and that to make themselves a difficult target, while their AAA belched forth shells by the hundred. Phillips did not radio for air support.

With over 80 planes attacking, it was only a matter of time before bombs hit the *Repulse* and *Prince of Wales*. Still Phillips did not ask for air support.

At 11.44am torpedo bombers arrived, a much more dangerous prospect. Phillips knew that Japanese torpedo bombers had wrought terrible destruction at Pearl Harbor just 57 hours earlier, but he still did not ask for air support.

At 12.01 the *Repulse* took a torpedo. That was enough for her captain: he broke radio silence and radioed Singapore for aid: 'Enemy aircraft bombing my position 134NYT22x99.'

When Pulford was informed he sent a squadron of Buffaloes at once.

The *Repulse* attracted most of the enemy planes and over the next few minutes she took another four torpedoes.

At 12.33pm she rolled over: her crew spilling and jumping into the sea.

At 12.40pm Singapore received a message from the captain of the *Prince of Wales*: 'Have been struck by a torpedo on port side. Send destroyers.' Even now Phillips, who must have known of this message, and the ship's captain were not asking for air cover, but destroyers! One can only guess at the purpose – to tow the ship? To look out for submarines, while the battleship limped home?

In the next few minutes the battleship took six more torpedoes. At 1.04pm Singapore received two more messages: 'send tugs' and 'send destroyers'.

The first message from Phillips himself came at 1.17pm, that he was evacuating non-fighting personnel from the battleship to his destroyers and asking for '?' – the word was indecipherable.

Four minutes later Singapore received a message from the destroyer *Electra* of Force Z: 'HMS *Prince of Wales* sunk.'

As the Japanese planes flew off the four destroyers searched for survivors: of the 1,309 aboard the *Repulse* 513 were never found; of the 1,612 aboard the *Prince of Wales* 328 including Phillips were never found.

The Buffaloes arrived minutes later. The Japanese planes had had no fighter support, so if the Buffaloes had arrived in time they would have slaughtered the Japanese.

The British had been discussing the suggestion that had British admirals been in charge at Pearl Harbor the story would have been different. Now came the news of Phillips' fiasco. Some overly racist officers, unwilling to believe that the Japanese could be capable of such excellence, thought they might have been using German pilots on loan!

The Commander: Arthur E. Percival had begun his military service in a most unpromising manner. In 1914 at the age of 26 he had enlisted as a private to serve his country during World War I. He was commissioned and decorated for bravery and it was only after the conflict he thought of a military career.

He served in the Irish War 1919-1921 as an intelligence officer and had a reputation (not necessarily deserved) as a brutal interrogator.

In 1937 as a colonel and chief of staff to Lieutenant General Dobbie, commander in Malaya, he helped draw up the Dobbie report on the state of Malaya's defences.

In 1939 he was promoted to brigadier and given the 43rd Division, but saw no action. In April 1941 he was appointed ground commander Malaya and promoted to lieutenant general.

In Malaya his most important subordinate was Lieutenant General Sir Lewis Heath, and there was speculation as to whether the two would get along, because Heath, who was Indian Army not British Army, had recently led a division in battle against the Italians.

Strategy: The defence strategy for Malaya and Singapore was for the army to protect the airfields, which existed so that air power could protect Singapore naval base and the fleet when it was within range, the fleet being there to protect the colony and its sea routes. However, if there was no fleet, the whole rationale for the strategy was removed.

Of course the colony was valuable to the British and had to be defended, but when compared to Brunei, Sarawak and North Borneo which had only about 2000 defenders between them, and Burma which had about 6,000, the garrison of Malaya of almost 100,000 is evidence that its prestige was much more important than its tin and rubber. To be exact the prestige lay in Singapore, therefore Percival knew he would be expected to trade space in Malaya to extend the life of Singapore.

In 1938 the Dobbie Report (which had Percival's input) had suggested a defensive strategy of holding until the fleet came to the rescue. Initially Dobbie and Percival thought the Japanese not only could, but would use the monsoon as cover for their attack, but following a paper exercise they decided this would be too difficult. However, they did reach the conclusion that the Japanese would invade Thailand first, then advance south into Malaya along the west coast of the colony, which did not have impenetrable jungle. They emphasised the importance of air power and tanks in the colony's defence. The 1938 government replied with such phrases as: 'provision of a tank unit not justified,' and 'little money for rearmament', but said the fleet would come to the rescue 'regardless of the situation in European waters'!

Following the Dobbie Report a compromise was attained, that the two-division garrison would fight a withdrawal southwards, holding each position as long as possible, until the fleet arrived in Singapore. Dobbie ordered a line of pill-boxes built in Johore, the Malay province opposite Singapore.

Dobbie's successor Lieutenant General Lionel Bond asked for an additional two divisions, two tank battalions, extra anti-tank guns and anti-tank mines, but he stopped the work on the Johore Line.

In March 1940, completely aside from the military planning, a civil servant, C. A. Vlieland, wrote that he expected the Japanese to invade the east coast of Thailand, charge to the west coast of Malaya, then advance south along the west coast towards Singapore. He suggested holding northern Malaya even at the expense of Singapore, which if without a fleet was just another island. Naturally the military did not listen to this civilian.

It was, therefore, no coincidence that in April 1941 Churchill appointed Percival to take command of Malaya's ground defence. Upon inspection Percival requested Malaya's garrison be increased to 582 modern aircraft and 48 infantry battalions and one tank battalion.

In August Brigadier Ivan Simpson, Percival's chief engineer, suggested the army start training native guerrillas in case of Japanese occupation of part of Malaya. Percival was appalled. He had fought guerrillas in Ireland and had no wish to train a potential enemy. Simpson also asked for a defence line to be built, perhaps the incomplete Johore Line. Percival refused. He thought it would be bad for morale to build a defence position so far from the Thailand border.

The Defences: Percival never got his 582 modern aircraft: by December he had seventeen Hudson and three PBY reconnaissance planes, 34 Blenheim and five Shark light bombers, 27 obsolete Wildebeest and four Swordfish biplane torpedo bombers, ten Blenheims rigged as night fighters and 41 Buffalo day fighters. The Buffalo was a good fighter, but required about eleven minutes to reach 20,000 feet, whereas the Zero could reach that height in seven and a half minutes and could outpace the Buffalo on the level.

Ground reinforcements were much more forthcoming, though there was no sign of tanks. Heath's Indian Army III Corps, with headquarters at Kuala Lumpur, controlled the defence of north Malaya, using the 11th Division in the northwest: headquarters at Sungei Patani near two airfields with its 6th and 15th

Brigades on the Thailand border, one near an airfield; and the 9th Division in the east: headquarters at Kuala Lumpur with its 8th Brigade at Kota Bharu near two airfields and 22nd Brigade at Kuantan near one airfield. In corps reserve were the 28th Brigade at Ipoh and 12th Brigade at Port Dickson, both borrowed from the two divisions.

Defending south Malaya was the Australian 8th Division with its 22nd and 29th Brigades at Mersing on the east coast and its 27th Brigade at Kluang guarding an airfield.

Singapore was defended by the Malay Division of the British Army.

Indian and Australian divisions were equipped and structured like British Army divisions, normally: an armoured car battalion, a signals company, four engineer companies, three artillery battalions of 24 medium range 18- or 25-pounders each, a machine-gun and mortar battalion, and three brigades of three infantry battalions each. A division contained 13,863 personnel. An infantry battalion contained 813 personnel armed with bolt action .303in calibre rifles, 50 machine-guns and six mortars.

Indian Army personnel were natives of the Indian sub-continent, though almost all officers and certainly senior officers were ethnically British born in India. Usually an Indian division's artillery and a third of its infantry battalions were on loan from the British Army.

However, the élite infantry of the Indian Army were the battalions of Gurkhas, tribesmen from Nepal who were technically mercenaries, but who fought more for honour than pay.

The Indian Army had a proud heritage, but recently Britons from Britain had been allowed to enter the army as officers, men who did not understand the language, religion or culture of their soldiers, and this caused problems. Furthermore, most of the Indians sent to Malaya were new recruits with little training. This was bad enough, but ethnic Indian officers were not admitted to the (white) officers' clubs, nor could they travel in the same rail compartment as a white man. They may possess the rank of lieutenant or captain, but it was obvious that even a white British corporal 'outranked' them socially.

Indian troops suspected that in combat flanking British troops would desert them. British troops suspected that flanking Indians would run away at the first shot.

On 1 December Brooke-Popham had mobilised his local reservists (all were members of the British Army): the Federated Malay States Volunteer Force (FMSVF), the Singapore Straits Settlement Volunteer Force (SSSVF), and some regional militias. The SSSVF troops were Chinese and the others were Malays and Tamils with a few Chinese, but the officers, sergeants and technical personnel were drawn from the 5,000 conscripted British colonists.

A good number of the Chinese had succumbed to the radical philosophy of Communism and the army screened every Chinese recruit for party membership, refusing to take in anyone of dubious loyalty.

The colonists did not have much faith in their native troops. All colonial powers were racist to a degree that ranged from virulent hatred to kind paternalism, and the British were in fact one of the most gentle of the imperialist powers. However, oppression is in the eye of the oppressed not in the eye of the oppressor. British officers wrote descriptions of Malayan troops and workers as 'soft', 'idle', 'no martial qualities', 'lack stamina and courage', and over a gin and tonic they used much more derogatory phrases. They openly did not trust native soldiers and the latter knew it.

The Malay Division was a real hodgepodge, containing: an infantry brigade of one FMSVF, one Indian and one British battalion; a second brigade of two British battalions and one Indian; a third brigade of two Indian battalions and one British; three battalions of British artillery; two batteries of Indian artillery; SSSVF engineers and signallers; and British rear-echelon troops.

Attached to the Malay Division were three battalions of the SSSVF and two battalions of Indian States Forces (ISF), that is members of autonomous Indian state armies, not the Indian Army. Some Malayan militia and a company of the FMSVF were attached to the 9th Division and two companies of the FMSVF were attached to the 11th Division. The remainder of the FMSVF – three infantry battalions, six labour battalions, some artillery, engineers and rear-echelon – were spread around Malaya, as were regional militia companies and a transport company of the SSSVF. On Penang Island off the north-west coast was a battalion of the SSSVF.

The Australian division was all-Australian, and when they arrived in Malaya they were astonished to find white colonists behaving as if there was no war. They knew Britain was a land of strict rationing and air raids with conscription of males up to 45 years old, and they knew that the other three divisions of Australia's overseas expeditionary force were deeply enmeshed in combat, but in Malaya and Singapore the colonists lived the life of Riley, relying on cheap native labour, residing in beautiful homes with servants, spending their time in clubs, tennis courts, cricket grounds and polo grounds, their every desire catered for. It made the Australians angry that they had been brought here to defend these upper class toffs and their property.

Such were Percival's defenders: 35,000 Indians, 15,000 Australians, 14,000 British, 12,000 Malays, 5,000 British colonists, 3,000 Chinese, 4,000 Tamils and 2,000 ISF.

Causes of Arrogance: Malaya had been judged to be impregnable from invasion as long as its defenders were determined to resist, owing to the poor road network on the Thailand border, 7000-foot mountains in the centre and several fast flowing rivers.

The monsoon was an added complication for any invader. Invasion by sea was ruled out as long as the air force and fleet existed. Fortress Singapore, as Churchill called it, had no mountains, but did have a battery of 15-inch guns that could sink any ship.

The Japanese would be fighting on strange ground, but the defenders knew it well. The Japanese factory worker from Tokyo did not understand the jungle any better than the mechanic from Sydney or the clerk from London, but among the defenders were colonists and Malays who knew the jungle intimately and how to survive in it.

Above all, no one expected the Japanese to fly well, sail well, march well or fight well.

The Enemy: Vice Admiral Ozawa's task force of two battleships, eight cruisers and 26 destroyers plus transports brought the Twenty-fifth Army to the shores of Thailand and Malaya. Supporting the 35,000 assault troops were 560 aircraft.

General Tomoyuki Yamashita, the 56-year-old commander of the Twenty-fifth Army, was apprehensive, though this overweight, pensive individual did not let it show. He was confident in his troops, though he was wary of the Imperial Guards who had been primarily a ceremonial unit. He was keenly aware his superiors would be watching his performance, for he was a political general and had never seen action.

The 18th Division's 56th Regiment landed at Kota Bharu, the 5th Division landed in southern Thailand, the 55th Division landed in central Thailand and the Imperial Guards Division invaded Thailand overland from Indo-China. The 56th Division was in reserve.

A Japanese division normally consisted of a reconnaissance battalion (trucked infantry, some armoured cars and horse cavalry), an artillery regiment of 24 short-range 75mm and twelve medium-range 105mm guns, an engineer battalion, a signals battalion, a transport regiment of 50 trucks plus several hundred horses, and three infantry regiments of a battery of 75s and three battalions each. An infantry battalion contained 677 riflemen armed with the Arisaka 6.5mm bolt action rifle, 40 machine-guns and twelve heavy machine-guns, and 50 small and four medium mortars.

Yamashita also had a battalion of tanks equipped with the Chi-Ha four-man tank weighing 16 tons, with a top speed of 24mph, carrying a 47mm gun and two machine-guns. A diesel, it was hard to set afire, and only an anti-tank gun could penetrate its armour. It could ford a stream 3ft 3in deep and cross an 8ft ditch.

Morale was extremely high, for the army had never been defeated in its ten year war in China. Current Japanese thinking was that it was such a disgrace to be defeated that death was preferable.

The Battle: In the early hours of 8 December Brigadier B. W. Key of the 8th Brigade was alerted to the invasion at Kota Bharu. His superior, Major General A. E. Barstow at divisional headquarters 180 miles the other side of the mountains could do little to direct the battle. Key, his brigade and a handful of guns were on their own. By 2.00am his infantry were in action. The Japanese fought in a light brown uniform with round helmet or soft peaked cap. Allied troops wore sand coloured shirt and shorts or trousers with usually a flat helmet or broad brimmed hat. Some Indian troops wore turbans.

At dawn Hudsons and Wildebeests flying from the two nearest airfields attacked the invasion task force and sank a transport.

At 7.30am these airfields were hit by Japanese planes, while the British ground crews were refuelling and bombing up their aircraft for a second attempt at the task force. There was much destruction.

By noon the lead Indian battalion, 3/17 Dogras, had retreated ten miles, and at 7.30pm the airmen deserted Kota Bharu airfield.

This same day in north-west Malaya the 3/16 Punjab battalion invaded Thailand, hoping to gain a secure forward defence position, but three miles into the country they encountered Thai border guards who resisted them!

On 9 December the 8th Brigade retreated from Kota Bharu, and Japanese aircraft began using the captured airfield: the retreating airmen had not holed the runways or demolished the facilities.

On the 10th Pulford declared his bombers would make no more daylight raids and he ordered the abandonment of all airfields in northern Malaya. Kuantan airfield on the east coast was also abandoned.

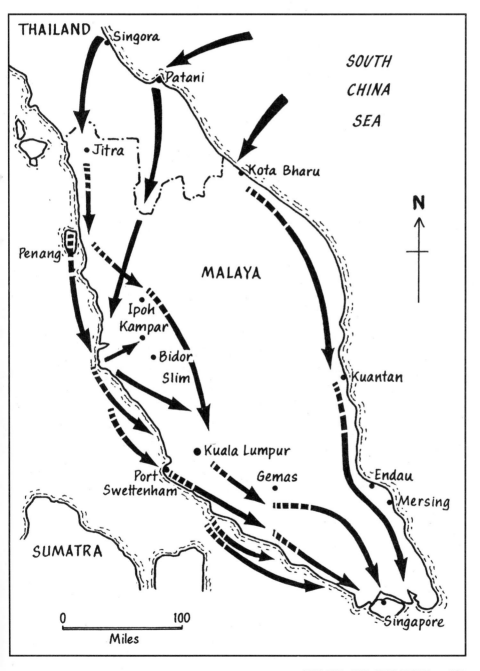

By the 11th the 3/16 Punjabis were falling back under attack by the Japanese 42nd Regiment of the 5th Division. Major General Murray-Lyon commanding 11th Division noticed this and realised that already his right flank had been turned. In other words he held north-west Malaya and Key held the north-east, but only the 3/16 Punjabis held the north.

That day his 11th Division was attacked by the Japanese 5th Division (minus 42nd Regiment) and under the cover of a heavy rain the Japanese advanced with ten tanks and two battalions of infantry in trucks. At 4.30pm the 1/14 Punjabis were overrun by this force at Nangka: they had been extended out on a limb without support. The Punjabis scattered into the forest. Then two miles south at Asun the 2/1 Gurkhas were attacked by this force. For three hours the Gurkhas bravely battled, but they were defenceless against tanks. They too scattered eventually.

At 8.00pm the Japanese assault force reached the main Jitra Line, which Murray-Lyon had dug north of the Jitra River, manned by the 6th and 15th Brigades (two British and two Indian battalions along a ten-mile front, with two Indian battalions in reserve) The Japanese were stopped by British troops.

On the 12th the whole line repelled a Japanese assault, while survivors of the previous day's fight straggled into friendly lines: a quarter of the 2/1 Gurkhas and half the 1/14 Punjabis. However, the line began to crumble fast and, while Heath authorised the retreat of the 3/16 Punjabis from Thailand, Murray-Lyon requested permission to fall back 30 miles. Heath passed this request to Percival, who passed it to Brooke-Popham, who refused. However, Murray-Lyon kept pressing Heath – the official report describes the 11th Division as 'exhausted and disorganised' – so Heath approved a slight withdrawal.

That was enough: the troops crossed to the south bank, abandoned much of their transportation and fled into the forest and rice paddies. They trudged in heavy rain across soggy fields and swollen streams, while the excellent Japanese engineers built bridges and regraded roads in record time. Some Japanese advanced on bicycles!

The two-day fight had been a fiasco. When Murray-Lyon reassembled his division on the night of the 13th he found over 3000 men were missing, as were 50 artillery pieces, 300 vehicles and tons of supplies. Japanese fatalities in this operation were 27!

On the 14th the 11th Division dug in 30 miles south of Jitra, but found the Japanese on them almost at once. Heath arrived to visit Murray-Lyon and agreed that both the 12th Gurkha Brigade, currently 200 miles to the south, and the 28th Gurkha Brigade, 100 miles south, should be brought up. That night the 6th Brigade was in danger of being overcome and the 15th Brigade had to send elements to aid it.

Next day Murray-Lyon ordered another retreat, to the Muda River. One shortage that affected events was of anti-tank mines: it seemed impossible to get them out of their warehouses at Kuala Lumpur!

Percival authorised the evacuation of Penang Island. The islanders had been under air attack since the 11th suffering over 600 casualties: they had no fighter cover or AAA. Many of the police (Indians) had abandoned their posts. The order was for all whites to evacuate, but not natives!

A convent of nuns thought this a despicable order and refused to budge and had to be practically manhandled aboard ship. The islanders and 500 soldiers of the SSSVF were left behind. The British fled so quickly they failed to institute a scorched earth policy, leaving full warehouses, equipment and boats for the Japanese. The islanders did not panic and maintained essential services until the Japanese arrived.

On the 17th Murray-Lyon asked for permission to retreat again, though he had been joined by the 28th Brigade. Permission was granted. Percival decided to hold a new line by falling back from Ipoh along the main road through Kampar, Bidor and Kuala Lumpur. 11th Division clerks burned anything they couldn't carry as the divisional headquarters was evacuated.

On the 23rd Brooke-Popham left Singapore, his tour of duty over, glad to be relieved by Lieutenant General Sir Henry Pownall.

There were other changes that had not been scheduled: Heath replaced Murray-Lyon with Brigadier Paris. The 6th, 15th and 28th Brigades all had new commanders, the previous ones being wounded.

By now the 12th and 28th Brigades were holding a mountain position 10 miles north of Ipoh, while the 6th and 15th Brigades grabbed some rest, having retreated 200 miles in eleven days.

On the 26th, the 12th Brigade, despite having only two anti-tank guns, held off an enemy attack.

Percival had been approached again by Brigadier Simpson about completing the Johore Line and he had refused, claiming it would be bad for morale. On the 27th he abruptly changed his mind and asked the colony's Public Works Department to finish the line between Muar and Mersing. Like most government workers they set to with no great sense of urgency.

By the 28th the 12th and 28th Brigades had fallen back to the Kampar position.

The following day the 12th Brigade was hit by a severe attack including dive bombers and was given permission by Paris to retreat across the Kampar River. British armoured cars gave them covering fire. The brigade, which had incurred 500 casualties in a week, went into reserve, while the 6th, 15th and 28th Brigades manned the new position around Bidor.

On New Year's Eve the 28th Brigade repelled an attack. Next morning everyone held their positions under fire.

However, the Japanese landed on the west coast south of the Perak River using portable boats they had brought with them and boats captured at Penang. Neither Allied planes nor ships interfered with the landing.

On 2 January the 12th Brigade counter-attacked the beachhead, but failed, and on the main front the 1/8 Punjabis counter-attacked strongly, but that night all were told to retreat.

The troops fell back to the Slim River, where on the 5th the 12th Brigade repelled a Japanese probe.

On the afternoon of the 6th 20 Japanese tanks, some engineers and a battalion of trucked infantry of the 42nd Regiment advanced along the main road as if on parade. The 2/1 Gurkhas were shot up by them and had to let them pass. After dark the Japanese drove over no less than five bridges: there were no Allied engineers assigned to blow the bridges, nor had anyone been warned by the 2/1 Gurkhas. Local natives saw the tanks and ran yelling to the nearest Allied soldiers: no one believed them. The Japanese were allowed to advance so far that an AAA battery was shot up by them. By dawn even the Allied reserve, the 28th Brigade, had been bypassed by the Japanese: they had advanced 19 miles!

Percival was a worried man by now. He had already planned to withdraw to the Johore Line, but not this early. He received news that the 11th Division and the two brigades were fleeing southwards, swimming and rafting across swollen rivers, having abandoned vehicles, guns and equipment. The latest strength reports stated that the 12th Brigade had but 500 riflemen and the 28th Brigade just 600, and the 6th and 15th Brigades were only slightly larger. The 2/1 Gurkhas had been wiped out.

Meanwhile Churchill had authorised a new command structure for the Far East, ABDA named for the Australians, British, Dutch and Americans involved in this war against Japan, and he gave command of ABDA to Indian Army Field Marshal Archibald Wavell, who set up his headquarters on Java. Pownall became his chief of staff.

Wavell approved Percival's retreat to Johore, and Percival replied by saying he planned to defend that line with the Australian 8th Division and the British 18th Division, soon to arrive, because III Corps was obviously done for. However, Wavell wanted every man in line and to beef up III Corps he assigned the Australian 27th Brigade to it. Major General Gordon Bennett, the outspoken commander of the Australian division, was annoyed by this: he did not want his Aussies frittered away under 'foreign' commanders.

To placate Bennett, Percival and Wavell agreed to give him in exchange the newly arriving Indian 45th Brigade and the Indian 9th Division, which had been methodically retreating down the eastern coast of Malaya, effectively making Bennett a corps commander. Later though, Wavell asked Bennett for his 22nd Brigade also to join III Corps.

Bennett was quickly exasperated by the British generals: they seemingly had no concernabout esprit de corps, communications or lines of supply.

Percival was in fact keenly aware of these and he wanted all of the Australians to remain on the eastern end of the line, close to their headquarters at Mersing, and III Corps to a man on the western end as most of them were approaching from the north-west, but Wavell overruled him.

During these discussions Brigadier B. W. Key was given command of 11th Division.

On the 11th Kuala Lumpur the capital of Malaya was abandoned, when it was learned that the Japanese had landed 25 miles to the west at Port Swettenham. At neither town was a scorched earth policy enforced.

On the 13th the British 18th Division began arriving at Singapore.

Next day Bennett set up an ambush at Gemas less than 140 miles north of Singapore. The Aussies let the Japanese 5th Division walk right in, then hurt them badly.

However, next morning the Japanese landed on the west coast south of the Muar River, outflanking the Australians. Brigadier Duncan was ordered to counter-attack the beachhead with his fresh Indian 45th Brigade until Bennett could extricate his men. A few Australians rushed up to help the Indians and the British 53rd Brigade of the 18th Division sent a battalion to the scene. Between them they held back the Japanese invaders for 24 hours, but it cost them one man in three killed, wounded or missing.

On the 16th another Japanese amphibious invasion near Batu Pahat outflanked everyone. At the same time part of the Japanese 18th Division landed on the east coast at Endau: two Allied destroyers interfered and one was sunk.

By these two landings the Johore Line was outflanked.

Against Wavell's orders Percival ordered III Corps to move back to the west, while the Australians and others in the east withdrew southwards.

On the 19th an Australian battalion and the 45th Brigade found a Japanese unit blocking their retreat. They attacked desperately, but could not break through and were forced to abandon their equipment and walk into thick forest. Only a quarter of the Australians, Britons and Indians reached safety. Brigadier Duncan was killed.

Percival's intention was to man the line Batu Pahat–Mersing with in the west the 11th Division and 53rd Brigade, both under III Corps, and in the east Bennett's Australian division.

On the 20th 51 newly arrived Hurricane fighters went into action in daylight. Their aim was to capture air supremacy: within a few days 26 had been shot down.

Meanwhile the Indian 44th Brigade was arriving at Singapore along with an Australian machine-gun battalion and thousands of British, Indian and Australian replacements. The remainder of the British 18th Division was to arrive soon.

The exhausted retreating troops had only just settled into their new defence line when they were attacked on the 25th. Within hours the 6th and 15th Brigades reported they were in a bind and Percival authorised a retreat.

Throughout the night these fellows pulled out, but before dawn found they had been cut off by infiltrating Japanese of the 5th Division. Heath told the British 53rd Brigade to help, but their counter-attack failed. The trapped troops were ordered by radio to abandon their equipment and vehicles and sneak through the countryside. That day the Australian 22nd Brigade stopped the Japanese 18th Division at Mersing.

On the 27th Percival asked for permission to abandon Malaya and retreat onto Singapore Island. He had known this day was coming, but it choked him up all the same. Wavell approved. Percival assigned the Indian 8th Brigade, who had fired the first shots in the campaign, to be the last to leave along with the Indian 22nd Brigade, both of Barstow's 9th Division.

That evening and over the next three days soldiers wearily stumbled southwards over the causeway that linked the island to the mainland. Some of these men had walked 515 miles!

Barstow was going forward to check on his rearguards when he ran into the Japanese: he was killed.

Survivors from the 8th Brigade managed to get across the causeway before the engineers blew a gap in it at 8.15am on the 31st, but the 22nd Brigade was abandoned.

This gave everyone on Singapore a breather. The population had increased by 50 per cent with refugees, and troops were wandering around looking for their units. Equipment was haphazardly stored and parked until the supply officers could create some sort of order out of this chaos. Japanese air raids, which had been continuous since 8 December added to the confusion. However, there was no wholesale panic among the civilians.

Just as troopships had been able to reach Singapore, so other vessels had been able to leave with refugees and wounded.

Percival took stock of his army. So far he had suffered 11,000 wounded and 14,000 missing or dead, and was missing 50 armoured cars, 330 guns and 800 vehicles. (He did not know it, but Japanese losses were 1,793 killed and 2,772 wounded.)

However, he had been reinforced, so that he now had more men than ever before: over 131,000 army, navy, air force and police, counting the sick and wounded.

He expected the Japanese to land on the north coast, east of the causeway near the naval base, which was still his primary defensive charge, therefore he installed in the east the 2nd Malay Brigade and on the north-east coast between Changi and the naval base the Indian 8th Brigade and the 11th Division, which controlled remnants of the 6th, 15th, 28th and 45th Brigades. Holding the base itself was the British 18th Division, which apart from its 53rd Brigade was new to action. The causeway was protected by the Australian 29th Brigade. All of these forces came under III Corps.

Defending the north-west was Bennett's Australian division (minus the 29th Brigade), which had the 27th Brigade just west of the causeway and the 22nd Brigade further west. Guarding the west coast was the fresh Indian 44th Brigade and on the south coast was the 1st Malay Brigade.

In reserve were the SSSVF, a group of ad hoc forces under the 12th Brigade, and DalForce (2,000 recently recruited Chinese including some Communist companies).

Percival controlled 51 infantry battalions: 15 Indian Army, 15 British, 9 Australian, 5 SSSVF, 2 FMSVF and one each from the autonomous Indian states of Mysore, Jhind, Kapurthala, Hyderabad and Bhawnagar. There were also some independent companies and the naval base was defended by marines and sailors, including survivors of Force Z. Many of the units were without adequate equipment. A few tanks had at last arrived, but they were in need of an overhaul before use!

Believing the island too small to trade space, Percival emphasized the need to stop the enemy at the water's edge.

At noon on 8 February the defenders came under a fierce artillery bombardment. Allied artillery replied, but Singapore's 15-inch guns remained silent: they pointed out to sea and could not be turned around.

That night the Australian 22nd Brigade opened fire on barges and rafts approaching them: here the terrain was swampy and extremely difficult to cover. Searchlights had been promised, but were inoperative. The Australians inflicted great slaughter on the invaders, but they kept coming oblivious of losses, 21 battalions of them from the 5th and 18th Divisions.

At dawn the Aussies found themselves outflanked by infiltrators, so they began to fall back.

Percival and Bennett decided this must be the main effort and they rushed reinforcements to the west at once: DalForce, the 12th Brigade and the 6th and 15th Brigades.

During the day the Australian 22nd Brigade fell back towards Tengah Airfield: the airmen fled leaving food on the tables!

By dusk the Aussies and DalForce were holding, as was the 44th Brigade on their left flank.

Not wishing their ground crews at the three remaining airfields to be overrun, the air force abandoned Singapore altogether, flying and sailing to Sumatra.

Just after dusk the Australian 27th Brigade west of the causeway was attacked by barges and rafts filled with the Japanese Imperial Guards Division. The struggle was fierce and the Aussies were forced inland. A company of Chinese did well here.

Percival had received several instructions from Churchill, such as: 'every inch of ground to be defended' and 'no question of surrender'. On the 10th he received the instruction to fight to the death without thought of sparing troops or the civilian population.

The same day the 27th and 29th Brigades fell back from the causeway, which the Japanese were now able to repair and use. Within hours they were crossing in trucks, horse drawn wagons and on bicycles.

Wavell flew in from Java and spoke with Percival and Bennett under shellfire. Wavell was later to say he sensed a lack of 'fighting spirit'.

Bennett placed his division and DalForce along Mandai Creek, while the Indian 12th Brigade on his left flank at Bulim fought a withdrawal action eastwards towards Bukit Panjang. Further south the 15th and 44th Brigades were falling back eastwards towards Bukit Timah to anchor with the 1st Malay Brigade, whose British, Indian and Malay troops had refused to withdraw.

On the 11th Percival was asked by Yamashita to surrender: he refused. The western third of the island had been lost and combat was taking place inside the naval base, and the Australian division and DalForce and a British battalion were holding the area of Bukit Panjang and the race course, but the 15th Brigade and part of the SSSVF had been cut off by an enemy night advance. Its left flank uncovered, the British 18th Division withdrew, abandoning the naval base. On the north-east coast the 11th Division was under assault by a landing of Imperial Guards.

By the 12th the 1st Malay Brigade was holding the south coast just west of Singapore City. To their north the 44th Brigade, then the Australian 22nd Brigade and a British battalion were also holding. They all faced the Japanese 18th Division. North of them the Australian 27th Brigade was west of Cluny Hill facing north against the 5th Division. East of the hill the British 18th Division, with 54th Brigade in reserve, was holding back the Imperial Guards, with to their east the depleted 11th Division, 8th Brigade and 2nd Malay Brigade all similarly holding back the Imperial Guards.

On the 13th a Malay battalion of the 1st Malay Brigade on the south coast was all but wiped out by a ferocious Japanese attack, having refused to retreat. The survivors of the brigade were withdrawing eastwards towards Alexandria Barracks; the 44th Brigade was retreating towards the biscuit factory; the Australian 22nd Brigade towards the golf course; DalForce and the Australian 27th Brigade towards Cluny Hill; and the 18th British Division towards Bukit Brown. All others were holding.

Percival called a council of war and for the first time Heath suggested surrender. Bennett agreed. Their intent seems to have been to avert a bloodbath. Percival, recalling his orders, refused. Indeed he suggested a counter-attack – but with what, the others asked: there were no reserves?

By the morning of the 14th the 1st Malay Brigade had fallen back 4,000 yards in the last two days to the brick works, Alexandria Barracks and the military hospital. Over the same period the 44th Brigade had retreated 3,000 yards to the biscuit factory; Australian 22nd Brigade 1,500 yards to the golf course; Australian 27th and 29th Brigades and the remnants of DalForce 1,500 yards to Cluny Hill; British 54th Brigade had entered the line to the right rear of the Aussies between Cluny Hill and Adam Park; the rest of the British 18th Division had withdrawn 1,800 yards to Bukit Brown cemetery, and some elements only 1,000 yards to Thomson village. This placed the Australian division into a bulge of about four square miles. The 11th Division, 8th Brigade and 2nd Malay Brigade had not retreated since the 12th.

On this day Percival refused another call to surrender, even after his staff and civil servants urged him to do so, but he had his mind on the water problem. Three reservoirs were in danger of being overrun and the bulk of Singapore's water supply came along an aqueduct from the mainland! It had been damaged by shellfire.

On the morning of the 15th the 1st Malay and 44th Brigades fell back another 2,000 yards and the British 55th Brigade lost the cemetery, but otherwise the troops were holding back the Japanese.

Percival received orders from Wavell to resist as long as his troops were physically capable of doing so, but allowing him the ability to judge. Percival decided his troops were no longer capable of doing so and he radioed Yamashita asking for a truce and talks. Without waiting for a reply he told his men to cease fire at 4.00pm. By radio Yamashita agreed to cease attacking.

The two generals met at the Ford factory at Bukit Timah at 5.15pm and Percival signed a conditional surrender at 6.10pm, effective 8.30pm.

Between 8 December 1941 and 15 February 1942 an army of over 145,000 had disappeared: 67,500 Indians including ISF, 38,450 Britons including colonists, 18,350 Australians and 21,000 Chinese, Malays and Tamils. About 6,000 had been killed in Malaya and 2,700 on Singapore and perhaps 3,000 escaped by boat to Sumatra (though many were captured there). Maybe 2,000 locals melted into the population to become guerrillas. Thus about 125,000 marched into captivity on Singapore to join the 6,000 or so already imprisoned. On Singapore the Japanese captured 354 guns, 200 armoured cars, a few tanks, 1,000 vehicles and 100 AAA guns.

The Japanese had lost 684 killed and 1,352 wounded just getting ashore on Singapore the first night and then 1,030 killed and 2,026 wounded up to the surrender.

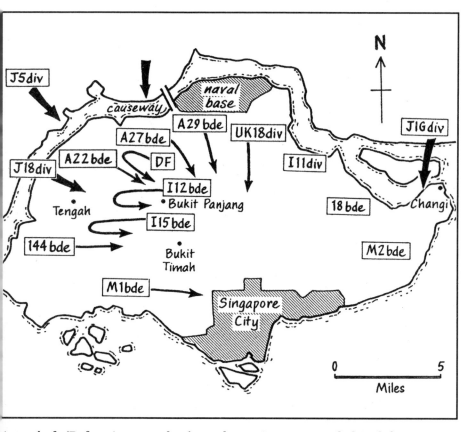

Appraisal: 'Defeat is an orphan', so the saying goes, and this defeat was no exception. Everyone blamed everyone else. Wavell blamed Percival and his commanders. Percival blamed the air force. Bennett blamed the Indian troops, bad morale among British officers and the poor quality of the British 18th Division, but praised his Australians, said the Malays fought well and the Chinese with 'great stoicism'. The Americans thought Wavell was inept.

At the heart of this squabbling was the realisation that everyone had been extremely arrogant leading them to commit major errors in seventeen categories: grand strategy, timing, firepower, intelligence, reconnaissance, communications, command structure, strategy, dispersal, supply, morale, training, ground, specialists, reserves, tactics and command ability.

From the beginning the grand strategy was flawed. Malaya and Singapore were defended not because they were a valuable colony – Burma was equally valuable and was sent only two divisions. They were defended in order to hold onto, what has been described as, 'Britain's virility symbol': the Singapore naval base. Prestige is the worst possible reason to defend a position.

Every commander wants to be able to choose the timing of battle, specifically to fight only when he is ready. Having made the decision to hold onto Singapore at all costs the governments of Neville Chamberlain and then that of Winston Churchill proceeded to deny themselves the choice of timing by wasting the time allotted them by an unprepared Japan: namely they denied the defenders of Singapore the tools to defend this 'symbol'. Of the planes requested only a quarter were provided and most of them were obsolete: no tanks were sent until it was too late; and above all just enough capital ships were sent to offer a sacrifice.

Once the fight had begun the timing of each attempt to halt the Japanese on a line was ruled by the delay of the Japanese to reach that line, but this breathing space was wasted with the failure to implement a scorched earth plan. During their retreat the Allied troops destroyed so little, that the Japanese found the colony's resources, facilities and goods awaiting them as if they had bought the colony.

The primary firepower of the defenders was the warplane and it was completely misused. Phillips's refusal to ask for air support doomed him and his ships to a suicide run. Pulford's restriction of air raids to night time after just a few hours of battle may have saved planes, but night bombing at this stage of history was notoriously inaccurate. The decision effectively removed the Allied air force from the equation. The Australian, British and New Zealand air crews were brave, but the British ground crews lacked firm discipline and the responsibility for the decision to swiftly abandon airfields lies on their shoulders and those of their commanders.

Another crucial shortage of firepower was anti-tank guns and anti-tank mines. They were few in number or sent to the wrong location. Having said that, those that were in position seemed to have been misused. The 25-pounder artillery piece could knock out a tank if used in an anti-tank role, but Japanese tanks overran artillery batteries whose gunners were sheltering from the rain!

The command structure was impossible even before the fighting began. Brooke-Popham could not directly command his air, sea and ground leaders: he could only commit Matador with Phillips's approval; Percival planned to fight the war using Heath's corps headquarters, thereby duplicating his own headquarters to no purpose; but Heath was situated 250 miles from his 11th Division headquarters, yet almost across the street from his 9th Division headquarters; the latter was almost 200 miles south of one of its brigades; and over 100 miles west of its other brigade.

Once combat began Bennett was treated as a de facto corps commander, but never given the signals equipment and supply system to cope with this new task. Brooke-Popham knew he was going home and his replacement, Pownall, arrived two weeks into the battle, but was superseded two weeks later by Wavell. Percival was very much the real commander at this time, whether he was aware of it or not. Churchill certainly treated him as such.

Intelligence gathering and appraisal was excellent, and reconnaissance was good, but both were often useless because the commanders did not react accordingly as exemplified by Percival's leaving the colony for an inspection of Sarawak at the critical moment; Phillips's lack of urgency that removed him from Singapore for three vital days; Brooke-Popham's dithering about Matador; British officers refusing to believe natives who saw Japanese tanks. The false report of an invasion at Kuantan kept Force Z at sea too long.

Communications were excellent. Churchill on the opposite side of the planet was kept up to date. However, communications were selectively used: Pulford not telling Brooke-Popham early enough of the missing PBY; Brooke-Popham not telling Churchill of the Blenheim incident; Phillips's insistence on retaining radio silence even after he knew the Japanese were watching him.

The strategy was flawed from day one, for it had the word 'retreat' built into it. Strategy normally leads to an attack, a defence, a defence until reinforcements arrive for a counter-attack, or a short withdrawal to a defensive strongpoint. A strategy of 'retreat at once until your back is to the sea' is doomed to failure.

This brings us to dispersal. It is true that such a large colony cannot be wholly defended, so units had to be selectively placed for defence. However, Percival committed his units to airfield defence, the worst possible use of infantry. Thus instead of forming a defensive pocket the troops were scattered all over, for example, between the 8th Brigade and the nearest friendly troops was 180 miles of mountainous jungle.

This points out the supply problem. In static warfare normally the supply route from corps headquarters to division should be about 20 miles, with 10 miles at most between division and brigade, therefore 30 miles from corps to brigade. The shortest supply route in Malaya was 100 miles between III Corps and 22nd Brigade, and the longest was 270 miles between III Corps and 6th Brigade. Moreover the road network was primitive and some routes led over inhospitable mountains, and all were under enemy air control.

Considering how arrogant the senior commanders were it is all the more unsettling to learn how low morale became. High morale without foundation always collapses at the first shot. The eagerness of British ground crews to abandon airfields is evidence. The morale of British troops was shaken by the knowledge that the Royal Navy with all its sophistication and technology could be decisively defeated, that the Royal Air Force could be vanquished, and British Army generals could be frightened, and all by Orientals.

In the past eighteen months the British Army had retreated in Norway, Belgium, France, Somaliland, Greece and Crete, and each time the good old navy had rescued them. But with every step in retreat across muddy Malaya, the soldiers suspected there would be no naval evacuation this time. They became convinced of this on Christmas Day when told that the 12,000-man garrison of Hong Kong had been overrun.

Hitler said man does not die for business, but for ideals. In Malaya the soldiers felt they were being asked to die for business, for the plantations and farms owned by rich colonists and wealthy private companies.

Among non-white troops racism accounted for much bad morale. For the official history to describe the 11th Division as 'exhausted and disorganised', because it had waited in the rain for a week and then fought for one day, is an alarming indictment. The Indians were not enthusiastic fighters, especially when nearby British battalions pulled out (under orders to do so). As early as the first week of action some Indians had defected to the enemy! Eventually, almost 40 per cent of the Indian prisoners joined the Japanese to fight the British!

It is, therefore, surprising how well the Malays and Chinese fought and that anti-British activity by the civilian population was more rumour than fact.

Among the generals as soon as the retreat began the bubble of arrogance burst. They consoled themselves with the belief that they were up against five enemy divisions and that the Japanese were jungle experts. In truth the Japanese used only one division and a few extra battalions for several weeks and never more than three divisions and never needed to call upon their reserves. As for the jungle, most of Malaya is not jungle and anyway jungle was as much a novelty to the Japanese as it was to the Queenslanders and Yorkshiremen.

Good training could have offset bad morale to an extent, but frankly training was sorely lacking: some British troops went into action without rifle instruction. Small unit tactical training was practically unknown. Some of the brigades had not had brigade manoeuvres and none of the five Allied divisions had ever enjoyed divisional manoeuvres. The shifting of battalions from brigade to brigade only exacerbated this problem: for example, the troops of the Malay Division spoke nine different languages.

Time and again ground was misused. The 11th Division was in the lowlands, where it could be easily overrun, not in a mountainous 'castle' where it could hold out. Defensive positions were dug on the wrong side of rivers, with their supply routes leading over precarious bridges. The purpose of choosing a river is to block the enemy with it, not block one's own line of retreat. Once the enemy had broken through and taken a bridge everyone north of the river was lost. The Japanese breakthroughs on the Jitra Line and the Slim Line were textbook examples of an enemy taking advantage of his opponent's poor use of ground.

There were colonists and natives available who knew the countryside like the back of their hand. Small guerrilla teams of jungle and demolition specialists left behind could have wrought merry hell with Japanese supply lines and added to Yamashita's worries.

Reserves were totally misused. Survivors of 6th and 15th Brigades were angry to find later that while they were bearing the brunt of the enemy attack for many days, the Indian 22nd Brigade and an Australian division were still in barracks. The Allies began the campaign with ten brigades on the mainland, but for the first month the enemy only had to contend with four of these.

The tactics of colonels and brigadiers were hopeless. Using entire battalions as trip wire units was not only a waste of needed manpower but it dangled them like bait: too small to survive, too large to evade and return to safety.

This leads us to an assessment of command ability. It does seem that Percival passed the buck too many times at first, perhaps feeling he was supposed to, and the decision of Heath to allow a partial retreat shows that either he did not realise such an order would cause a complete rout or he did realise but felt the need to disobey Brooke-Popham. Wavell's switching of brigades like they were ships in a fleet in primitive country under monsoon rains was rash to say the least, especially as he went against their tenuous lines of supply. Percival's re-switching to accommodate the supply officers at a time when any movement of units risked their dislocation and destruction only compounded Wavell's error.

Alternatives: The immediate alternative that comes to mind is not to have fought at all, but to have left the colony to the enemy in the manner that others were. Japan was a naval power and as such could only be defeated at sea, which included the seizure of island airfields. Never again was Malaya conquered by battle. In August 1945 the Japanese, their sea lanes commandeered by the Allies, their cities under air attack from island airfields, called it quits and handed back their conquered territories.

However, once Churchill had made up his mind to defend the colony the defenders of 1941 had the option of choosing the mountainous spine of Malaya for their final stand or flat indefensible Singapore. MacArthur held out on Bataan Peninsula in the Philippines for three and a half months and that was without pre-stocked supplies. Had the defenders of Malaya planned a mountain strategy and stockpiled supplies, they may have held out for several months.

Was Churchill right to ask for 'no surrender'? This is an academic question, but it is interesting to note that in Singapore the Japanese were seriously out-numbered and on 12 February they made five separate advances with an average of 830 yards per advance, on the 13th five advances averaging slightly less, on the 14th four advances of an average of 750 yards each, and on the 15th up to 4.00pm only two advances of 2000 yards each and one of 200 yards. The Japanese rate of advance was definitely slowing down. Their continuance of heavy air raids showed that the Japanese did not expect to capture the island so soon. Indeed on the 15th Yamashita was considering a retreat as he was almost out of ammunition and he and his chief of staff Colonel Masanobu Tsuji were caught completely off-guard by Percival's message!

Consequences: The immediate result of the defeat was the enslavement of the native population of Malaya and Singapore. If they had thought themselves oppressed by the British, well they were soon praying for the return of the British. Murder of innocents, slave labour, enforced prostitution was the reality of Japanese rule.

As for the military prisoners many wounded were murdered by the Japanese: shot, bayoneted and beheaded. Women soldiers were brutally raped before being murdered. Everywhere there was butchery. The prisoners of war and 15,000 civilian white colonists (men, women and children) were placed in prison camps without access to medicines or adequate food: they died like flies.

Percival endured his captivity with courage and after his liberation at war's end he retired owing to ill health. He spent his retirement defending his conduct of the battle.

Wavell was in Java when Percival surrendered and he flew to India to take up a political position.

Bennett, despite asking Percival to surrender, did not do so himself, but made his way with a few followers by boat all the way to Australia. He was treated with revulsion by the Australian public.

The Battle's Place in History: Churchill called it: 'the worst disaster and largest capitulation in British history', but it was more than that. It was the death knell of the British Empire, perhaps all white supremacist empires. It taught the dark-skinned people of the planet that a white army could be demolished by a non-white army. Every anti-colonial revolt from 1942 onwards drew inspiration from 'Singapore'.

1943

Kasserine

The Army: The United States Army shrank after World War I to a point where it could barely man the border if a crisis arose, let alone send expeditions abroad. It consisted of three components: regulars, reserves and the National Guard.

The regulars contained two types of individual. The most numerous were the work-shy, who took from the army far more than they put into it, content with evenings and weekends off duty and days spent painting or digging or marching. Men who had reached colonel in the war were reduced to major and below after it, and top sergeants to corporal. In the 1930s to retire after twenty years' service having had only one promotion was common. Officers were happy if they made captain within their first twenty years. It was an easy life if you could cope with mindnumbing monotony.

The other type of regular was the warrior, of whom there were few: men like George S. Patton, who had once gunned down a Mexican 'bandito' with a quick draw of his pistol and had led tanks in World War I; or Terry Allen, who didn't let a little thing like a bullet in the jaw curtail his ambitions.

The second component of the army was the reserves, but in the 1930s reservists rarely made meetings and almost forgot they were in the army.

The third component, the National Guard, was an American peculiarity. These reservists were soldiers of their state, not the nation, and were in fact the old militia under a new name. Usually their only call to duty was to put down riots and prevent looting after storms. Although they were soldiers of their state, collectively their units were components of the Federal army and like the militia of old could still be called upon to fight wars: in World War I a third of American divisions had been 'state' units.

Wary of the turn of events in Europe in 1939 the army under the command of General George Marshall created new tank units and once again Patton was called upon to help whip them into shape. The tanks were placed into armoured divisions, which were structured as follows: signals company; engineer battalion; three artillery battalions, each with eighteen self-propelled 75mm guns (SPGs); a reconnaissance battalion with armoured cars, eighteen Stuart tanks and infantry carried in half-tracks; two armoured regiments of three tank battalions each; and an armoured infantry regiment of three battalions.

Each tank battalion consisted of 53 tanks, six 105mm SPGs and seventeen armoured cars. Each armoured infantry battalion carried nine 57mm anti-tank guns, three 105mm SPGs and three companies of riflemen in half-tracks.

The bulk of American divisions were infantry, consisting of: signals company; engineer battalion; three battalions of twelve 105mm howitzers each and one battalion of twelve 155mm howitzers; a reconnaissance company of armoured cars; and three regiments of six 105mm howitzers, twelve 57mm anti-tank guns and three infantry battalions each. Each infantry battalion was divided into a headquarters company, heavy weapons company and three rifle companies, manning 32 machine guns, nine 60mm mortars, six 81mm mortars, three 57mm anti-tank guns plus 324 actual riflemen in twelve-man squads each of which had one automatic rifle. American infantry divisions were highly mobile compared to German or Italian, for there were no less than 2,017 motor vehicles for 14,253 personnel, and no need for horse-drawn wagons.

Once the Japanese attacked Pearl Harbor, followed a few days later by declarations of war by Germany and Italy, the Americans knew they were well and truly participants in World War II, which the British had been fighting for two years.

Marshall was already in the process of overseeing the expansion of the army from half a million regulars, reservists and National Guardsmen to a requirement of over eleven million. Initially men in their twenties were conscripted and others allowed to volunteer. Anyone with adult education was commissioned and anyone who did well in the entry exams was sent to cook school, engineer school, artillery school, radio school etc., after a couple of months of which they graduated as sergeants. The army grew overnight, and by summer 1942 it was quite common to find an entire company with no one in it from captain to private with over six months' service.

With so many 'civilians' in uniform it was decided that America's opening campaign should be fought by the regulars of the 1st and 2nd Armoured, 1st, 3rd and 9th Divisions, plus the 34th Division made up of state soldiers from South Dakota, Iowa and Minnesota. However, all these units had taken in reservists and conscripts to meet required strengths.

Grand Strategy: The reason why the desert was the first choice of battlefield was not because that is where the enemy was, but because that is where he was not.

To be precise, Churchill talked Roosevelt into attacking French North Africa (Morocco, Algeria and Tunisia) with four aims: win a victory in Britain's (but not America's) war with France; put Allied troops in Tunisia, in the rear of the Italian-German Panzer Army Afrika in Libya; and if handled right, to convince the French to defect to the Allied cause, thereby making North Africa a springboard for an Allied invasion of German-occupied southern Europe.

Japan did not figure in this picture and Churchill emphasized that Germany and Italy should be defeated before Japan was tackled. Roosevelt agreed.

Roosevelt and Churchill certainly handed their admirals a headache: to transport 100,000 men and women 4,500 miles from the USA to Morocco and 2,900 miles from Britain to Algeria and 3,300 miles from Britain to Tunisia and land them under fire, with the only land-based air support coming from tiny Gibraltar 500 miles from Algiers.

Obviously they would have to rely on aircraft carriers, but the admirals were loath to risk these precious vessels in the Mediterranean, where they were vulnerable to German, Italian and French planes, ships and submarines. After much wrangling the admirals agreed to sail as far east as Algiers but no further. The troops would have to reach Tunisia overland from Algeria.

Battlefield: Not only did the Allies have to reach Tunisia before the Germans and Italians cottoned on and entered that country, but they had to beat the winter rains. American GIs would find that the African desert was nothing like that portrayed in the movies. Sure, there were some sand dunes, but most of the terrain was similar to the American deserts: high bare rocky mountains, sharp ridges, gullies (called wadis in Africa) and scrub grass that barely kept alive the small herds of sheep tended by the local nomads. The coastal belt was often lush and green with cultivated fields and vineyards, but the British got that territory: the Americans got the inhospitable desert. Nor was it hot, but downright cold at night, and in December the rains and hail would turn the roads (almost all of them dirt) into streams of liquid mud.

The Commanders: As Roosevelt was bringing the most toys to the party he got to choose the commander. Many were surprised by his choice: Lieutenant General Dwight D. Eisenhower, who bragged that he was a simple Kansas farm boy. Preferring to be called Ike, Eisenhower had never seen action, had never commanded a unit larger than a battalion, and had been a lieutenant-colonel as recently as 1939. Roosevelt chose him because he was a good planner. General MacArthur had another word for it: 'Best clerk I ever had.'

The generals who would be taking America's army into battle against the European enemy were Major Generals George S. Patton, Charles Ryder and Lloyd Fredendall. In these men's hands lay the prestige and honour of the army, for their mistakes could damage home front morale at the outset, already suffering a terrible knocking from Pearl Harbor and the abandonment of the Philippines.

Ryder was an unassuming man, but Patton and Fredendall were such loud, flamboyant, outspoken, blustery characters, it is a wonder they had not been thrown out of the conservative army. The reason they had been retained was that each had 'delivered' when required, Patton in combat and in his tank expertise and the 59-year-old Fredendall in his ability to train troops and handle major exercises with panache.

The landings in North Africa were divided into three commands: Patton would take the 2nd Armoured, 3rd and 9th Divisions into three amphibious invasions of Morocco; Fredendall would land the 1st Armoured and 1st Divisions at Oran, Algeria; and Ryder would take his 34th Division, some 9th Division men and British troops into Algiers.

On 8 November 1942 the Americans in their brown woollen uniforms and new round helmets hit the beaches. French troops in their own version of brown uniform fought back. Despite initial losses, Ryder secured a surrender of Algiers on the first day, but Patton had a rough air, sea and ground fight on his hands.

Under Fredendall Major General Orlando Ward's 1st Armoured Division and Major General Terry Allen's 1st Division landed near Oran and advanced against light resistance for 30 miles before dusk.

The following day Fredendall's troops captured La Senia airfield, but the French counter-attacked. Fredendall's staff noticed a potential weakness here: Fredendall talked of retreating! However, next day the French in North Africa opted for the Allied cause. The fighting was over.

It was now the turn of the British First Army to disembark in Algeria and drive into Tunisia. In command was a 51-year-old Scot, Lieutenant General Kenneth Anderson, who had a reputation for being dour and unlikeable. He had distinguished himself in World War I, but apart from commanding a division in the Dunkirk evacuation, he had never led a large force in action.

Causes of Arrogance: The Americans had won their first action and this always makes an army slightly cocky. However, cooler heads tried to point out that most of the French had welcomed the Americans and had made it difficult for their fellow countrymen to resist, while others had surrendered after token resistance. Few had fought with ardour. In other words this was not a real test of American military prowess.

Still the press loved it and Roosevelt and Marshall were well pleased. They authorised a battle star decoration for the three-day operation and handed out a few medals. In victory generals do not as a rule sit down to study why they won. Therefore, lessons that could have been learned were ignored.

One reason for American arrogance was their weaponry. American film newsreels made for public consumption explained that American tanks were the best in the world, without offering any proof in support. Similar films were made about their planes. The troops saw these films too.

The army had settled upon three basic designs of tank. The M3 Stuart was a 12.5-ton vehicle, which could glide down a smooth road at 35mph. In its cramped compartment it carried four crewmen and the turret mounted a 37mm gun and two machine-guns. The Stuart could shoot through the armour of every known German and Italian tank at up to 500 yards' range.

The M4 Sherman was a 30-ton vehicle of which the Americans were very proud. Despite its weight it could reach 24mph and its five crewmen operated a 75mm gun and three machine-guns.

The Sherman could shoot through anything at 1000 yards. The M3 Lee was in essence a combination of the other two, a 27-ton vehicle carrying six crew who operated a 75mm gun firing from the hull, a 37mm gun in a turret and four machine-guns, one in a mini-turret atop the turret.

In reserve and not assigned to armoured divisions were battalions of tank destroyers. This fanciful term was used for the M10, a 30-ton tank manned by five men and firing a 3-inch gun.

The infantry were well equipped too: the .50in and .30in calibre machine-guns, though left over from World War I, were extremely reliable and accurate; every twelfth infantryman had an automatic rifle; riflemen were issued the brand new .30in calibre Garand rifle, which could fire its eight-round magazine without manually operating the bolt; and Americans were liberally provided with grenades.

Two other factors lifted American morale. On 4 November British General Montgomery and his Eighth Army soundly trounced Rommel's Italian–German Panzer Army Afrika in Egypt, and two weeks later the Soviets surrounded a German army at Stalingrad. It seemed the enemy was on the ropes already and all the Americans had to do was deliver the knockout punch, a repeat of America's role in World War I.

A further factor in American morale at this time was lifestyle. Americans had arrived in Britain and Northern Ireland to find a land primitive by American standards. Almost every American family owned a car and was thus able to move to better neighbourhoods or even better towns as their income rose, and though these young Americans had grown up through the terrible depression, the city boys among them still found the homes of the British to be of poor quality compared to their own, for the British working class maintained several generations in tiny two up two down terraced houses with outside toilets, no gardens and crammed together under soot-filled skies. However, the homes of native Africans, basically overcrowded hovels, were primitive by British standards! The Americans (not for the last time) mistook possession of material goods as a sign of military efficiency.

Another reason for American arrogance was that 85 per cent of Americans were descendants of immigrants who had fled Europe for the freedom and promise of America. In American minds this spoke wonders – America must be better than Europe – and as the enemy was European, well the conclusion was obvious. Just like their fathers in World War I, the Americans were going to kick the living hell out of the 'Krauts'.

The Enemy: At the news of the American landings Hitler and Mussolini realised that only Tunisia stood between the Allies and the rear of Rommel's army, now retreating into Libya. German planes began flying troops to Tunisia at the rate of 1,000 a day and Italians sailed to Tunisia and drove in from Libya. They would eventually constitute Fifth Panzer Army under General Jürgen von Arnim, an ad hoc force made up of: the 10th Panzer (armoured) Division, 334th Division, a provisional division, the Hermann Göring Division manned by airmen, the Italian Superga Division and the Italian 50th Brigade.

These units would not fight homogeneously, but would be farmed out in battle groups as needed. Their punch was the German tank arm: Mark IIIs with 50mm guns and Mark IVs with 75mm guns. The crisis was so severe that Hitler authorised the use of three Tiger tanks straight from their brand new assembly line. No one had faced a Tiger before and the Germans put much faith in the new vehicle: the 55-ton monster carried an 88mm gun and could not be knocked out by any Allied tank gun hitting the turret or front.

The Campaign: Logistics was the biggest problem for Anderson's First Army of the 6th Armoured and 78th Divisions, some paratroopers and commandos and Ryder's American 34th Division, and it was six days before the British reached the Tunisian border. They found the French Tunis Division in combat with Germans and Italians and they joined the battle at once.

Over the next two weeks the combined force of Britons, Americans, French and Tunisians advanced 25 miles, which put them only 12 miles from the city of Tunis and the coast. The campaign seemed to be won.

But on 1 December the Germans counter-attacked, leading with their three Tigers: the British lost 55 tanks and 1,000 men and were forced to withdraw.

Anderson asked for reinforcements and Eisenhower sent him Ward's 1st Armoured Division. British officers were muttering under their breath that it was time for the Yanks to put their money where their mouth was.

However, Ward's 2/13 Tank Battalion was completely defeated by a few 88mm AAA guns and some Mark IV tanks, and one of his armoured infantry battalions retreated after an air raid! On the 10th Ward's tanks stood up to sandy-uniformed German infantry, but fled when German tanks approached. The British were not impressed.

On the 22nd, despite heavy rains having turned the ground into glutinous mud, Anderson ordered an offensive. The American 18th Regiment of Allen's 1st Division was brought up and told to occupy Longstop Hill, which was in British possession. The American riflemen blindly stumbled uphill in the rain to find the Germans waiting. The next three days were marked by a shambles of communication. The Americans blamed the 'Limeys' for their 350 casualties, and the British blamed the 'Yanks' for their 200 losses.

Eisenhower had a serious problem on his hands. British and American common soldiers were getting along very well with each other, but their officers were butting heads. American officers complained that Anderson had badly mishandled them. It did not help that Anderson appeared unsociable.

Eisenhower decided to separate the nationalities by confining Anderson to control of British only under his First Army: 6th Armoured and 78th Divisions, the soon-to-arrive 46th Division and miscellaneous units. Lieutenant General L. Koeltz would receive control of French XIX Corps: the Tunis, Moroccan, Algiers and Constantine (Algerian) Divisions, consisting mostly of natives from those colonies with French officers and support troops.

Eisenhower placed the Americans under Fredendall as II Corps: 1st Armoured, 1st and 34th Divisions, the 60th Regiment of 9th Division, 1st Ranger Battalion, 1st Tank Destroyer Group of four battalions of M10s, four regiments of combat engineers, a battalion of anti-tank guns and two battalions of SPGs. He would also have some British and French reconnaissance troops. Fredendall got the best weather, for the south was still comparatively dry, whereas Koeltz to the north and Anderson still further north would be dealing with mud all the way.

It would take a week or two before the units were reassigned and of course these three commanders needed a ground commander above them and Eisenhower took that job himself. He would direct the land battle from Algiers 400 miles away, while also directing air and sea operations and dealing with Churchill and Roosevelt who were constantly offering suggestions.

The American and British press now expected big things as the Americans were at last under their own commanders.

However, before the transfer could be fully made a battalion of Stuarts was ambushed by German tanks and retreated after losing four tanks, abandoning French and British infantry. There were reports that the French were so angry, they fired upon the Americans!

Stuart crewmen found that while they had to wait until the enemy was within 500 yards to guarantee destruction, the enemy could blast away with tanks and 50mm anti-tank guns at 1,000 yards.

Another problem that had not revealed itself until now was that the Stuart stood 8 feet 3 inches high, offering a high silhouette in the open desert and it was difficult to hide in a wadi or depression. The M10 was 8 feet 5 inches high. The Sherman was 9 feet high as was the half-track 75mm SPG, the M7 105mm

SPG was 9 feet 5 inches, and the Lee was 10 feet 3 inches! Whereas the British Crusader tank was 7 feet 4 inches: and of the enemy only the Mark IV at 8 feet 7 inches had a high silhouette; the Mark III was 7 feet 9 inches as was the Italian M13; and the excellent Italian Semovente 75mm SPG was only 6 feet. German and Italian towed anti-tank guns could be hidden behind a bush four feet high.

Fredendall's staff were surprised when he announced he would set up his headquarters at Tebessa, for it was not even in the same country as the battlefield. It was in Algeria, 120 miles from the front. He then dismayed many of his officers by calling upon engineers, who were badly needed elsewhere, to build a bunker system to rival the pyramids, his excuse being the danger of air raids. Once ensconced he did not venture forth from his bunker, creating a siege mentality.

When Ward reported to Fredendall he complained that Anderson had never used his 1st Armoured Division as a unit, but had doled out its components in penny packets. If Fredendall heard him, he took no notice for he proceeded to divide the division into two combat commands CCA and CCB, and gave Ward command of CCA only. Fredendall claimed CCB as his own reserve to be based at Sbeitla 25 miles from the front, alongside Ward's headquarters.

Fredendall decided to hold a line stretching from the Ousseltia Valley with the 1st Division and 60th Regiment, which anchored on the French corps, then 50 miles southwards across precipitous rocky mountains through outposts at Pichon to the Sidi Bou Zid-Faid track, still temporarily held by men of the Constantine Division, then southwards across 40 miles of open desert to Maknassy held by a few men of CCA, thence fully 50 miles south-west to Gafsa where an airfield was held by the Rangers and some British and French reconnaissance troops. In other words south of Pichon there was no continuous front line. Fredendall chose to hold only specific passes through the mountains and even directed where individual companies should be placed, all from his maps without ever visiting the terrain.

On 20 January the French Corps got into trouble and Eisenhower ordered Fredendall to help. He sent his reserve, CCB under Brigadier General Paul Robinett, but the message Robinett received from Fredendall was so intricate that he had to study it and get advice, even after it had been deciphered! Fredendall used words like 'elephants' and 'big boys' to describe tanks.

Believing he understood, Robinett led CCB northwards from Sbeitla, and asked the French for instructions (their French was easier to understand than Fredendall's English). He was told to advance down the road through desert mountains towards Ousseltia.

On the afternoon of the 21st CCB ran into Germans and was stopped by artillery fire, whereupon the French told Robinett to turn north, but he answered that he needed to refuel first, upon which the French replied that he should go back home. Robinett refuelled and then did as told, returning to II Corps. The French then complained to Eisenhower.

Eisenhower knew that Rommel's army would eventually drift into Tunisia, but was not worried as long as Montgomery had his teeth in Rommel's pants and on 23 January Montgomery reported that Rommel had just left Tripoli, 300 miles from Tunisia.

On the 31st elements of the Constantine Division still holding the Sidi Bou Zid-Faid track were struck by the 21st Panzer Division, one of Rommel's units. Both Eisenhower and Fredendall were alarmed: obviously Montgomery had been wrong. The Constantine troops pleaded for aid immediately as they were about to be overrun, and Fredendall called upon Ward to send CCA from Sbeitla under Brigadier General Raymond McQuillin.

It took all day for CCA to cover the 30 miles, possibly because McQuillin was a World War I veteran, who moved methodically as if still fighting that war. During the drive their strung-out column in bright sunshine was strafed by German planes and then by American planes. Thoroughly dispirited by this, some machine-gunners fired at their own planes!

It was dark before CCA reached the scene of battle, by which time the French and Algerians had already been overrun. McQuillin decided not to attack for he knew his tanks were blind at night, something that infantry never appreciated.

He attacked next morning, but the Germans had put anti-tank guns in his path. He retreated.

By now the French and British were complaining of Eisenhower's handling, and to prevent the shaky Allied alliance from falling apart Eisenhower agreed to let Anderson command the whole ground battle.

Anderson issued orders to Koeltz and Fredendall at once: the Constantine would be reunited under Koeltz, who would also receive elements of the US 1st and 34th Divisions, and Anderson commandeered Ward's CCB as his own reserve. This left Fredendall without one complete division.

Having lost his reserve, Fredendall ordered Ward to divide his CCA into a new CCA at Sidi Bou Zid under McQuillin and CCC under Colonel Alexander Stark at an exposed position 40 miles north of CCA. The 168th Regiment of the 34th Division took over the Sidi Bou Zid-Faid track. Fredendall picked these dispositions himself – in his bunker reading from a map.

The Battle: Eisenhower was worried about the constant switching of units and on 12 February, despite no longer being ground commander, he visited Fredendall in his bunker, expressing his concern for the loose and extended front line. However, far from gaining consensus, he found Fredendall complacent and his staff downright haughty. In addition to the loneliness of each desert outpost, Eisenhower was worried about the fact that field grade officers would have to fight the next battle on their own, without the benefit of the experience and knowledge of generals. Fredendall seemed not to understand, yet Eisenhower found Ward effectively without a job and twiddling his thumbs.

Eisenhower had cause to worry. Rommel had been dismissed from his command because of his retreat, but he had convinced Hitler to let him go to Tunisia to control a limited attack on the Americans by borrowing units from his old Panzer Army Afrika and from von Arnim's Fifth Panzer Army. Rommel chose three routes of advance: Faid Pass through Sidi Bou Zid to Sbeitla, and Maknassy towards Sbeitla, using battle groups from the 10th and 21st Panzer Divisions; and Gafsa towards Feriana using battle groups of the 15th Panzer and Italian Centauro Divisions: committing a total of 205 German and 23 Italian tanks and about 5,000 German and 1,000 Italian infantry.

In the early hours of 14 February a few miles east of Sidi Bou Zid Lieutenant-Colonel John Waters, Patton's son-in-law, was trying to keep his head down in the middle of a sandstorm. On a hill he had a battalion of the 14th Armoured Infantry Regiment (1st Armoured Division) and an infantry battalion of the 168th Regiment (34th Division). On a nearby hill Colonel Thomas Drake commanded the remainder of the 168th. Suddenly they came under artillery fire and as the sand ceased to blow they were assaulted by German infantry. The battle was on.

McQuillin in his headquarters, a collection of vehicles and tents in a cactus patch a mile from Sidi bou Zid, was responsible for this sector and he knew something was up when his radio calls went unanswered. Then as the sandstorm cleared his headquarters was attacked by German planes. He gathered his 51 tanks and some SPGs and sent them under Colonel Louis Hightower eastwards to assist Waters and Drake.

American desert tank tactics were for the tanks to advance side by side with the centre of the line a little further ahead, making a slight V shape, as if the tanks were horse cavalry. The Germans watched them with binoculars and moved their tanks and anti-tanks guns to the flanks. They quietly allowed Hightower's tanks to come in closer and closer until they had passed the Germans on the flanks.

The Americans were totally unaware and were not looking for the enemy, for they had not yet reached Waters' and Drake's positions. In an instant the Americans were completely surprised as on their rear flanks innocuous looking scrub bushes suddenly turned into anti-tank guns and tanks appeared out of dips in the rolling ground. One by one American tanks were destroyed: some exploded in flames as armour-piercing shells struck their petrol tanks; others shattered into pieces with turrets tossed into the air as shells struck their stored ammunition; and others simply came to a groaning halt as an armour-piercing shell bored through the hull and then spun around at lightning speed like a marble in a tin, smashing all in its path. Only seven tanks managed to withdraw. Hightower escaped his burning tank and managed to outrun German infantry.

The 81st Reconnaissance Squadron (battalion) was at McQuillin's headquarters, but after being attacked again by aircraft and then shelled by German tanks, the squadron's Stuarts, armoured cars and half-tracks fled northwards. McQuillin ordered an evacuation at noon and his staff packed up in record time and drove northwards under air attack. Some vehicles were strafed and bombed, but others were abandoned because they ran out of fuel: no one stopped to tow them. It was a sad sight. The tail end of the column was shot up by German reconnaissance vehicles.

By nightfall McQuillin had lost four battalions of infantry, 44 tanks, 26 SPGs, 59 half-tracks and 24 other vehicles.

Once Ward in Sbeitla was told of the affair he reported to Fredendall that nothing stood between his divisional headquarters and the Germans, except the shaky survivors of the morning's encounter and his own rear-echelon. Fredendall could not send his reserve to aid CCA as CCA was his reserve. Meantime McQuillin had driven 16 miles before setting up his headquarters in another cactus patch: he had fifteen vehicles left.

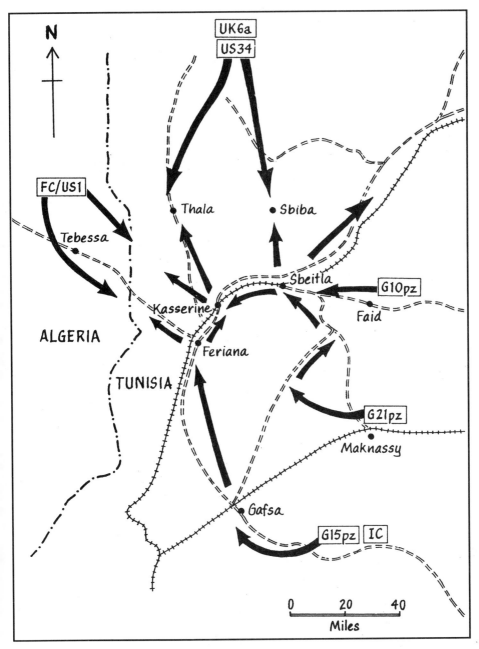

Fredendall had to ask Anderson for help, and Anderson responded with the 2/1 Tank Battalion from CCB and he authorised Fredendall to evacuate Gafsa. Fredendall decided one tank battalion was not enough, so he ordered Stark to abandon his section of the line 40 miles north of Sidi bou Zid and with his CCC rush to the rescue.

Fredendall passed on the message to Gafsa and here the small force of Americans, Britons and French packed their belongings into vehicles, destroyed what they could not carry and retreated north. At the nearby airfield air force ground crews did the same.

It was the following morning, the 15th, before CCC and 2/1 Tank Battalion reached Sbeitla, where Stark conversed with Ward, and mid-morning before they could all move out to meet the enemy. Stark was an infantry officer, not a tanker, so he allowed Colonel James Alger to take command of the assault: 58 Lees, a few hundred infantry in half-tracks, some SPGs and a few M10s.

They came under air attack at once, and the vehicles scattered wide into the flat desert scrub, bouncing in and out of wadis. The half-tracks carrying infantry and equipment, the half-track 75mm SPGs, the 105mm SPGs and the M10 tank destroyers were all vulnerable to aerial strafing as they had no roofs. It took hours to regroup.

Following reorganisation Alger ordered his tanks to take up the side by side V formation. He had confidence in his tanks for they could give as good as they got at up to 1,000 yards' range. He pressed ahead, awaiting the report that one of his tanks had sighted the enemy. At 4.00pm American tanks suddenly began to explode. Not knowing where the fire was coming from Alger ordered a withdrawal. It was too late. One by one the tanks blew up or creaked to a halt. When Alger's tank blew up, he extricated himself and was captured. Only four tanks escaped.

Stark reported the incredible news to Ward, who informed Fredendall, who called Anderson, who telephoned Eisenhower. Anderson's and Eisenhower's joint decision was that II Corps had to hold the line Feriana–Kasserine–Sbeitla, 50 miles behind the original front. This line would hinge on Sbeitla, so that village must be held at all costs. Anderson also let Fredendall have the remainder of CCB: Fredendall ordered them to Sbeitla at once.

For the moment McQuillin was to bear the brunt of the next enemy assault using a motley collection of his survivors under Hightower's command and a fresh tank battalion under Colonel Ben Crosby.

On the morning of the 16th McQuillin's SPGs opened fire on the approaching Germans and temporarily stopped them.

This day Fredendall gave Drake and Waters permission to retreat: far too late, of course.

That evening, having done better than he thought he would, McQuillin asked for permission to pull back to Sbeitla, but before he received an answer his position was attacked in the dark by German infantry. The Americans repelled them, then withdrew at midnight, using SPGs to keep the Germans at arm's length.

By morning of the 17th the 1st Armoured Division's components were all united three miles east of Sbeitla under Ward, and at noon they met the advancing Germans with all arms in and around an olive grove. After four hours of major battle Ward asked permission to withdraw and Fredendall approved it. At 5.00pm everyone began pulling out, including divisional headquarters, under air attack. Fredendall radioed Stark to take elements of CCB and CCC to Kasserine 20 miles to the south-west, while the rest of the division retreated to Sbiba 20 miles north.

This same day the mixed troops who had retreated from Gafsa were attacked at Feriana by Italian and German tanks and infantry. Within an hour they were pulling out towards Tebessa, joined by air force ground crews from the nearby airfield.

Before dusk the airmen at Thelepte airfield were also fleeing towards Tebessa, their aircraft and stores only partially destroyed.

Fredendall was worried that the Germans were now just 40 miles from his bunker in Tebessa and shaken because in two days Eisenhower's new front line had been turned on the south flank and pushed in on the north flank. He ordered a new II Corps headquarters set up at Kouif, which placed him closer to his northern front, but out of the path of the enemy at Feriana.

He demanded more help, so Anderson assigned him the remainder of the 34th Division, a French regiment and the British 1st Guards Brigade (of Major General Keightley's 6th Armoured Division) to help the remnants of the 1st Armoured Division hold Sbiba, the new hinge of the line. Anderson also ordered British Brigadier Nicholson to take command of the threatened front, though Sbiba was to remain in Koeltz' sector. Anderson appointed Brigadier Charles Dunphie's British 26th Armoured Brigade (of Keightley's division) as a reserve for Nicholson. To reinforce Stark at Kasserine Anderson sent a regiment of Major General Welvert's Constantine Division and the 18th Regiment of Allen's 1st Division. Fredendall had already put the 19th Engineer Regiment there. Lastly Anderson put the remainder of Welvert's and Allen's divisions around Bou Chebka between Feriana and Tebessa in case the enemy tried to outflank Kasserine and drive into Algeria.

Eisenhower ordered his rear-echelon combed for non-essential personnel, who were to be trucked to II Corps and, despite having no combat training, assigned to combat units as replacements. Eisenhower also told Brigadier General Irwin, artillery commander of 9th Division, to take his guns to the threatened sector: it would mean a road trip of 735 miles!

Fortunately for the Allies the Germans and Italians did not press their attack on the 18th: von Arnim and Rommel were bickering as to what to do next. Rommel won the argument when Field Marshal Kesselring gave him total command of the battle.

On the 19th the defenders of Sbiba and Kasserine were attacked by battle groups of Germans and Italians. The combat was extremely rough, being fought in cold wind over bare rocky ridges and around huge boulders. There was little sandy soil to dig foxholes and few bushes to hide behind. At Kasserine Americans, French and Algerians fought shoulder to shoulder, in some cases literally. The engineers fought as infantry and did remarkably well – these were Combat Engineers, organised and trained as infantry – but they could not prevent some ridges from falling into enemy hands. French artillerymen manned their 75s until almost overrun, then limbered up their horses, withdrew a few yards, and resumed firing. Rommel personally directed the fight at Kasserine.

At Sbiba French, Algerians, British and Americans fought shoulder to shoulder. Though American and British senior officers often argued, the ordinary British 'Tommy' and American 'Yank' soon made friends.

That night Brigadier Dunphie was ordered by Anderson to take a group of all arms from his 26th Armoured Brigade to Kasserine and take command. Dunphie had Crusader tanks, 19-ton vehicles able to reach 40mph on the flat, and which, with a 2-pounder gun firing solid shot only, could give as good as they received in a tank battle.

Fredendall managed to scrape up a battalion of tanks and some infantry and sent them to Kasserine, and he sent a message to Robinett to advance with his division through Thala to approach Kasserine from the north-west, take command of all Americans there and report to Dunphie. Robinett actually controlled the remnants of CCB (some tanks of the 2/13 Battalion, a low strength battalion of armoured infantry and some SPGs), therefore he wondered what 'division' Fredendall was talking about, and assumed it was Fredendall's usual manner of encrypting messages.

Eisenhower knew that Anderson's manner grated on the French and Americans, and yet Tunisia needed a ground commander, so he had compromised with the British and offered the role of ground commander to General Sir Harold Alexander, currently Montgomery's boss. Alexander, an easy-going fellow who preferred making suggestions rather than giving orders, would take over Anderson's First Army as well as Montgomery's Eighth Army. To the Americans Eisenhower's compromises appeared to be pro-British. Patton called him: 'the best general the British have.'

On the 20th in light rain and thick mist Americans, French, Algerians and British fought off several attacks by German and Italian infantry. Many positions were overrun, but the Allies only fell back a few yards to begin the battle again. In the late afternoon at Kasserine American engineers fell back too far and French gunners had to destroy their horse-drawn 75mm guns and run. However, this short gain cost the enemy considerable casualties including the Italian commander.

Meanwhile Robinett was trying to reach Kasserine: encountering retreating American stragglers from a score of outfits he organised them into provisional units to follow him.

Anderson's chief of staff, Brigadier McNabb, was told by Anderson to make some sense of Kasserine, so he drove along rough tracks dodging trucks until he encountered Robinett who had just reached Dunphie. Dunphie willingly deigned to serve McNabb as his superior in jobs (though not in rank), but he was surprised to hear Robinett ask for orders. Robinett had been told to obey Dunphie, but he had no instructions about McNabb. Stark knew nothing of this chain of command and thought he was in charge at Kasserine. Nicholson continued to give orders as he thought he was in charge of both Kasserine and Bou Chebka, though not Sbiba as Koeltz was in command there. At Bou Chebka, Welvert and Allen were both in command. To add to the confusion McNabb ordered that Fredendall should remain in command of the whole sector.

Dunphie, Robinett and McNabb did at least agree on tactics: they would defend Kasserine by putting infantry on the high ground and tanks on the low ground. This does seem rather basic common sense, but so far no one had thought of it.

On the 21st elements of Robinett's CCB and the 1st Division fought Italians and Germans near Bou Chebka, in part because Americans of both units became lost in a downpour and struck the enemy's flank accidentally. American tanks battled Mark IIIs in a cactus patch. Eventually the Germans and Italians were stopped just five miles from the Algerian border.

At Sbiba and Kasserine the mixed-bag defenders fought off heavy attacks. However, the British Crusaders were completely defeated: the ten surviving Crusaders retreated from Kasserine and did not stop until just outside Thala, 15 miles north. The other defenders of Kasserine clung on like grim death.

That evening Brigadier General Irwin arrived at Thala with his 9th Division artillery and conferred with the British tank commander. Irwin told his men to dig in the guns; they could not rest yet, though they were thoroughly exhausted from their four-day drive.

On the following morning Irwin's forward observers watched through binoculars as tanks of the 10th Panzer Division approached. The ten British tanks moved out to do battle, while Irwin's guns gave covering fire. In the deadly encounter seven Crusaders were knocked out, but the Germans could not stand up to massed artillery and they withdrew.

This same day the defenders of Sbiba and Kasserine fought off several attacks by tanks, SPGs and infantry.

That evening Anderson moved his own headquarters and ordered Sbiba abandoned! Possession of Sbiba would enable Rommel to outflank Thala and break through into Algeria or turn north and strike the French Corps in the rear.

Fredendall left his new headquarters at Kouif to visit Welvert, and as soon as his back was turned quite a few of his staff officers fled into Algeria! Eisenhower had ordered Major General Ernest Harmon to Tunisia to help Fredendall straighten out the situation and he arrived at Kouif at 3.00am on the 23rd. He was welcomed by Fredendall, who immediately placed him in command of the battle with the words: 'The party is yours.'

However, come dawn there was no resumption of the battle and on the 24th the Allies realised Rommel had called off his offensive.

Over the next few days the Allies sorted themselves out, units searching for their parent unit, soldiers searching for their commanders, and everyone breathing a tremendous sigh of relief.

The battle had cost the French and British about 500 killed and wounded each. American losses were much more grievous: 3,400 wounded, 5,550 dead or missing, and about 345 tanks and SPGs, 200 guns and 530 vehicles.

Appraisal: Ernie Pyle was there. He shook hands with generals and slept alongside privates in foxholes: he ate with sergeants and rode with corporal jeep drivers; and dodged shells and bullets with everyone, while taking their names and addresses for his newspaper column. He was no military expert, but he wrote after the debacle: 'We Americans were so smug with our cockiness.'

He decided that the courage of Americans was not in question, but the army needed to spread themselves thicker on a front line, and streamline the command structure for quick and positive action.

If he could see this, probably many a soldier could too. Therefore, it is all the more shocking that the generals could not see it in time.

The errors of the Allies in the first three months of the Tunisian campaign were constant, but the affair beginning on 14 February, known thereafter as the Battle of Kasserine Pass, unveiled these errors to all and sundry. They fell into nineteen major categories: command structure, grand strategy, strategy, specialists, intelligence, reconnaissance, psyops, dispersal, supply, ground, counsel, morale, training, tactics, equipment, firepower, communications, command ability and reserves.

No army or civilian corporation likes to alter the chain of command, for it causes disruption. In Tunisia the chain of command from Eisenhower as Expeditionary Commander to troops of CCB changed four times in nine weeks and then ten times in one week! Moreover the names of the commanders changed: initially involving four persons and eventually involving eleven, and none of these changes was brought about by sickness or casualties. When it is realised that each individual along the chain of command had the authority to move, weaken or strengthen CCB, then the confusion becomes apparent.

Other units suffered similar command changes to the point that the troops did not know if they were coming or going, or who was in charge. Some soldiers had two different chains of command at the same time!

Six Allied divisions fought in the battle, but not one divisional commander led more than two thirds of his division, and Ward was practically ignored.

The grand strategy of invading North Africa to woo French troops to the Allied cause and suddenly appear behind Rommel like an illusionist in a theatre was a good idea, and if its accomplishment was a little haphazard it worked nonetheless, with one exception: the navy's fears left the troops 400 miles short of Tunis, and the Germans and Italians beat them to the finish line. This failure to win the race to Tunis caused further complications when Eisenhower decided to stick to the original goal. As early as late November the Allies were reduced to butting their heads against a wall.

Eisenhower's strategy to take Tunis settled into the age old siege pattern, whereby the fellows outside sat in the rain awaiting spring. The problem with this was that von Arnim's supplies came 250 miles by ship from Palermo, whereas Eisenhower's came 4,500 miles by ship from the USA to Casablanca and thence 1,100 miles by road. Furthermore, everyone knew Rommel was approaching. In other words Eisenhower could not afford a wait and see siege strategy.

Specialists, such as Montgomery's Long Range Desert Group, were available, but were ignored for the most part. A good reconnaissance force like this one could have formed a trip wire unit between von Arnim and Rommel. Rangers and commandos were also on hand, but instead of being assigned solely to sabotage raids, they were distracted by being sent on patrols of the large southern desert or to attack outposts like Sened. There is evidence that the Americans owe the slowness of Rommel's advance to a brave British specialist unit. Fredendall used 200 engineers to build his bunker, while Allied planes were stuck on muddy airfields, unable to fly, because of a shortage of engineers to create all-weather airstrips. Patton was the number one tank specialist in the US Army, yet throughout the first three months of the campaign he sat at a desk in Morocco.

There is no question that the onslaught of 14 February came as a total surprise. Eisenhower was assured by his own intelligence service and by Montgomery that Rommel's army was still hundreds of miles away and was being dogged by Montgomery. Yet the appearance in Tunisia of one of Rommel's key divisions on 1 February proved Allied intelligence was not wholly accurate. Rommel's attack on the 14th with three of his best divisions, plus the 10th Panzer borrowed from von Arnim, exposed the truth that Montgomery was at best only in contact with Rommel's rearguards and often not even that.

Yet Allied reconnaissance planes could have made things clearer, had they been able to fend off enemy fighters and had they been provided with all-weather airfields. Allied ground reconnaissance had not been sent far enough east to watch the coast road. Had they done so they would have seen Rommel's army arriving.

Allied psychological operations were at their worst in the early part of the campaign. Rommel was enticed to attack the Americans because of their poor showing to date. In December some use of the full weight of American armour would have overwhelmed small enemy detachments and given the Germans the impression that the Americans had unlimited strength. In fact Rommel came to the conclusion that they were not much stronger than he was. The reality was that Rommel on the 14th only had a preponderance of artillery: he was matched by infantry and outnumbered by tanks 2:1, and by the 19th he was outnumbered in tanks 2:1, artillery 1½:1 and infantry 4:1. Had Allied psyops managed to convey this ability to throw in heavy reserves they might have convinced Rommel not to attack at all.

Dispersal was a serious problem. That there was an outpost at Gafsa was no worry, for they could pull out instantly, and did so. But at Gafsa was a manned airfield, and much valuable material was abandoned. Worse happened at Feriana and Thelepte. Why were these airfields manned without protection? Normally airfields are in the rear of the front line not on it.

The truth was II Corps's front was too long for its resources: eleven infantry battalions manning a line longer than that manned by the other 64 Allied infantry battalions.

Additionally, this dispersal of units was made without regard to parental integrity, creating a nightmare for supply teams (supply depots, administrators, truck drivers and military police traffic directors). A narrow road cannot handle two truck convoys at the same moment, one must await the other, but which one? Also every convoy that uses a road must return on it. The Feriana-Sbeitla road was used by two divisional supply teams: the Tebessa-Thala track was used by two American divisional supply teams and II Corps's own team; the Thala–Kasserine road was used by five supply teams from a British, a French and two American divisions and II Corps; the Le Kef-Thala road was used by one British, one French and one American divisional supply teams; the Le Kef-Sbiba road was used by a British, a French and two American divisional supply teams; and the Tebessa–Feriana road was used by seven supply teams from two American divisions, a French division, American, British and French reconnaissance units and the American air force. As if this was not enough, these traffic jams were subjected to air raids.

If unit integrity had been maintained, then after the 14th the Tebessa-Feriana road would have been used by one divisional supply team, the Tebessa-Thala track by two divisional teams, the Thala-Kasserine road by two divisional teams, the Le Kef-Thala road by one divisional team and the Le Kef-Sbiba road by two divisional teams.

The choice of ground was poor: for example, the manning of mountains overlooking Faid Pass by four battalions of infantry was commendable only if tanks and anti-tank guns had been blocking the pass. Without them the infantry might as well have been in the nightclubs of Algiers for all the good they did. Their courageous fight only served to hold up German supply trucks a few hours. In any case German advances from Maknassy and Gafsa outflanked the pass immediately. This is what comes of picking ground by reading an unreliable map instead of visiting the scene.

Heaven knows Fredendall had been offered enough counsel to enable him to correct mistakes. His attitude to counsel can best be exemplified in his refusal on the 12th to take Eisenhower's worries seriously. If he would not listen to his superior, it is obvious he was not listening to his subordinates. If he had, perhaps he would not have suffered such a disaster.

This brings us to morale. It is ironic that though arrogant the Americans had poor morale. There were few warriors among them. They seemed evenly divided between 'lifers' in the regular army, who had been on a free ride for far too long, and the newly recruited sergeants and lieutenants who barely knew how to issue orders. The instant something went wrong, neither lifers nor newcomers had the know-how to get them out of a jam.

Poor training was one reason for poor performance. The purpose of an army is to fight and when not fighting to train to fight. The US Army had done no fighting and darn little training between the two world wars. Only in 1939 were major exercises brought to life again. Almost every man below sergeant had only received on the job training, and that from others of the same capability. The new sergeants who had gone to schools to learn demolition, gunnery or reconnaissance etc, had not been taught how to teach others. Therefore, it is no surprise that the standard of discipline and training was higher among National Guardsmen than it was among regulars, reservists or conscripts.

Fredendall made no effort to remedy any of these failings, despite his previous reputation as a trainer. When Patton saw II Corps after the battle, he wrote: 'have never seen so little order or discipline.'

When it came to tactics senior officers were as much in the dark as the corporals. Most tank commanders were ex-cavalry and as such treated their machines like horses, hence the cavalry style charges. The result was suicide. The Germans and Italians were astonished.

The equipment of the Americans was not nearly as good as they professed. Their description of the M10 as a 'tank destroyer' was a joke and would remain so until its crews were taught how to fight enemy tanks. With an open top its crew was vulnerable to strafing and shrapnel. The armour of American armoured vehicles was inadequate. The enemy enclosed from all angles and struck American vehicles in their rear and sides, where their armour was far thinner than the front and turrets: on the Stuart 25mm compared to 38mm. The problem of high silhouettes has already been mentioned.

As to firepower, the American reliance on the 75mm SPG offered the 1st Armoured Division less explosive power and range than was required. The 105mm was better, but the divisions still possessed no long range 155mm guns.

The 37mm gun of the Stuart and Lee was hopelessly too small, and though the Lee had a good 75mm weapon it could not fire it until the entire vehicle faced the enemy, by which time the enemy had already fired. The Sherman carried its

75mm in a turret, so it could survive an encounter with enemy tanks. The British in the desert had been issued with Lees and Stuarts as a stopgap measure a year earlier and had told the Americans of their shortcomings. The Americans had not listened.

Fredendall was in a powerful position as a corps commander, but he diluted much of his impact by poor communications, especially when he personally gave orders. His obsession with enemy 'listeners' moved him to create his own personal code system, and to be doubly secure he told no one how to decipher it. Hence the recipients of his orders were not only confused, but they assumed their corps commander was an idiot, which he was not.

Eisenhower bears responsibility for the misuse of reserves. It is astonishing that an engineer regiment and mobs of cooks, clerks and mechanics had to be thrown into the line as infantry, while Eisenhower retained the 2nd Armoured and 3rd and most of the 9th Divisions hundreds of miles to the rear. His decision to bring up the 9th Division artillery was correct, but the fact that it saved the day literally in the nick of time shows what a close-shave Eisenhower's forces had.

Command ability could have offset some of these errors, but it was sorely lacking. True, Ward was bypassed by Fredendall's orders, but he did not attempt to seize command either (like Arnold at Saratoga). McQuillin was slow to advance, quick to retreat. Stark was right to give command of an armoured battle to Alger, a tanker, but then why was this infantry-minded officer in an armoured division in the first place?

Fredendall informally abdicated command to Anderson and told his Americans to obey British officers, most of whom had no more experience than did the Americans, and he formally abdicated command when Harmon arrived. However, it can be said Fredendall abdicated his command as soon as it was given him, when he decided that enemy planes were a danger to him personally.

Six divisions fought the battle, but not one divisional commander was given responsibility for a major sector of the line. Instead the battle was fought by Anderson, Fredendall, Koeltz, one American brigadier general, three colonels and two lieutenant-colonels and three British brigadiers.

Eisenhower could have straightened this out, but at this stage of his career he was not confident enough in his own ability to be able to give unpleasant orders to officers like Fredendall, who until recently had outranked him.

Consequences: The immediate consequence of the battle was the complete restructuring of the Allied forces in Tunisia. Once Alexander took charge he sorted the British, French and Americans into national sectors.

Anderson remained, but was very much under Alexander's influence for the remainder of the campaign, after which the Montgomery faction made sure he never commanded an army in combat again.

Fredendall was sent home by Eisenhower, ostensibly to help trainers with his combat knowledge, but behind the scenes everyone knew the truth. He was replaced by Patton, thus the Americans switched from their worst tank commander to their best. Patton wrote privately: 'I cannot see what Fredendall did to justify his existence.'

According to the GI slang of the day, Patton seized II Corps by the scruff of the neck and began 'kicking asses and pulling passes', going through 'after action reports' like 'crap through a goose' and sending deadweight sergeants and officers, including McQuillin and Stark, home by the 'boatload'.

Marshall restructured the army, the most important changes being the attachment of a tank and AAA battalions to every division in the European theatre and an increased allotment of artillery to every corps. He also made chains of command and lines of supply inviolable.

Alternatives: The immediate alternative that comes to mind is to have used paratroopers and amphibious landings to seize Tunis in the first two days after the French change of heart in November 1942. This could have been done by a secondary naval task force with Allied aircraft flying from French airfields in eastern Algeria.

If the Allies had still lost the race to Tunis, they should not have continued to batter their heads against the 'walls' of Tunis, but could have made a swift tank charge, aided by paratroopers, south eastwards for 70 miles to Enfidaville on the coast to prevent any junction of Rommel and von Arnim. This would also have given the Allies the coastal plain for a quick attack northwards into Tunis.

The use of the indirect approach would have been far less costly than the direct battering ram approach adopted by Eisenhower.

The Battle's Place in History: The battle does not have much of a place in history because the Americans tend to mitigate their failures and publicise their victories. The Allies entered Tunis in May 1943, six months after they had come within twelve miles. They claimed a great victory and the Allied public, eager for any good news, accepted this without questioning the butcher's bill of 75,000 Allied casualties.

Eisenhower, Patton and Montgomery remained popular and were to be victorious again on future battlefields.

1950

Osan-Taejon

Background: Korea was annexed by Japan at the beginning of the twentieth century and during World War II Koreans were conscripted to serve as labour troops for the Japanese. Korea suffered American air raids and in August 1945 the north was invaded by Stalin's Red Army. A week later the Japanese surrendered.

American troops entered southern Korea and met the Red Army near the 38th Parallel, which more or less divided the nation in two. The two Allies shook hands once, then settled down to stare at each other with loaded weapons.

The problem was that the Americans did not trust Stalin, understandably so as he had invaded seven neutral nations since 1939. Furthermore, Communist rebellions sprang up throughout Asia in the aftermath of the Japanese surrender, which the Americans assumed were controlled by Stalin, the most important being China, where the long standing Communist army of Mao Zhe-dung turned against Chiang Kai-shek's regime; Indo-China, where communists rebelled against the French; East Indies, where communists (and others) revolted against a British-Dutch army; and Malaya, where communists rose up against the British. It did seem like Stalin wanted to create a communist Asia.

American marines were stationed in China to protect business interests and were under orders not to intervene in the civil war, but in 1949 Chiang Kai-shek's defeated army began a mass evacuation to the island of Taiwan. The defeat of a long-time friend of the USA was a shock to the American people and they wondered what on earth the US government was doing: had they gone soft on communism?

In Korea Stalin created a clone of his own USSR, choosing Kim Il-sung as the Korean dictator.

Kim was born in 1912 near Pyongyang, the north's largest city, and had either become a communist revolutionary fighting against Japanese oppression, or had become a petty bandit, depending on whether one believed the communists or anti-communists.

Either way, he certainly drifted into communism and was hand picked to study political indoctrination in Moscow. In his 29th year he joined Stalin's Red Army, probably as a political commissar for units recruited in Mongolia and Siberia, and according to the communists he performed bravely at Stalingrad.

In August 1945 following Stalin's occupation of northern Korea Stalin chose Major Kim to lead the fledgling North Korean People's Army (NKPA) and in 1948 appointed Kim premier of an independent People's Republic of Korea, which claimed to rule all Korea, but which at the moment only held sway in the north, ruling a population of 10 million.

Meanwhile in South Korea the Americans had created an American-style democracy and had chosen Syngman Rhee to head it. The Americans claimed

Syngman was the opposite of Kim: never a soldier he had been born 37 years before Kim. However, in truth he was extremely similar for he was America's version of Kim. Growing up in Korea before the Japanese conquest, a devout Christian, he went to the USA in 1904 to study theology at Harvard and Princeton, gaining a PhD. Returning to Korea, he spoke out against the Japanese and eventually had to flee. He spent the rest of his life in the USA (Hawaii). Following the American occupation of southern Korea he was brought in by the Americans and in 1948 made President of the Republic of Korea.

Both Kim and Syngman had gone abroad to study the basic philosophy of the host nation, both had then taught that philosophy and both had returned home to lead their nation. There was another similarity. Kim claimed to be a communist, a man of the people, but instead of helping them he butchered them like the good little Stalinist that he was. Syngman claimed to be a Christian and a lover of democracy, but he ruled with a vicious police and would not tolerate outspoken political opponents. He murdered and tortured to keep his position.

Syngman ruled the southern half of Korea and 20 million souls, but like Kim, he claimed to rule all Korea – he was himself a northerner – and this meant that Korea had two rulers, each with his own army. This state of affairs could not last long.

A few American diplomats and military officers suspected that the two Korean armies might become gladiators of the USA and USSR, turning Korea into a battleground for a war by proxy. They were deeply concerned when both the Red Army and US Army withdrew from Korea in 1949, unshackling Syngman and Kim. These Korea watchers expressed their concerns through the proper channels, but they were voices crying in the wilderness.

In fact on 20 January 1950 Dean Acheson, US Secretary of State for Foreign Affairs, publicly stated that Korea was outside the US defence perimeter. This sent a signal to Kim!

The Commanders: Harry Truman was no general: indeed he boasted that his military career consisted of running an artillery battery during World War I. However, he had been a member of powerful Congressional armed forces committees during World War II, and vociferous and uncouth enough in his public complaints that Roosevelt took a shine to him, picking him as his running mate in 1944. Victorious, Truman was sworn in as Vice-President, but in April 1945 received the shock of his life when Roosevelt died. Truman told the press: 'Pray for me.'

Four months later the United States ended World War II with a bang – an atomic bang. Truman, a Missouri farmer and home town politician was now the leader of the most powerful nation on earth.

Truman did better than anyone had a right to expect, but it does seem he was particularly naive about Stalin, not realising how dangerous that dictator was until it was too late.

Once he did realise, he sent military equipment and advisers to the Greeks who were fighting communist rebels and he managed to argue the Red Army out of Iran, but he 'lost' Eastern Europe and China. His 'war' on communism was very similar to Roosevelt's 'war' on Germany and Japan prior to Pearl Harbor.

The American armed forces were controlled by a navy chief, an army chief and an army air force chief, the three sitting as the Joint Chiefs of Staff, accompanied by a representative of the President, who was the commander in chief, but this pitted army against navy, interservice squabbling that had damaged American potential for years. In 1949 a new structure was created, whereby the President did not have a representative and the chairman would be picked from each branch of the service in turn on a rotation basis. However, the squabbling became worse for the air force was now independent of the army and this caused a three-way argument, most violent when it came to fiscal allocation. General Omar Bradley, named as the first chairman of the joint chiefs, had a great war record: he succeeded Patton as commander of II Corps in Tunisia and Sicily, then became Patton's boss in France, then directed three armies in the conquest of Germany. He was acceptable because he was a live and let live fellow, popular with the common soldier.

Representing the army was General 'Lightning Joe' J. Lawton Collins, who had proven his worth battling Japanese and Germans. The navy was represented by Admiral Forrest Sherman and the new air force by General Hoyt Vandenburg. Sherman also spoke for the Marine Corps.

While Eisenhower controlled American occupation forces in Europe, the man who commanded American power in the Far East was General of the Army Douglas MacArthur, who had achieved icon status among the folks at home. The son of a Civil War hero, MacArthur was born four years after Custer died and he grew up in the forts of the wild west. He fought hand to hand with Filipino rebels, battled Mexicans in 1914, served as a fighting general in World War I, commanded the army, retired with honour, became a Filipino field marshal, in 1941 took command of all American and Filipino forces defending the Philippines against the Japanese, escaped in a patrol boat following a direct order from Roosevelt, then led American forces in a three-year campaign to push the Japanese all the way from the shores of Australia to the Philippines. He topped this by directing the Japanese surrender ceremony on the battleship *Missouri* in Tokyo Bay 2 September 1945.

Following this he was made Far East Commander and de facto dictator of Japan, where he recreated a healthy nation out of wartorn chaos, gained the respect of the Japanese and introduced democracy, social programmes and women's liberation. Many Americans wished he would run for president.

Besides his two hats of 'dictator' and FECOM, he was also his own ground forces commander. He was also one of the most insufferable egomaniacs who ever wore a uniform. Roosevelt had sarcastically nick-named him 'His Majesty'.

By 1950 Japan was still under occupation by the US Eighth Army, currently commanded by General Walton H. Walker.

At 61 Walker was nine years younger than MacArthur. As a horse cavalryman he had fought Mexican cavalry in 1916 and had battled in the trenches of World War I. Following this he gained knowledge of the Oriental mind by serving in China for many years. During World War II he entered tank service and became one of Patton's top corps commanders.

Walker's leading Korea expert was Major General William Dean. Dean was a warrior, who had shown bravery in World War II and had been made military governor of Korea in 1947 with responsibility for overseeing the nation's transition to a sovereign government and the establishment of a viable defence force. Unhappy in an administrative role, in 1948 he switched to command of the 7th Division, one of the occupation units in Korea, and took that division to Japan in 1949. Walker made him his chief of staff, but Dean was an infantryman not a desk jockey, and he requested he be sent back to the infantry. When command of the 24th Division in Japan became vacant Walker gave it to Dean in October 1949.

The Battlefield: At 85,000 square miles Korea is about the size of Britain, but with two thirds the population. The eastern side of the nation is less populated and the cities of Pyongyang, Hungnam and Wonsan in the north and Seoul, Pusan, Inchon, Taejon and Taegu in the south accounted for no more than a tenth of the inhabitants in 1950. The majority of Koreans were farmers with small plots and rice paddies, barely large enough to feed their families and there were a few village craftsmen. Christianity flourished but the majority of the people were Buddhist.

The nation was surrounded by water except for the north which bordered on China.

The first thing the Americans noticed was that it stank. Natural fertilizer was liberally used and this plus poor sanitation gave it an air that could be choking in high summer when the temperature in the interior reached 100˚F. The mountains were cooler, but in winter they turned inhospitable with temperatures well below freezing. Rainfall was plentiful in winter turning the dirt roads into rivers of mud.

No one knew it at the time, but with every foxhole newly dug or earth turned over by an artillery shell long dormant diseases were released which were to soon devastate soldiers and civilians regardless of political affiliation. American disease casualties were far higher than on the malaria-infested jungle-clad islands of the Pacific.

Causes of Arrogance: One of the biggest causes of military arrogance in history has been the possession of a greater weapon than the enemy, be it a longer spear, firearms, artillery, a battleship or planes with bigger bomb loads. The Americans of 1950 had the ultimate superior weapon: the atomic bomb.

Not without logic, the Americans believed that as long as they had 'the bomb' no nation would ever dare attack them or their friends. The fact that the British and French had the bomb too was no problem for they were allies.

Even the discovery in the late 1940s that Stalin had the bomb too did not deter the Americans from this feeling of security, for it was believed that the concept of the Americans and Soviets fighting each other with atomic bombs in their arsenal would be rather like two men fighting with grenades inside a closet: neither would dare pull the pin.

Another major reason for American arrogance was their recent victory in World War II. They had smashed the power of Japan, Italy and Germany, and the Americans had been led to believe by propaganda that they had practically done it alone, with the possible exception of British courage. The suggestion that the

Soviets had made the major contribution to victory was in 1950 considered seditious gossip.

The loss of Eastern Europe and China to communism were perceived to be political defeats, for which the right wing blamed Truman, but they were certainly not military defeats. The concept that Americans could be defeated militarily was inconceivable.

Of course there were still bones of contention: Berlin, Vienna, Trieste were high on the list. Korea was not even on the list. American advisers knew how poor Syngman Rhee's army (ROK) was, but they took comfort in the assumption that Kim Il-sung's army (NKPA) was equally bad, because they were drawn from the same ethnic group. The Americans said they could see why the Japanese had never used Koreans as combat soldiers.

Last but not least there was another major cause for arrogance. Communism denied the existence of God. Therefore, anyone who believed in God was certain communism could never triumph.

With such arrogance the Americans did not mind declaring their willingness to defend other nations, for no one thought they would actually have to do it.

The Army: The US Army in the late 1940s was the most unusual army ever created in history for it was more than a ceremonial body yet it did not expect ever to have to fight again. This was owing to one single factor, the atomic bomb. Some politicians asked why armed forces were even necessary any longer, and eager to show their voters that they had reduced spending and therefore taxation they cut the armed forces down to the bone, then smashed the bone to powder, then blew the powder away. Of the scores of divisions with which the Americans had won World War Two, only a handful were retained and none at full strength.

The bulk of the infantry divisions were on occupation duty in Japan and Korea to see that those people behaved themselves: they did.

When the 1st Cavalry and 7th Divisions were withdrawn from Korea in 1949 they were sent to Japan, not so much to reinforce America's commitment to defend that subjugated nation, but because the generals thought that if the divisions reached the States, they would be disbanded by cost conscious politicians.

As it was, the divisions had already been emasculated. Each was supposed to contain nine infantry and four artillery battalions, but the 7th and 24th Divisions only had six infantry battalions, the 1st Cavalry (really infantry) Division had six infantry and three artillery battalions, and the 2nd, 3rd and 25th Divisions had only four infantry and three artillery battalions.

Combat support and rear-echelon units were even worse off: for example AAA battalions had only one battery instead of three. So, although the regular army had 591,487 men and women in June 1950, this size was misleading: for example Eighth Army stood at 48.8 per cent strength in combat formations and 25.9 per cent in rear-echelon formations!

What kind of person was it who served in this redundant army in these naive days? Some were war veterans who knew nothing but soldiering and were afraid of taking their chances in the wide world. Known as 'lifers', those among them who achieved sergeant grade (NCO - non-commissioned officer) - were nicknamed NCO - No Chance Outside.

Others had put eight or so years in already, owing to the war, and decided they could handle at least another twelve, which would enable them to retire on half pay at a relatively young age.

Others came from poor families and saw that the army offered education, training and status and they did not want to go back home to poverty. Many women served for this reason.

Others were negroes from the south, who saw a chance for equality undreamed of back home. They remained in the army because it gave them dignity. Negroes served in their own units sometimes with white officers, but native American Indians and people of Asian race served in 'white' units without racial distinction.

A few had enlisted to see a foreign country, having been too young for World War II.

Others had left the army after the war, found hardship during the post-war economic depression and because of pressure from wives had 're-upped' to become 'retreads' in order to grab that steady paycheck.

However, so few of the millions who wore World War II uniform had remained in the army that selective conscription was in force. It took in just enough recruits to keep units active. These men aged between 18 and 26 spent their two years dreaming of home. As the most recent call up had been in January 1949 they were due to go home in January 1951.

It seemed no one was in the army because he wanted to fight.

Unit training in such an atmosphere was impossible. No unit larger than a battalion could hold unit manoeuvres.

Initial training of recruits was good, but once completed a soldier was lucky if he received more than one week per year of field training, and most did not get that. As a result the troops became soft, lazy and physically unfit. It was joked that if there was another war it would take one man to fight and five to bring up the Coca-Cola.

In addition to the regular army, there were 184,000 personnel serving in organised reserve units, which supposedly made monthly meetings, but it was easy to miss a meeting for 'personal' reasons. Another 416,000 men and women were on a reserve list, unpaid and not required to meet.

There were also 325,000 National Guard (state soldiers), organised into 27 divisions and 20 independent regiments. Having served well in World War II, they now expected to be called up, at most, for a riot, flood or storm.

Just about every member of the organised reserves or National Guard was in it for the extra money.

The Marine Corps was different in that it still had esprit de corps. Many marines spent the post-war years in China in the middle of a civil war, where they suffered eleven killed in three years. However, by 1949 even the marines could not perform large manoeuvres for there was no marine unit larger than a regiment.

In June 1950 there were still 470 American advisers aiding Syngman Rhee's army, the ROK, which was divided into eight divisions of three regiments, of three infantry battalions, each. The divisions were short on engineers and only had one battalion of artillery, and contained no more than 10,000 soldiers.

The Enemy: Kim's North Korean People's Army (NKPA) consisted of 135,000 troops divided into a tank brigade, ten divisions, two regiments and five brigades.

A division consisted of: three regiments of six 120mm mortars, four 76mm howitzers and three infantry battalions each; an engineer battalion; and a powerful artillery force, an obvious result of Red Army influence, of twelve 122mm howitzers, 24 76mm howitzers, twelve 45mm anti-tank guns and twelve 76mm self-propelled guns. Infantry battalions were well armed with a plethora of automatic weapons.

The tank of the NKPA was the excellent Soviet-built T-34/85-II, which at 32 tons, 7 feet 10 inches high, 110mm armour on the front and turret and 75mm on the sides, a top speed of 30mph, a range of 186 miles, five crew, an 85mm gun and two machine guns, was far better than the American vehicles. The American Chaffee carried only a 75mm gun and only 63mm of armour up front; the Sherman had a 76mm gun and 50mm armour; and the M36 tank destroyer carried a 90mm gun, but had a thin skin of 50mm. American tanks had petrol engines, whereas the T-34/85-II was diesel, meaning it did not catch fire as easily. Only the American Pershing with its 90mm gun and 114mm armour and the new Patton could match the NKPA tank.

Whereas few of Syngman's troops were combat veterans, Kim's cadre had fought alongside communist Chinese forces against the Japanese. Some men as young as 37 had fourteen years' combat experience.

A handful of Soviet advisers remained with technical units.

The War: At 4.00am on 25 June 1950 (3.00pm on 24 June in Washington) the NKPA invaded South Korea and the hundred aircraft of the NKPAF began bombing and strafing barracks and traffic choke points. North-west of Seoul the ROK Capitol Division was shelled by a brigade and a regiment of the NKPA. North of Seoul the ROK 1st Division was struck by the 6th and 7th NKPA Divisions: here eighteen ROK 105mm guns were unable to interfere with the pounding by 96 NKPA artillery pieces. To their east the ROK 7th Division was assaulted by the NKPA 3rd and 4th Divisions and the 105th Tank Brigade. NKPA I Corps directed these attacks.

In the centre of the country near Wonju the ROK 6th Division was attacked by the NKPA 2nd and 7th Divisions, and on the east coast the ROK 8th Division was bombarded by the NKPA 5th Division, while an independent regiment outflanked the defenders with an amphibious invasion. NKPA II Corps directed these assaults.

The ROK 2nd Division was rushed to the line immediately, but before the day was out was caught up in a retreat.

The following day Truman ordered all American advisers of Korean Military Advisory Group (KMAG) to extricate themselves from the conflict immediately. Some joker renamed the unit Kiss My Ass Goodbye. All American civilians were ordered to leave the country.

Syngman Rhee formally asked Truman and the United Nations Security Council for assistance, and fortunately the Soviets were currently boycotting the council, otherwise they could have vetoed any aid. This was a strong indication that

Stalin had known nothing of Kim's plan! However, the Americans were so terrified of 'Reds under the bed', that they simply assumed the invasion was Stalin's idea.

MacArthur asked for military aid for the ROK Army. Truman only agreed that MacArthur could use his air and sea forces of FECOM to enable American and neutral citizens to get out by ship.

However, after reading the latest reports of the retreat of the ROK Army and NKPAF raids on the evacuation ships, Truman authorised MacArthur to use aircraft and warships to aid the ROK forces.

On the 27th the United Nations Security Council asked its members to repel the NKPA invasion. Immediately Truman authorised Brigadier General John Church to go to Korea to set up an advisory mission. He also issued the first of many emergency decrees. However, he was adamant that there would be no public use of the word 'war', preferring 'conflict' or 'police action'.

On the 28th ROK troops reported significant sabotage and guerrilla activity by communists in civilian clothing or ROK uniform. This helped explain why Seoul was abandoned quickly, though the ROK were right not to fight for the city and endanger its inhabitants. However, before the ROK could fully retreat southwards across the Han River, ROK engineers blew the bridges!

On this day the British agreed to honour the UN request. Truman stated that his government would honour the request.

On the 29th MacArthur flew to Suwon, Korea, his plane landing just minutes after an air raid, and he talked with Syngman, Church and Ambassador John Muccio. There was a sense of urgency, yet one of almost arrogant amusement: how dare this insignificant little nation attack one of America's friends. MacArthur also took a look at the Han River and flew over the enemy to get the feel of the task ahead.

Immediately he returned to Japan MacArthur requested of Truman: 'full utilisation of the army, navy, air team'. In effect he was asking for America to go to war again, just 58 months after World War II.

Congress began to argue how to call up the necessary reservists, realising they had created one hell of a mess for themselves: they could not use atomic bombs in a civil war, yet did not have an army large enough to defeat an enemy of 135,000 and still maintain existing commitments.

The Battle: The call went out for troops: the 1st Cavalry and 24th Divisions to move to Korea at once. The air force also had to call on reservists and asked the states for aid: each state had its own air unit, part of the National Guard. The marines were ordered to assemble a brigade, but replied they would have to call up reservists to fill it!

Everyone needed the latest intelligence picture, but the Americans had to rely mostly on the ROK: only two members of US military intelligence spoke Korean.

Lieutenant-Colonel Charles Smith had been told to take command of the headquarters of 1/21st Regiment, B and C Companies, two recoilless rifles from M Company and two 4.2-inch mortars from regimental headquarters and take them to Korea. On 2 July he reached Taejon, about 110 miles south of Seoul. There he met Church, who told him President Truman had authorised the use of ground troops at 5.47pm the previous evening, and he was to take his 406 men, plus a company of tanks under Lieutenant Leonard Gewin of the 78th Battalion and a battery of 105s from the 52nd Battalion to join the ROK three miles north of Osan and to delay the enemy.

Smith's men felt awful lonesome and must have wondered where the half million strong American army was: and where were those atomic bombs everyone kept yelling about?

They boarded ROK trucks and rode north across a hot, dusty, humid, smelly, hilly cultivated landscape. Americans always judge battlefields like a prospective buyer and they quickly concluded this land was not worth dying for. The roads were poor and the men bounced around until they ached. The trucks moved slowly and several times stopped to let refugees pass.

Then the ROK drivers refused to go any further! This damaged the morale of the Americans even more: they had come to help these people! They jumped into the drivers' seats and drove on, leaving the Koreans by the roadside.

One of Smith's columns was strafed by aircraft. This damaged morale even more: fortunately the Americans thought they had been enemy planes: they were Australians!

While stuck in a jam, some of Smith's GIs watched from the back of their truck as ROK military police executed someone. For most of the men, several of them teenagers, this was their first experience of death.

Morale was very bad by the time they reached their destination on the night of the 4th, only to find there was no ROK line: they were alone. In uniforms little different from World War II and with that war's weapons, they dug foxholes in the rain. For the few veterans it was all too familiar.

At 7.00am the following morning the men of Task Force Smith saw tanks approaching from the north and they opened up with everything they had, but their rifle and machine gun bullets, tank and artillery shells and bazooka rockets bounced off the tanks like ping pong balls. Gewin's tanks did their best, but they had been provided with low-yield training ammunition. Not having been informed that T-34/85-IIs were vulnerable from the rear, the Americans fired from the front and then had to let them pass, but the tanks swerved to chew up the Americans. One 105mm crew seemed glued to their gun and they fired point blank into two tanks, stopping them. A third tank gunned down the crew. The tanks shot their way right through the defences and kept on going.

Though cut off now, Smith calmed his men and ordered them to stay in their foxholes.

At 11.00am they were attacked by tanks and infantry of the NKPA 4th Division and 107th Tank Battalion: the battle raged for several hours.

At dusk Smith studied the situation: with 98 killed and wounded, Gewin dead and his tanks destroyed, and some men bugging out to the rear, Smith called it a day. He ordered his men to destroy their guns and mortars, abandon the vehicles, and make their way south across country as best they could.

While Task Force Smith was delaying the enemy Major General Dean was trying to turn his 24th Division into a division in fact as well as name. He managed to acquire an artillery battalion, an engineer battalion and an AAA battery, but he was desperately in need of three infantry battalions: he was sent individuals

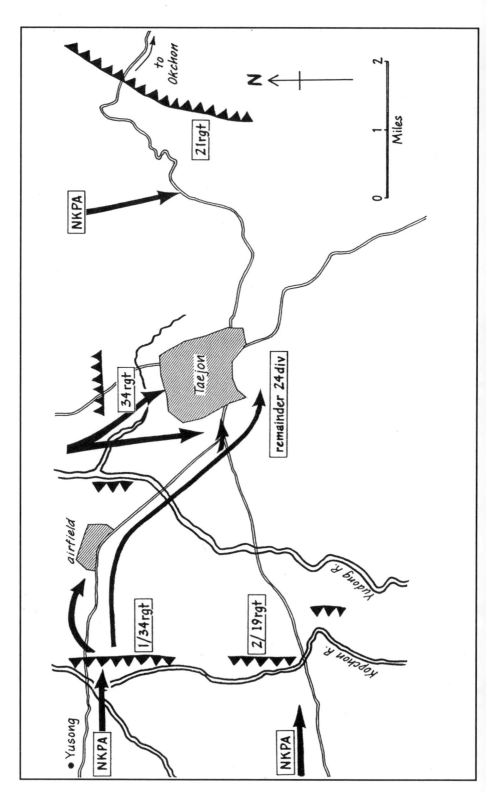

from rear-echelon units and told to create the battalions from them. The division sailed to Korea in elements. Obviously there was no time for training and the newly created battalions were little more than mobs.

Dean flew into Taejon on 3 July with orders to fight a delaying action only! Thus he had no intention of holding this city of 130,000 panicky people: it was just another town to him. He was also made responsible for all American forces in Korea.

When the 1,981 men of his 34th Regiment arrived on the 5th he sent half northwards to Pyongtaek under Lieutenant-Colonel Harold Ayres.

Next morning Ayres' men were struck hard by a major NKPA tank/infantry assault using heavy and accurate artillery fire. For hours Ayres held, but remembering his orders to delay only, and not wishing to be trapped like Smith the previous day, he asked permission to withdraw. The 34th's commander approved and Ayres' men retreated.

However, Dean himself drove up in a jeep and angrily ordered the men to halt and dig in where they stood. He raved at Ayres that he had not approved a retreat and when he learned who had, the regimental commander, he fired him! He gave the replacement commander instructions to fight like hell.

On the 7th the entire 34th did as ordered and held back enemy infantry.

Meanwhile Dean assigned one of his brand new battalions to hold Chonan. Often not knowing their officers or sergeants by name these men were terrified.

On the 8th the 34th Regiment was assaulted by NKPA tanks. The new regimental commander obeyed Dean's order and stood his ground until a tank shot him down.

Meanwhile on the 7th the United Nations asked the United States to control UN forces in Korea. This was logical, for the Americans would provide the bulk of the troops, and the Americans had created the UN, paid for it, housed it and scrutinised all prospective employees. The UN could hardly ask someone else. However, they did suggest the war should be run by a committee. Wisely, Truman refused: he wanted one man in charge and that man to be MacArthur. The UN acquiesced and on the 8th MacArthur assumed command of all UN forces in Korea. However, he remained in Tokyo and continued to 'wear' his other three hats.

The average American did not like what he saw of Korea and quickly became alienated from the Koreans. Many Americans believed the ROK was not fighting and they also traded stories of communist guerrillas operating behind the lines, massacring innocents and prisoners. As the communists were of the same race as the ROK, the Americans soon became racist in their attitude to all Koreans. After all, it was only five years since the 'genocidal' war against the Japanese, and Korea had been part of the Japanese empire, had it not? Koreans were referred to as 'slopes', 'gooks' or other epithets.

On the 8th Dean brought up the 21st Regiment to hold Chori and Chochiwon, while the 34th was allowed to fall back past them towards Taejon. Within hours the 21st was in heavy action.

As ever Dean was driving around in his jeep giving everyone hell. His staff, who often could not contact him, were frustrated, never knowing what he was doing or what he wanted.

On the 12th Dean brought up the 19th Regiment and put them along the Kum River, which hopefully would be deep enough to stop tanks, while the rest of the division was allowed to retreat into Taejon.

However, next day General Walker arrived at Taejon, declaring his Eighth Army was taking over all UN operations in Korea. He conferred with Dean, studied the maps and decided that Taejon could be held for another week. Dean was somewhat surprised by this conclusion, for the situation did not look good: there were still only 18,000 US troops in Korea; the ROK was claiming 40,000 casualties so far, almost half their army; guerrillas were harassing Dean's supply line to the port of Pusan; UN air cover was good but often uncoordinated; and last but not least Dean had lost over 1,000 casualties and three of his battalions were brand new. Nonetheless, the order stood.

On the 14th Dean placed the survivors of the 34th Regiment alongside the 19th Regiment. NKPA infantry was already infiltrating across the river and artillery pounded the Americans.

The 25th Division had been ordered to Korea and to beef it up to a reasonable strength it received the 24th Regiment, 77th Engineer Company and 159th Artillery Battalion. This came as a shock to the division for these were negro outfits.

The vast majority of the division's soldiers were glad of any assistance, but the white southerners were appalled they would have to fight alongside negroes – they used other epithets. The division also received a battery of AAA and a company of tanks.

There was no time for unit training and on the 14th the first elements entered a rearguard position at Sangji.

The Kum River did not stop the T-34/85-IIs. They could ford a stream 4 feet 4 inches deep and in Korea's hot July the Kum was shallower than that. The 24th Division reluctantly fell back towards Taejon. Dean hated to admit he would not be able to hold for the entire week, that is until the 20th.

On the 14th Syngman gave control of the ROK armed forces to MacArthur (his fifth hat), who assumed command of all ROK ground forces too (his sixth hat). MacArthur refused to give up any of them. However, he did give Walker operational control of all ROK and UN ground units.

Of far greater benefit to the infantry than this manipulation of their chain of command was the issue of 3.5-inch rocket launchers to replace their bazookas. A good weapon, the 3.5 could knock out a T-34/85-II, especially if it struck the side or rear. All it took was courage.

On the 18th Walker visited Dean in Taejon again to find him ready to pull out. Walker demanded Dean hold at least until the 20th, when the 1st Cavalry Division would arrive. Dean described his division: his 1/21st was almost non-existent; his 1/19th was at 50 per cent strength; 3,800 of his men had been killed or wounded and 2,400 were missing. He had barely 4,000 men left, including cooks and clerks. Walker did not change his mind.

Dean placed the 2/19th behind the Kopchon River four miles west of Taejon, the 1/34th four and half miles north-west of the city, and the 21st Regiment and some tanks on the Okchon Road four and a half miles to the east. Inside Taejon and to the immediate north was the remainder of the division. Practically every engineer and rear-echelon soldier was in line alongside the infantry.

On the 19th all positions were pounded by NKPA artillery, while the outposts fought off enemy scouts. The engineers fought well that day.

On the morning of the 20th the artillery barrage became heavier as the 1/34th was struck by the NKPA 105th Tank Brigade and an infantry regiment. Within minutes the Americans had to fall back or be overrun. Running for a mile they reached the airfield and stopped to dig in, determined to at least halt the NKPA infantry. They did so and even managed a counter-attack later in the morning; but the enemy tanks rumbled past them towards Taejon oblivious of flanking fire.

Meanwhile the 2/19th was hit by the entire NKPA 3rd Division and at once they had to flee eastwards towards Taejon. Halting at the Yudong River, they tried to set up another defence line. Under assault for two hours, they knew they could not hold and eventually began to run southwards away from Taejon. This allowed the NKPA 3rd Division to enter Taejon, where they joined with their tanks.

Rather than flee Dean ordered every man into the streets to fight and he grabbed a 3.5-inch rocket launcher and began tank hunting. The battle was ferocious as the soldiers desperately fought house to house while the terrified civilians fled or hid. Tanks smashed through buildings and literally crushed the defenders. Many Americans fought without orders, for Dean disappeared and within minutes men were running southwards and eastwards out of the town. Those moving southwards across the hills reached safety. Those running eastwards, expecting to find the 21st Regiment, instead ran into an NKPA roadblock, which had been set up the previous night without hindrance from the Americans. The 21st, isolated now, escaped by moving eastwards towards Okchon.

The 24th Division was destroyed. Eventually 3,010 men, 228 of them wounded, reached safety: 48 were known to have been killed that day and 874 including Dean were missing.

Inside the city the NKPA arrested the civilian population and shot anyone who could think such as doctors, lawyers, managers, landlords, artists, teachers and politicians, killing about 7,000. They also tied the hands of 42 American prisoners then shot them in the head.

In the meantime Walker had decided that the only major natural barrier ahead of the NKPA was the Naktong River, and he hoped to be able to fall back to it in good order, keeping safe his lifeline to Pusan 130 miles south-east of Taejon. To this end he ordered rearguard actions and counter-attacks: the first was launched on the 20th at Yechon by the fresh 24th (Negro) Regiment.

Aftermath: Next day the 1st Cavalry Division arrived, a day too late to save Dean's division. The cavalry had been speedily reinforced by an artillery battalion, a battery of quad .50s, a reconnaissance company and about 3,000 trained infantrymen borrowed from the 3rd Division who were placed into three new battalions. Without time for unit training or to spy out the land, the cavalry counter-attacked Yongdong. The fight was rough.

By the 23rd the 25th Division had to throw in its 27th Regiment at Hwanggan to enable the 24th Regiment to withdraw from Yechon.

On the 29th only after a week of tough action did Walker allow the 1st Cavalry to retreat. They were grateful for this order and pleased with the reinforcement of two tank companies, but saw that alongside the new Pershings were some obsolete Shermans, and owing to a shortage of personnel all the crews were instructors.

However, no one liked Walker's next order: once they reached the Naktong all Americans were to 'stand or die'.

On the 30th the 27th Regiment was allowed to withdraw to Masan, which it was ordered to hold for four days. This was a desperate order, as was Walker's decision to send the 24th Division back into combat. As this division had almost no infantry, he lent it the fresh 5th Regiment, 3,307 strong.

On 4 August the 1st Cavalry and 25th Divisions and the 5th Regiment began retreating over the Naktong. Walker wanted to appear aggressive from behind this barrier, so just three days later he launched the 25th Division into a counterattack through Chinju Pass, accompanied by the 1st Marine Brigade. The marines had put this brigade together in record time using their 5th Regiment, a battalion of artillery and a tank company. All members were marines; new recruits, China veterans, reservists, even embassy guards.

The fighting along the Naktong was terrifying: for example, within a week the 2/5th Marines was down to 98 riflemen, and on the night of the 18th alone the marines suffered 345 casualties.

However, reinforcements were pouring in. The 1st Cavalry Division was reinforced by three trained infantry battalions, and the 2nd Division arrived, having taken in men from every source to create an additional three infantry battalions and had willingly accepted negroes (in their own battalion of course). The division also took on three extra artillery battalions, one of which was negro, and an AAA battalion. Furthermore, recruits and reservists arrived to replace casualties. Many reservists brought valuable World War II experience with them.

Walker finally came to the conclusion that the enemy offensive had been stopped.

Consequences: Americans have a habit of losing their first battle: Detroit, Bull Run, Pearl Harbor, Bataan, Kasserine, and now Osan-Taejon; but then bouncing back with a vengeance. The delaying actions at Osan and Taejon gave the UN enough time to establish defences on the Naktong, which held out until other UN forces were able to make an amphibious landing at Inchon near Seoul on 15 September. By then the NKPA had stretched its supply lines 200 miles and had suffered two thirds casualties, so the 'moment of balance' of the campaign had already been achieved. Inchon simply underlined it.

The consequences of the NKPA offensive were felt throughout the United States: not only did the Americans send an expedition to Korea of seven divisions, but they sent four divisions to Germany in case Stalin attacked there: evidence of their continuing belief that Stalin was responsible for the Korea offensive.

The armed forces enjoyed an incredible expansion – suddenly in Congress money was no object: existing conscripts were informed their service was extended by a year; conscription was reintroduced, taking in 50,000 men in September alone; 934 army reserve units manned by 138,600 personnel were activated, plus 244,300 individual army reservists were recalled.

Over 20,000 marine reservists were called up in just a few days. The navy activated individual reservists and 22 reserve aircraft squadrons. The air force called up 100,000 individual reservists and activated 30 reserve squadrons. In addition to these Federal forces the states mobilised eight divisions, three regiments and 66 aircraft squadrons.

Appraisal: Failures in fourteen major categories led to the disaster, which can be designated: counsel, psyops, intelligence, grand strategy, command structure, morale, training, manpower, reserves, firepower, communications, tactics, strategy and command ability.

The first failure was that of Truman, Acheson and the joint chiefs to listen to those Korea watchers who suggested Korea would be the next battleground. The ROK and NKPA were already trading shots in border skirmishes, so there was a sound basis for this suggestion: they were not just crying wolf. Syngman and Kim both claimed all of Korea, and the USA and USSR gave each of them the tools with which to conquer the other. It was incredible naivety on the part of Stalin and Truman to think these two Koreans would 'toe the line'.

Three other nations had been divided after World War II, Indo-China into a French south and west and a communist north, Germany into a Soviet east and an Anglo–American–French west, and Austria in the same manner as Germany. Neither sectors of Austria or Germany possessed their own armies (as of 1950), but both the communist Indo-Chinese and the French did and their agreement to divide the country only lasted a year before brutal war broke out in 1946.

The same was going to happen in Korea and the super powers should have foreseen it.

Having ignored counsel, the Truman administration then compounded the issue in 1949 by pulling out of Korea all US troops, followed by Acheson's statement that Korea was not inside the US defence perimeter. The Americans could hardly have done more to invite Kim to invade. This was psychological operations at their worst.

This was followed by a total intelligence failure. Kim could not invade without extensive military preparations, but most of these went undetected, and those that were ignored. The Americans were too finely focused on Stalin and on what he might do next to notice what his disciples might be planning.

Once hostilities began American intelligence assumed Stalin was behind it, though there was evidence to the contrary, and continued to aim at the wrong target. This of course suited Stalin to a tee and he claimed he was in control of Kim. In truth he had only a marginal influence on the Korean dictator.

American grand strategy in case of such a scenario was flawed from the outset, because it relied on 'the bomb'. Truman had used this weapon against the Japanese, therefore his generals never suspected he might baulk next time. However, they did know he was on a limited term of office and the next President might not be so obliging. Yet the generals did not realise that for the first time in history American generals would have to go to the President for permission to use a weapon, and if he refused then they had better have something up their sleeve. When Kim called their bluff, the Americans were embarrassed to reveal they had nothing up their sleeve.

Once the war was under way the Americans fought it with the most unusual command structure ever devised. This was a result of two factors: the necessity to keep up the facade that this was somehow an international crusade and not an American show; and the egocentrism of MacArthur.

The United Nations ground forces consisted solely of American troops for the first two months. In fact, though seventeen nations eventually sent troops to help the ROK, American casualties were fifteen times greater than all of theirs put together.

MacArthur's willingness to take on responsibilities became silly: for example if the ROK ground commander (MacArthur) needed additional reinforcements he would ask his armed forces commander (MacArthur) to ask the UN commander (MacArthur) to ask FECOM (MacArthur) to ask FECOM ground commander (MacArthur) for those units, and with every request a different group of staff officers was involved. At the same time he still held political sway in Japan and commanded air, naval and ground forces in the Philippines, Japan and Okinawa. In mid-September he took another hat: Korea ground forces commander! Even if he was omnipotent, his staff was not and was confused and frustrated.

The arrogance of MacArthur had been matched by all American soldiers up to June 1950, but after the first shot, as has so often happened before, arrogance without firm foundation turned to depression and a feeling of abandonment.

American morale was bad because no one expected to fight. Regulars were angry at the politicians who would not use 'the bomb'. Reservists were angry that the regulars had not been sufficient. Ground troops were angry at the initial poor air support. All were angry at the ROK troops, because apparently they would not fight. Every American in Korea thought he or she was there because some-one else had not done their job. Like most prejudice, the anti-ROK feeling was based on fiction: the NKPA had lost 58,000 casualties by early August, most of them inflicted by the ROK!

Truman bears a major responsibility for bad morale, because he proscribed use of the word 'war', preferring 'conflict' or 'police action'. This is one of those ideas that sounds great in the boardroom, but out in the mud and blood it was the worst insult ever levelled at American troops by their commander. No soldier likes to risk his life when his commander in chief does not have the guts to call a spade a spade. In its casualties, firepower and complexity, the Korean War was one of the largest wars in history. For Truman to try to suggest otherwise was idiocy.

It is not surprising that not one American who reached an enemy prisoner-of-war camp escaped and many simply lay down and died, completely devoid of hope.

The lack of training was disgraceful. For the US Army to be caught with its pants down was disappointing. For this to happen just eight years after Pearl Harbor was unforgivable.

Prior to June 1950 Walker could not hold corps exercises, because his Eighth Army possessed no corps. Not one American divisional commander could hold divisional exercises, because none possessed a complete division. No regimental commander could hold regimental exercises for the same reason. Many engineer and AAA battalion commanders were in the same situation.

In World War I the army did not like committing a division to battle until it had had a year of divisional training. In 1950 divisions were committed without so much as a single day of training.

Bazooka teams were not informed that T-34/85-IIs were vulnerable from the rear, thus they died trying to knock out these monsters from the front. Clerks, cooks, drivers, mechanics, technicians and such were thrown into infantry combat without infantry training, unable to take over from a dead machine-gunner, because they did not know how to operate the weapon. Entire battalions were created from strangers and thrown into combat at once. Flabby reservists were sent into mountain combat without retraining. This was not a professional army.

Truman, Bradley and Collins, and to a lesser extent MacArthur and Walker, bear the responsibility for allowing the army to become a retirement home for boozers, users and losers.

No manager likes to begin a project without sufficient manpower, yet the generals who were ordered to defeat the NKPA were restricted by a shortage of personnel that bordered on the criminal. The assimilation of a new regiment into a division was no real problem, for American soldiers owe their loyalty to their company, not battalions and certainly not regiments or divisions, but for a division to go into action with only two thirds of its infantry allocation, while attempting to create the missing third out of strangers, severely limited the division's combat potential. It was September before the 25th Division had more than two thirds of its infantry allocation.

Every division went into action with an insufficient provision of AAA, tanks and qualified rear-echelon personnel. It was like trying to stage a play by hiring the actors on opening night.

The ridiculousness of negro segregation was more evident than at any other time in American history, for while negro volunteers were refused, because the negro battalions had no room for them, white battalions were desperately short of manpower.

All national armies maintain a field force and a home force if the nation is wealthy enough to keep both on full-time duty. In 1950 the United States was certainly wealthy enough to do this, yet when the crisis arose there was barely enough of a field force, let alone a home force. Truman was forced to call upon reservists for his marines, army, air force and navy, borrow state units, reintroduce conscription and ask for volunteers all to fight an enemy of just 135,000.

Firepower is essential to an army, otherwise it becomes no more effective than a horde of tourists. The American high command had decided in 1943 that an infantry division should have an attached tank battalion, yet seven years later divisions were entering combat with only a third of a tank battalion Four battalions of artillery per division were deemed essential in 1939, yet eleven years later divisions entered action with only three. The 3.5-inch rocket launcher was available, but sat in warehouses while GIs were crushed by enemy tanks.

The basic method of American combat was to keep the enemy's head down through firepower, a tactic developed in the Indian wars, where the enemy's firepower was poor. So, most American infantry never used the bayonet, and at the first sign of enemy presence the call went out for mortars and artillery. Thus the emasculation of firepower cut straight to the heart of American-style fighting.

Dean failed in his use of communications. He must have been one hell of a battalion commander, but a regiment was too big for him, let alone the responsibility for 18,000 men and women in 1950. Instead of commanding from his headquarters with periodic visits to the front, he was driving around in his jeep like a war correspondent. A commander who is unable to command because he removes himself from the centre of communications is a useless commander. Fredendall was the opposite type: he never left his headquarters. What is needed is someone who can balance the two requirements of command. In essence Dean was born four centuries too late: he was a medieval style commander, who led his army from the front and fought as a warrior. His tank-hunting in Taejon was brave and it was also foolhardy. His men needed him more than ever at that moment. He failed them. His exploits as a guerrilla over the next month until captured are legendary, but if three-quarters of his men could reach safety in hours how come he could not in 30 days? Perhaps he deliberately abdicated his responsibility.

Certainly his tactics at Taejon were poor. He left a gap wide enough for an entire enemy regiment to set up a roadblock between his headquarters and a third of his men. If his perimeter was too long he should have shortened it.

MacArthur later said that he had devised the strategy of an amphibious counter-offensive at Inchon as early as that day in June on the Han river, though this was perhaps a typical MacArthur exaggeration: in June he gave no instructions to planners or asked for advice from the navy, did not mention it to the joint chiefs until 7 July, and when the marines arrived instead of reserving these amphibious experts he threw them into the Naktong battle.

The Inchon landing has been hailed as one of the greatest military moves in modern warfare, but this is a result of MacArthur's successful public relations. After all it does not take a genius to figure out that a battlefield surrounded by water on three sides might benefit from an amphibious landing. The NKPA had used one in their offensive: surely it was logical the UN forces should use one in their counter-offensive?

The miracle of Inchon was not a product of MacArthur's genius, but it was a product of the US Navy's magnificent planning ability.

If MacArthur was economical with the truth, it was to hide the fact that for the first weeks of the war he had no strategy.

Bradley was a nice guy, but he should never have been put in the position of defending the army against Congressional budget cuts, for he was not strong enough and not willing to jeopardise his career over it. As a result the army was decimated and its new weapons programme almost ceased.

In contrast the air force received the money to become a sovereign branch; it cost several million dollars just for new uniforms; and its aircraft procurement programme was mindblowing: from the B-17 to the B-52 in just six years.

In comparison the army got new but barely adequate tanks and not enough of them, was still armed with the World War I .30in calibre machine-gun and Browning Automatic Rifle, and the only significant infantry addition was the 3.5-inch rocket launcher.

Because of the above problems the command ability of everyone was put to the test under near impossible circumstances. It is not surprising that some failed.

The Battle's Place in History: One of Roosevelt's favourite sayings was: 'We have nothing to fear but fear itself.' Unfortunately Truman was no Roosevelt and he allowed the fear of communism (which was really fear of the unknown) to rule every aspect of American life, while his public relations teams tried to hide the truth about the unpreparedness of the military in June 1950, emphasising the bravery of 'the few', without mentioning why so few had to bear the burden in the first place.

In World War II the Americans had thrown their own citizens into prison camps because they were of Japanese race. However, the enemy was now the communist, who could not be visually recognised. Thus everybody became a potential enemy.

To complain of injustice was deemed kowtowing to the communists, so everyone in America pulled together and lied to themselves as well as to each other. Children underwent air raid drills at school; stores advertised they had turned their basements into bomb shelters; citizens were encouraged to root out communists among their neighbours. Members of the professional classes were fired, ostracised and some driven to suicide because of something someone thought they may have said.

The place in history of the Battle of Osan-Taejon was to herald in America a decade of mistrust and create a breeding ground for reactionaries, fascists and secret cabals at the highest level.

1950

Chongchon-Changjin

Grand Strategy: On 15 September 1950 the US 1st Marine Division invaded the west coast of Korea at Inchon (see previous chapter), and together with the US Army's 7th Division liberated Seoul, while the Republic of Korea (ROK) and United Nations (UN) forces in the Naktong Bulge counter-attacked.

Harried by UN air power, the remnants of the NKPA retreated northwards, abandoning guns, trucks and tanks. UN forces and the ROK liberated countless villages at almost no cost. Signs of devastation and atrocities were everywhere. Many NKPA prisoners proved to be South Koreans, recently conscripted at gun point by the NKPA. These prisoners volunteered for the ROK at once.

The UN debated whether or not simply to liberate South Korea or to occupy North Korea and hand it to Syngman. When NKPA opposition was found to be minimal, the Americans and Syngman urged the UN to consider occupying North Korea. On 3 October Chou En-lai, the Chinese premier, warned the UN not to cross into North Korea, or China would aid the NKPA. The UN ignored this threat and ordered MacArthur to proceed into North Korea.

While Walker marched his Eighth Army north-west above Seoul, the troops who had landed at Inchon, known as X Corps, were transferred by sea for a second amphibious invasion on the east coast at Wonsan on 26 October, which was unopposed. Then X Corps advanced northwards towards the Chinese border. Between X Corps and Eighth Army were 50 miles of mountains.

The Commanders: MacArthur was still in possession of his various hats and he had added the hat of ground commander to control personally the ROK, the Eighth Army and X Corps. Walker was still in command of Eighth Army.

MacArthur had given his FECOM chief of staff, 58-year-old Major General Edward Almond, command of X Corps, and like his illustrious boss, Almond decided he could wear more than one hat and both lead a combat corps in Korea and manage the FECOM staff in Tokyo at the same time. Almond, who was seen by some as a sycophant, was a southerner who had commanded a negro division in World War II. Resenting that assignment, owing to his racism, he had not defended his men when they were mistreated.

The Army: X Corps consisted of the army's 3rd and 7th Divisions and the 1st Marine Division, the latter of which Major General Oliver Smith had created from the 1st Marine Brigade, by adding the 1st and 7th Marine Regiments and support units. The division also contained some British and ROK marines.

7th Division had been given several hundred ROK troops to serve in their own infantry platoons alongside American platoons. Language was a problem, but the experiment seemed to be working.

In reserve Almond had the 3rd Division and on his coastal flank and under his orders was ROK I Corps, a weak formation containing the survivors of the Capitol and 3rd Divisions.

In September had come Lieutenant General John Coulter with his I Corps headquarters culled from V Corps in the USA and Lieutenant General Frank Milburn with his IX Corps headquarters. Then for some unfathomable reason these two officers swopped commands. Both reported to Walker.

Milburn was ordered to take several units northwards: the 24th Division, which had been rebuilt with new personnel and had the 5th Regiment on loan, was to follow the coast as it curved west from the mouth of the Chongchon River; the British Brigade and 1st Cavalry Division would advance on the right (eastern) flank aiming towards China; and the ROK 1st Division was to protect their right flank.

On Milburn's right (east) was the ROK II Corps (6th, 7th and 8th Divisions), which under Walker's orders cautiously moved northwards through foothills towards China. Their right flank was wide open. Walker was an armoured warfare expert, taught to ignore flanks, and he was not concerned.

In reserve was Coulter's IX Corps controlling the 2nd and 25th Divisions, a Turkish brigade and a Commonwealth brigade (British, Australians, New Zealanders and Canadians).

Causes of Arrogance: MacArthur was on a roll. His amphibious counter-offensive seemed to have totally destroyed the NKPA, who retained an estimated 25,000 men at most and no heavy equipment.

MacArthur was aware of Chou En-lai's threat, but intelligence and aerial reconnaissance had so far noticed no unusual movement from China across the Yalu River into Korea. Still he urged Walker to forge ahead and occupy the south bank before the Chinese could intervene.

One thing that did bother him was that no NKPA officer higher than colonel had been captured. The NKPA staff eluded him and until they were in his hands there would be no surrender.

With thirteen divisions almost within sight of the Yalu, MacArthur did not believe it was tempting fate to tell his troops they would be home for Christmas.

The Enemy: Mao Zhe-dung had led Chinese communist troops since the 1920s and had waged constant warfare either against warlords, the Japanese or the Nationalists of Chiang Kai-shek. His wars culminated in his expulsion of most of Chiang's troops, who fled to the island of Taiwan in 1949.

Having achieved cult status among his followers, Mao had no doubts that the rank and file would follow him to the ends of the earth, but his leading generals and politicians were a back-stabbing bunch and he knew he had to make good his word at every turn or lose control.

Chou En-lai had threatened the UN in Mao's name, but the UN had ignored Chou and still refused to recognise Mao's rule in China, so he felt he had to back up Chou's words, otherwise lose face, which could be fatal for him.

By October 1950 some of Chiang's troops still held out in southern China and Chiang was appealing to the US Navy for aid to re-invade the mainland. Mao knew the Americans were not buying Chiang's 'everyone wants me to return' routine, but in the light of MacArthur's recent victory they could change their mind. What guarantee was there the UN forces would stop at the Yalu? Mao felt he had no alternative but to enter the Korean War.

Mao appointed Peng Dehuai, his deputy minister of defence, to command the expedition. Peng had been an officer in the Chinese Republican Army in the 1920s and had gone over to the communist forces (CCF), rising to senior general. He had almost 30 years' combat experience.

He divided his expedition into the 9th Army Group of fifteen divisions under General Song Shilun, which was to attack US X Corps, and 13th Army Group of eighteen divisions under General Li Tianyu, who replaced Lin Piao who had been taken ill, which was to attack Eighth Army. The NKPA would be taken into reserve and Kim Il-sung was to be publicly praised and privately ignored.

A CCF division consisted of: three regiments, of three infantry battalions each; and one artillery battalion using mixed guns: 75mm, 76mm, 105mm, 122mm, 150mm; reflecting the CCF capture of artillery from the Japanese and Chiang's American-supplied army. CCF infantry were issued with a considerable number of automatic weapons, reflecting the Soviet influence, but their firepower came from a variety of captured firearms including pre-World War I items. Most CCF troops were tough uncomplaining warriors who had not witnessed much compassion, though fewer than a third were communists.

CCF divisional commanders normally reported to an army commander, who was comparable to an American corps commander. Army commanders reported to army group.

The Battle

First Stage: On 24 October just north of Unsan the ROK 1st Division was counter-attacked. The UN command had been expecting some last ditch counter-strokes by NKPA die-hards and this news did not alarm them. The ROK held.

Next day the ROK 6th Division on the extreme right of Walker's army was counter-attacked by enemy forces coming down from the mountains on the open eastern flank between Onjong and Huichon. This too was not alarming for intelligence knew these mountains had not yet been cleared and were bound to contain some NKPA holdouts. The 6th Division was forced to withdraw under pressure, yet the ROK 7th Regiment on its lonesome 40 miles north was told to continue to advance towards the Yalu: there was no need for concern!

Even the revelation that two enemy prisoners were Chinese not Korean did not trigger an alarm: intelligence replied they must be volunteers.

Second Stage: By the first morning in November Walker's units were strung out across a wide frontage: the 21st Regiment at Chonggo-dung 20 miles south of the mouth of the Yalu; the 19th Regiment at Kusong 30 miles to their east; the 5th Regiment ten miles north of Kusong; the British Brigade at Taechon fifteen miles south-east of Kusong; 1/5th Cavalry Regiment at Yongsae-dong fifteen miles south-east of Taechon; ROK 15th Regiment on their immediate east flank; 8th Cavalry Regiment on their north-east flank; the remainder of the ROK 1st Division at Unsan; the ROK 6th Division was still to the north with its 7th Regiment stuck out like a sore thumb; and the ROK 7th Division that had held the south-east flank at Yongwon was withdrawing westwards. The ROK 8th Division was in reserve.

At dusk on 1 November the ROK 7th and 8th Divisions and 15th Regiment and two infantry battalions of the 8th Cavalry Regiment (US 1st Cavalry Division) were each assaulted by two divisions of the CCF 39th Army. The combat was extremely rough in freezing weather and by midnight ROK troops were streaming to the rear and the American 1/8th and 2/8th battalions were each surrounded.

The 1/8th reported that they were quickly running out of ammunition, so many were the targets, but the Chinese seemingly did not mind losing men by the hundred in human wave attacks. Therefore, the battalion was given permission to break out southwards towards the 3/8th in reserve. In the dark the men stumbled through brush and trees, running into Chinese everywhere.

At dawn the 3/8th and regimental headquarters were attacked by thousands of Chinese infantry. Radio operators frantically called up air strikes at once, but the jets with their rockets, bombs and napalm only momentarily halted the hordes of Chinese.

1st Cavalry Division ordered the 1/8 and 3/8 to retreat while the 5th Cavalry charged to the rescue.

There were thousands of Chinese in the American rear: the 9th Artillery Battalion was forced to abandon their 105mm howitzers; and the 5th Cavalry was soon stopped, taking 350 casualties. However, by 3 November the 2/8 had held and the remainder of the regiment had fought their way to safety: the 1/8 reporting 265 dead or missing and the 3/8 reporting 600 dead or missing.

Staring at his maps Walker realised that the Chinese had infiltrated into Korea without anyone noticing, had travelled almost a hundred miles without anyone noticing, had dug in their artillery within range of his troops without anyone noticing and had attacked in such a manner that they had reached Wonri just fifteen miles from the mouth of the Chongchon River. If they reached the mouth they would cut off the US 24th and 1st Cavalry and ROK 1st, 6th and 8th Divisions and the British Brigade. Already the supply line for these formations was under CCF artillery fire.

He ordered a complete retreat to the south bank of the Chongchon.

MacArthur's intelligence staff now believed the Chinese had entered Korea with five divisions, say 70,000 men, and they also re-estimated the strength of the NKPA at about 80,000.

MacArthur ordered Almond to capture the Changjin Reservoir area as a method of forcing the Chinese to withdraw units facing Walker to defend the reservoir. Almond's marines captured their targets by 7 November at a cost of 400 casualties. They also took prisoner 62 Chinese of the 124th Division, Fortysecond Army, XIII Army Group. This was the first real hard evidence that the Chinese had entered Korea in force, yet intelligence was slow to accept it.

Third Stage: By 26 November Walker had settled his Eighth Army into new positions along the Chongchon River: from west to east the 24th Division, Commonwealth Brigade, 25th Division at Kunuri, the 2nd Division south of Wonri with the Turkish Brigade in its midst and the 1st Cavalry Division holding the eastern flank facing east. He was obviously no longer relying on ROK units. Further east many ROK troops were still retreating from the north.

On X Corps front Almond had placed Colonel Allan MacLean on the eastern shore of the Changjin Reservoir with a task force made up of the 31st Regiment (minus a battalion), the 1/32nd Regiment, a company of Pershings, an artillery battalion, and eight quad .50in calibre machine-guns on half-tracks: 2,500 Americans plus 700 ROK in their own platoons.

In the rear at Hudong were other elements of the 7th Division: two infantry battalions, two artillery battalions and a few tanks. In divisional rear was a battalion of the 31st Regiment and an artillery battalion.

On the western shore of the reservoir were the 5th and 7th Marine Regiments at Yudamni. At the south end of the reservoir at Hagaru was the headquarters of the 1st Marine Division and along the line of supply to the rear at Kotori was the 1st Marine Regiment, with its 1st Battalion further south at Chinhungni. These towns were linked by narrow valleys through mountains, which were snow-coverd by late November.

Despite there now being over a hundred miles of open front between Walker and Almond, MacArthur ordered another attack by Almond to relieve pressure on Walker. He probably felt he had to do something, for his men were obviously not going to be home for Christmas and this was obviously not the end of the war. In the USA politicians and press were angry at the delay. He proudly named his new offensive 'the end of the war offensive'.

On the morning of the 27 November Almond's attack by the 5th and 7th Marines and Task Force MacLean went well, though MacLean lost contact with his reconnaissance platoon.

However, just after dusk MacLean was counter-attacked by the CCF 80th Division, and the 5th and 7th Marines were assaulted by three divisions! Pounded by artillery the Americans found hordes of Chinese upon them even before the enemy guns ceased fire, screaming and blowing bugles. F Company 7th Marines was surrounded almost at once. MacLean's men held their foxholes in the snow, but within a few hours Lieutenant-Colonel Don Faith of the 1/32nd reported he had 100 casualties and the 3/31st also reported high loss.

At dawn MacLean ordered his Pershings to clear out the enemy from his front, but they ran into Chinese troops armed with captured bazookas and 3.5-inch rocket launchers: the Pershings withdrew. Disgusted, MacLean's infantry continued to battle on, and fortunately the Chinese were loath to show themselves too much in daylight in full view of forward artillery observers and air controllers.

At dusk MacLean told Faith to pull back into the 3/31st's lines, but as his battalion did so Chinese infantry moved with them, infiltrating the line: MacLean was shot and captured and the commander of 3/31st was wounded. Faith learned that command of the task force now fell on him.

MacArthur studied the maps, reports and aerial photographs and the stark truth hit him like a thunderbolt. He announced that Korea had become 'an entirely new war', and he authorised a retreat if necessary.

On the 29th, Faith sent the Pershings into action, and again they withdrew in the face of anti-tank rockets. Faith reported to division that his casualties were steadily mounting and some men were down with frostbite: at night it was –35˚F.

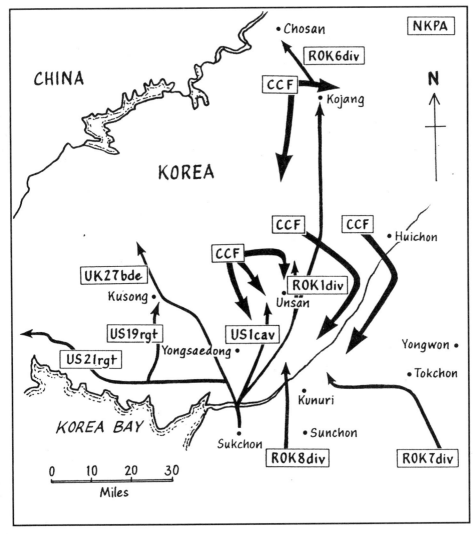

The marines were also under heavy pressure and their supply trucks were under fire from artillery and snipers. As Smith's divisional headquarters at Hagaru was also under fire, this meant that the 5th and 7th Marines and Faith's forces, together about 6,000 men, were all cut off.

Smith began to fly out sick and wounded from Hagaru airfield, while he ordered the 5th and 7th Marines to retreat. F Company was rescued: they had suffered 29 killed, 89 wounded and 40 crippled by frostbite, almost 100 per cent loss.

On the 30th Faith received the order to fight his way southwards to Hagaru, but he immediately replied this was impossible: he had 500 wounded and others crippled by frostbite and to move them in trucks along icy roads under a gauntlet of fire would be suicide. He declared he would stay and fight. That night his men suffered another 100 casualties.

Meanwhile Smith decided he had to clear his supply road between Hagaru and Kotori eleven miles to the south, so he ordered Lieutenant-Colonel Douglas Drysdale, commander of the British 44 Royal Marine Commando at Kotori to take over a company of the 1/31st and anyone else he could find and advance northwards.

Drysdale gathered 900 men all told and they shuffled along, some of them with rags around their feet to fend off frostbite. It was not long before they encountered enemy infiltrators.

Meanwhile Walker had decided to retreat again as it was only a matter of time before the Chinese built up enough pressure to crack his line.

The main problem was that the Chinese were not attacking his front but his open flank, devastating retreating ROK units as they did so. He ordered Major General Lawrence Keiser to block this flank with his 2nd Division, reinforced by ROK troops and the Turkish Brigade, while the Eighth Army fell back along the Sukchon and Sunchon roads, both leading to the city of Pyongyang.

Keiser put his 9th and 23rd Regiments on the left (north-east), the ROK 3rd Regiment in the centre (east) and the 38th Regiment and the Turks on the right (south east) supported by a battalion of 8-inch howitzers.

The Turkish Brigade was a powerful force of infantry, engineers and artillery, 5,455 strong, but their commander, Brigadier General Tahsin Yazici, was concerned that his soldiers were green. He had fought the British in World War I and the Greeks in the 1920s, but had had no occasion to extend his combat experience since then.

On 29 November Keiser's force was hit by waves of Chinese. The 24th and 25th Divisions and the Commonwealth Brigade had not completed their withdrawal south of Sunchon, so Keiser told his men they had to hold.

However, the Turks were struck by the entire CCF 113th Division and within hours they broke: Chinese poured through. This upset the whole apple cart, for if the Chinese reached Sunchon just ten miles south of the Turkish position they would trap all of Keiser's command and the 24th Division.

Keiser ordered an immediate retreat and told Colonel Paul Freeman to rush his 23rd Regiment and 15th Artillery Battalion from the extreme left to the extreme right to stop the enemy. Keiser got permission for the Commonwealth Brigade to swing eastwards through Sunchon then advance northwards to meet Keiser's men as they marched south.

On the 30th the Commonwealth Brigade did as ordered, but just north of Sunchon they ran into major Chinese elements. Keiser's command was cut off.

With just six miles of mountainous, icy road between them and the Commonwealth troops, the Americans, ROK and Turks fought to break through, abandoning their vehicles and taking to the hills, but the wounded could not do this, of course. In tiny groups Keiser's men trickled into the lines of the Commonwealth Brigade. On 1 December Faith was told to withdraw. The entire UN front was now in bloody, freezing, dispirited retreat.

Faith placed his sick and 600 wounded in trucks, hoping they would not freeze to death, and his men began to fight their way south. During the day they were strafed by American planes, machine-gunned by Chinese from the hills, shelled by artillery (whose identity they did not know) and periodically assaulted by hordes of Chinese charging down the snowy mountain sides.

The Pershings pushed on and managed to get through to Hagaru.

Almond did not know it, but his two divisions on both sides of the reservoir were surrounded by fifteen CCF divisions.

Drysdale reached Hagaru from the south: 200 of his 900 had fallen back, but the others had pressed on over eleven miles of icy battleground and with himself wounded he reached Smith's command post, having suffered 361 casualties (61 of them British).

On 1 December Walker manned the line Sukchon–Sunchon with the 25th and 24th Divisions, the Commonwealth Brigade and to the east of Sunchon the 1st Cavalry Division. Survivors of Keiser's command continued to drift in and Freeman's rearguard fared well, for instead of moving to his right (south) as ordered he swung way to the west and retreated through Sukchon. Everyone was gravely depressed to hear that the morrow's orders were to retreat further.

On the 2nd Walker had the 187th Airborne Regiment and the British Brigade take the place of the 25th and 24th Divisions as rearguards, while everyone funnelled through Pyongyang to the south.

A roll call of Keiser's command could now be taken: his 23rd Regiment had 485 casualties; 9th Regiment 1,267 casualties; 38th Regiment 1,075 losses; the engineer battalion 561 casualties; his divisional artillery and rear-echelon 1,561 killed, wounded and missing. The Turks lost 1,080 men. The ROK 3rd Regiment was too tore up to take roll call. Moreover, the survivors were without equipment, ammunition, hot food or medical supplies and were sick with respiratory ailments and frostbite.

Meanwhile at Hagaru Smith watched the 5th and 7th Marines trudge into the town on the 4th. He knew he had to take his whole division and the remains of the 7th Division southwards. Task Force MacLean was done for: Smith learned that as the survivors of MacLean's 3,200 strong force reached Hagaru only 385 were capable of further resistance. They brought Faith's body with them. Having flown out 4,316 stretcher cases, on the 6th Smith gave the order to retreat.

That same day Walker withdrew his army from Pyongyang and Koksan with orders to make for the Imjin River in South Korea. He also ordered a complete scorched earth policy: nothing was to be left for the enemy.

For 38 hours non-stop the 5th and 7th Marine Regiments, 1st Marine Division headquarters and survivors of Task Forces MacLean and Drysdale battled and cut their way through the enemy along the mountainous icy road in a bitter cold wind. It cost 616 casualties, but they covered the eleven miles and reached Kotori, which was held by elements of the 1st Marine Regiment.

Here they received unbelievable news from MacArthur: they were to proceed to Hungnam probably to be evacuated by the navy. They were shocked that the United States Armed Forces was to suffer a 'Dunkirk'.

After a few hours' rest, on the 8th Smith's force marched on, led by the 1/7th Marines, while to their south from Chinhungni the 1/1st Marines were fighting towards them and the 3rd Division held Chinhungni.

They all linked up 24 hours later, but it cost the 1/1st 112 casualties.

At Wonsan and Hungnam the army, navy and air force began evacuation. They were also pestered by countless civilians who had no wish to live one more minute under Kim's evil regime. They scrambled onto navy ships, passenger vessels, ferries: anything that would float.

On the 11th Smith led his troops into Hungnam: they had fought and walked 70 miles; now ROK units and the 3rd Division manned a rearguard. In two weeks the 1st Marine Division had suffered 800 dead or missing, 3,000 wounded and 7,300 maimed with frostbite. Some 200-man companies were down to 30 men. It was the most calamitous loss in US Marine Corps history.

Offshore two cruisers and the battleship *Missouri* gave covering fire. Aircraft flying from South Korea, Japan and seven carriers were bombing, rocketing and strafing the Chinese to hold them at bay.

The marines evacuated, the last climbing aboard ship on the 15th: then the ROK were shipped out; between the 17th and 21st the 7th Division left; followed by the 3rd Division, until not one man was left.

Aircraft flew out 3,600 personnel, 196 vehicles and 1,300 tons of provisions and equipment, and ships embarked 105,000 personnel, 91,000 civilians, 17,500 vehicles and 350,000 tons of provisions.

Aftermath: Walker had retreated 130 miles. Almond had retreated 70 miles by land and 130 by sea. Alongside the retreating soldiers went a million North Korean civilians. The Chinese were stopped in South Korea by a combination of stiffening resistance, UN air power and a 200-mile-long supply line over icy roads. More to the point, Peng Dehuai had accomplished his mission: namely, rescue Kim's North Korea. He had no orders to advance further.

Consequences: Walker relieved Keiser of command. Many lower ranking officers were also dismissed. Almond was forced to give up his Tokyo job.

On 23 December Walker was killed in an accident on an icy road. No doubt this saved MacArthur the embarrassment of relieving him.

Walker's replacement was General Matthew Ridgway a veteran paratrooper. Ridgway demanded X Corps too, which would take one of MacArthur's hats away from him (ground forces commander). An unusually depressed MacArthur did not argue. The 1st Cavalry and 2nd Divisions had suffered badly: the former losing in a few days the equivalent of a quarter of its World War II loss and the latter the equivalent of half its World War II loss. They were blamed for their failure to hold, and while the 2nd managed to throw off the shackles of shame within a year, the 1st Cavalry were burdened with it for fifteen years.

The marines on the other hand were praised for their courage. In two weeks the 1st Marine Division had suffered two and a half times the casualties of its namesake in four months on Guadalcanal in World War II. The marines reminded the public they had been placed into an untenable position by army generals not marine generals. Smith was not dismissed: he was decorated.

Racial segregation, already on its way out, had been shown to be a drawback when front line battalions were pleading for replacements. Over the coming year the US Army was desegregated. The immediate consequence of the defeat was that the war went on for another two and a half bloody years.

Appraisal: Errors within the United Nations, the White House, the Joint Chiefs, FECOM, Eighth Army and X Corps led to the disaster. They fall into fifteen major categories: planning, counsel, psyops, command structure, grand strategy, morale, ground, strategy, dispersal, intelligence, reconnaissance, supply, reserves, command ability and tactics.

In terms of planning, it was not strict adherence to a plan that got the UN force into trouble, but flagrant disregard of it. The nations currently sending troops, equipment and money to the UN in Korea were doing so to restore the sovereignty of South Korea, not to dissolve the sovereignty of North Korea. There is no doubt that the American politicians and generals became greedy. They perceived no enemy opposition in front of them and they were still thinking in World War II terms of total war and unconditional surrender. However, World War II was an exception in history. Wars are rarely so neat and tidy in their conclusion.

The UN invasion of North Korea was a whole new ballgame with new rules, but the Americans did not understand this truth in time.

There were of course plenty of China watchers who foresaw a Chinese invasion, but, as expected when voices speak against the flow of prevailing opinion, their counsel was ignored.

The statement by Chou En-lai was the sort of 'hands off' warning that the USA and UN themselves made from time to time, yet now that the shoe was on the other foot the USA and UN ignored it.

Had the UN decided to invade North Korea while wary of Chou's warning, they could have launched a major psychological operation to convince the Chinese that it would not be in their interest to go to war. Mao was certainly not looking for another war: his nation was devastated after 24 years of struggle and he still had not rounded up all of Chiang's die-hards. The UN and USA could have offered a compromise deal, perhaps recognising Kim's right to run a political party if not a government. They could have assured Mao that they had no intention of crossing the Yalu.

However, the USA, and therefore the UN, were not even on speaking terms with Mao and were ostracising him and his envoys. They made no attempt to offer him a face-saving formula.

If MacArthur's habit of collecting hats in July could have been excused by the urgency of the situation, by September there was no excuse for him to hang on to them. In fact he added a seventh hat, that of ground forces commander. Certainly Eighth Army and X Corps were so far apart that an overall ground commander was needed, but not one who had so many other responsibilities.

It is said that no man can serve two masters. What would MacArthur have done if his three masters, the US government, the UN and Syngman Rhee had given him conflicting orders?

When Almond was allowed to keep his job in Tokyo at the same time as leading combat troops in Korea, it flew in the face of every known management structure. What corporation would allow an executive to manage the construction of a building in one country while heading an office in another on a day to day basis, especially in the pre-computer era?

Indeed the question arises, should a staff officer be given command of a fighting formation? Within the German Army staff officers and commanders enjoyed separate lineage and were respected equally. Only in an emergency would a staff officer take command. A regimental staff officer knew his next step up the ladder of promotion would be as a member of a divisional staff, then a corps staff, then an army staff. However, within the US Army the jobs of commander and staff officer were open to all without previous experience or training being taken into consideration. This made for poor judgement at times, when an officer more attuned and capable for staff work was thrown into a life or death command position.

Once the decision to invade North Korea was made a grand strategy was formulated, namely a hell bent for leather charge northwards with the goal of the Chinese border, but what guarantee did this strategy offer Mao that the UN would stop at the border? For example, the UN offered no suggestion of a demilitarised zone stretching 30 miles either side of the Yalu. For the UN to advance with an army towards the border of an ideological enemy, who is ruling a country illegally according to the UN, and for the UN to expect that enemy not to be alarmed is quite frankly not just bad grand strategy, it is stupidity.

MacArthur risked the morale of his men. MacArthur knew that unless the NKPA staff was captured there would be no surrender, yet he informed his troops that his final push heralded the end of the war and they would be home for Christmas. These statements placed the morale of his troops on a knife edge: his failure to deliver did not just destroy their morale, but it destroyed any faith they had in his abilities.

The racial antagonism between Americans and Koreans was becoming a serious morale problem. The attempt to remedy this and at the same time train the ROK by placing ROK platoons among American companies was a poor move. Every infantryman is terrified his buddy in the next foxhole will run out on him or his neighbouring squad or platoon will do so, and if the neighbouring platoon is of a different nationality, which could not understand calls for help yelled in a different language in the heat of battle, then the infantryman becomes even more tense. He is apt to bug out if the going gets rough. The first large scale experiment of this nature was the 7th Division's Task Force MacLean, and this force was wiped out in its first battle! The 7th Division was the only American division to accept large numbers of ROK troops and the programme was continued, but only on an irregular basis.

Once the grand strategy was in place MacArthur decided to ignore the central mountainous part of the country and advance along the coastal plains. Logistically this was a good choice of ground, but strategically it was not, because the NKPA was basically an infantry force and knew these mountains intimately. MacArthur did not place any light infantry here, who could have combed the area for signs of enemy build ups, but relied almost exclusively on aerial reconnaissance.

If MacArthur's choice of ground was flawed, this could have been offset by the strategy of placing strong units to protect the continually extending inland flanks of X Corps and Eighth Army. Coastal flanks could take care of themselves for the UN navy controlled the waters.

However, Walker was an armoured warfare expert, who thought in terms of road networks. He ignored the interior mountains and placed poorly armed, depleted survivors of the ROK on this flank. Almond had nothing to protect his inland flank. The Chinese could not believe their luck when they attacked.

Walker's successor, Ridgway, was a paratroop expert, who thought in terms of light infantry able to go anywhere regardless of roads. In other words he thought like the Chinese and he was never caught out in the same fashion.

Having made a strategic mistake, Walker proceeded to compound it by dispersing his forces in the face of the enemy. At one time he had five regiments advancing on a front of 70 miles, an average of one 30-man rifle platoon every quarter mile with no reserves. Moreover, on his inland flank he had gaps as wide as 30 miles.

He might have changed his dispositions if military intelligence had told him he was up against fresh Chinese and not defeated NKPA, but MacArthur's intelligence boys were asleep again. Had they taken the time to investigate they would have realised that the counter-attack which hurt the ROK 6th Division on 25 October could not have been a riposte by whipped NKPA. It had to be a new force. Their explanation that the two Chinese POWs were volunteers is startling.

Of course intelligence was relying primarily on aerial reconnaissance, as was everyone else. Air power in Korea was essential and it prevented many a unit from being overrun, but despite the fact that aircraft were over the Yalu and North Korean mountains every day taking photographs they did not see 33 divisions cross the river, nor did they see those divisions traverse the mountains for up to a hundred miles, nor did they see the supply lines of those divisions. This is all the more incredible when it is realised that many of the hill slopes were bare and by mid-November were snow covered.

Within hours of the beginning of the Chinese second stage of their offensive, 1 November, Eighth Army's supply line was in danger. Walker was using a handful of bridges along a ten-mile stretch of river to supply five divisions and a brigade. This bottleneck crippled his logistics and their lack of protection was such that within 24 hours they were under artillery fire and in danger of being overrun. Walker's order to retreat was given because his supply line was in danger, not because his front had broken.

Walker's reserve consisted of a corps of two divisions and two brigades, but this entire corps was in fact hors de combat, totally useless to him as a reserve, because of their position far below the Chongchon River. He did not order them to counter-attack against those Chinese who were south-east of the river, nor to rush to the aid of their beleaguered colleagues north of the river, nor to swing to the east and advance through Tokchon towards the Chinese east flank, but simply told them to dig in and await their retreating comrades.

Walker was not a bad general, but his command ability had been lulled into a false sense of security. Indeed his order to retreat took courage in light of how shocking he knew it would be to the American public. However, once he had given this order, it does appear that it set the tone and he retreated again at the end of November and thereafter his army did not stop retreating, bar rearguard actions, for nine weeks.

Certainly Walker was failed by Keiser's tactics, when he placed green Turkish troops to hold a crucial point in the rearguard with the result that they broke in hours and nearlytwo divisions were cut off. Keiser had kept nothing in reserve to plug the gap. However, it must be noted that Keiser's dispositions were no secret to his superiors who did not correct him in time.

Alternatives: The alternatives open to the UN forces were first of all not to have made any of the above errors. Secondly, they still possessed the largest navy in the world, and one wonders why a repeat of the Inchon operation was never made.

Before retreating fully from the Chongchon, Walker could have sent his reserve corps through Tokchon to Huichon to strike the Chinese on their eastern flank, though that would have been a gamble, and from 27 November onwards the American generals were loath to gamble anything. In fact their future operations were noticeable for a distinct lack of audacity.

The Battle's Place in History: The immediate problem for the US Army was how to portray the disaster in the best light. For the first time since 1814 their attempt to invade another country had been thwarted. Armed with an excellent public relations team and the belief among the American public that to complain too much would be to sound like a communist, the army was surprisingly successful in its efforts. Changjin was America's Dunkirk. Chongchon was America's version of Greece 1940. Yet two generations later neither are remembered.

In part this is because Americans do not like to remember their defeats. In addition the war fizzled out inconclusively, the opposite of the World War II-style ending the American public wanted. The result was they turned to other interests, such as classic cars, Hollywood and rock 'n roll. It was 42 years before an official war memorial was erected.

In January 1951 the immediate concern was how to correct the situation, and here MacArthur proved he was as bankrupt in military strategy as Truman was in political strategy.

Truman washed his hands of the affair, claiming that all along his goal was to merely ensure the security of South Korea. This was couched in political speak, but he could not hide the fact that it was a climb down of major importance. The USA had lost the war for North Korea.

It was up to MacArthur to win the war for South Korea. However, MacArthur hated to be thrown out of any place, and he began sounding like the MacArthur of old, the MacArthur who had once been thrown out of the Philippines, but had come back with a wrathful vengeance. In his cry for revenge he separated from Truman. The President was not after revenge, but security. Syngman Rhee wanted both.

Over the next three months MacArthur made public complaints to the press about Truman's war policy and privately he wrote to politicians explaining his requirements: the use of atomic bombs on Chinese supply bases just north of the Yalu and US support for an amphibious invasion of China by Chiang Kai-shek's forces.

This was too much for Truman. On 11 April 1951 he relieved MacArthur of every one of his hats, with the explanation that MacArthur was: 'unable to give his wholehearted support to the policy of the US government.'

No relief of an American general has caused so much argument and soul searching. The army, which had already been angered by Truman's talk of Korea as a 'police action', took MacArthur's dismissal as a personal affront. This was the beginning of a split in American political life, with the reactionary militant faction assuming a secret role in addition to its public face. A year later Truman lost his argument with the military when he failed in his re-election attempt: he was succeeded by a general: Eisenhower.

Dien Bien Phu

Background: The French began to turn Indo-China into a colony in 1858. An area of diversity, it contained 17,500,000 Vietnamese, 6,000,000 Cambodians and 600,000 Laotians, each living in their own land. Over 1,000,000 Chinese lived in the cities as shopkeepers or as tribesmen along the Chinese border in the north. There were also about 700,000 tribesmen of various ethnicities, known as Montagnards.

The Vietnamese cities were Hanoi in the north, the nearby port of Haiphong, and Saigon 850 miles by road to the south. There were many provincial towns, and the rural people lived in hamlets and went out daily to tend rice paddies and small plots.

Most Indo-Chinese were Buddhist, but the 80,000 French colonists converted many natives to Catholicism. The Vietnamese have a tradition of religious tolerance. Besides churches, the French built schools and hospitals, brought sanitation and irrigation, established plantations and introduced modern amenities to the cities, but they did not tolerate rebellion. In 1931 following a revolt by communist Vietnamese the French executed 782 prisoners.

In September 1940 Indo-China was invaded by the Japanese, who after a short fight with the French gained permission from them to remain through a deal using Hitler as a middle man. Despite American air raids, the Franco–Japanese truce lasted until March 1945 when the Japanese suddenly attacked the French, slaughtering many and imprisoning the rest.

In August 1945 the Japanese were forced to surrender to the Allies, and in September British forces under Major General Douglas Gracey arrived in southern Vietnam to take the surrender of the Japanese, but Gracey found himself in the middle of a political demonstration in Saigon. The Vietnamese did not want to be ruled by the French again, but he had no authority to prevent the French colonists, whom he freed from Japanese prisons, from taking over.

When Gracey refused even to talk to delegates from the people, riots broke out and in response Gracey rearmed the Japanese and sent them into the streets.

Weeks later troops from France under Major General Philippe LeClerc arrived in Saigon to replace the British and Japanese. The people of southern Vietnam resisted the French and open warfare broke out.

The Army: Following France's costly fratricidal involvement in World War II the most unpopular move a French government could make would be to conscript young men to fight in Indo-China. Therefore, the government relied on three sources for its manpower: regulars who volunteered to fight; colonial subjects who had a similar mindset; and foreigners who served in the famous Foreign Legion.

Unlike regulars in most armies, the French possessed a large number of true warriors, who believed it was their duty to fight as long as they wore a uniform; no barracks spit and polish for them. Colonial troops were drawn from Indo-China and Africa, primarily Algeria, Morocco and Senegal, and these fellows too considered themselves to be members of a warrior élite.

The Foreign Legion of late 1945 contained a wide variety of personnel: veteran legionnaires, who had fought in World War II; German veterans of Hitler's army and SS, who needed a home while their nation was being rebuilt from rubble and who wanted to get out of prisoner-of-war camps; French who had chosen the losing side in World War II and needed a refuge; veterans of Mussolini's army; eager teenagers of many nations who had been too young to see action in World War II; war veterans who could not adapt to peacetime, including Americans and Britons; refugees from communism; and criminals fleeing the police. Most legion officers were French who loved the legion: to be transferred to another unit was seen as a disgrace. According to veteran legionnaires the best soldiers were Germans, Italians and French in that order. Many legionnaires, certainly the criminals, served under a *nom de guerre* and hid their past.

However, there were few warriors among the French generals and staff officers in Indo-China. Remaining in Saigon some spent more time with their fancy cars, women, luxurious villas and music concerts than they did at work.

The Enemy: The Vietnamese peasant Nguyen Sinh Cung had been educated by the French and had then travelled to Europe to discover if he had been told the truth. Working in London and Paris as a waiter, he met the common folk and became enthralled by communism.

Returning to Vietnam he became a revolutionary, eventually calling himself: 'the one who enlightens', Ho Chi Minh.

After the Japanese invasion he gathered together a tiny band of guerrillas, ostensibly to fight the Japanese, but they spent most of their time in political discussion. Their first attack was not made until Christmas Day 1944 with 34 men: and they attacked a French outpost.

Ho recognised one of his number, Vo Nguyen Giap, as a potential leader. Vo had been born in 1911 into the literate mandarin class and on the one hand he gained from the French willingness to educate the peasantry and on the other he suffered from their political oppression. Before he was ten years old his father and sister were murdered by the French and as a young man, training to be a history teacher, his wife and sister-in-law were murdered by the French.

In March 1945 following the Japanese attack on the French, Ho and Vo began raids on the Japanese and managed to contact the Americans who in May sent them instructors who came by parachute.

When Ho learned of the Japanese surrender he marched his hardy band into Hanoi and declared the Viet Nam Independence League (Viet Minh) Government of National Unity. The inhabitants flocked to his banner by the thousand and they confiscated weapons from the bewildered Japanese.

The War: Throughout late 1945 and early 1946 LeClerc led his troops to defeat rebels in southern Vietnam and Cambodia, but as yet made no effort to enter northern Vietnam. In fact the French offered Ho Chi Minh a deal: if he would allow French troops to enter northern Vietnam, they would recognise his government. It seemed too good to be true, but Ho accepted. In May 1946 French troops entered peacefully.

Ho was in fact much more concerned about gaining the support of the rural Vietnamese: to this end he murdered 350 village chiefs who spoke against him.

By June 1946 the French had pacified all of Indo-China, but then they announced that South Vietnam would become an autonomous state, not under Ho's rule. Seeing this as a repudiation of their agreement, Ho went to Paris to negotiate, where he was assured that he would be left alone in North Vietnam.

However, the French soon had 39,000 troops in Indo-China (legionnaires, Africans, Vietnamese and regulars) and were inclined to ignore Ho. On 20 October 1946 French troops opened fire on Ho's Viet Minh soldiers in Haiphong, bringing into play a warship and aircraft: an estimated 20,000 civilians were killed or wounded in the bombardment! Thus full-scale war broke out between the French and the Viet Minh.

On 27 November the French captured Hanoi, so Ho and Vo took their troops into the countryside to wage guerrilla war. Since arriving in Indo-China thirteen months earlier the French Army had suffered 3,200 killed in action and thousands wounded. They thought the conflict was now over, but it was just beginning.

In France the public knew little of the combat in Indo-China, because they were too busy trying to forget war and learn to live at peace again. Careers, marriages, childbearing had been interrupted by World War II, and now they wanted to get back to normal. Only the communists among them were concerned about the struggle in Indo-China, taking Ho's side of course, and even they were more concerned with events in Europe. The press kept the lid on the Indo-China conflict as much as possible, in part to please the government and partly so as not to appear to be spoiling the fun of the French people. Government statements about the war were watered down generalisations.

Yet the war did not go away: in 1947 4,081 French Army personnel were killed in action. Most of them were Indo-Chinese, Africans and Foreign Legionnaires, whom the French public did not care about. As for the French regulars who were killed, the feeling was 'they asked for it'.

However, by 1948 there were 100,000 French troops fighting in Indo-China, of which 42,000 were actual Frenchmen, and the year's casualties of 4,821 killed were starting to make an impact on public opinion.

In 1949 the Indo-China garrison was increased to 150,000, this time including some conscripts, though few of the 4,872 killed that year were conscripts.

That year a new French government granted independence to Vietnam, Laos and Cambodia, each to have its own armed forces. Working in conjunction with the Vietnamese the French now began a policy of 'Vietnamisation' of the war.

The outbreak of the Korean War in 1950 changed the attitude of the French public, as they came to the conclusion that the communist conspiracy was larger than they had thought; believing Korea was simply a continuation of the communist attempt to control Asia, which had begun in Indo-China. The French sent a battalion to Korea and the public started to ask about Indo-China.

1950 also changed the war for the Viet Minh, for China had fallen to Mao Zhe-dung's communist forces, and Mao was able to provide Vo Nguyen Giap, who was now commander of the Viet Minh Army, with equipment, supplies, advisers and a rest centre on the China side of the China–Vietnam border. This translated into an increase in casualties among the French-controlled forces: 7,150 killed that year.

By now almost every French regular was being sent on a tour of duty to Indo-China, but as yet few conscripts had been sent. With the increased danger, the French planned to evacuate all French women and children from Vietnam, but a new commander took over, General Jean de Lattre de Tassigny, who cancelled this order and brought his wife. His attempts to shore up morale worked, and the French soon began to win some heavy actions.

Unfortunately, he had to depart in late 1951 through ill health, and was replaced by General Raoul Salan whose tour was marked by a series of defeats and half-victories. He called for more manpower.

By 1952 the French were fighting the Viet Minh with: 54,000 French regulars and a few conscripts; 48,000 Africans; 20,000 legionnaires; 53,000 Indo-Chinese; 5,000 navy and marines; 10,000 air force; 55,000 French colonists serving as part timers; 150,000 regulars and 50,000 reservists of the Vietnamese Army; 15,000 regulars and reservists of the Laotian Army; and 10,000 regulars and reservists of the Cambodian Army; a total of 470,000 reservists were called upon periodically.

However, they were outnumbered by the Viet Minh, which stood at 125,000 regulars, 75,000 regional defence troops and 350,000 home defence militia. Not all Viet Minh fought willingly and few were communist. Vo had been forced to resort to conscription of all men aged 16–55 and women aged 18–45. All female conscripts were used as porters. Male conscripts could be drawn for the regu-lars, regional forces or the militia as soldiers or porters. Any who refused con-scription had to flee to a 'French' garrison or be executed. Many a Viet Minh had a brother in the opposing army.

The Commanders: In 1953 the French sent a new commander. Henri Navarre, now in his 55th year, had entered the army as a cavalry officer and had seen action in World War I and against the Riffs in the 1920s. He missed the 1940 German invasion of France, being stationed in Africa, and he later joined the intelli-gence branch and directed agents in German-occupied France by radio. In 1944 he was promoted to colonel of a Spahi Regiment (French and Moroccan armoured vehicles). Helping to chase the Germans out of France he then partic-ipated in the invasion of Germany and won praise for his capture of the town of Karlsruhe.

Upon the German surrender he returned to staff duty, was promoted to brigadier general in 1947 and to divisional commander two years later. By 1952 he was chief of staff of NATO Central Forces.

Arriving in Indo-China in May 1953 he established a routine of working from maps in his air conditioned office in Saigon, occasionally flying out to his units to give pep talks.

Navarre's deputy was Major General René Cogny, an academic with degrees in law and politics. He was not known as a warrior.

However, there was no shortage of warriors. Navarre's golden boy was Christian Marie Ferdinand de la Croix de Castries, who despite his noble name was born into a Parisian family of reduced means in 1902. Too young for World War I, he entered the army as a private, gained recognition and was commissioned. One advantage was that he represented the army in equestrian sports and became a world champion. In 1940 as a captain he fought the Germans, was captured and escaped on his third attempt. Reaching Allied territory he joined Navarre's Spahi regiment as a major and fought in France and Germany.

He volunteered for Indo-China and by 1953 had earned his eighteenth decoration for bravery and the rank of colonel.

Another of Navarre's warriors was Maurice 'Bruno' Bigeard, who had never envisaged a military career: in fact he hated his conscripted service in the 1930s. In 1939 aged 23 he was recalled as a sergeant, fought the Germans and evacuated to Britain. Training as a saboteur, he parachuted into German-occupied France with the 'rank' of major and led a band of guerrillas.

Upon the German surrender he was offered a regular commission, accepted and volunteered to go to Indo-China with LeClerc. When his tour was over he refused to return to France and specialised in commanding paratroopers and training Montagnards. A charismatic leader he never carried a weapon, preferring to rely on his men's loyalty.

Another warrior was the paratrooper leader Pierre Langlais. Not content with some hairy escapades during World War II, by 1953 he was on his third Indo-China tour.

Yet another was Brigadier General Charles Piroth, an artillery specialist, who had volunteered for Indo-China despite the loss of an arm.

Strategy: Successive French governments were embarrassed at their failure to win in Indo-China, especially as France had not fully recovered from World War II and could not afford the war: by 1953 almost three-quarters of the bill was being paid by the American taxpayer!

Navarre's orders were to 'Vietnamise' the war by slowly withdrawing French forces so that the Vietnamese, Laotians and Cambodians could defeat the Viet Minh by themselves.

His first major move was to create four Groupes Mobiles: one of Montagnards, two of Africans and one of Frenchmen, including veterans of Korea; who were to be fully supported by air power. Their mission was to seek out the Viet Minh and fight them on their own terms.

However, Navarre's primary intention was to break the back of Vo's regular army. He felt that if he could goad Vo into launching human wave assaults against a fixed position he could devastate the Viet Minh, to the point that the Vietnamese could mop up the survivors.

The Battlefield: For this great battle Cogny suggested the Nam Yum Valley along Route 41 at a site known as Dien Bien Phu (it means Northern Administrative Centre) in northern Vietnam just seven miles from the Laotian border. The site lay on an ancient trade route between Vietnam and Laos, and Cogny and Navarre judged that if Vo wished to reinforce his guerrillas in Laos, he would have to use this valley. Additionally this was a major opium producing area, and Navarre knew the Viet Minh gained much of their supplies by trading opium to the Chinese. By moving into the valley the French could threaten Ho's economic lifeline.

Only two miles wide and overlooked by hills as high as 2,500 feet, the valley nonetheless had enough small hillocks to house a defence force and enough flatland for two airfields. It seemed ideal to Navarre.

Causes of Arrogance: Intelligence warned Navarre that Vo could attack with four divisions, but that is precisely what Navarre wanted: human wave assaults. This is because of his arrogance, which was based on his belief that he possessed superior firepower, superior mobility, superior men and superior leadership.

His firepower consisted of 105mm and 155mm artillery, tanks and impressive air power: land-based Marauders to bomb the enemy night and day and, flying from carriers at sea, Bearcats, Helldivers, Hellcats and Corsairs to bomb, napalm, rocket and strafe.

His mobility came from his vehicle columns, spearheaded by tanks, and his air power: Sikorsky helicopters that could land almost anywhere and Dakotas, which could land at small airfields or drop troops and supplies by parachute.

For this operation he would use only the best men.

As for leadership, his officers and sergeants were professionals of the highest calibre, many with thirteen years' combat experience. Most of his officers came from the best military schools and he himself had been entrusted to command British and American troops in NATO, had he not?

As for his enemy, the Viet Minh were always low on ammunition, were without armoured vehicles or air support, and possessed nothing heavier than 75mm howitzers. Navarre and his staff agreed that the Viet Minh could never carry their 75mm howitzers over the summit of the hills overlooking Dien Bien Phu, and even if they could they would soon run out of shells, because their supply line was so long – over 500 miles to their depot in China. The Viet Minh shortage of radios meant they had to use couriers to redirect gunfire. These peasant soldiers in their green uniforms and pith helmets were illiterate and understood nothing of politics, their best 'general' was a school teacher and their political leader was an ex-waiter.

With such confidence Navarre was able to inform his staff: 'A year ago none of us could see victory. Now we can see it clearly, like light at the end of the tunnel.'

Countdown: On 20 November 1953 colonial paratroopers under Bigeard's command jumped onto Dien Bien Phu and captured it from the local Viet Minh, killing 200 for a cost of 40 killed. Over the next few days more paratroopers arrived and two airfields were prepared to take Dakotas.

Within a week Bigeard had five battalions of paratroopers (two of Frenchmen, two Vietnamese and one of legionnaires), a battalion of T'ai (Montagnard) tribesmen, two French and one Laotian artillery battery, a legion mortar company, and two French engineer companies, totalling 4,907 personnel.

Navarre flew in to inspect the base and was pleased. He declared Colonel de Castries, ably assisted by such warriors as Bigeard, Langlais and Piroth, would command the defences in anticipation of an enemy attack.

However, several officers offered polite objections, suggesting they pull back and bomb the enemy: they feared being surrounded, but Navarre explained this was exactly what he wanted.

In Saigon on 3 December Navarre ordered de Castries to hold the base at all costs. In reply the colonel asked for reinforcements, whereupon Navarre said he was loath to increase the garrison above 13,000, otherwise Vo might not be enticed to attack. Naturally, he told de Castries, if he got into trouble he would send in his reserve of 44 battalions by road and air. He told de Castries not to worry for Dien Bien Phu would soon be an 'impregnable fortress'. De Castries was not worried and replied: 'We'll demolish the Viets when they come down from the hills.'

However, it appeared that Vo had not taken the bait, for in December the Viet Minh launched major assaults along the Laos border and in January they attacked installations in central Vietnam. In February they launched an offensive inside Laos. With each attack Navarre responded by sending units from his dwindling reserve. Thus by March 1954 Navarre's reserve stood at 20 battalions.

It was a pity, Navarre thought, that Vo had not accepted his challenge at Dien Bien Phu, because the base really was an 'impregnable fortress' by this date. With a perimeter of over eight miles, it contained no less than 49 mini-forts divided among nine bastions. Brigadier General Charles Piroth had placed his artillery in such a way that every square inch was covered. De Castries had given the nine bastions the names of women – the soldiers joked they were the names of de Castries' mistresses – Gabrielle, Anne-Marie, Beatrice, Huguette, Francoise, Claudine, Eliane, Dominique and shy Isabelle, who hid from the others by remaining two and a half miles to the south.

The Dakotas brought barbed wire and concrete to build bunkers and trench systems. Each item had to be flown in and every day no fewer than 80 Dakotas landed at one of the two airfields.

To give his men a clear field of fire de Castries had cut down all the trees around the perimeter, and to remove the chance of tree bursts from enemy artillery he cut down the trees inside the perimeter too. Thousands of mines were laid. Inside the perimeter the troops spent their days digging alongside five bulldozers. They wore camouflage uniforms with either broad brimmed slouch hats or berets or American-style helmets. Most of the Africans wore turbans.

De Castries knew the enemy was watching: his patrols were always encountering them and sometimes serious engagements had taken place. His patrols were suffering an average of six casualties a day.

On 12 March Navarre was tensely awaiting news from another battlefield, when he received surprising news from Dien Bien Phu: as Major General Cogny's plane took off, his inspection trip over, shells landed on the runway. Vo had at last taken the bait!

The Battle: By now Dien Bien Phu had been expanded to 1,509 Frenchmen, 2,872 legionnaires, 2,854 Africans, 2,575 T'ais and 1,004 Vietnamese, for a total of 10,814, divided into four battalions and two companies of legion infantry, a battalion of legion paratroopers, a French paratrooper battalion, three battalions of Algerians, a battalion of Moroccans, two battalions of T'ais and eleven Groupes

Mobiles companies of T'ais, two companies of French engineers, a French mortar company and eight 105mm and four 155mm batteries manned by Frenchmen. Isabelle had three tanks and the others seven tanks. There were also air force ground crew at the Isabelle and Dien Bien Phu airfields. Lastly there were a dozen or so Vietnamese and Algerian prostitutes, who now began serving as nurses: they showed courage and dedication.

Vo was in the hills and he had brought with him the 304th, 308th, 312th and 316th Divisions, plus an extra regiment, making 37,500 assault troops, 50,000 rear-echelon personnel, 800 supply trucks and 200,000 porters who were hauling supplies on their backs, in carts or on bicycles all the way from China.

General Vu Hien's artillerymen had manhandled their guns for a week up and over the high summits to put them into position in the forested hills overlooking the valley. Hien had some Chinese advisers with him. Once in position his gunners stared in disbelief. The French had cut down most of the trees in their base, so the gunners had a perfect view of every bunker, and they could tell which ones were command centres from the radio antennae. They had little need for couriers for redirecting artillery fire, for the gunners could see for themselves.

Navarre had expected the Viet Minh to muster perhaps 24 75mm howitzers, but Hien had brought 48 such guns, and for the first time in the war he had 105mm howitzers, 84 of them, and 60 75mm recoilless rifles, 48 120mm mortars and four 120mm Katyusha launchers each able to fire a salvo of a dozen rockets. Thus Vo's army outgunned the French below in 75mm and above, 288 tubes to 82, counting artillery, tanks and mortars.

Vo also had a surprise for French planes: 36 37mm AAA guns.

This first night Viet Minh artillery opened fire just before dusk: time enough for them to correct the fall of their shells, but close enough to dark for them to be safe from the prying eyes of French planes. French artillery under Piroth's direction and aircraft replied, but struck the reverse slopes of the hills, for the French assumed they must be on that side, still considering it impossible for the enemy to have carried guns across the summit. Undetected the Viet Minh artillery continued.

Suddenly Navarre's arrogance could bolster him no longer: he inquired of his staff the best way to withdraw the 10,000 men. They replied that by road he might save at best four battalions (2,000 men), and that he could not evacuate by air because the runways were under artillery fire. Like the monkey with his fist grasping nuts inside a jar, Navarre could not let go by surrendering, nor could he withdraw his fist. He was well and truly stuck.

Early on the 13th Beatrice on the north-eastern perimeter was assaulted by Le Trong Tan's 312th Division. Protecting her was just one legion battalion under Lieutenant-Colonel Gaucher. The legionnaires were at a decided disadvantage in that the Viet Minh looked right down on them. Nonetheless, they stood their ground and with automatic weapons and radio-directed artillery they slaughtered the charging enemy in great heaps. Despite this, some legionnaires had to pull in a bit or be overrun. Nearer dusk they pulled in further, and during the night de Castries gave permission for Gaucher to evacuate Beatrice. They had inflicted 600 fatalities on the Viet Minh and wounded over 1,000.

The following morning Dominique on the eastern perimeter identified Viet Minh creeping closer, but it was Gabrielle, a hillock position a mile to the north of Beatrice held by a company of legionnaires and an Algerian battalion, that caught the full brunt of an attack by Vuong Thua Va's 308th Division. Here the slaughter was even more prodigious as rifles, machine-guns, artillery and aerial bombs and rockets laid low hundreds of Viet Minh, but they kept coming and at times were so close to the trenches that artillery and air strikes could not be used. Moreover, Viet Minh artillery was accurate and heavy.

Navarre, who was in radio contact, was fearful his plan might not work he ordered a battalion of paratroopers to parachute onto Dien Bien Phu airfield.

At 2.00am next morning in rain Gabrielle was attacked again by a horde of Viet Minh. By 6.00am they were through the wire and charging from bunker to bunker shooting the occupants. At this instant de Castries attempted a rescue with infantry and tanks from the main camp, but Viet Minh artillery fire drove them back. Within minutes Gabrielle's survivors were running for the safety of Anne-Marie on the north west perimeter and Huguette on the west, shells dogging them all the way.

Navarre's intelligence staff was working overtime, calculating bad and good news: the bad news, that at this rate of attrition the remaining seven bastions would be overrun in a week; the good news that Vo would run out of manpower in four days.

Throughout the 15th every bastion was shelled, but none was attacked. The garrison was thankful, but this upset the intelligence calculations.

On the 16th another battalion of paratroopers jumped onto the airfield. Pilots reported seeing trenches snaking their way towards the perimeter. This was alarming news for Navarre, for apparently Vo had realised his human wave assaults were too costly (Gabrielle had cost Vo over 6,000 casualties). Therefore, he would continue shelling the defenders while at night his men were digging trenches ever closer to the wire.

On the 17th Viet Minh officers approached Anne-Marie under a flag of truce, offering de Castries 86 French wounded who had been captured at Gabrielle. Naturally he accepted, appreciating this was an excellent move on Vo's part, for the wounded simply added to de Castries' burden, because medevac planes had tried to fly out his wounded, but when one was shot down the service was abandoned.

This same day some T'ai defenders of Anne-Marie surrendered! De Castries sent a few tanks to the position to corset the remaining T'ais and legionnaires, but the tankers could not stand the artillery fire and withdrew.

Day after day the battle continued: artillery barrages 'took out' segments of the defences; supplies were parachuted onto the airfields; reinforcements and replacements parachuted onto the airfield, then ran for cover under a barrage of shells; aircraft strafed and rocketed the hills – invariably the wrong slopes – and French artillery replied continuously, often without aim to keep up the morale of the garrison. Every night the Viet Minh dug a little closer. Viet Minh leaflets blew in the wind, asking the T'ai and Vietnamese to defect. Other leaflets written in French addressed the Africans and still others written in German asked the legionnaires why were they fighting for the French? As the days went by soldiers

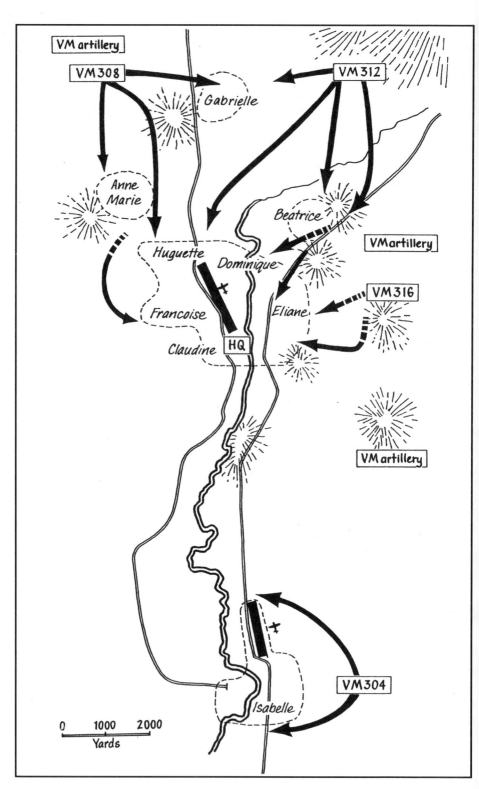

of various nationalities left the line and began to set up 'neutral zones'. De Castries left them alone.

On the 21st at Eliane on the south-east perimeter a Moroccan and a T'ai battalion, a French engineer company and some mixed paratroopers fought Le Quang Ba's 316th Division to a standstill, inflicting 150 casualties.

On 30 March at 5.00pm Dominique on the east, defended by an Algerian battalion, some mixed paratroopers, twelve French manned 105s and two quad .50s manned by Vietnamese, was assaulted by the 312th Division, while Eliane was attacked by the 316th Division. There was hand to hand action at Dominique within minutes.

By nightfall Eliane was in danger of being overrun, so Bigeard grabbed a motley band of about 80 men and led them straight into the Viet Minh. The ferocity of his charge shocked the Viet Minh into retreating, but almost every one of Bigeard's little band was hit.

Paratroopers and tanks counter-attacking from the airfield restored the situation at Dominique and Eliane by dawn.

But come sunset the whole performance was repeated at Dominique, with bitter fighting between the exhausted combatants. In the dark men fought blindly, only able to tell friend from foe by the sound of their weapons. No doubt many were shot by their own side. Fortunately the tanks arrived on cue and restored the situation once more. Came dawn on 1 April the field was quiet except for the moans of wounded. Approximately 350 Viet Minh bodies lay in front of Eliane and over 800 in and around Dominique.

A few days later the Viet Minh trenches were within grenade throwing range of Dominique and Eliane. Bigeard and Langlais did not like sitting still and 'taking it', so on occasion they led small raids into the enemy trenches to the astonishment of the Viet Minh.

It was heartbreaking for the defenders to watch helplessly as precious parachuted supplies drifted into Viet Minh lines, and they cussed out the air force who could not hit anything with a bomb or a parachute. They also blamed their artillery commander. Why were they outgunned, they asked Piroth? He had no answer and must have felt the responsibility keenly every time he saw a casualty being painfully carried to the aid station to join the hundreds lying on stretchers. It became too much for him. With his one arm he awkwardly pulled the pin from a grenade and blew himself up!

To keep up morale someone started a rumour that American troops were on the way. In truth a few American transport pilots were all that Uncle Sam was going to send.

After dark on 4 April Huguette on the north-west, linking Anne-Marie with the main compound, was assaulted by the 312th Division. The combat was bitter and hand to hand in places as a legion battalion and six 105s fought like wildcats. Reinforced by paratroopers the defenders counter-attacked.

Meanwhile other paratroopers and T'ais charged out of Francoise on the west to strike the 308th Division. To and fro the struggle for the two bastions continued, hour after hour, relentlessly, into the morning, all day, all night, the combatants losing all sense of time, and only in the 96th hour did the shooting cease. The defenders had inflicted over 2,000 casualties on the Viet Minh.

Navarre did not know what to do next. If he allowed de Castries to reinforce the defences nearest the enemy trenches, he risked weakening other segments of the perimeter. If he allowed de Castries to shrink the perimeter, he would offer the enemy artillery a compact target and more parachuted supplies would fall into enemy hands. If he tried to break through with an armoured force, would he end up with two trapped expeditions? He came to the conclusion that Dien Bien Phu had become the Verdun of the Indo-China War. For morale reasons at home he could not abandon the fight, therefore he chose to reinforce massively by the only method possible, by parachute.

Over the next three weeks three battalions of paratroopers and a battalion of parachute artillery, plus medical teams, dropped onto the airfield. After 12 March a total of 1,429 Frenchmen, 931 legionnaires, 30 Africans and 1,901 Vietnamese joined the battle by parachute.

By 23 April de Castries had made major changes. Over 500 of his men had been killed and as many captured. Over 1,500 were nursing wounds. Thus a quarter of his original force was lost to him in 41 days of combat. He now held Claudine on the south-west with 400 legionnaires under Major Clemencon, who had a large artillery position behind him. To the west Francoise had retracted somewhat and was defended by several companies of T'ais and air force ground crew under Captain Duluat. Huguette on the north-west was defended by Major Guiraud with 600 legionnaires and 1,540 Africans. Anne-Marie was abandoned. Manning the northern edge of the perimeter were 250 Moroccans and a mixed group under Major Nicolas. Dominique on the north-east was barely held by Major Tourret's 530 mixed infantrymen. Eliane was by far the strongest position, held by 1,800 paratroopers. Lonely Isabelle's 1,400 defenders under Colonel Lalande were still in good condition.

On the southern perimeter of Dien Bien Phu the Viet Minh had dug their trenches close enough to easily snipe at anyone crossing the runway. To neutralise these snipers, on the 24th the garrison concentrated their artillery on them, followed by a sortie with infantry and tanks. They massacred Viet Minh by the score, but made no major impression and had to withdraw.

This attempt to save the runway was rather futile, for the air force was afraid to land; they had lost too many planes trying it.

On the evening of May Day, a communist festival, the defenders on the entire southern and eastern perimeters were shattered by an artillery barrage followed by charging Viet Minh of the 308th, 312th and 316th Divisions. Isabelle too received a major assault from Hoang Minh Thao's 304th Division.

This death or victory battle continued into 2 May and 3rd, and that evening the north-west came under attack. By now Viet Minh were being shot down just 300 yards from de Castries' command bunker. On and on the battle raged.

On the morning of the 6th a hundred French and Vietnamese paratroopers volunteered to jump onto Dien Bien Phu: some fell among the Viet Minh.

That evening a terrific explosion blew away part of the southern perimeter: the Viet Minh had tunnelled underneath and planted a mine. Before the dazed defenders could regain their senses a mass of Viet Minh was overrunning their positions. De Castries pleaded with Navarre for aid, but there was none left. He was expected to console himself with a promotion to brigadier general.

By the morning of the 7th the perimeter was two miles north to south, but only 600 yards east to west and the combat was continuous. That afternoon the Viet Minh launched another human wave assault and for the first time every defender – combat troops, cooks, clerks, radio operators, wounded – was involved in hand to hand combat. At 5.30pm the headquarters staff threw up their hands when Viet Minh entered their bunker.

After dark a mob of several hundred defenders tried to break out into the countryside, but they ran into Viet Minh everywhere. One by one and in small groups of a few dozen or so the entire garrison was captured.

Only Isabelle still stood and its garrison surrendered formally next morning.

Aftermath: Between 12 March and 8 May the defence of Dien Bien Phu (and Isabelle) soaked up 15,105 soldiers of the French and Vietnamese armies, including those who parachuted in on the 6th, of which 1,142 were killed (269 Frenchmen, 318 legionnaires, 206 Africans, 261 Indo-Chinese in French uniform, and 88 in Vietnamese uniform), 1,606 were captured prior to the 7th, many of them too wounded to resist (180 Frenchmen, 738 legionnaires, 434 Africans, 156 Indo-Chinese in French uniform and 98 in Vietnamese uniform) and 4,436 were wounded (974 Frenchmen, 1,266 legionnaires, 1,036 Africans, 955 Indo-Chinese in French uniform and 205 in Vietnamese uniform). Thus by the afternoon of the 7th de Castries had suffered over 7,000 casualties, which was two thirds of his original strength and 45 per cent of his total numbers. The defenders inflicted casualties on the Viet Minh of about 7,900 killed and 15,000 wounded.

On the 8th the surviving defenders walked, limped or were carried by their friends into Viet Minh captivity. It took several weeks of agonising travail to reach their destination, a prison camp.

Appraisal: The errors of Navarre and de Castries were committed because of an arrogance based upon a flawed belief. It was not racism, but elitism. They assumed that peasants without any military education could never win a pitched battle against an army of France, a nation that had pioneered so much military thought. The Bigeards of the army thought differently, but Bigeard and his ilk were seen as cannon fodder not as men who had invaluable advice.

These errors fall into seventeen major categories: grand strategy, ground, counsel, timing, strategy, intelligence, supply, command structure, specialists, dispersal, firepower, reconnaissance, morale, tactics, reserves, psyops and command ability.

Navarre was sent to Indo-China to put the army on the road to victory to enable the Vietnamese to take over, but he soon returned to Paris selling his Dien Bien Phu plan, which called for a defensive grand strategy. It says little for the government that they accepted his plan, for it assumed Vo would take the bait, and that was the flaw in the plan: what if he did not? Valuable troops would sit out the war in Dien Bien Phu, and the longer the war lasted the greater the chance of a Viet Minh victory. To wage war by waiting for the enemy to make the next move is not the way to swift and sure victory. Navarre had forgotten the creed of one of France's greatest commanders, Lazare Carnot: 'L'audace, l'audace, toujours l'audace!'

Moreover, Dien Bien Phu was the worst possible choice of ground. Navarre and Cogny broke every rule in picking this battlefield: the approach highway could be blocked easily by snipers and artillery; the narrow trails in the area led through marshy fords, impassable to trucks and tanks; the highest hills would be in enemy hands, so that every French position would be under observation and within rifle range; and the two airfields were vulnerable to artillery fire.

Navarre listened to plenty of advice before he made his fateful decision to stand at Dien Bien Phu; some counselled air strikes without a ground defence; others wished to rely on the Groupes Mobiles; others suggested like with like by training their men to fight as guerrillas man to man with the Viet Minh. Navarre and the politicians who supported him bear the responsibility for ignoring this counsel.

In effect Navarre challenged Vo to a duel at Dien Bien Phu, but he put no time limit on it, leaving it up to Vo to choose the date of battle. This enabled Vo to assemble his attackers at little monetary cost – it cost almost nothing to feed a porter – while Navarre had to assemble his defenders using precious aviation fuel to carry everything, whether a bullet or a pair of socks.

Only when Vo was ready did the battle begin – in the rainy spring when clouds and squalls would restrict air resupply, air support and aerial reconnaissance, and soggy ground would restrict tanks.

Dien Bien Phu called for airborne strategy from start to finish, and in every successful airborne operation such as Norway, Netherlands, Sicily, Normandy, Eindhoven-Nijmegen, Corregidor and the Rhine in World War II, and Sukchon and Imjin River in Korea, success came because normal infantry were able to approach by land or sea to rescue the airborne troops. At Arnhem in 1944 British paratroopers were defeated in a week, because the infantry failed to break through. True, in 1941 German airborne troops on Crete succeeded alone, but this had not been planned: the amphibious invasion was repelled at sea; and though victorious, the losses among the airborne troops were so great Hitler refused to consider further airborne operations.

The Chindits in Burma 1943–1944 were successful alone, because these glider-landed troops were given leave to travel to enable them to escape encirclement and to keep building airfields out of artillery range, and were able to contact friendly guerrillas, and ultimately even they were rescued by forces approaching overland.

Thus Navarre's strategy flew in the face of every major airborne operation in history: to put his men behind enemy lines with no method of rescue.

Navarre's intelligence staff were not completely at fault. They warned Navarre that Vo could attack with four divisions, and that is precisely what happened. However, their belief that Vo possessed nothing larger than 75s and few of those was completely wrong, as was their estimation that the Viet Minh porters and artillerymen did not have the stamina to pull guns over the hills.

Furthermore, their conclusion that Vo's supply line was too long underestimated the power of the human being. A modern French division liked to have a supply line of no more than ten miles to its corps depot, for two reasons: first, a modern division required a tremendous amount of consumables such as water, various foods, fuel, ammunition, medicines, lubricants, cleaning materials and mail; and second, each division only possessed about 500 supply personnel. Navarre's intelligence staff did not realise that the Viet Minh really needed only ammunition and a few bags of rice, and each of their divisions possessed 50,000 supply personnel!

A 500-mile journey divided among 200,000 porters equals 400 porters per mile or one every four and a half yards. In other words a human conveyor belt could have been set up passing low weight items such as artillery shells from man to man. When one adds the carrying capacity of carts and bicycles, not to mention the few trucks possessed by the Viet Minh, the establishment and maintenance of such a supply line does not seem all that impossible after all, if there are no other draws upon it and if it is left alone to operate in peace for five months, as happened at Dien Bien Phu. This was undoubtedly a magnificent feat of logistics, but one that was mathematically possible and therefore deemed by Vo's staff to be humanly possible. This should have been recognised by Navarre's people. It has been said the Viet Minh's best weapon was the Peugeot bicycle.

This brings us to de Castries' supply line. Quite simply it did not exist. Navarre threw 10,000 men into a bottomless pit, cut off from land supply immediately and from air supply as of the first shellburst. Resupply by parachute was not adequate, because the weather cancelled many a flight, high winds blew parachutes into Viet Minh lines, and as planes often had to fly lower than the hilltops into a shooting gallery with thousands of enemy infantry firing at them and AAA less than a mile either side, their pilots were not always concentrating on accuracy: 48 planes were shot down and 167 badly damaged, with the loss of 139 airmen.

Navarre was an armoured warfare man, but Dien Bien Phu was not an armoured battle, nor could it ever become one with just one tank for every 3,700 attackers. Yet as part of his command structure Navarre chose as his commander on the scene an armoured warfare man, de Castries. Furthermore, de Castries was a colonel, a rank that normally commands 3,000 or so troops. Why was such a crucial battle in the war given over to so junior an officer? A battle involving over 10,000 men surely required three or four generals and a host of colonels.

There was obviously resentment from the other colonels and lieutenant-colonels, because they were expected to treat de Castries like a divisional commander. Furthermore, they were specialists in either parachute tactics, artillery or infantry defence. With just ten tanks among them it seemed odd to give command to a tank man. In any case, paratroopers are a close-knit bunch and do not like 'outsiders'. This did not make for a comfortable command structure.

Specialist infantry exist because normal infantry are not trained to do everything, nor can they be in a twentieth century army. Groupes Mobiles were specialists in moving through jungle-clad terrain living off the land and what they could carry and paratroopers were specialists in jumping on and grabbing a position, which they then handed to the infantry. Neither were trained or equipped to defend ground: that was not their job.

Therefore, Navarre was going against normal practice by asking such specialists to help defend a fixed immobile position. On 12 March no less than a third of the defenders were specialists, and by the end half were specialists. This is a criminal waste of specialists: first, because they cannot be in two places at once, so operations that could have benefited from them were denied them; second, they suffered casualties, thereby denuding Navarre of experienced specialists; and third, they were not trained or equipped to fight such a siege and suffered disproportionately as a consequence. It was tantamount to using architects as bricklayers – a waste of education and one ends up with a crooked wall.

The dispersal of the defenders into Beatrice, Gabrielle, Anne-Marie, Isabelle and the remainder was foolish. Beatrice did not last a day: Gabrielle less than two days; Anne-Marie was untenable. While the enemy left Isabelle's runway unharmed, her defence was necessary, but the instant that first shell fell Isabelle's runway was inoperative and, though her artillery was always beneficial to the whole battle, her two battalions of Algerians and legionnaires were unable to aid the defenders of Dien Bien Phu itself. The Viet Minh did try her once or twice and suffered about 1,500 casualties as a result, but once Dien Bien Phu had fallen Isabelle was given up.

Navarre was assured the garrison would have superior firepower. In fact the defenders were outgunned. Navarre had to grudgingly admit this and reinforce them with a battalion of parachute artillery.

A modern French division normally contained nine infantry battalions and four battalions of artillery, approximately 7.3 tubes per battalion. If one looks at de Castries' force in these terms, Navarre had given him the equivalent of fifteen battalions of infantry at 4.2 tubes per battalion, rising to twenty battalions of infantry at 4.1 tubes per battalion. In other words Navarre talked big about firepower, but gave his troops only 57 per cent of their normal artillery entitlement. Counting the weapons the Viet Minh used as artillery, they had eight tubes per battalion.

Of course, Navarre had air support, but that brings us to the reconnaissance failure. Intelligence told everyone the Viet Minh could not carry artillery across the hills, therefore aerial reconnaissance never looked for guns on the forward slopes. Far too many bombs and rockets were wasted on the reverse slopes, before this error was realised. French air supremacy does not appear to have been a major concern of Vo.

Considering the fact that the defenders of Dien Bien Phu were all volunteers, their morale was poor. Some defected to the enemy; others surrendered; still others declared 'neutrality'.

Frenchmen who had been fighting the Viet Minh for years knew the French public were not behind them. The role of the civilian in wartime is not just one of materially supporting the soldiers, but morally supporting them. As French soldiers departed for Indo-China they saw that the French people were concentrating on employment, housing, fashion, music and films not on war and warriors. The atmosphere was not conducive to giving a man a good send off. Letters from home asking why the war had not been won yet, indeed why it was being waged at all, together with newspaper articles asking the same, added to the drain on army morale.

Ironically by 1954 the French public had begun to morally support their men at the front, but the latter did not know this.

Legionnaires fought for the legion not for France, but they too were susceptible to morale problems, especially as the die-hard warriors among them died, leaving a residue of doubters.

The African soldiers wondered why their own homelands had not been granted independence like the Vietnamese; a question that suggested the French had less respect for them.

The Indo-Chinese troops hated the Viet Minh, but knew their families were at risk from Viet Minh murder squads. One wonders how many defected in order to save their families?

All the defenders were disgusted that there was but one general, Piroth, among them. Generals, they knew, preferred to remain in Hanoi, Haiphong and Saigon, drinking the best wines, eating gourmet dishes, sleeping with beautiful mistresses, attending concerts, rarely giving a thought for the poor fellow in the muddy trench way up in the highlands on the Laotian border.

De Castries' tactics leave a lot to be desired. Obviously he and Navarre expected the enemy to conform exactly to plan, a very dangerous assumption. When Vo called off his human wave assaults and substituted siege tactics of the kind that had been perfected by the Frenchman Vauban two centuries earlier, it came as a surprise to Navarre and de Castries, neither of whom were able to rethink their original plan.

De Castries made a couple of counter-attacks, but neither was a major effort to ensnare a portion of the enemy by a pincer movement. At no time did he launch assaults to link up with Isabelle to enable that garrison to join him. Langlais, Bigeard and others who kept the enemy on their toes by raids did so without de Castries' approval. By continuing with his original plan de Castries subjected his men to the steady attrition of artillery fire, which not only killed and maimed but sapped morale.

Between December and March it did not occur to Navarre that Vo was deliberately draining his reserve pool by attacking in diverse locations. Navarre fell into this trap and allowed his reserves to be frittered away on operations that were not crucial, so that by the beginning of Vo's assault on Dien Bien Phu Navarre's reserves had been halved. This is most evident when it is realised that on 12 March, the day Vo began the siege, Navarre was launching a full-scale offensive elsewhere and when he chose to reinforce de Castries by parachute, he was so short of jump-qualified personnel that 680 of the reinforcements were not paratroopers and were making their first jump!

During the war French psyops got better all the time: the granting of independence was the best move; but it is hard to know what psyops the French could have used to prevent the Chinese supporting the Viet Minh. The best time for a peace conference was before July 1953, for that month the United Nations gave up in Korea, settling for a stalemate along the 38th Parallel. Kim Il-sung did not get South Korea, but neither did Syngman Rhee get North Korea. Ho Chi Minh and Chou En-lai concluded that if the United Nations could not wrestle North Korea from communism, France on her own could not wrestle North Vietnam from communism. The French knew this too and their only hope was to accept peace talks, scheduled for May 1954, and to attend them with a victory under their belts. As it was, the Viet Minh are the ones who attended the talks in Geneva boasting of a recent victory, Dien Bien Phu. Thus from July 1953 onwards the best psyops cards were in Ho Chi Minh's hand.

Navarre's command ability can be summed up by the incident where he chickened out at the beginning of the battle only to find he was irreversibly committed.

Apart from courage, de Castries exhibited little else of note. His allowance of deserters to declare 'neutrality' is evidence that he was bankrupt of ideas and had abdicated responsibility for his men. To be fair to him he was in over his head and should never have been placed in this impossible position.

Alternatives: Navarre should never have thrown his troops into the deep end with a 'sink or swim' attitude.

He did not know it, but his Groupes Mobiles had begun to hurt the Viet Minh. If he had kept up their incisive surgical offensives while also using guerrillas to fight guerrillas he may have succeeded in Vietnamising the war, which was his goal.

However, once he had committed his men to Dien Bien Phu there was still another alternative. A company of paratroopers dropping on top of the Viet Minh supply line could have caused Vo to reconsider his battle. Four or five such drops in succession at various places along Vo's supply route might have caused him to withdraw. These would not have been suicide missions, for these paratroopers could have been equipped to accept parachuted supplies at selected sites along their escape route. No one knows if this would have worked, but to be sure, dropping them on top of Dien Bien Phu was suicide.

Consequences: The loss of 15,000 men in one incident was a shock to the French public, but much more than this was the knowledge that when Navarre threw down the gauntlet he did so in the name of the French Union, an empire of state of the art technology, science, culture, and great sophistication, and a peasant army had taken up that gauntlet and beat Navarre fair and square in a knock down toe to toe fight. France had suffered humiliation in 1940, when she was conquered by Germany, and further humiliation when she was liberated by the Americans and British in 1944. Now had come another humiliation.

France went into mourning. The government closed all cinemas and theatres. What made it worse was that the very day the terrible news reached France, 8 May, French delegates sat down with Viet Minh and Chinese envoys in Geneva to begin talks. It seemed the Viet Minh had planned their victory down to the very hour. The Chinese envoy, Chou En-lai, spoke with elegance and conviction and with the calm deliberation that one has when one knows victory is already in the bag.

The public wanted to blame someone, of course, and one scapegoat was the German legionnaires – one legionnaire in four was German. With the sort of logic that idiots love they blamed these Nazis for selling out to the communists, forgetting two things: one, Nazis don't like communists; and two, by 1954 few of the Germans in the legion were old enough to have been Hitler's soldiers.

Others, on slightly firmer ground, blamed French communists for treason and undermining morale. Still others blamed the press for reporting the truth!

Navarre was brought home in disgrace, his career in ruins. Soon his mistakes would be used in military schools as an example of how to lose a war.

The almost 14,000 prisoners taken at Dien Bien Phu were released five months later, but only one in five (including de Castries) survived this short but brutal captivity!

The Battle's Place in History: The Geneva negotiations resulted in a deal similar to that in Korea. Cambodia, Laos and Vietnam remained independent, and an election would decide who should rule Vietnam, the Viet Minh or the pro-French government under Emperor Bao Dai. Until the election could be held, in two years' time, Ho would be allowed to rule Vietnam north of the 17th Parallel and the Emperor's government would control Vietnam south of it.

Needless to say the elections never took place. First Ho solidified his rule in the north through terror, and then he organised a guerrilla force, the Viet Cong, which just five years after his victory at Dien Bien Phu began a new conflict for control of South Vietnam: the Vietnam War.

The French defeat had already sparked another war in 1954. The Algerians watched as France was defeated in battle, angry that so many of their sons had died in Indo-China. They demanded independence and when France refused to let go her grasp, Algerian rebels began a war of liberation just days after the prisoners from Indo-China came home.

1991

Kuwait

Background: Iraq is an Arab nation, though a seventh of its population is Kurdish and there are minorities of Assyrians, Turcomans, Azerbaijanis and Iranians. In 1990 the state religion was Islam of the Sunnite variety, but most citizens held to the Shiite sect.

Iraq is the oldest known civilisation, its history being divided into three eras. The first was the rise of great empires known as Mesopotamia, Babylon and Assyria, led by such emperors as Hammurabi and Nebuchadnezzar and concluding with the Persian (Iranian) invasion. A history of antiquity is woefully incomplete without the story of these empires and the great cities that launched them. The second era was that of Moslem Iraq. A history of the world between the seventh and seventeenth centuries is incomplete without reference to the great Moslem city of Baghdad. The third era was one of depression, for the state fell under the Turkish Empire and was reduced to a backwater of primitive hovels. By the early twentieth century the descendants of the great empires were a pitiable lot living in poverty.

However, in 1918 they were liberated by the British and for a few heady weeks the inhabitants let their dreams run wild, until they realised the British had come to stay. They revolted and were easily defeated in inglorious skirmishes. The Iraqis were humiliated by the British victory.

Yet, in 1932 the British entrusted Iraq with independence, but retained British troops there just in case. To celebrate the Arabs massacred Assyrians.

In 1941 following a Fascist revolution in Baghdad, the British responded by attacking the Iraqis and destroying their armed forces in a month-long war and establishing a favourable government at a cost of less than 50 British casualties. Again the Iraqis felt humiliated.

On 19 June 1961 Britain gave Kuwait independence. A week later Iraq claimed Kuwait, whereupon the British sent troops to Kuwait and the Iraqi government backed down. The Iraqis saw this as yet another humiliation at the hands of the British.

The Commander: Saddam Hussein was born in 1937 in al-Ouja a poor village. Possibly illegitimate he was raised by a cruel stepfather. He received better treatment from his blood relatives, marrying a cousin in an arranged marriage and on behalf of his uncle/father-in-law murdering a rival. Through family connections he entered university, studying law of all things, but drifted into revolutionary politics as a member of the Baath party. In 1959 he attempted to assassinate the president, was wounded and forced to flee, first to Syria then Egypt.

In 1963 the Baath seized power in Iraq, and Saddam came home, but the party quickly dissolved into factions and Saddam was soon in hiding again, operating as a terrorist. In 1968 Saddam's faction seized power.

Though taking the job of deputy president, 31-year-old Saddam was the true strong man in Iraq. He modelled himself on Hitler – he kept a portrait of the Nazi dictator in his office – and he created a state in the Hitler mould with a secret police, concentration camps and torture chambers. One favourite tactic was to torture the children of suspects rather than the suspects. However, Saddam had to move cautiously as would-be assassins lurked even within his inner sanctum.

In March 1973 his troops seized two Kuwaiti border posts to test international opinion: the reaction was so swift that he backed down.

In October that year he loaned a few brigades to the Jordanians to attack Israel: the result was ignominious defeat; the Israelis declared the Iraqis to be the weakest Arabs they had ever faced. Saddam lost much prestige over this, and his star began to slide further when his troops were defeated by rebel Kurds.

He concluded he had to restructure his army and, swallowing his pride, he asked the USSR for help, who at once began an all out modernisation programme. Despite much Soviet influence, Saddam reorganised his armed forces not on communist lines, but on Hitlerian lines.

On 16 July 1979 Saddam tired of publicly taking a back seat to his puppet government and he turned on them in an incident known as the Night of the Long Knives (in reference to a similar event in Hitler's régime). In fact the butchery lasted several weeks as Saddam had hundreds of leading politicians shot, including his deputy prime minister. He commanded many of the firing squads himself.

Meanwhile the Ayatollah Khomeini, an Iranian Shiite whom Saddam had once deported from Iraq, seized power in Iran and turned against the world, bearing a special grudge against Saddam. Saddam, seeing himself as a saviour of the world, and actually being treated as such by wishy-washy foreign diplomats, ordered a full-scale invasion of Iran on 22 September 1980. He expected his new armed forces to stomp the Iranian revolutionaries within days.

It did not quite work out this way: the Iraqis were sorely hurt at Khorramshahr. Saddam fired several officers and executed a few, but he could not change the military situation, which settled down to a trench stalemate reminiscent of France in World War I.

Saddam always liked to have aces up his sleeve, and three of these were his work on biological, chemical and nuclear weapons, all top secret. However, the Israelis learned the truth and humiliated Saddam by bombing his nuclear facility. Naturally Saddam dismissed the 'responsible' military officers.

Despite announcing he would withdraw from Iran the war dragged on: casualty lists lengthened beyond reason with nothing to show for it; and in 1984 the Kurds took advantage of this to revolt again. In 1986 Saddam staked all on an offensive into the Fao Peninsula: it failed with terrible loss.

The Iranians had begun to attack neutral oil tankers in the Persian Gulf with missiles and mines, because some of them carried Iraqi oil, and the British and American navies responded by taking up a 'big brother' role to the tankers, thereby becoming *de facto* allies of Saddam.

In March 1988, fed up with having to siphon troops away from the Iranian front to fight Kurds, Saddam ordered poison gas used on the Kurds: in the village of Halabja 5,000 people were killed. The international outcry was loud, which probably surprised Saddam, for no one had cared when he gassed Iranians.

He did have some good news, though. This spring General Saadi Tuma Abbas defeated a major Iranian offensive aimed at Basra.

On 3 July owing to the failure of their offensive and the growing American and British response at sea, the Iranians asked for a truce with Iraq. Saddam was only too happy to agree. Naturally he claimed victory, but even the most rabid Saddam supporter knew it was a draw at best.

The Armed Forces: Saddam's army had been equipped and trained by Soviet advisers into their manner of warfare, but during his war with Iran Saddam had gained considerable weaponry from others: for example, his armoured vehicles consisted of tanks, armoured cars, infantry fighting vehicles (IFVs – tanks that carry infantry) and armoured personnel carriers (APCs) either bought from or built under licence from Yugoslavia, the USSR, Hungary, Brazil, Czechoslovakia, China, Italy, Britain, France and the USA.

By 1990 the army was divided into the reservists and the regulars, the latter 590,000 strong and among whom was the famed Republican Guard, modelled by Saddam on Hitler's *Waffen SS* and consisting of one special forces, two armoured and five mechanised divisions and a marine brigade, either fully formed or in training. The remainder of the regular army consisted of four mechanised, six armoured and 50 infantry divisions and 47 brigades, either fully formed or partially formed and awaiting recalled reservists.

An infantry division consisted of: a command battalion; four towed artillery battalions (two 85mm, one 100mm and one 122mm); four mortar companies (60mm, 82mm, 120mm, 160mm); three anti-aircraft artillery (AAA) battalions (one 37mm, one 57mm and one of twin and quad 14.5mm and 23mm); two engineer battalions; a battalion each of reconnaissance, anti-tank guns, signallers, supply and transport; a chemical defence company; a military police company; a tank battalion; and three brigades of three infantry battalions each.

An infantry battalion consisted of five companies: one headquarters; one support of four anti-tank guns and four 82mm mortars; and three rifle, each containing three rifle platoons and one weapons platoon of four machine-guns, twelve rocket propelled grenades (RPG) and three 60mm mortars. A tank battalion possessed a headquarters and a support companies and 27 tanks.

A mechanised division was similar to an infantry division, minus the tank battalion, plus a SAM 9 (surface to air missile) battalion, and each of its three brigades contained a company each of signallers, engineers, supply, transport, reconnaissance, chemical defence, mortars and commandos, as well as one tank and three mechanised infantry battalions.

A mechanised infantry battalion consisted of five companies: headquarters, support and three mechanised infantry. Each of the latter contained a weapons platoon and three platoons of three APCs each, carrying eight infantrymen apiece.

An armoured division was the same as a mechanised division except that each brigade contained three tank and one mechanised infantry battalions.

A corps controlled several divisions, plus each corps possessed in its own right several artillery battalions with a mixture of guns (107mm, 122mm, 127mm, 180mm and 300mm); an artillery observation battalion; AAA batteries of missiles and guns; and battalions of anti-tank guns, engineers, reconnaissance, radar, signals, support, transport and medical; plus helicopter squadrons.

The Republican Guard (RG) differed in that their provisions and equipment were far superior, plus each mechanised brigade had an extra mechanised infantry battalion, each mechanised infantry battalion had an extra mechanised infantry company, the mechanised infantry used IFVs (73mm BMP-1s and 30mm BMP-2s) instead of APCs, each armoured brigade had an extra tank battalion, and all artillery was self-propelled 90mm, 122mm, 152mm and 155mm.

Thus an army infantry division contained 27 second-rate tanks (T-54s, T-55s, T-59s or T-69s with 100mm guns or Vickers and Centurions with 105mm guns); a mechanised division contained 81 tanks, mostly second-rate, but with some first-rate (T-62s with 115mm guns, Chieftains with 120mm guns and T-72s with 125mm guns); an armoured division contained 243 second- and first-rate tanks. Republican Guard mechanised divisions had 81 first-rate tanks and armoured divisions had 324 first-rate tanks.

In total the Republican Guard possessed 1,053 first-rate tanks and 2,376 IFVs, and the remainder of the army had 3,132 first -and second-rate tanks and 1,458 APCs.

Saddam had also created the Popular Army, based upon Hitler's storm troopers, consisting of 850,000 part-timers organised into battalions and brigades. Much of the AAA of Air Defence Command was manned by these fellows, using the Soviet supplied surface to air missile (SAM) 2, 3, 6, 7, 8, 9, 13 and 14 systems and the French Roland system, plus Soviet supplied guns – twin and quad 14.5mm and 23mm, and single towed 37mm and 57mm.

Saddam's strategic capability was Scud Command using the highly inaccurate and low yield Scud missile. As a battlefield weapon the rocket was useless, but as a psychological weapon against a populated area it had some merit.

By 1990 Saddam's army was the fourth largest in the world and the most combat experienced.

His air force was also state of the art with 48 MiG-29s, 20 MiG-25s, 50 Xian/MiG-23s, 150 Xian/MiG-21s, 116 Mirage F1s, 80 Su20s, 40 Xian/MiG-19s and 50 helicopter gunships.

However, the navy was but a small coastal force with eight minesweepers, six corvettes, five frigates and a few minelayers and patrol boats.

Causes of Arrogance: The number one cause of Saddam's arrogance was the fact that he seemed invulnerable. He had lost count of the number of times someone had tried to kill him. Like Stalin his ego received a boost every time he escaped injury.

Another reason for his sense of invulnerability was that the USA and Britain had become *de facto* allies during the Iran War and both they and the French had sold him arms, the British even breaking their own rules to do so. It appeared to him these governments would not let anything stand in the way of keeping Iraq powerful and Saddam in control: for example, in May 1987 an Iraqi pilot mistook an American warship, the *Stark*, for an Iranian and put a missile into her, killing 37. There is no doubt it was an error, but it impressed Saddam that President Reagan and Vice-President George Bush meekly accepted the explanation.

Another example came in 1989 when he arrested two Britons for spying: the protest by British Prime Minister Margaret Thatcher was weak.

In January 1990 George Bush, now President, announced the US Navy would no longer keep a carrier force in the Persian Gulf. This sent a signal to Saddam that the Americans were no longer interested in what happened in that part of the world.

In March 1990 Saddam executed one of the British spies: again Thatcher's protest was weak.

In April four powerful American Senators met with Saddam to protest about his biological–chemical–nuclear programme, but their words were so shallow, Saddam decided they were just going through the motions to gain votes back home.

In May the Arab League agreed to hold its summit in Saddam's capital and all the member states celebrated his powerful role in the Arab world.

On 18 July Saddam claimed Kuwait was stealing his oil by angular drilling and trespassing: he also claimed sovereignty over Kuwait; he demanded they cease aggression toward his troops; and he demanded they cancel his $15billion debt to them. The Kuwaitis responded by agreeing to talks.

At this time the US Navy re-entered the gulf for exercises with the United Arab Emirates, but on the 25th US Ambassador Glaspie assured Saddam of no hostile intent and that the Americans were not concerned with Arab versus Arab disputes.

Armed with this assurance Saddam bullied the OPEC council into raising the price of oil from $18 to $21 a barrel.

If anyone could mastermind a coalition against Iraq it would be the USA, but Saddam was not concerned for three reasons: the USSR would not allow its ally Iraq to be crushed by the capitalist Americans; the USA could not do it without Saudi Arabian and other Arab support, and as long as the USA was an ally of Israel no self-respecting Arab state would join the USA; and the Americans had had their fingers burned in the disastrous sixteen-year Vietnam War, ending in 1975.

In 1983 the Americans had kicked out a rebel government on the tiny island of Grenada, but that operation was a noted fiasco, and the same year an American–British–French–Italian intervention in the Lebanon Civil War was quickly curtailed following two bomb explosions that killed a few hundred Americans and Frenchmen. In December 1989 the Americans had responded to a declaration of war by Panama's President by invading that nation and capturing him, but the American public immediately began to question the morality of the move and its implications. They were also overly concerned about the handful of American dead. Saddam decided that the American people would no longer support a long war or a short but high casualty war.

Britain was another concern, if history was anything to go by, but here too there was no cause for worry for four reasons: the USSR would not allow the British to attack; Britain had come within a whisker of defeat just crushing one division of Argentinians in 1982; the British still had Commonwealth commitments and 15,000 men on operations in Northern Ireland; and in any case Saddam's army outnumbered the British Army ten to one.

Saddam had no worries about the French, for they would not put conscripts into a war: their disasters in Indo-China and Algeria had put a stop to that; and they had insufficient regulars to fill more than a couple of divisions.

The Syrians were a threat, but Saddam did not see them participating in an American-led coalition. They had fought the Americans as recently as 1983.

The Egyptians had cause to dislike the Iraqis, but President Mubarrek had internal security problems and his army had not fought a major battle since 1973, when they had been decisively defeated by the Israelis.

The Turks were also a threat, but with potentially hostile Greece and the USSR on their borders, and their own Kurds in rebellion, Saddam did not believe the Turks would risk a conflict.

By August 1990 Saddam believed he could do anything.

The Invasion: At 2.00am on 2 August 1990 the Republican Guard Medina, Hammurabi and Tawakalna Divisions invaded Kuwait. Tanks charged along roads, many of them almost bereft of ammunition to make them lighter and therefore faster, while marines landed on the coast. The Iraqis reached the Emir's palace in Kuwait City within hours. However, the Emir had fled. The Iraqis had to be content with shooting his brother.

While the small Kuwaiti Army and British advisers fought a withdrawal action towards Saudi Arabia, the Republican Guard did not press them – in truth most of the Iraqis were too busy looting everything from jewels and money to computers, tape recorders and lamps. Anyone who resisted was gunned down or beaten.

Next day the United Nations Security Council voted 14-0 to condemn the invasion. By the 4th most of the Kuwaiti troops had surrendered or reached Saudi Arabia, and some organised a guerrilla force. Additionally thousands of civilians and over a million foreign workers fled Kuwait, but the Iraqis prevented all 'Western' citizens from leaving, including 2,500 Americans and 4,000 Britons.

Countdown: On the 7th President Bush announced US troops would go to Saudi Arabia at that government's request. He was obviously worried that Saddam would push on and capture the oil-rich gulf. Thatcher followed Bush, and Mikhail Gorbachev, the Soviet leader, ordered the 8,000 Soviet workers in Iraq to down tools.

Next day Saddam annexed Kuwait. This was followed by a French decision to send troops to Saudi Arabia, whereupon Saddam ordered his border guards to detain all 'Western' foreigners trying to leave Iraq.

The biggest blow to Saddam came on the 10th when twelve of the twenty Arab League states voted to join the coalition to defend Saudi Arabia.

Saddam hoped most of this was purely show and when Saudi and American reconnaissance planes began flying over Iraq he ordered his forces to leave them alone.

Saddam never did anything without several aces up his sleeve, and now he introduced the first one. He said he would withdraw if Israel withdrew from her conquered territory.

These days in Baghdad Saddam was receiving a stream of diplomats, unofficial emissaries, pacifists and radicals from the coalition countries. Apparently he saw this as a major indication of the weak will of the coalition, and to reinforce his position he introduced a second ace: he announced a treaty with Iran, thus making everyone aware that he was no longer afraid of an Iranian stab in the back while he faced the coalition.

Saddam then drew his next ace, stating he would allow foreigners to leave Iraq and Kuwait if the Americans withdrew from Saudi Arabia and the UN lifted its new trade embargo on Iraq. To add punch to this statement he arrested foreigners and placed them at potential bombing targets in Kuwait and Iraq. Three days later he appeared on television with hostage children. The world's news teams covered it. Saddam had become the greatest TV star in the world. Suddenly as a goodwill gesture he allowed all foreign females and children to leave.

When Bush dismissed his air force chief for publicly bragging about the plan to bomb Iraq, Saddam possibly saw this as evidence that Bush had no real intention of attacking him.

Meanwhile the coalition nations were plagued with scaremongers, some of whom were ecologists who warned that Saddam had the power to 'destroy' the world. In response Saddam declared he would destroy Kuwait's oilfields if attacked, an act which, said the scaremongers, would cause a 'nuclear winter' by blocking out the sun and killing everyone and everything.

However, none of this stopped the coalition forces from assembling in Saudi Arabia, and in November Saddam mobilised his reservists aged 17 to 33: 480,000 of them.

On the 29th the UN ordered Saddam to leave Kuwait by 16 January 1991 or face military action. This was a war ultimatum, and Bush and Thatcher were strongly behind it.

By now Saddam was receiving very conflicting signals. The Americans wanted talks and Gorbachev was saying he could get a deal, yet coalition reconnaissance planes were still overflying Saddam's airspace and raiders were loose in his desert: in a skirmish three French soldiers were caught. Hoping for a climbdown by the coalition, Saddam released the Frenchmen, and on 6 December he announced all foreigners could leave.

Realising he may well have a major war on his hands after all, Saddam promoted General Saadi Tuma Abbas to Minister of Defence. Saddam had no intention of letting go of the military reins: he would direct this coming battle personally; but probably he needed a scapegoat in case things went wrong, hence Saadi's promotion.

As one last attempt to escape retribution he threw another ace onto the table: he declared he would use chemical weapons if attacked.

On 7 January came a major provocation: British and American raiders captured a SAM site in entirety and lifted the equipment back to Saudi Arabia in helicopters. Saddam did not let this impudence goad him into attacking.

On 12 January the US Congress finally voted to support Bush if it came to war. Saddam must have known now that Bush had to strike.

The Enemy: The anti-Saddam coalition building up inside Saudi Arabia was the most international effort since the Korean War. The Gulf nations provided: a mechanised brigade and 20 warplanes from Oman; an infantry company and 36 warplanes from Bahrain; a mechanised brigade and 50 warplanes from the United Arab Emirates; a mechanised battalion and eighteen warplanes from Qatar. These nations also supplied ships, rear-echelon units and money.

Other Islamic nations had joined: an Afghan company, a Bangla Desh brigade, a battalion each from Morocco, Pakistan, Niger and Senegal.

The Kuwaitis had put together a liberation army of one armoured and four infantry brigades and a few warplanes.

The Saudis had a large army of one airborne, four armoured, three mechanised and four infantry brigades and 30 independent infantry battalions.

However, apart from some of the Kuwaitis and Afghans none of these forces had any serious combat experience. In fact one of the Saudi armoured brigades was made up of Moroccan volunteers and another of Pakistani volunteers. The Pakistanis and a Saudi mechanised brigade were busy watching the Yemen border. British and Americans who were training the Arab forces often shook their heads in frustration.

However, the coalition also contained élite Arab forces: Syrians and Egyptians. The Syrians placed an armoured division, an AAA brigade and three infantry battalions in Saudi Arabia and ten brigades on the Syrian–Iraqi border and mobilised their air force. The Egyptians sent to Saudi Arabia an armoured and a mechanised divisions, a AAA brigade, a ranger brigade and two commando battalions.

The French 'Daguet' Expeditionary Force consisted of one tank, two mechanised, two paratrooper and four infantry battalions plus rear-echelon units, ships and planes.

The British 'Granby' Expeditionary Force included many ships, a hundred warplanes and the 1st Armoured Division possessing the equivalent of five tank, five mechanised and five SPG artillery battalions, plus a host of rear-echelon troops.

Turkey had declared neutrality, but maintained ten divisions on Saddam's northern border, and there were American planes based in Turkey.

The following nations provided ships, aircraft, rear-echelon units, equipment or facilities: Singapore, South Korea, Sierra Leone, Sweden, Spain, Romania, Philippines, Portugal, Poland, Norway, New Zealand, Netherlands, Italy, Hungary, Honduras, Greece, Germany, Denmark, Czechoslovakia, Canada, Bulgaria, Belgium, Argentina and Australia.

However, the Americans were the glue that held everyone together. They provided for their Desert Shield/Desert Storm expedition a greater force than they had ever fielded since World War II, drawing upon reservists and National Guard: in the air 1,400 warplanes and 600 helicopter gunships; at sea a plethora of warships that could bombard the Iraqis with missiles or gunfire and land an amphibious force on the coast thereby outflanking Saddam's defences on the Kuwait–Saudi border. American ground forces consisted of the equivalent of one airmobile, one airborne, two marine, two mechanised and four armoured divisions, and two marine, two armoured and two mechanised brigades, plus nine artillery brigades and a host of special forces and rear-echelon units. Indeed there were more Americans than all other coalition troops put together.

Strategy: Saddam knew that unlike the Iran War the coming conflict on his southern flank would be an armoured battle (the 'mother of all battles' he told his people) and he was confident that he stood in good condition to fight it, with 4,200 tanks against the coalition's 3,200 (two thirds American, about 360 Egyptian, 250 Syrian, 200 British, 200 Saudi, 200 Kuwaiti, about 50 French, and a few Omani) and 2,400 IFVs against the coalition's 1,250 (900 American and about 250 British).

Nor was he worried about his Iranian, Turkish or Syrian flanks. His only vulnerable flanks were the air and the sea, because Saddam had only 500 warplanes to the coalition's 1,900, and 50 helicopter gunships to their 800, and they possessed an amphibious force offshore.

Saddam preached confidently that the will of the Iraqis was stronger than that of the coalition: once his fighters and AAA defences began knocking coalition planes out of the sky and his Scuds began hitting Saudi cities and the world public began to see civilian bomb damage in Iraq on their television screens, he believed the coalition would cease attacking, rendering their aerial supremacy redundant. He kept secret his deal with Iran to fly some of his planes there, where they would claim sanctuary. Obviously he risked their confiscation, but that was a chance he was willing to take, if the only option meant losing them to bombs.

By January he had amassed eight divisions on the Turkish border and nine on the Syrian border, not so much in case these nations invaded, but rather to warn them off. For the same reason he had ten divisions on the Iranian border.

He maintained Republican Guard elements in Baghdad as he suspected the coalition was fermenting a revolt against him. Once the conflict began he would be constantly on the move, spending each night at a different command centre.

Six of his divisions were on the Kuwaiti coast staring, figuratively speaking, at the coalition fleet which had a division and two brigades of marines still afloat. On the Kuwait–Saudi border he had ten divisions with another three extending the line into the desert along the Iraq–Saudi border, a total front of 200 miles. The Iraq–Saudi border was 500 miles long, but so arid was the interior desert that he was assured no mechanised force could invade across it.

His first reserve was in southern Kuwait: a mechanised and three armoured divisions: his second reserve was a mechanised and two armoured divisions in northern Kuwait and an armoured and an infantry division west of Kuwait; and in southern Iraq between Basra and the Kuwait border was his third reserve of an armoured and two infantry divisions plus the Republican Guard with a special forces, two armoured and four mechanised divisions. Several Iraqi divisions had additional brigades. One faint hope was that as the Republican Guard was not actually in Kuwait the coalition might not bomb it. In any case Saddam surely had to keep it far to the rear in case of an amphibious invasion; he wanted them to meet the invasion not be outflanked by it. Thus Saddam had 38 divisions and eighteen brigades awaiting an attack by fifteen divisions and 26 brigades.

Saddam's troops at the front were told to remain in deep bunkers and only man their trenches when they knew enemy infantry were approaching. Life for these soldiers, in mixed uniforms of green, brown or sand-coloured, was boring to say the least. Rations were already short and mail did not always arrive on time. Their officers were dulled by the monotony and made every excuse they could to take a trip into Kuwait City or even home.

The UN ultimatum would expire on 16 January and Saddam knew he only had to hold out until mid-February, for then the Shamal began, the seasonal sandstorms that blinded pilots and troops. On 17 March Ramadan would begin and Saddam hoped Islamic armies would not wage war on fellow Moslems during that month-long religious festival; though he certainly had never had such qualms.

Last but not least Saddam was sitting down to this game with four aces up his sleeve: he could make war on Israel, thus causing the Arabs to think again about fighting him; he could burn Kuwait's oil wells, turning the sky into an impenetrable fog; he could loose oil into the sea and clog up an amphibious invasion attempt; and lastly he could inflict such heavy losses on the Americans they would call off the war in response to the public outcry.

The War: At 2.00am on the 17th an Iraqi patrol fired shots at unidentified helicopters flying overhead. At 2.38 a radar site 40 miles south-west of Baghdad was strafed by helicopters. Saddam, currently in one of his command centres, was notified. Thirteen minutes later Baghdad was bombed. The city's AAA began firing at once, but they could not understand their radar scopes (the enemy was in fact a squadron of F-117s that could not be seen on radar, followed by a flight of drones). The gunners, therefore, switched to Plan B: they stuck their guns towards the most likely approaches and began to fire blind. In seconds the sky above Baghdad was lit up like a fireworks display as the tracers, usually every fifth round, of 14.5mm, 23mm, 37mm and 57mm visibly streaked upwards from 3,000 guns!

Along the front line Iraqi artillery and missiles began firing on suspected enemy concentrations. The coalition forces preferred to retaliate using helicopters and planes.

This first night the Iraqi Air Force scrambled 53 fighters to engage the attackers, but twelve were lost. The coalition claimed to have lost four aircraft, though the Iraqis were certain the figure must be greater.

The citizens of Baghdad were heartened that enemy aircraft stayed away during daylight, though the city was struck by Tomahawk missiles, which snaked along their path like robot pilots, which of course they were.

At dusk Baghdad was hit by planes again and by midnight 116 Tomahawks had struck the city.

On the 18th the first Iraqi Scud was fired at Saudi Arabia, landing on Dhahran, and that night Saddam played one of his four aces: he sent Scuds towards Israel.

Many of his airfields reported they were temporarily out of action and this second night of the war only 23 Iraqi fighters could take off.

By the 19th it looked like Saddam's strategy was working, for the coalition expressed concern over the Scud attacks on Saudi Arabia for their psychological impact and on Israel for their political impact. Saddam now sent Scuds towards Bahrain.

By the 20th Saddam had lost radar sites, vehicle parks, railyards, bridges, supply dumps, weapons factories, oil tanks, power stations, machinery plants and countless smaller targets, but his commanders were still confident for their troops at the front had been hit hardly at all. Yet there was one problem. Some installations were not reporting in. Couriers had to be sent, some driving hundreds of miles. It was obvious the coalition air forces were concentrating on knocking out Saddam's communications. He was already fighting the war blind as he could not see the damage for himself. He would soon be fighting it deaf too. However, he consoled himself with the thought that having chosen a simple waiting strategy his fractured communications would not hurt him too much.

Yet, it was not just messages that were not getting through. At the front AAA guns were running out of ammunition, and the troops were running short of water, food and fuel for heaters and electricity generators. Some were forced to plug into vehicle batteries. It was frustrating for the junior officers, because they did not know what was happening. The world public sitting in armchairs in front of television sets knew more about the progress of the war than did the front line Iraqi soldiers.

Saddam began his psyops again: displaying captured airmen for the television cameras and then sending foreign journalists to see homes destroyed by the bombing. Coalition public relations officers were making much of their guided bombs, but were not mentioning that not only did a quarter of the guided bombs miss but 90 per cent of the bombs were not guided and as a result homes were inadvertently hit. Naturally, Saddam's psyops teams claimed the homes were struck deliberately.

On the 21st Saddam played his third to last ace, ordering the Kuwait oil wells to be set afire. Within a day the sky over southern Kuwait was black even at noon, to the point that no aircraft dare fly into it. When foreign ecologists complained of the environmental damage this would cause, Saddam must have lapped it up: his plan was working.

On the 22nd an Iraqi oil tanker was bombed and began to loose oil into the Persian Gulf. Coalition spokespersons claimed Saddam was responsible. This was a precursor of his second to last ace and on the 25th he used it: his troops opened oil pipelines at the water's edge and the oil poured into the Gulf and began floating south at a speed of 20 miles a day.

However, Saddam had to make a decision he had dreaded. He authorised his planes to fly to Iran. He had dispersed his planes as much as possible, placing some in the middle of villages, but they were being destroyed on the ground one by one. He also agreed that his surviving ships could sail to Iran.

The first three aces were not working: Israel had not retaliated despite suffering hundreds of casualties; and the ecologists were having no effect on the coalition leaders, so the oil spill continued to spread and the wells continued to burn. It was time to play the fourth and last ace: to inflict casualties.

The method was an offensive, something he believed the coalition would not expect. On the night of the 29th the fassault began: on the coast the 5th Mechanised Division attacked the abandoned Saudi town of Khafji, while a mechanised brigade attacked 30 miles inland, and 60 miles inland a mechanised and three infantry brigades advanced southwards.

At Khafji only artillery fire greeted the Iraqis, but at the other two locations they came under fire in the dark from American marines armed with TOW (wire-controlled missiles). Several vehicles blew up, and after a two-hour fight the Iraqis were subjected to a night raid by American helicopters. The Iraqis halted.

Came daylight the Iraqis in all three locations were pounced by aircraft of all sizes and suffered hellatious casualties. In Khafji they held on by hiding in buildings, but in the open desert they were sitting ducks.

The morale of the Iraqis sank quickly. They did not press their attacks and one company just west of Khafji negotiated with Saudi troops for a couple of hours: when the talks broke down the Iraqis withdrew!

The fourth prong in the assault was an amphibious attack in seventeen boats, ploughing through the oily water. However, they were detected by the British navy and the boats were all sunk by warships and helicopters, but for three which beached. Hundreds of Iraqis floundered in the oil slick, choking and drowning.

On the night of the 30th those Iraqis holed up in Khafji were counter-attacked by Americans, Saudis and Qataris and throughout the night there was wild firing. The Iraqis fought in little groups from buildings, shooting out of the windows at anything that moved. When enemy soldiers came rushing through the doors, most of the Iraqis gave up. No one wanted to die for Saddam!

By 5.00pm on the 31st the Iraqis had lost Khafji: 429 of them had surrendered and 37 wounded were captured. About 50 Iraqis had been killed. Out in the desert scores of Iraqis were killed before the brigades retired to their original lines. The coalition claimed to have lost only 84killed and wounded in the entire offensive of which only 11 of the dead on the ground were Americans (plus 14 in the air). Obviously these were not the sort of casualties that would inflame American public opinion. The whole affair was sorry from start to finish.

Along the front Iraqis were already deserting, a few every night. After the Khafji offensive coalition air raids started to concentrate on the front line: the Iraqis heard or saw bunkers go up in smoke, their 50 or so occupants burned or disfigured beyond recognition, a result of bombs from aircraft no one saw. The Iraqis were terrified. This was not an enemy they could see, shoot, stab and grapple with: this was like an angel of death. Abandoning their bunkers, wrapped in overcoats if lucky, they drifted north dodging their own patrols. Many officers joined them. A few went south to deliberately surrender, believing they would be safer in Saudi hands that if caught by their military police.

There were now small skirmishes all along the front, for example an Iraqi patrol fought Syrians on 4 February.

By the second week of February every front line battalion had been struck at least once by aircraft and the reserve positions were also under bombardment. Tanks were protected on three sides by sand berms, but enemy bombs seemed to home in on them like a magnet. Fortunately their crews were bunkered down a few hundred yards away and were unhurt. By now it was suicide to drive a supply truck to the front, thus stockpiles of provisions lay unused. In some parts of the line the infantry were living on nothing but rainwater! Starvation was a real possibility.

On the 13th 334 civilians were killed in British and American air raids. Saddam thought surely now the international public outcry would curtail further air strikes. Coalition raids did in fact reduce in intensity, but only because they were running out of targets and were concentrating on the front line and the Republican Guard.

Indeed on the 16th the deaths of 173 civilians in a British air raid did not seemingly affect the coalition for they were obviously planning a ground offensive soon. In fact that very night coalition troops began preliminary assaults: along the Iraq-Saudi border just west of Kuwait troops of the 25th Division engaged advancing elements of the US 1st Division, while the 48th Division fought the American 2nd Armoured Cavalry Regiment (ACR).

The Battle: On the 20th the 27th Division reported it was under attack by helicopters, tanks and artillery (US 1st Cavalry Division) six miles north of the Kuwait–Saudi border just east of Wadi al Batin. Saddam's staff wondered if this might be a feint. If the Americans advanced northwards from this point they would be safe from counter-attack on their west, because of the wadi, but not their east. Armoured and mechanised troops in the first reserve were alerted.

Unknown to Saddam this same day a position of the 45th Division in second reserve way out in the western desert was assaulted by helicopters until American airborne troops jumped out of helicopters, yelling for the occupants to surrender. After some brief shots they did: all 435!

By evening elements of the following divisions were under American shellfire: from the coast westwards the 18th, 8th and 29th, to their north the 14th and 7th, thence westwards the 20th, 36th, 16th, 30th, 26th, 27th, 25th and 48th. (Actually the 16th and 30th were shelled by Egyptians)

At dawn on the 22nd twelve miles north of the Kuwait–Saudi border and 50 miles inland the 29th Division was attacked. Iraqi artillery laid down a barrage on the advancing enemy (US 1st Marine Division), but their forward observers had trouble seeing what was happening and communicating what they did see. However, the American artillery fire and helicopter strikes were deadly accurate. Iraqi riflemen ran to their trenches, which were only about four feet deep, with the dirt piled behind them, not realising this piled dirt presented a visible target to American machine-gunners. Many were hit and some lay down and hid. Only a minefield kept the Americans from closing in.

Throughout that night Iraqis deserted to the Americans by the hundred. Some even helped the Americans find paths through the minefields.

In the early morning darkness of 24 February the 14th and 7th Divisions reported the enemy was approaching using the cover of a foggy rain (US 2nd Armoured and 2nd Marine Divisions – Saddam thought the 2nd Marines were at sea).

By now the survivors of the 29th Division were fighting bravely – the fainthearts having deserted – but in the night fog it was difficult to identify targets and every rifle shot seemed to be answered by artillery. Urgent radio calls by junior officers for reinforcements fell on deaf ears.

While it was still dark way out in the desert an outpost of the 45th Division was under assault. The defenders directed their artillery onto the attackers, but the enemy's guns (US and French) were more numerous and more accurate. Whenever there was a break in the firing scores of Iraqis jumped up and fled in the dark. When a sandstorm arose, hundreds escaped under its cover.

By 6.00am the infantry of the 14th and 7th Divisions were shooting at Americans trying to dig their way through a minefield.

Came daylight the 18th Division on the coastal end of the Kuwait–Saudi front reported enemy engineers trying to cut through the wire, and Iraqi artillery responded immediately, but the enemy (Saudis, Kuwaitis and Qataris) returned fire with artillery and mortars.

Five miles inland the 8th Division reported a similar scene (they faced Saudis and Omanis).

Far to the rear 300 rear-echelon troops were suddenly assaulted by helicopter-borne infantry (US 101st Division). Totally surprised they surrendered.

With so many Iraqi units under attack it was obvious the long awaited enemy ground offensive had come.

By noon 3,500 members of the 45th Division had surrendered to the French! At this moment the 29th Division was battling an American bayonet assault: hundreds of Iraqis threw up their hands. In the 14th and 7th Divisional sectors Iraqis were running in both directions, either fleeing or surrendering. Some watched the US 2nd Armoured Division drive past them apparently not seeing them, though the fog had cleared by now. The Iraqi 3rd Armoured Division in first reserve was ordered to await the Americans. They did so, their hands tensely gripping their gun controls.

At 3.00pm the 8th and 18th Divisions began to disintegrate.

At this instant the 25th Division, who had suspected their firefight of a few nights earlier had been a ruse, and who had been under artillery fire ever since, felt relief at being attacked, for finally they had something to shoot at (US 1st Division). However, their trenches were only three feet deep with sandy earth piled in front. This gave the infantry a good firing position and cover from small arms fire, but with the backs of their torsos exposed it offered no protection whatsoever from mortars or artillery exploding behind them. Furthermore, three feet is not a high climb for a scared man and too many Iraqi riflemen took advantage of this and ran. Perhaps half remained to continue firing. The noise was tremendous, so much so they did not hear an American armoured bulldozer moving towards them from the end of the trench: it simply followed the line of the trench, ploughing the earth back in. Standing men were caught unawares and had to jump out of the trench and thus fully exposed were shot down, and kneeling men or wounded were suddenly buried beneath the earth. Within twenty minutes of the start of the shooting, 150 Iraqis had been gunned down or buried alive and 500 threw up their hands in surrender, while hundreds more fled.

By late afternoon the 16th Division was under assault by Egyptians (3rd Mechanised Division), and the 36th and 20th Divisions by Kuwaitis and Saudis.

By sunset on this calamitous day, from east to west the 18th and 8th Divisions had been unable to prevent enemy forces from advancing through them; the 29th Division had fallen apart, some 4,000 men surrendering and others wandering around in the open; the 14th and 7th Divisions had collapsed, over 4,000 of their members surrendering, and only a few were holding out in isolated pockets; the 3rd Armoured Division had opened fire on the advancing enemy (US 2nd Armoured Division) and was momentarily halting them; the 20th and 36th Divisions were falling back under artillery fire; the 16th Division was holding the Egyptians for the time being; the 30th Division was under fierce air and artillery bombardment; the 27th Division was in danger of being surrounded; the 26th Division's flank was being probed by the enemy (US 1st Division); the 25th Division was all but destroyed; and the 48th Division at the westend of the line was unable to prevent enemy armour (US 2nd ACR) from passing its right (west) flank.

At dawn on 25 February in a rainy fog the 26th Division received a full-scale attack on its right (west) flank (US 1st Armoured and 3rd Armoured Divisions). The Iraqis did not stand a chance.

This morning survivors of the 8th and 18th Divisions capitulated as soon as enemy troops appeared. They actually tried to joke with the enemy, but these were Kuwaitis and were not in a joking mood.

The 20th Division was assaulted by a full-scale Kuwaiti-Saudi attack, the 16th Division was assaulted by the Egyptian 3rd Mechanised Division and the 30th Division by the Egyptian 4th Armoured Division.

As these battles were taking place the last of the 45th Division gave up almost without a shot to advancing French troops.

The Iraqi 5th Mechanised Division was ordered to restore the situation, a laughable order, but they obeyed and drove westwards hoping to strike the enemy flank. They did in fact catch American marines unawares, because they were able to approach unseen through As Subayhiyah, a planted evergreen wood, the only one in Kuwait. However, the Americans quickly rallied and by noon the Iraqis had lost 150 armoured vehicles and several hundred infantry to American tanks, IFVs and helicopters. Against orders the Iraqis withdrew.

In mid-afternoon on Highway 8 between Basra and Baghdad fully 175 miles behind the front line astonished Iraqi truck drivers were arrested by Americans (101st Division), who had just arrived by helicopter.

Thisevening the Iraqi 12th Armoured Division in second reserve was still trying to acquire adequate information as to the enemy's location when scouts reported a major formation approaching them from the south-west. It was the British 1st Armoured Division! The Iraqis ran to their tanks and guns, which were divided among several desert camps each surrounded by high berms. Infantry of the 47th Division helped man some of them. Within minutes heavy combat broke out and lasted all night.

On the morning of 26 February the 16th Division collapsed, allowing the Egyptian 3rd Mechanised Division to pour through. Within an hour just west of them the 30th and 27th Divisions were surrounded by the Egyptian 4th Armoured Division and Americans, and just east of them the 36th and 20th Divisions were surrounded by Egyptians, Kuwaitis and Saudis.

By mid-morning one camp of the 12th Armoured Division had been overrun by the British, another was being overrun and a third was still resisting. Some smaller pockets of Iraqis were approached by what they thought were tanks and they surrendered, only to find these were British artillery SPGs. By this time bypassed Iraqis were surrendering to truck drivers!

By noon two more camps of the 12th Armoured Division had fallen to the British: the 1,200 defenders fought for perhaps fifteen minutes then threw up their hands.

Saddam was obviously at a loss as to what to do. He knew he had been defeated, but had no idea how badly. He ordered the Medina and Tawakalna Divisions of the Republican Guard to advance into battle to aid the 12th Armoured Division, which was obviously in difficulty, while the remainder of the army including the Republican Guard was ordered to make for Basra. Saddam explained

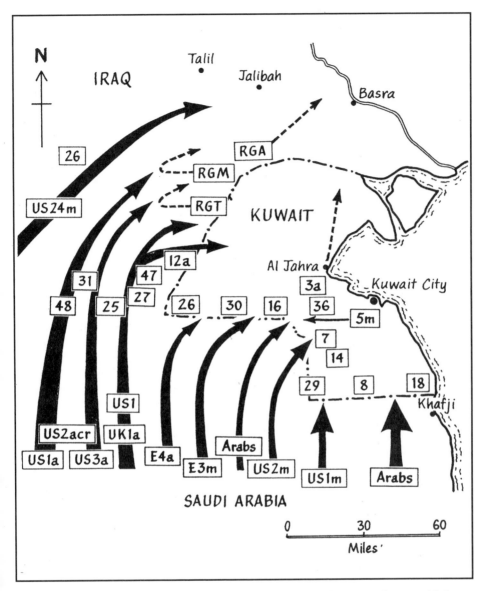

this by announcing he was complying with the UN resolution and was withdrawing from Kuwait.

Those Iraqis who heard the news began to flee north along the coast road between Kuwait City and Basra, passing through the bottleneck of Al Jahra. Those without vehicles stole them from the Kuwaitis and within hours a convoy of passenger cars, trucks, fire engines, jeeps, motorcycles, indeed anything that rolled was heading northwards in a mad scramble, almost continuously under strafing and bombing from coalition planes and helicopters: many vehicles swerved off the road and drove across the relatively flat coastal plain.

Several hundred members of the 15th Division holding Al Jahra watched as the vehicles sped past them. Suddenly without warning they saw enemy tanks appear from behind a ridge (US 2nd Armoured Division): 50 Iraqis who tried to fight were shot down, then the rest surrendered. The loss of Al Jahra trapped the 1st Armoured, 5th Mechanised, 6th, 7th, 8th, 11th, 14th, 15th, 18th, 29th, 31st and 42nd Divisions!

At 3.00pm in a howling sandstorm on the north flank of the 12th Armoured Division T-72s of the RG Tawakalna Division started to explode. Many did so unseen and unheard by other tanks. The slaughter continued for a half hour and most members of the division did not even realise they were under fire until they saw the glow of flames through the blowing sand. Their attackers were the US 2nd ACR and 3rd Armoured Division approaching from the west.

Some coalition forces were so far behind Iraqi lines by now that at 4.00pm the Iraqi Army Desert Warfare School was under attack. Here, the sandstorm over, one element of the RG Tawakalna Division fired at enemy muzzle flashes in hazy visibility (US 2nd ACR), but could not prevent their own tanks from blowing up at an alarming rate. Unlike the Iraqis, the Americans were equipped with thermal imaging sights and could 'see' square images representing vehicles. In 23 minutes the Iraqis lost 28 tanks, sixteen APCs and 39 trucks. Not one American vehicle was hit by Iraqi fire.

A similar fight took place nearby at 4.30pm when the 50th Brigade of the 12th Armoured Division and an element of the RG Tawakalna Division were struck by part of the 2nd ACR. After an hour of one-sided massacre the RG Tawakalna decided they had to get closer to see their enemy – visibility was about 1,500 yards – but they ran into more enemy tanks (US 3rd Armoured Division) and the battle raged furiously. Within six hours at least 120 Iraqi armoured vehicles were knocked out.

North of the Tawakalna the RG Adnan Division was trying to withdraw north-wards when its left column was struck on the west by enemy tanks and artillery (US 1st Armoured Division). About 6.00pm another camp of the 12th Armoured Division was overrun by the British: 285 Iraqis gave up.

Soldiers at Al Abraq Barracks west of Kuwait City were overawed to see Egypt-ian tanks appear in their midst. They capitulated at once.

After dark the survivors of the RG Tawakalna began to fall back eastwards, while to their south two more desert camps were overrun by the British.

During the night north-west of Basra on Highway 8 Iraqi troop convoys were shot up: over 1,200 Iraqis surrendered to the US 24th Division which had driven this far without hindrance.

Saddam's staff officers stared at their maps: with Highway 8 cut, if coalition aircraft could blow the causeways and bridges over the river at Basra, then the 26 divisions between Basra and Al Jahra would be cut off from Iraq.

While it was still dark on the morning of the 27th part of the RG Tawakalna Division and the 12th Armoured's 50th Brigade were caught by the Americans (US 1st Division and a brigade of the 2nd Armoured Division). The Iraqis turned to fight and called for artillery support. As daylight approached the remainder of the RG Tawakalna was caught by the US 1st Armoured and 3rd Armoured Divisions

North-west of Basra four commando battalions at Jalibah Air Base were sur-prised by tanks and infantry: within minutes the base was in the hands of the US 24th Division.

North of Al Jahra elements of the 21st Division, still believing themselves to be in second reserve, were overwhelmed by Egyptian tanks and APCs.

Minutes later stragglers of the 11th Division inside Kuwait City were surprised to see Kuwaiti troops entering. They resisted with small arms, but were hunted down building by building. Kuwaitis and Palestinian workers who had collaborated with the Iraqis were arrested and shot.

So far the RG Medina Division had not been attacked, but just after noon its 2nd Brigade espied tanks approaching from the west (US 1st Armoured Division). In hazy visibility the Iraqis aimed at enemy muzzle flashes, while they suffered terrible damage from extremely accurate enemy tank and artillery fire. After just 40 minutes, 60 Iraqi tanks and dozens of IFVs were blazing. The dozen or so surviving tanks and hundreds of 'unhorsed' personnel began running towards the east.

That afternoon Talil Air Base in Iraq, about 45 miles from Jalibah, was overrun by the US 24th Division. Here too the Iraqis wondered how the enemy had managed to come this far.

Just after dark Iraqi troops crossing a causeway west of Basra came under artillery fire. They could not believe it. How could enemy artillery shell them 50 miles north of Kuwait? Obviously the Americans were between the Iraqi Army and safety?

The remnants of the RG Medina and RG Tawakalna Divisions ran past a logistics camp, which was abandoned that night, and by morning the two divisions were about 30 miles south-west of Basra.

At 4.00am on the 28th a terrific artillery bombardment spurred the Iraqis on their way – direct hits turned trucks into scrap metal – and by 8.00am the remnants of several divisions were in the Safwa area when the noise of gunfire ceased.

Throughout the day the troops got the word. The coalition had ceased fire. The Iraqis continued to retreat towards Basra.

Saddam was approached for an armistice. He could hardly refuse, for the Americans were only 200 miles from Baghdad and he had nothing in their path!

All day long and throughout the night and the next day Iraqi and coalition diplomats argued by radio. There was still some combat as Iraqi artillery fired upon the stationary Americans, and fleeing Iraqis were shelled in turn.

In the early morning hours of 2 March the RG Hammurabi Division tried to sneak past the US 24th Division. They were heard and the Americans opened fire with everything. At dawn the Hammurabi were also assaulted by helicopters. All day the battle raged until the last of the Iraqis escaped out of range. The Hammurabi lost 177 tanks and IFVs and 400 trucks.

On the 3rd Saddam sent Lieutenant Generals Mohammed Abdez Rahman and Sabin Abdel-Aziz to sign the armistice agreement in front of General Norman Schwarzkopf. Naturally Saddam refused to attend himself. In fact as there was no Iraqi surrender he told his people this was a victory. The Iraqi soldiers knew the truth. It had been a massacre.

When Iraqi war casualties were totalled Saddam's generals were stunned: air strikes throughout Iraq and Kuwait had killed about 2,300 civilians (including workers at military sites) and 25,000 uniformed personnel. About 76,000 were wounded.

In the ground battles Iraqi losses were around 10,000 killed, 10,000 wounded and 89,000 captured up to the evening of 2 March. Fewer than 500 coalition personnel had died in the entire air/land/sea conflict and that included accidents.

Appraisal: One's first response to an appraisal is to wonder what mistakes Saddam did not make, his conduct being so appalling, but with careful thought one can discern that they fell into fifteen major categories: counsel, command structure, intelligence, firepower, psyops, grand strategy, equipment, strategy, dispersal, pace, training, morale, tactics, reserves and command ability.

Saddam's communications were excellent, hence the coalition spending so much effort trying to destroy them. He certainly had sufficient troops and had placed more than adequate reserves within range.

As for his timing one can look at that two ways. Some say he timed his invasion of Kuwait a year late, for the Soviets of 1989 might have defended him. But he cannot be blamed for not knowing they would refuse in 1990. The Americans were as surprised as he to find the Soviets abandoning their client, and at worst one can only say that Saddam received bad counsel from the Soviets.

Oddly enough the only counsel he took was from the Soviets, for he never willingly took advice from his own people, and in fact everyone was too afraid of him to offer it. All brutal dictators are cut off from the objectivity of scientists, engineers, economists and other professionals that make nations like France or Britain so viable. Saddam had brilliant minds in his nation, but none who could speak objectively.

This leads us to his command structure. Quite simply it was primitive for he ruled absolutely. During the Iran War he had executed officers for failure and also for success in an attempt to remove would-be successors. As a result no officer wanted to make decisions and if possible always passed the buck. Saddam was not a MacArthur who wore all the hats he could find, but he might as well have been.

Saddam's greatest failing was his lack of sound military intelligence, coupled with his refusal to listen to anything that contradicted his opinions. He underestimated the French, thinking they could not fight and therefore would not fight, but he forgot to take into consideration French pride. The French could not let the Americans alone rule a coalition involving most of Europe and the Arab nations. They had to participate as a matter of honour, and to give the appearance they were influencing events even if they were not.

Saddam underestimated the British, believing Margaret Thatcher was weak, possibly as she was a woman, and misunderstanding Britain's crippling effort to regain the Falklands. The Falklands lesson was not that the British military had shortcomings, but that in spite of them they pressed on to victory. Thatcher had gained popularity as a result. In 1990 she was no longer popular and was fighting off a revolt in her own party. Saddam's invasion of Kuwait was just what the doctor ordered. Thatcher charged into the affair and not only followed Bush, but often led him. Moreover, the British people supported the war wholeheartedly, owing to their sense of injustice and respect for the underdog, in this case the Kuwaitis.

Saddam certainly underestimated the Americans politically. Bush was on a roll: he had just toppled Noriega in Panama, had won the Cold War, and knew that if he showed firm resolve over Kuwait he would win Arab friends, something no President had been able to do (though Carter came close). Most importantly the Soviet Union was tottering. Bush had to remain bullish, because the Iraqi army was a Soviet client, equipped and trained to fight Red Army style. By defeating Saddam's army in open battle, Bush would be defeating the Red Army by proxy, which no one had done except MacArthur who defeated the NKPA in 1950. If Bush refused to fight, some hawkish Soviet faction might see this as American fear of a Soviet trained army, and seize power in Moscow and reverse Gorbachev's process of reconciliation. It is no coincidence that the Soviet Union collapsed just months after Saddam's defeat.

Saddam also underestimated the Americans militarily. Vietnam was not only behind the Americans, but the junior officers who had fought and bled in that conflict were now generals and they at least knew what not to do. Just as the Germans had rebuilt a new army following their defeat in World War I, so the Americans had built a new army after Vietnam. With no conscripts and no room any more for users, boozers and losers, the army had become a dedicated 'lean mean fighting machine' as the soldiers joked. Even the reservists and National Guard sensed a new dedication, which they had never experienced before. In Vietnam entire platoons had been sacrificed. Now a whole battalion would work to rescue one life. Each soldier was precious. Saddam had plenty of cannon fodder. Bush had none.

Most Americans in the war were new to combat and individually they made serious mistakes that resulted in loss of life, but their degree of professionalism was so high that no entire unit made a mistake. Much of the USA is desert, so the Iraqi desert offered no obstacle, and the Americans had trained for generations to fight a Soviet style army in an air/land battle. It is ironic that they only fought this battle after the end of the Cold War. The enemy might be Iraqis, but their vehicles and tactics were Soviet, hence there were no surprises.

Saddam not only failed to read the character of this new American army, but he failed to consider major discrepancies in his own firepower. Even by World War II standards Iraqi divisions were artillery poor, each fielding two short range, one medium range and one extra medium range battalions, compared to the American division's one medium range and three or four long range battalions. Only at corps level did Iraqi artillery look equal.

An Iraqi tank battalion possessed 27 first- or second-rate tanks, but an American armoured cavalry battalion fielded 43 first-rate tanks, as did a British armoured battalion, an American armoured battalion had 58 first-rate tanks and a marine tank battalion possessed 70 second-rate tanks.

An Iraqi infantry battalion contained four anti-tank guns, four 82mm and nine 60mm mortars, twelve light machine-guns, 24 RPGs, about 270 riflemen and no armoured vehicles, but they were assaulted by American marine infantry battalions possessing eight 81mm and nine 60mm mortars, four heavy and eighteen light machine-guns, eighteen RPG equivalents and 360 riflemen and a number of armoured vehicles on loan and by American mechanised infantry battalions possessing six 4.2 inch mortars, 250 riflemen and 54 armoured vehicles armed with an assortment of wire guided missiles, 25mm guns and machine-guns.

Saddam had 50 helicopter gunships, but the sky was denied them, whereas the coalition had 800 available to shoot every Iraqi in sight and to observe their movements even at night.

Mathematics alone should have told Saddam he would have one hell of a massacre on his hands if he attempted to fight.

Saddam's psyops was the worst possible. Most dictators make a show of appearing genial to outsiders. Saddam took the opposite course. When he invaded Kuwait the people of the world labelled him 'aggressor', but that did not mean they would leave their cosy homes to risk death in opposing him, especially as Kuwait was no shining light of democracy. As a result of such luke-warm concern most aggressors go unchallenged. However, Saddam's troops, apparently with his permission, looted Kuwait like a plague of locusts, so add to Saddam the label 'thief'. Then he refused to allow Americans and Britons the right to leave Kuwait and Iraq, so add the label 'kidnapper'. Then he placed hostages at potential bombing targets, so add the label 'disrespectful of life', which reminded the British of his execution of one of their journalists, so add the label 'murderer'. Then he appeared on television with hostage children, one of them an obviously frightened little English boy, so add the label 'child abuser'. Then he threatened to destroy Kuwait's oilfields, so add the labels 'vandal' and 'environmental polluter'. Then he said he would use chemical weapons, which reminded the world of his gas attacks on Kurds, so add the label 'mass murderer'.

After all this the world was ready to make sacrifices to defeat him.

Following his invasion of Kuwait his grand strategy was to claim to be a defender of Islam and of Arab rights, but the Kuwaitis had enough influence in the Arab world to challenge his claim, and his war on Kurds and Iranians exposed his lack of love for Moslems. Only Yasser Arafat and Muammar Gaddafi the Palestinian and Libyan leaders seriously supported Saddam, the former because his headquarters was in Baghdad and the latter because he did not want Saddam to steal his thunder. Jordan and Yemen gave lip service to Saddam.

Saddam's equipment was excellent, but it came from too many sources. By late 1990 his armed forces were scrounging for spare parts for their foreign equipment. His greatest equipment defect was the lack of thermal imaging sights. His tank gunners could only shoot what they could see through optical sights, and they could not see an enemy who kept beyond 1,000 yards in a haze, a fog or at night. Had they been able to close the range at once, they may have stood a chance.

His strategy was to await a counter invasion of Kuwait. He was prepared for the massive aerial onslaught, but he seems to have become fixated on the allied fleet and the Kuwait–Saudi border and to have dismissed the possibility that the coalition would launch a major desert flanking sweep to the west to strike his Republican Guard in third reserve without having overcome the entire Iraqi front line, thereby cutting off Kuwait from Iraq like plucking an apple from a tree. Saddam's strategy was akin to bolting the door but leaving the window open.

Furthermore, he dispersed units to the point that they were redundant. The 25th, 26th and 48th Divisions which stood alone to the west of Wadi al Batin might as well have been in downtown Baghdad for all the good they were doing there. What purpose did the 45th Division serve alone in the desert?

His pace was completely off. He had become locked into the leisurely pace of the eight-year Iran War. The endless coalition air strikes without any sign of a ground offensive lured him further into this languid pace. Therefore when the coalition offensive began on 24 February it came like a whirlwind: within six hours the second reserves 45th Division was destroyed; by the seventh hour the front had been broken – it took only twenty minutes for the Americans to bust through; by the ninth hour four divisions were retreating; by the twelfth hour eight divisions were disintegrating and a first reserve division was under attack; by the 35th hour rear-echelon forces behind the third reserves were being rounded up; by the 54th hour the entire army was in retreat; by the 57th hour a third reserves division was under attack; and by the 58th hour twelve divisions were surrounded. Bush called a halt after 100 hours.

The Iraqis were obviously not trained to handle a battle of such speed. Indeed many reservists were not trained at all. Some of them had only been called up in November and sent straight to their desert bunkers. However, even Iran War veterans found this war a whole new kettle of fish. The Republican Guard were the best trained, but only two of their divisions were ordered into battle.

In this kind of struggle morale is of the essence, but Saddam's troops had none. Tens of thousands deserted and tens of thousands surrendered after no more than one burst from their rifle. Hardly any of Saddam's soldiers wanted to die for Saddam: neither Kurds, Turcomans, Assyrians, Azerbaijanis nor the Shiite Arabs from the southern marshes, nor the Iran War veterans who thought one more battle would be pushing their luck, nor those who were angry that the Republican Guard got the best of everything, nor those whose relatives had been imprisoned and tortured by Saddam's police, nor those who thought this was a war about oil wealth, nor those who thought Saddam's anti-Islamic record was sacrilegious, nor those who just could not stand one more minute of aerial bombardment, nor those who thought they had been driven into the desert as sacrificial lambs and abandoned without food or water.

Iraqi tactics were hopelessly obsolete. Educated only to make and receive infantry charges they had nothing in their thought processes to combat a mechanised war. The battle for Kuwait was won on wheels and treads, not in trenches.

In reserve Saddam had nine armoured, six mechanised, one special forces and three infantry divisions, plus the six coastal divisions, yet he only ordered one armoured and two mechanised divisions to counter-attack. No one but Saddam can be blamed for misusing his reserves in such a cowardly manner.

This leaves us with Saddam's command ability. Once the ground offensive had begun his only effective order was to retreat. As General Schwarzkopf said: 'He's no soldier.'

Consequences: The war left a sour aftertaste in everyone's mouth. The Arab people were astounded at the ferocity of the attack on Iraq, at the deaths of so many fellow Arabs and the humiliation of an Arab state. However, the people of the West thought the war had been called off at half time. They wanted a World War II style ending with someone hanging upside down or in a war crimes court. Instead they had to watch helplessly as Saddam took out his frustrations on his own people.

Some hoped the war would at least warn off potential aggressors elsewhere. It did no such thing. Within months the Americans were being humiliated in Somalia and the British and French in Bosnia.

The Battle's Place in History: The 100-hour offensive 24-28 February 1991 was the largest armoured battle in history, far greater than Kursk, Normandy or Stalingrad. In manpower it was the largest battle fought by British, French or Americans since World War II, the largest ever fought in a desert and the largest in Iraq's 4,000 year history. In total casualties (killed, wounded and captured) it was larger than Alamein, Neuve Chapelle, Antietam or Waterloo.

It was also one of the most one-sided affairs in military annals. One has to go back to Pakenham's defeat at New Orleans for a comparison. It was the most reported battle in the history of journalism. By any standards it was one of the great battles of history.

Yet in the West, just five years on it has already been consigned to the dustbin of memory like the hoola hoop, the 1980 Olympics, or the question 'who shot J. R.?', a mere diversion from the drudgery of life.

It is up to future generations to place the battle into context.

SUMMARY

So what have we learned? Commanders make errors because of arrogance. We knew that already. However, we have learned that one does not have to be arrogant in order to make errors caused by arrogance; for example, there is no evidence that Pakenham, McDowell, Harmar, Chelmsford and Short were arrogant men. Therefore, can we identify those who will make errors owing to arrogance, before we place them in command?

Nationality apparently has nothing to do with it. The commanders we have studied were English: Burgoyne, Chelmsford, Brooke-Popham, Phillips, Percival; Scottish: Braddock, St Clair, Anderson; Irish: Pakenham; American: Harmar, McDowell, Custer, Kimmel, Short, Eisenhower, Fredendall, Dean, Walker, Almond, MacArthur; French: Navarre, de Castries; Italian: Baratieri, Mussolini, Visconti-Prasca; Polish: Rydz; Russian: Meretskov; Georgian: Stalin; Iraqi: Saddam Hussein.

Age also seems to have no bearing (food for thought for many an employer): at the time of the battles in our study MacArthur was 70, Braddock, Short, Brooke-Popham, Walker and Stalin were in their 60s, McDowell and Meretskov in their 40s, Custer, Harmar and Pakenham in their 30s and the others were in their 50s.

The age of their opponents reflects the same age span: Beaujeu was in his 30s, Giap was 42, Peng Dehuai was 52 and Mannerheim was 72.

One would assume that experience of battlefield command, indeed any combat experience, would be factors. Yet St Clair, Custer, Almond, Chelmsford, Baratieri, Mussolini, Anderson, Fredendall, MacArthur, Walker and Saddam had previous experience leading large formations in battle; and Braddock, Burgoyne, Harmar, Pakenham, McDowell, Rydz, Meretskov, Stalin, Visconti-Prasca, Short, Brooke-Popham, Phillips, Percival, Dean, Navarre and de Castries had some if not considerable combat experience.

Did the era in which these commanders lived have anything to do with their type of errors? Evidently not, for their lives extend from the late seventeenth century to today. Braddock was born in 1695, Burgoyne in 1722, St Clair 1736, Harmar 1753, Pakenham 1778, McDowell 1818, Chelmsford 1827, Custer 1839, Baratieri 1841, Brooke-Popham 1878, Stalin 1879, MacArthur and Short 1880, Kimmel 1882, Mussolini and Fredendall 1883, Rydz 1886, Percival and Visconti-Prasca 1887, Phillips 1888, Walker 1889, Anderson 1891, Almond 1892, Meretskov 1897, Navarre 1898, Dean 1899, de Castries 1902 and Saddam 1937.

Is it possible that, as we are dealing with errors caused by arrogance, an attacker makes more errors than a defender? Certainly Braddock, Burgoyne, Harmar, St Clair, Pakenham, McDowell, Custer, Chelmsford, Baratieri, Stalin-Meretskov, Mussolini, Eisenhower-Anderson-Fredendall, MacArthur-Walker-

Almond, and Navarre-de Castries were all waging offensive war. However, Rydz, Kimmel-Short, Brooke-Popham-Percival-Phillips, Dean–MacArthur–Walker and Saddam were on the strategic defensive. Moreover, of those waging offensive war St Clair, Chelmsford, Baratieri, Eisenhower–Anderson–Fredendall and Navarre-de Castries were on the tactical defensive, and the others, bar Pakenham, were thrown onto the tactical defensive by enemy counter-attacks.

As armies have become ever more sophisticated in terms of transportation, communications, resources, equipment and firepower, have we seen different errors committed and if so are these more complicated than those of 1755?

We have divided battlefield errors into 23 categories: inadequate training, a failure to maintain or restore morale, no or ineffective psychological operations, bad choice of ground or failure to use it, refusal of counsel, no or poor reconnaissance and/or ignoring reports, no or poor intelligence and/or ignoring reports, disregard of the plan, flawed grand strategy, faulty strategy, inefficient tactics, an inappropriate choice of time/date, dispersal of troops, insufficient manpower, insufficient firepower, misuse of specialists, incorrect use of reserves, improper or shoddy equipment or failure to use, inadequacy of supply line or failure to protect it, unwieldy command structure, misjudging the pace, poor communications or their misuse, and low command ability.

The question is do new categories appear as mankind progresses technologically?

What is immediately apparent is that it only takes one error in one category to risk defeat, and mistakes in two or more categories can be disastrous. Pakenham scored errors in only three categories, but suffered one of the most ignominious defeats in military history, whereas Fredendall, Anderson and Eisenhower at Kasserine Pass managed to make mistakes in nineteen categories, yet their army survived and won the campaign.

Inadequate training was a major cause of defeat for the British/Americans on the Monongahela, the Unionists at Bull Run, the cavalry at Little Big Horn, for Stalin's generals in Finland, for Mussolini's reservists in Greece, for American regulars at Pearl Harbor, for British Empire troops in Malaya, for America's regulars and new recruits at Kasserine, for America's regulars at Osan and Taejon, and for Saddam's veterans and reservists.

Morale was a key factor in several of our studies. Braddock did nothing to maintain it. St Clair expected low morale and got it. Custer deluded himself into thinking his regiment had high morale. Chelmsford made no attempt to instil morale in his native soldiers. Mussolini thought propaganda would create high morale. Stalin and Saddam thought fear of the secret police was a valid substitute for morale. The Americans, British and French thought that putting on a uniform automatically made one want to fight, a belief shattered at Pearl Harbor, Kasserine, Malaya and Dien Bien Phu. In 1950 the Americans told their soldiers never to expect a war again, then sent them to fight one, but tried to convince them it was not a war, and then months later tried to convince them that the war that was not a war was over, and followed this by announcing the war that was not a war that was over had become a whole new war.

Psyops (psychological operations) sounds like a new discipline, but it is as old as warfare itself. There are examples of it in the Bible. In our studies Braddock,

Harmar, St Clair, Chelmsford, Stalin and Mussolini launched invasions without making any attempts to woo or divide their enemy with gifts or promises. At times the Americans ignored psyops, thereby giving Rommel the impression the Americans were vulnerable and without reserves, giving Kim the impression he could invade South Korea with impunity, and giving the Chinese no option but to fight. Saddam attempted psyops, but was so bad at it he gained another enemy every time he spoke publicly. The French had good psyops in Indo-China, but missed the boat: it was all for nought after the truce in Korea.

Every army fights on ground: it is the one constant factor in all land battles, yet it is consistently misused. Braddock let the enemy have the only hill. McDowell treated Bull Run like a water barrier, when he should have realised it was a highway. In Malaya the British chose to defend both banks of rivers, thereby sacrificing whole battalions. Reno retreated to a rocky bluff and survived: Custer chose a bald slope and did not. Stalin chose the forested land mass of Finland and Mussolini a craggy Greek mountain range, when both could have outflanked their enemy by sea. Fredendall chose his ground from maps known to be inaccurate. MacArthur allowed the enemy to occupy the mountains, where they could assemble in peace. Navarre picked the valley floor and gave the hills to enemy artillery.

Good advice is precious and bad advice is better than none at all, for at least it confirms one's better judgement, yet often combat commanders ignore counsel at their peril: Braddock, St Clair, Custer, Chelmsford, Stalin, Mussolini, Marshall, Fredendall, Saddam, Navarre, and the entire American establishment throughout 1950.

Reconnaissance is the eyes of the army: yet battle commanders often do not look or they disbelieve what they see. Braddock, Burgoyne, St Clair, Pakenham, McDowell, Custer, Baratieri, Stalin-Meretskov, Mussolini and his generals, and Fredendall did not look; Rydz and Saddam could not look; Harmar in Ohio, the Americans at Chongchon-Changjin and the French at Dien Bien Phu looked, but did not see; Chelmsford looked and saw, but did not believe; likewise for the Americans and British in 1941.

Intelligence is the basis of all planning. To quote Wellington: 'All the business of war is to endeavour to find out what you don't know from what you do.' Harmar and St Clair thought they could live without it. Braddock, Burgoyne, Custer, Chelmsford, Rydz, Stalin, Mussolini and Navarre believed only the intelligence reports that suited their purposes. McDowell assumed he was the only general who knew how to use a locomotive. The Americans and British in 1941 compiled intelligence data, but did not disseminate it. In 1943 the Americans relied on Montgomery's intelligence reports instead of their own sources. Throughout 1950 the Americans had a complete intelligence breakdown, as did Saddam in 1990–1991.

Attacks always begin with a plan. However, Braddock disregarded his own plan to move cautiously. Custer disregarded the plan, and in September 1950 MacArthur convinced Truman to ignore the geographic boundaries of the plan.

Most grand strategies are good, because they are the creation of many concentrated minds, but some are flawed. Stalin and Mussolini made the error of attacking overland hundreds of miles from the enemy capital, when they could have landed by sea and taken the cities in hours, and by attacking Mussolini simply endangered his own oil supply. In Malaya the British chose to defend Singapore for its symbolism rather than its usefulness. Eisenhower was reduced to a land advance on Tunisia because of navy fears. In 1950 the Americans hid the hollowness of their military behind the atomic bomb, a grand strategy that was shown to be an illusion. Then once MacArthur created a real army he led it towards an ideological enemy expecting no response. Saddam's grand strategy was to challenge the world to an all or nothing battle, like a gambler who bets high on a low hand.

Strategy on the other hand can be the product of just one person or of a small committee. It too can be faulty. McDowell was pushed into a strategy of the direct approach, invariably risky. Baratieri actually chose this strategy, sticking his head into the lion's mouth and daring him to bite down. Stalin and Meretskov stuck to the logging trails, ignoring the forests and therefore occupied only inches of a country hundreds of miles wide. Mussolini sent his troops down valleys ignoring the mountains. MacArthur faced a Korean offensive with no strategic contingency plans, then in his counter-offensive sent his armies along Korea's coasts ignoring the interior. Rydz chose to defend the Polish Empire instead of the Polish nation. In Malaya the British opted for retreat from the word 'go'. In Tunisia Eisenhower butted his head against Tunis, bankrupt of any other ideas. Navarre chose the famed hill and valley strategy, but did it backwards: one is supposed to occupy a hill and dare the enemy in the valley to knock you off, not occupy a valley and dare the enemy on the hill to leap on you.

Inefficient tactics lose many a battle. Braddock went into battle with the tactics of the parade ground. Pakenham thought that walking into the enemy's firepower was a manly thing to do and would frighten the enemy. St Clair did absolutely nothing, which in itself is a tactic. McDowell tried a flanking manoeuvre, but was so slow that he ended up making frontal assaults, though he could have called them off at any time. Burgoyne and Custer attempted flanking manoeuvres, but did so without knowing where the enemy flank was. Chelmsford acted like he was on Hyde Park, and his subordinate, Pulleine, did the same. Baratieri so confidently expected his firepower to wipe out the enemy, he made no tactical contingency plans. Stalin and Meretskov willingly sent their infantry into massed charges, because manpower was the one cheap item in their arsenal. Mussolini's generals pushed their combat units down the valleys, leaving no one to protect their lines of communication, so that once attacked they had to counter-attack to the rear. The Italians did not so much retreat from Greece as advance backwards into Albania. Kimmel's tactics were to present his ships to the enemy without protection, and Short presented his airfields without AAA or fighter cover. In Malaya the British retreated when enemy tanks penetrated their lines, instead of remembering, as the Finns did, that all tanks run out of fuel eventually. In Tunisia the Americans used tanks like horse cavalry, presenting their rear to bypassed German anti-tank guns. In Korea Dean failed to cover his flanks, and the UN almost lost several divisions because Keiser manned his key rearguard with untried troops without reserves. De Castries' tactics were those of a defeatist, allowing the enemy to dig trenches without launching efforts to pinch off protruding trench lines. Though Saddam's armour had tactical know how, his infantry tactics were barely adequate to fight off human wave assaults.

The time or date of a battle is a key factor. McDowell advanced too soon, before his army was ready. Chelmsford advanced when the Zulus were already assembled. Baratieri advanced at night, fatiguing his own men and resting the enemy. Mussolini and Stalin attacked in the season of freezing weather, fog and darkness. Rydz, Kimmel, Short, Brooke-Popham and Percival all strongly suspected they would be attacked, but wasted precious time doing nothing. Navarre threw down the gauntlet then gave the enemy all the time in the world to pick it up.

Dispersal of one's troops is dangerous: but Burgoyne did it to hunt for provisions; Harmar, Chelmsford and Custer to seek the enemy; Stalin to capture useless forest hamlets; St Clair to chase deserters; Percival to protect airfields; and Braddock, Burgoyne, McDowell, Pulleine, Rydz, Fredendall, Walker, Navarre and Saddam dispersed their forces in the face of the enemy. On the other hand dispersal of mobile equipment is imperative. Kimmel's and Short's failure to disperse their battleships and aircraft doomed them.

Sufficient manpower seems obvious, yet Custer and Visconti-Prasca refused additional troops, lest they be forced to share the glory. Braddock refused Indian allies. In 1950 the Americans thought they could fight a war with every unit well below strength, even refusing volunteers because they were the wrong colour.

Specialists are only specialists when used as such. Chelmsford, Pulleine and Navarre used light infantry as line infantry. Mussolini fought a mountain war without his mountain divisions. Fredendall sidetracked engineers to build his own bunker. Eisenhower left his best tank specialist sitting at a desk. Percival refused to form guerrillas. Rydz misused every one of his specialist formations.

Reserves are only reserves if within reach: McDowell, Custer, Percival, Walker and Eisenhower left theirs too far away; Rydz's reserves were immobile; Visconti-Prasca attacked with too few; Navarre frittered his away; Chelmsford allowed his to be attacked; Short and Martin left their planes unarmed and unfuelled; Kimmel left his anti-submarine force with cold boilers; Truman's reserves were still in civvy street; and Saddam thought his reserves too valuable to risk.

The enemy is only impressed when being shot at. Phillips refused air power; Rydz refused tank power; Navarre refused artillery power; and Custer refused Gatling power. Pulford sacrificed soldiers to save his planes. Stalin sent his army into battle with insufficient automatic weapons. President Grant armed his cavalry with single shot carbines. Churchill left his Malaya defenders with no tanks and few anti-tank guns and mines. Marshall sent his army to Africa with undergunned tanks. By 1950 the US Joint Chiefs had created an army with insufficiency in everything,

As for equipment: Burgoyne took along too few horses; Stalin's and Marshall's armies had tanks that were too bulky; Stalin's and Mussolini's equipment froze and their troops' thin uniforms could not prevent frostbite; Kimmel refused anti-submarine nets and anti-torpedo nets. Saddam's armour had no thermal imaging sights and the equipment he did have relied on too many international spare parts inventories.

Supply is the most boring part of fighting a battle, but often the most crucial: shortages caused Chelmsford to call off 40 per cent of his invasion; Pulleine's,

Kimmel's and Short's troops were bereft of ammunition as it was locked up; the supply lines of Burgoyne, Rydz, Stalin, Percival and Eisenhower were too long; Navarre's line of supply was non-existent; Anderson and Fredendall jammed their supply lines; Stalin, Mussolini, Walker and Saddam did not protect theirs.

An unwieldy command structure can destroy an army: Custer, Chelmsford, Rydz and MacArthur refused to delegate; Stalin and Saddam instilled such fear their generals could not accept responsibility; Eisenhower and Mussolini allowed their structure to be changed so much it became ineffective; in Malaya the British structure was too rigid; and Navarre's insistence on placing an armour colonel in command of a crucial division-sized airborne operation speaks for itself.

The pace of an army is important: Burgoyne, McDowell, Pakenham, Chelmsford and Visconti-Prasca moved too slowly; Custer moved too fast; and Baratieri's units too irregularly. Saddam's forces fought at a pace so much slower than the coalition they might have been in a different time dimension.

Poor or misused communications destroy all good intentions. Custer, Chelmsford and Fredendall issued incomprehensible orders. Rydz and Meretskov had inadequate equipment. Baratieri's generals deliberately cut themselves off from their superior, as did Dean. Marshall's staff refused to use navy communications.

Sometimes an army falls into an almost irreversible position, but a leader pulls them through: witness St Clair's ability to rally and fight his way out, despite a severe attack of gout. High command ability can save the day. Low command ability can blow it. On the 'day of battle' Braddock was stubborn; Burgoyne indecisive; Custer rash; Chelmsford dithering; Baratieri panicky; Rydz escapist; Stark and Marshall failed to impress upon Kimmel and Short that they were on a war footing; Kimmel and Short failed to realise why they had been sent to Hawaii in the first place – it was not to play golf. Percival, Phillips, Pulford and Brooke-Popham moved as if in a dream. Wavell played chess with brigades. Fredendall and Anderson deputised others to pull their chestnuts out of the fire. Bradley and Collins were not strong enough to stop Congress decimating the army. Dean was out of his league. Walker and Almond lived with a false sense of security. Navarre knew only to throw good money after bad. Saddam was an excellent dictator, but no general.

What becomes apparent is that he number of errors is not as important as the number of categories in which those errors fall, for example nine errors in one category might not have as much impact as one error in each of three categories.

There are obvious differences between the commanders we have studied, yet a similarity between their errors. True, the ones we have studied were all men, but there has never been any indication that women could fight battles differently. Catherine the Great, Boudicea, Eleanor of Aquitaine, Lakshmi Bai and a few others notwithstanding, women have not been given the opportunity to destroy and maim to the same extent as men. That lies in the future. So we must fall back on the one constant among our studies to explain this similarity of errors: they were all human. If this is the only relevant factor then it means that military commanders of the future are going to make the same errors if they become stricken with the disease of arrogance. Providing them with such technology as laser guns, magnetic shields, instant visual communications between all personnel, computerised response, virtual reality training and android reconnaissance troops will have no more impact on the type of errors than has any other military invention to date since mankind first flung a rock at his fellow man.

The military sphere is not the only discipline that can be affected by these error categories. They are just as relevant in business, sports, politics, science, education, religion, any human endeavour. None of us can afford arrogance, neither the scout alone in enemy territory, the battalion commander nor the admiral nor mighty general, nor the shopkeeper, marketing director, scientific investigator, police detective, medical doctor, teacher, priest, politician, whoever.

Arrogance makes fools of us all and like Braddock we shall finish up defeated, whispering in our last gasp: 'We shall better know how to deal with them another time.'

Suggested Reading

1755 — The Monongahela
Braddock at the Monongahela: P. E. Kopperman, Feffers, 1977
The British Army in North America: Robin May and G. A. Embleton, Osprey No. 39, London
Dictionary of the American Indian: John Stoutenburgh Jr., Random House, London
Encyclopaedia of North American Indian Tribes: Bill Yenne, Bison Books, London, 1986
Ill-Starred General: L. MacCardell, University of Pittsburgh, 1958
King George's Army: Stuart Reid and Paul Chappell, Osprey No. 285, London, 1995
The Orme Journal (1755): British Library, London.

1777 — Saratoga
Benedict Arnold: Patriot and Traitor: Willard Sterne Randall, Bodley Head, London, 1991
Cassell's Biographical Dictionary of the American War of Independence: London, 1966
General Burgoyne in Canada and America: Michael Glover, London, 1978
General Washington's Army: Peter F. Copeland and Marko Zlatich, Osprey No. 273, London
King George's Army: Stuart Reid and Paul Chappell, Osprey No. 285, London, 1995
Saratoga: the Decisive Battle: Rupert Furneaux, Allen & Unwin, London, 1971
Uniforms of the American Revolution: John Mollo, Sterling, New York, 1991
With Burgoyne from Quebec: an Account of the Life at Quebec and of the Famous Battle at Saratoga: Thomas Anburey, Macmillan, London

1790 — North West War
Dictionary of the American Indian: John Stoutenburgh Jr., Random House, London
Encyclopaedia of North American Indian Tribes: Bill Yenne, Bison Books, London, 1986
The Frontier in the Formative Years

1783-1815: Reginald Horsman, University of Wisconsin, Milwaukee, 1970
The Papers of Thomas Jefferson: Princeton University
The United States Infantry: Gregory J. W. Urwin, Blandford, New York, 1988

1814 — New Orleans
The British at the Gates: The New Orleans Campaign in the War of 1812: Robin Reilly, Cassell, London, 1976
Expansionists of 1812: Julius W. Pratt, Smith, Gloucester Massachussetts, 1957
A History of the War between Great Britain and the United States: G. A. Auchinleck, MacLear, Toronto, 1855
Life of Andrew Jackson: Marquis James, Craftsmen, Camden NJ, 1938
The Lion and the Union: the Anglo-American War of 1812-15: Kate Caffrey, Deutsch, London, 1978
The Naval War of 1812: C. S. Forester, Michael Joseph, London, 1957
New Orleans 1815: Tim Pickles, Osprey No. 28, London, 1993
Struggle for the Gulf Borderlands: Frank Lawrence Owsley Jr., University of Florida, Gainesville, 1981
The United States Infantry: Gregory J. W. Urwin, Blandford, New York, 1988
Wellington's Infantry: Bryan Fosten, Osprey No. 114, London, 1981

1861 — Bull Run
All for the Union: the Civil War Diary and Letters of Elisha Hunt Rhodes: Orion, New York, 1991
Battle Cry of Freedom: James M. McPherson, Penguin, London, 1988
Battle in the Civil War: Paddy Griffith, Fieldbooks, Mansfield, 1986
The Civil War: Volume 1, Gregory Jaynes, Time Life Books, Alexandria, 1986
The Civil War: Shelby Foote, Bodley Head, London, 1991
History of the Great Rebellion: Thomas P. Kettel, Stebbins, Hartford, Connecticut, 1866

Jeb Stuart: John W. Thomason Jr., Scribner & Sons, New York. 1929
Joseph E. Johnston: Craig L. Symonds, Norton, New York, 1992
Our Masters the Rebels: Michael C. C. Adams, Harvard University, Cambridge, 1978
Stonewall Jackson and the American Civil War: G. F. R. Henderson, Longman's Green, New York, 1898
Uniforms of the American Civil War: Philip J. Haythornthwaite, Blandford, Poole, 1975
The United States Infantry: Gregory J. W. Urwin, Blandford, New York, 1988
Voices of the Civil War: Richard Wheeler, Crowell, New York, 1976
War Memoirs: Jubal A. Early, Indiana University, Bloomington, 1969

1876 — Little Big Horn
The Battle of the Little Big Horn: Mari Sandoz, University of Nevada, 1966
Bury My Heart at Wounded Knee: Dee Brown, New York, 1971
Carbine and Lance: W. S. Nye, University of Oklahoma, 1942
Crazy Horse and Custer: Stephen E. Ambrose, Garden City, NY, 1975
Custer, Man and Myth: Michael Angelo, London, 1976
The Custer Myth: William A. Graham, Stackpole, Harrisburg Pa, 1953
Dictionary of the American Indian: John Stoutenburgh Jr., Random House, London
Encyclopaedia of North American Indian Tribes: Bill Yenne, Bison Books, London, 1986
Journal of the Sioux Campaign of 1876: Montana Historical Society, 1896
My Life on the Plains: George Armstrong Custer, Carol, New York, 1993
The Scouts: Capps, New York, 1975
Son of the Morning Star: General Custer and the Little Big Horn: Evan S. Connell, Michael Joseph, London 1985

1879 — Isandhlwana
Blood on the Painted Mountain: Ron Lock, Greenhill, London, 1995
Colonialism in Africa: L. H. Gann and Peter Duignan, Cambridge, 1969
The Graphic: London 1879
Invasion of Zululand: S. Clarke, Johannesburg, 1979
Narrative of the Field Operations Connected with the Zulu War: Intelligence Branch of the War Office, Greenhill, London

The Road to Isandhlwana: R. W. F. Droogleever, Greenhill, London
The Scramble for Africa: Thomas Pakenham, Weidenfeld & Nicolson, London 1991
Small Wars: C. E. Callwell, Greenhill, London, 1990
The Washing of the Spears: Donald R. Morris, Simon & Schuster, New York, 1965
The Zulu War: Angus McBride, Osprey No. 57, London, 1976
The Zulu War: Then and Now: Ian Knight and Ian Castle, Battle of Britain Prints International, London, 1993

1896 — Adowa
The Battle of the Lions: Adua 1896: Rafaele Ruggeri, Military History Illustrated, Vol. 24, London, 1990
The Campaign of Adowa: George Berkeley, London, 1902
Colonialism in Africa: L. H. Gann and Peter Duignan, Cambridge, 1969
Enciclopedia Italiana: Rome
The Graphic: London, 1896
The Life and Times of Menelik II: H. G. Marcus, Oxford, 1975
La Prima Guerra d'Africa: R. Bataglia, Turin, 1958
The Scramble for Africa: Thomas Pakenham, Weidenfeld & Nicolson, London 1991
Small Wars: C. E. Callwell, Greenhill, London, 1990

1939 — Poland
Destiny Can Wait: the Polish Air Force in the Second World War: Polish Air Force Association, London, 1949
Documents on Soviet–Polish Relations: Sikorski Historical Institute
The German Army 1933-45: Albert Seaton, Weidenfeld & Nicolson, London, 1982
The German Campaign in Poland: R. M. Kennedy, Washington DC, 1956
German Ground Forces: Poland and France: Brian L. Davis, Almark, London, 1976
The Great Crusade: H. P. Willmott, Michael Joseph, London, 1989
Guderian: Panzer General: Kenneth Macksey, MacDonald & Jane's, London
History of the Second World War: HMSO, London
History of the Second World War: B. H. Liddell-Hart, Putnam, New York, 1970
Hitler's War Directives: ed. H. R. Trevor-Roper, Pan, London, 1966

Memoirs: Field Marshal Wilhelm Keitel,
Kimber, London, 1961
*Oberkommando der Werhmacht War
Diary*: MS CO20, USAREUR
Panzer Leader: Heinz Guderian, Arrow,
1990
Poland in the Second World War: Josef Gar-
linski, Macmillan, London, 1985
The Polish Army 1939-45: Steven Zaloga,
Osprey No. 117, London, 1981
The Polish Campaign 1939: Steven Zaloga
and Victor Madej, Hippocrene, New York,
1985
*The Polish Contribution to the Ultimate
Allied Victory in the Second World War*:
Tadeusz Modelski, Worthing, 1986
Tanks of World War II: Chris Ellis, Octopus,
London, 1981
The War Hitler Won: September 1939:
Nicholas Bethell, Allen Lane, London,
1972

1939 — Finland
Finland 1939-40: A. F. Upton, London,
1974
Finland in the Second World War: Charles
L. Lundin, Indiana University, 1957
*Khruschev Remembers: the Last
Testament*: Nikita Khruschev Deutsch,
London, 1974
Memoirs: Mannerheim, C. G., London, 1953
Stalin and His Generals: Seweryn Bialer,
Souvenir Press, London, 1970
Stalin's Generals: Harold Shukman, Wei-
denfeld & Nicolson, London, 1993
The Winter War: V. Tanner, London, 1957
*The Winter War: the Russo–Finnish Conflict
1939-40*: Eloise Engle, Military Book Soci-
ety, London

1940 — Greece
The Battle of Greece: Alexander Papagos,
Athens, 1949
Dictionary of Modern Italian History: Frank
J. Coppa, Greenwood, Westport Conn.,
1985
Enciclopedia Italiana: Rome
Generale nella Polvere: Piero Baroni, Rome,
1989
The Great Crusade: H. P. Willmott, Michael
Joseph, London, 1989
Greece 1940-41: Charles Cruickshank, Uni-
versity of Delaware, 1976
*Greece and the British Connection
1935-41*: John S. Koliopoulos, Oxford,
1977
Historical Dictionary of Fascist Italy: Philip
V. Cannistraro, Greenwood, Westport,
Conn., 1982

History of the Second World War: HMSO,
London
*The Hollow Legions: Mussolini's Blunder in
Greece*: Mario Cervi, Chatto & Windus,
London 1972
L'Italia e La Seconda Guerra Mondiale: E.
Faldella, Capelli, 1960
L'Italia nella Seconda Guerra Mondiale: G.
Gorla, Baldini e Castoldi, 1959
L'Italia nella Seconda Guerra Mondiale:
Pietro Badoglio, Mondadori, Milan, 1946
*The Rise and Fall of the New Roman
Empire*: Glen Barclay, Sidgwick & Jackson,
London 1973
La Seconda Guerra Italiana: G. Gigli, Lat-
erza, 1951
Twentieth Century Caesar: Jules Archer,
Bailey Bros. & Swinfen, Folkestone, 1972
2194 Days of War: Cesare Salmaggi and
Alfredo Pallvisini, Mondadori, Milan, 1977

1941 — Pearl Harbor
Admiral Kimmel's Story: Husband E. Kim-
mel, Regnery, 1955
*Allies of a Kind: the United States, Britain
and the War against Japan*: Christopher
Thorne, Hamish Hamilton, London, 1978
*At Dawn We Slept: the Untold Story of
Pearl Harbor*: Gordon W. Prange, Pen-
guin, London, 1982
Attack on Pearl Harbor: Roger Parkinson,
Wayland, 1973
Betrayal at Pearl Harbor: James Rusbridge
and Eric Nave, O'Mara Books, New York,
1991
December 7, 1941: Gordon W. Prange, Har-
rap, 1988
*Double Edged Secrets: US Naval Intelli-
gence Operations in the Pacific*: W. J.
Holmes, Naval Institute, Annapolis, 1979
FDR and American Foreign Policy 1932-45:
Robert Dallek, Oxford, 1981
*History of United States Naval Operations
in World War II*: Samuel Morison, Little
Brown, Boston, 1957
Infamy: John Toland, Methuen, London,
1982
*Men of War: Great Naval Leaders of World
War II*: Stephen Howarth, Robert W. Love
Jr. and Kyoshi Ikeda
Naval Battles of World War II: Geoffrey
Bennet, B. T. Batsford. London, 1975
Pearl Harbor Ghosts: Thurston Clarke,
Morrow, New York, 1991
Race to Pearl Harbor: Stephen E. Pelz, Har-
vard, 1974
*Threshold of War: FDR and American
Entry into World War 2*: Waldo Heinrich,
Oxford, 1988

Very Special Intelligence: the Story of the Admiralty's Operational Intelligence Centre 1939-45: Patrick Beesley, Macmillan, London 1977

1941-42— Malaya-Singapore

Battleship: Martin Middlebrook and Patrick Mahoney, Allen Lane, London, 1977

Four Samurai: A Quartet of Japanese Army Commanders: Arthur Swinson, Hutchinson, London, 1968

The Great Crusade: H. P. Willmott, Michael Joseph, London, 1989

History of the Second World War: HMSO, London

Malaya 1941: Sir Andrew Gilchrist, Robert Hale, London 1992

A Matter of Honour: An Account of the Indian Army: Philip Mason, Cape, London, 1974

The Official History of the Indian Armed Forces in the Second World War: Bisheshwar Prasad, Orient Longman's, Bombay

Percival and the Tragedy of Singapore: Sir John Smyth, MacDonald, London, 1971

Seventy Days to Singapore: Stanley Falk, Hale, London, 1975

Singapore: Masanobu Tsuji, Oxford, 1988

Singapore 1941-42: Louis Allen, Davis-Poynter, London, 1977

Singapore: the Battle that Changed the World: James Leasor, Hodder, London, 1968

Spotlight on Singapore: Denis Russell-Roberts, Times Press, Douglas, Isle of Man, 1965

Tanks of World War II: Chris Ellis, Octopus, London, 1981

The Underrated Enemy: Britain's War with Japan: Adrian Stewart, Kimber, London, 1987

The War in Malaya: A. E. Percival, Eyre & Spottiswoode, 1949

War With Japan: Ministry of Defence; HMSO, London, 1995

1943 — Kasserine

Oberkommando der Werhmacht War Diary: MS CO20, USAREUR

Come fini la Guerra in Africa: Giovanni Messe, Rizzoli, Milan, 1946

Crucible of Power: Kenneth Macksey, Hutchinson, London, 1969

Crusade in Europe: Dwight D. Eisenhower, London, 1948

Enciclopedia Italiana: Rome

First Blood: The Battle of Kasserine Pass: Charles Whiting, Grafton, 1986

Generale nella Polvere: Piero Baroni, Rome, 1989

GI: the American Soldier in World War Two: Lee Kennett, New York, 1987

Here is Your War: Ernie Pyle, Holt & Co. 1943

History of the Second World War: HMSO, London

L'Italia e La Seconda Guerra Mondiale: E. Faldella, Capelli, 1960

L'Italia nella Seconda Guerra Mondiale: G. Gorla, Baldini e Castoldi, 1959

Le Operazione in Africa Settentionale: Mario Montanari, Ufficio Storico SME, 1985

The Plain Cook and the Great Showman: Gregory Blaxland, Kimber, London, 1977

Revista Militari: Anno XI-3: Pietro Palotta, 1955

Rommel's Last Victory: The Battle of Kasserine Pass: Martin Blumenson, Allen & Unwin, London, 1966

The Rommel Papers: ed. Basil H. Liddell-Hart, Collins, London, 1953

Rommel's War in Africa: Wolf Heckmann, Granada, London, 1981

La Seconda Guerra Italiana: G. Gigli, Laterza, 1951

Tanks of World War II: Chris Ellis, Octopus, London, 1981

Three Years with Eisenhower: Harry C. Butcher, London, 1946

The Tunisian Campaign: Charles Messenger, Ian Allen, London, 1982

The United States Army in World War II: Department of the Army, Washington DC,

1950 — Osan-Taejon and Chongchon-Changjin

American Caesar: Douglas MacArthur: William Manchester, London 1979

The British Part in the Korean War: Anthony Farrar-Hockley, HMSO, London, 1990

Enter the Dragon: China at War in Korea: Russell Spurr, Sidgwick, London, 1989

Kim Il Sung: Dae-sok Suh, Columbia, New York, 1988

Korea: the Limited War: David Rees, Macmillan, London, 1964

The Korean War: Max Hastings, Michael Joseph, London 1987

The Korean War: Robert Leckie, Pall Mall, London, 1962

Korean War Almanac: Harry G. Summers, Facts on File, New York, 1990

1954 — Dien Bien Phu

The Battle of Dien Bien Phu: Jules Roy,

Faber, London, 1965

Dien Bien Phu: the Battle that Ended the First Indo-China War. Peter A. Poole, Watts, 1972

The French Foreign Legion: Douglas Porch, Papermac, London, 1991

Giap: the Victor in Vietnam: Peter MacDonald, Fourth Estate, London, 1993

Hell in a Very Small Place: the Siege of Dien Bien Phu: Bernard B. Fall, Pall Mall, London, 1967

The Indo-China War. Edgar O'Ballance, Faber, London

1991 — Kuwait

All Necessary Means: Ben Brown and David Shukman, BBC Books, London, 1991

Armies of the Gulf War. Gordon Rottman and Ron Volstad, Osprey No. 45, London, 1993

Crusade: the Untold Story of the Gulf War. Rick Atkinson, Harper Collins, London, 1994

Desert Victory: Norman Friedman, Naval Institute, Annapolis, 1991

The Gulf Conflict 1990-91: Lawrence Freedman and Efraim Karsh, Faber & Faber, London, 1993

The Gulf War Assessed: John Pimlott and Stephen Badsey, Arms & Armour, London, 1992

Illusions of Triumph: an Arab View of the Gulf War. Mohammed Heikal, Harper Collins, London, 1992

Military Lessons of the Gulf War. Bruce W. Watson, Bruce George and Peter Tsouras, Greenhill, London, 1991

Saddam's War. John Bulloch and Harvey Morris, Faber & Faber, London, 1991

War and the Media: Propaganda and Persuasion in the Gulf War. Philip M. Taylor, Manchester University, 1992

Index